Professional **PERFORMANCE 360** *Special Edition:* **SUCCESS 2nd EDITION**

Published by CelebrityPress®, Orlando, FL

CelebrityPress® is a registered trademark.

Printed in the United States of America.

ISBN: 978-1-7322843-2-6
LCCN: 2018946015

This publication is designed to provide accurate and authoritative information with regard to the subject matter covered. It is sold with the understanding that the publisher is not engaged in rendering legal, accounting, or other professional advice. If legal advice or other expert assistance is required, the services of a competent professional should be sought. The opinions expressed by the authors in this book are not endorsed by CelebrityPress® and are the sole responsibility of the author rendering the opinion.

Most CelebrityPress® titles are available at special quantity discounts for bulk purchases for sales promotions, premiums, fundraising, and educational use. Special versions or book excerpts can also be created to fit specific needs.

For more information, please write:

CelebrityPress®
520 N. Orlando Ave, #2
Winter Park, FL 32789
or call 1.877.261.4930

Visit us online at: www.CelebrityPressPublishing.com

Professional
PERFORMANCE
360

SPECIAL EDITION:

SUCCESS
2nd EDITION

//CONTENTS

FOREWORD

By Dr. Jeffrey MaGee, Nick Nanton, Esq. & JW Dicks, Esq 11

THE WORLD OF VIRGIN PERFORMANCE ...
A Never Ending Quest for Success

An Interview with Richard Branson, Kt 14

TEN REQUIREMENTS FOR SUCCESS
How Do You Measure Up?

By Nido R. Qubein, PhD 19

BUILDING YOUR DREAM LIFE

By Reggie Chandra, PhD 23

AN ATTITUDE OF EXCELLENCE
Building the #1 Real Estate Sales Team

By Rudy Lira Kusuma 29

PREMIERE FASHION EXPERT LEARNS THE DEEPER MEANING OF SUCCESS

An Interview with Ulrich Kellerer 35

A M.A.P. FOR ACHIEVING HIGH PERFORMANCE

By Henrik Rosvall 41

SIX THINGS KITESURFING TAUGHT ME
About Being a Successful Entrepreneur

By David Lee 47

TRUTH OR CONSEQUENCES? YOU DECIDE!

By Harvey Mackay 54

EMPATHY IS AN ELEMENT OF HIGH PERFORMANCE

By West Seegmiller, Esq. 59

EXPERTS IN SUCCESS
An Interview with Nick Nanton, Esq. & J.W. Dicks, Esq. 65

EXPLORATION ...
Be Enchanted and Unlock a New You!
By Alan Weiss, PhD 73

OVERCOMING OBSTACLES THAT STAND IN THE WAY OF SUCCESS
An Interview with Nick Nemeth, Esq. 77

HIGH PERFORMANCE 360
My Quest For Success
By Steve Renner 83

THE SECRET TO BUSINESS SUCCESS
Fire Yourself Everyday
By Susan Sly 89

SUCCESS IS HAVING THE FREEDOM TO DO WHATEVER YOU WANT IN YOUR LIFE
An Interview with Brian M. Douglas 95

MALL WORLD, BIG SUCCESS
An Interview with Brenda R. McGuire 101

TEN STEPS TO MOVE THE FAMILY COMPANY FROM BUSINESS TO LEGACY
By Betsi Bixby 107

PLATFORM FOR SUCCESS
By David A. Hoines, Esq. 113

SECRETS OF SUCCESS
An Interview with Maria Quattrone 119

FINDING PURPOSE AND SIGNIFICANCE BY PUTTING PEOPLE OVER PROFIT
An Interview with Frans Trisnadi 125

TWENTY-FIVE REASONS WHY MY LAW OFFICE IS SUCCESSFUL
By Ken Nunn, Esq. 131

THE HAPPY WORKPLACE BLUEPRINT
By John P. Nicholls 139

BUILDING WEALTH AND RENDERING VALUE
Identifying Long-Term Investment Demand Trends
An Interview with Christian Koch 145

VETERAN TAX ATTORNEY STRESSES LIFETIME LEARNING AS A KEY COMPONENT TO A JOURNEY OF SUCCESS
An Interview with David Auer, Esq. 151

TRANSFORMING THE FACE OF HONDURAS, ONE CHILD AT A TIME
By Darold Opp, DDS 157

DECIDE YOUR WAY TO SUCCESS FOR GOOD
7 Decisions
By Janice L. Quigg 163

LESSONS FROM THE MASTERS
No One Makes it to the Top Alone
By Jim Collyer 169

THE EARLY BIRD CATCHES THE WORM
By Patricia E. Takacs, DMD 175

REACHING BILLIONS:
Finding Online Success with Your Business Platform
By Lindsay Dicks 181

BUILD A BIGGER, BETTER BUSINESS WITH FACEBOOK!
By James Dicks 187

HAVE YOUR CAKE AND RETIRE TOO!
By Leasha West 193

THINK IT, INK IT, AND ACT ON IT
The Power of FAST Implementation
By Dr. Diyari Abdah 201

THE FUTURE BELONGS TO THE YOUNG...
and Ambitious
By Greg Rollett 207

BEING A BEACON OF LIGHT FOR THOSE IN HIS CIRCLE OF INFLUENCE
An Interview with Troy Singer 213

A LASTING IMPRESSION
Your Life, Your Legacy
By Josie Tytus, CPC 219

DEVELOPMENT OF A SERIAL ENTREPRENEUR
An Interview with Anelia Sutton 227

BE AKUHLA YOU:
Supercharge what you want to do
An Interview with Nosh Marzbani 233

SMILING SUCCESS
An Interview with Dr. Joseph (Joe) Marcius 239

THREE PILLARS TO HIGH PERFORMANCE AND A CHAMPION LIFE
By Richie Jaynes 245

TEN WAYS TO WASTE YOUR TIME IN A NETWORKING GROUP!
By Dr. Ivan Misner 250

YOUR LEGACY PLAN:
A Building Block For Generational Success
By Marilyn Garner, Esq. 255

IF I BUILD IT, WILL THEY COME?
By Danette Gossett 261

GROWTH DOES NOT JUST HAPPEN BY ACCIDENT, YOU MUST WORK AT IT
By Perminder Chohan 267

TWELVE STEPS FOR QUANTUM HEALING
By Renata Angelo 273

DISCOVERING YOUR INNER MAVERICK AND NEVER TAKING NO FOR AN ANSWER
An Interview with Rod Walker 279

HONESTY, INTEGRITY AND A DETERMINATION TO SUCCEED
That Includes Giving Back and Helping Others
An Interview with Kevin Hodes 285

WALK THE TALK
At a World Class Level
By Sussi Mattsson 291

THE CYCLE OF INFLUENCE:
"7-E's" to Becoming a Master Communicator
By Pa Joof 297

FIVE WAYS TO BETTER HANDLE THE IMPACT OF SUCCESS FOR GOOD
By Dr. Kathleen Allard-Wasajja 303

ONE DEGREE TRAJECTORY CHANGE MAKES MONUMNETAL ROIs
By Jeffrey Magee 310

PURPOSE:
A Competitive Advantage in Business and Life
By Patrice Tanaka, Founder & Chief Joy Officer, Joyful Planet LLC 314

FOLLOW YOUR PASSION
By Shaunequa Jordan 320

SUCCEEDING BY HELPING OTHERS
By Brent Campbell 325

THE BLUE PRINT THAT OPENS THE DOOR TO A BETTER LIFE
By Kwesha Denice Neal 331

HOORAY FOR EPIC FAILS
Dollhouses, Long-Jumping and GMAT Scores
By Rosie Unite 337

OPENING THE PERFORMANCE DOOR TO BECOMING A CONSISTENT PERFORMER

By Terry Rasner-Yacenda 345

HOW TO WIN IN LIFE
Bouncing Back From Failure When Hard Work Just Ain't Enough!

By Michael Cheng 351

YOUR FINANCIAL SUCCESS PLAN

By Mike Riedmiller 357

LEADING WITH "WHY"

By Lizzie Dement, M.Ed. 363

1 LIFE, 1 MIRACLE

By 'B. Taylor' 369

FINANCIAL FREEDOM IS IN YOUR HANDS!

By Ella Rivkin 373

UPGRADE YOUR THINKING FOR GREATER PERFORMANCE

By Peter Wolfing 379

SUCCESS SECRETS BY ANALYSIS AND PLANNING
The 5 Prosperity Pillars

By Paul Fulford 384

FOREWORD

The science and art of personal success psychology reveals that whether looking at an individual or an organization, there are very distinct similarities. Through *PERFORMANCE Magazine* (www. ProfessionalPerformanceMagazine.com) over the past two decades we have chronicled this and seen repeatedly with star athletes, entertainers, business icons, political leaders, best-selling authors and entrepreneurs at every level, the DNA of success is clear and distinct. Not just success and achievement, but sustained and accelerated success and achievement are dependent upon:

1. Values that drive Vision and Strategy

2. An understanding of how Systems and Operational approaches are borne from #1

3. Tactical Behaviors to Execute

4. The Discipline and Accountability mechanisms to enforce greatness and hold one accountable

This special edition, hard cover version of PERFORMANCE 360-2nd Ed. on Success, and the collection of very selective Subject-Matter-Experts (SME) Chapter's, provides you with a cross-section of insights for application and accelerated success. While true success lies within ideas and approaches that are evergreen (withstand time) and allow for the situational changes, performance is also about a deep understanding of the mechanics necessary to be effective at what one does.

It is estimated by the Association for Talent Development (ATD), the Society of Human Resource Management (SHRM) and other Chief Executive and Chief Learning Officer organizations that by 2020, that nearly 60 percent of the individuals in managerial-supervisory-leadership-executive positions in business and government agencies across the United States of America will be retired or eligible for retirement – that intellectual experience knowledge drain may have catastrophic consequences to business and individuals.

The need for continued development and human capital development of others is a never-ending pursuit of performance excellence. That pursuit embodies both science and art for personal success, whether looking at an individual or an organization. Read and master the distinct ideas within this book and experience the best of your performance excellence.

"Think twice before you speak, because your words and influence will plant *the seed of either success or failure in the mind of another."* Napoleon Hill

THE WORLD OF VIRGIN PERFORMANCE

A Never Ending Quest for Success

PERFORMANCE: In a World of Performance and the search for or the Quest for Wealth, what does that mean to you? The world itself looks at wealth in monetary terms. So what is your interpretation of what that is we're looking for?

RICHARD: Well I think that a Quest for Wealth, *per se*, is not a particularly satisfying thing to do. But having a quest or quests is very satisfying. And if the by-product of those quests is that wealth is created, and you use that wealth productively, that's satisfying. And in my own particular case, I originally wanted to start a magazine. When I was fifteen years old, I wanted to put the world right. And the Vietnamese war raging, and I wanted to do my little bit to stop it. And in order for that magazine to survive, I had to become an entrepreneur. I had to become a businessman—I had to worry about the paper manufacturing and the distribution, the marketing and so on. And the end result was that it became successful. I could then set about to challenging myself to make a difference in other areas. I love music, so I found a particular band that I loved the music of, and we couldn't find anybody else to put them out, so I decided to form a record company. Now, the end product of forming that record company, the product of signing bands like the Rolling Stones, Genesis and Janet Jackson, was wealth. But that was not where I got my satisfaction. I got my satisfaction from creating a great record company that I was proud of.

PERFORMANCE: So, the old adage of follow your bliss, follow your passion, it's what's been leading you, really, all along.

RICHARD: Yes, and I think that the most successful people are the people who do not sit down and think, how can I make a fortune? It's people who have a passion for something, for instance when I moved into the airline business, I hated flying on other people's airlines, and I felt I could do it better. If I was looking for wealth from doing it, everybody would have advised me that I was mad. But my reason for doing it was creating the kind of airline that I'd like to fly. As it turned out, I created Virgin Atlantic that I liked to fly and other people liked to fly, and twenty years later it's enormously successful. We've managed to sell 49% of it to airlines that are worth billions of dollars, and we've made good money from it. But if I'd actually gone into it because I thought I was going to make good money, I don't think I would've made a penny.

PERFORMANCE: Well, you're doing things contrary to people's opinions. And that's part of the secret to your success. You're now entering the marketplace with Virgin America and everybody's saying, what?

RICHARD: I think the most successful entrepreneurs are the ones who do things contrary to opinion. The standard business school advice is stick to your onions, don't do anything to stray from that. Or Nike stick with shoes, Microsoft stick with computers. Coca-cola stick with soft drinks. At Virgin we love the idea of becoming a way of life brand, of challenging businesses in other areas. And we love doing that, it's more challenging, we learn a lot more. We meet a lot of people. And contrary to advice in business school, I actually think it makes a lot of sense. Because music shops were one of the first things we did. I doubt there's a great future in music shops with iPods and other methods of getting your music. So if we just did music shops, we wouldn't survive. But because we've moved into things like mobile phones, where a lot of kids' spending power is going…if one business is suffering from a lot of competition, or new technology, another one of our businesses can do well.

If you're doing something you're committed to, you've got a chance.

PERFORMANCE: So if you were to…at some point, I read something about your ten steps to success. I don't expect you to remember rhyming them off, but perhaps if you could sort of address that, from your experience?

RICHARD: Well, I mean I think the most important thing, if you're a father, if you're a businessman, is to lavish praise, is to look for the best in people. To be good to people, to inspire people, not to criticize people. And I suspect that's the #1 most important thing in a leader. If you end up criticizing people all the time, people shrivel up. If you praise people, people expand. And it applied to anybody. You know, you see a person who's cleaning a room, you've got a switchboard operator locked way upstairs. Well everybody needs a little bit of attention, a little bit of praise. And since so many businesses are not good at that, the loyalty that you can get back is enormous, and so it makes fantastic business sense. And there are lots of other things, like to advise people, but I wouldn't say that that's the #1 overriding thing.

If someone is setting up a business it's important that they go into something that is a passion, and again, really interests them. And if you're going to work day and night to make it work, it's important that you're interested in it. For the first few years, if you don't have financial backing, the only word that's going to matter to you is valuable. And a lot of businesses don't survive. But at least if you're doing something you're committed to, you've got a chance. If you don't survive, it's not the end of the world. It's the whole idea of limited companies. So if you try, you fail, you go to Chapter 11, you've got to pick yourself up and try again. There have been a lot of entrepreneurs that went through that financial process and then went back and created major   corporations, so don't be too frightened about failure.

PERFORMANCE: I think that's really what keeps a lot of people back. It is enormous fear. Whether it's enormous fear of success, or failure, and sometimes you don't know which it is. And I think that one's identity is so much tied in with that success. If you could just elaborate on that in terms of your own identity and your work. I read something that really touched me, that when you sold Virgin Records, you were very emotional about that and cried about that, but you had to do that in order to get the airline moving.

RICHARD: Yeah, you know I think that unless you're doing something in life that you feel passionate about, you feel passionate about the people, you shouldn't be doing it. In my own particular case, I had a record company. It was very successful, I had a fantastic group of people running it, I had an airline that was less successful that was being attacked by British Airways and they were desperately trying to put us out of business. And it came to a stage where I had to sell the record company in order to protect the jobs at the record company, and also to protect the airline. And it was bizarre, I sold it, and got a billion-dollar check in my pocket, I had seen the staff, and I was running down the street, tears streaming down my face. And past a newspaper that said, "Branson Sells For A Billion", and I did think it was quite amusing, if a photographer got a picture of this person blubbering his head off with a billion dollar check in his pocket. But I do believe that if you're human, you've got to care about people.

PERFORMANCE: So that was a defining moment for you?

RICHARD: It was…I've been fortunate enough in my life to have had quite a lot of defining moments. And a life full of incredible experiences, whether it be personal experiences or business experiences. And I suspect that's also helped me when things have gone wrong. I don't dwell on them too long, and as long as I've done everything I can to try to make them successful, I'll be able to sleep well at night and I'll move on to the next challenge. And I've had enough challenges to satisfy many lives. I've been incredibly, incredibly lucky, and for me to dwell on things when they didn't go quite right, I'd be a very, very, sad individual.

PERFORMANCE: So what do you think has been your core strength and has made you take all these enormous risks? I mean, the sort of dangerous element of the challenges you've taken on physically and in business? Is there something in your childhood that has driven you to these kinds of adventurous extremes?

RICHARD: I think the adventure side of me, I suspect, has been brought out by my mother, in particular. I remember age five we were driving to my grandmothers', and two miles before we got there she dropped me off in the countryside and told me to make my own way there. She would've gotten arrested today. And I got horribly lost, but it was her way of trying to get me to stand on my own two feet. Age eight, she doesn't even drive me, she puts me on a bicycle and tells me to ride 300 miles to granny's house. And so on, and so on.

BY NIDO R. QUBEIN, PhD

TEN REQUIREMENTS FOR SUCCESS

How do you measure up?

Benjamin Disraeli (the famous British prime minister) said: "The secret of success in life is for a person to be ready for his or her opportunity when it comes."

My research staff and I have discovered that there are ten basic requirements for success as a professional speaker and consultant:

(1) You must have a solid, marketable idea and the commitment to do whatever it takes to make it work.

(2) You must have the skills and expertise to translate that idea into concrete action.

(3) You must have a clear vision as to where you want to go – both personally and professionally.

(4) You must have a solid plan of action which is based on workable strategies.

(5) You must have or be able to create the resources to implement that plan.

(6) You must be willing and able to motivate and guide the people who can help you put your plan and ideas into action.

(7) You must be able to always keep the big picture in mind, yet be willing to get your hands dirty in day-to-day activities – to become involved in both the macro and the micro dimensions of running a successful business.

(8) You must develop the systems which make the right things happen at the right times.

(9) You must exercise the disciplines to constantly be doing the right things, at the right times and in the right ways.

(10) You must be able to measure your success in tangible terms and predetermined timetables.

To make it easier to grasp and remember, I've broken it down into four simple statements:

(1) Success grows out of a clear vision.

(2) Success results from a solid strategy.

(3) Success revolves around practical systems.

(4) Success comes through consistent execution.

In this column, let us discuss the first statement: **Success grows out of a clear vision.**

A vision is defined as "An object of the imagination." It starts as an idea in the mind of an individual and grows into a dream – maybe even an obsession. To provide the central focus needed to anchor a successful professional practice, it must meet several criteria:

(a) It must be clear. Vague visions lead to confused activities and lost motion. Be able to state the central, unique premise of your business in twelve words or less. The more specific your vision is, the better your chances of success are.

(b) The vision must be practical and workable. Most of us can come up with more ideas before noon each day than we can implement in a lifetime. The secret is to find the right idea – the one we can make work for us.

(c) It must be a vision that will capture our enthusiasm and enable us to inspire others. The key to all motivation is desire – we have to want it before we can make it happen. Money is seldom a strong enough motivator over the long haul.

(d) It must fit our skills, our resources and our strengths. I've seen many professionals fail because they were chasing the wrong dreams. Finding the right niche for your unique skills and resources may be your greatest challenge.

(e) It must be adaptable enough to survive the changes that will occur over the years. To have staying power, we must be able to constantly adjust our vision to meet new conditions.

(f) It must be marketable. The perceived value of an idea lies in its rarity. The more people there are who can do what you do, the less value it has. If you want a real revelation, look in the yellow pages of your local phone book and see how many professionals there are who describe themselves exactly as you do. What gives you your differential advantage in the marketplace?

(g) A vision must be an idea you can communicate effectively to others. People must be able to easily understand it, to need or want it, and be willing to pay enough for it to be profitable for you.

An idea (or vision) doesn't have to be new to work and be very profitable. For example, Henry Ford did not invent the automobile, or even the assembly line -- as many people think. Those ideas had both been around for decades. He took someone's ideas and adapted them to his own purpose – to build large numbers of automobiles that the masses of people could afford to buy. And, the rest is history!

Internationally known management expert Peter Drucker says, "The most important question any company can ask is: What is our business?" Probably the greatest reason professionals fail or don't become as successful as they could is that they lack a clear and specific vision of what they hope to achieve.

ABOUT DR. NIDO

Dr. Nido Qubein has served as president of High Point University since 2005. An accomplished business leader and dedicated philanthropist, he has led the university through an extraordinary transformation including major increases in undergraduate enrollment (from 1,500 to 4,000 students), the number of faculty (from 108 to 260), and the construction of 49 new buildings on campus with a total investment of a billion dollars.

Under his leadership, four academic schools have been added – the Nido R. Qubein School of Communication, the School of Health Sciences, the School of Art and Design and the School of Pharmacy. New programs in entrepreneurship, interactive gaming, and commerce were added along with new initiatives in physician assistant, pharmacy, and physical therapy. The university, during his tenure, moved to a doctoral degree granting institution and added masters and doctoral programs, invested heavily in state-of-the-art technology and resourced academic programs with personnel, facilities, equipment and budgets.

President Qubein is a successful, sought-after speaker who has delivered more than 6,000 presentations across the U.S. and beyond to corporations, associations and nonprofit organizations. But as someone who came from humble beginnings, he lives by a principle found in the Gospel of Luke: "To whom much is given, much is required." He teaches this principle to students through his Freshman and Senior Seminars, and works tirelessly to ensure that holistic learning and a values-based education remain the central focus of High Point University

BY REGGIE CHANDRA, PhD

BUILDING YOUR DREAM LIFE

You are at a funeral—yours! You are observing your own funeral from above. Who are all in attendance? From your vantage point, you can see everything. The undertaker has done a great job. You look peaceful and ten years younger as you rest in your casket. Your family is crying and so are some of your friends.

It is time for your eulogy and your friends and family are standing in line at the microphone to share what your life meant to them. As you wait with eager anticipation to hear what they have to say about you, a million thoughts go through your mind:

1. What will my children say about me?

2. What will my spouse/significant other say about me?

3. What will my friends say about me?

4. What will the people in my community say about me?

5. What will my peers say about my career?

6. How will I be remembered by my descendants and successors? (What is the legacy I leave behind for others?)

It is too late to change your life-story after the fact. Once you die, it is over; your legacy is written in stone. As you listen to your eulogy, are you full of regrets? Do you regret that you did not spend enough time with your daughter or your spouse? Do you regret that you did not spend enough quality time with your friends? What about volunteering for your community, as you had always wanted? What other regrets do you have?

What would happen if suddenly the Creator gave you a second chance to live so you could address these pain points and positively impact your future? What if you came back to life so that you could build your Dream Life and not have any regrets at the end of your life? The first step in creating a Dream Life is to ask yourself these questions while you are still alive and take powerful and immediate action to create the eulogy you want to hear at the end of your life. Dream Life cannot be created on autopilot or by accident. It requires intentional design and development.

There are six pillars that support the Dream Life. Each pillar needs to be deliberately developed so that we can build the best version of "us." The Dream Life can be built by anyone; we simply need insight and inspiration into what is required to build it.

I. DREAM HEALTH

Our bodies are amazing machines, capable of extraordinary activity. As with any machine, we must take care of our bodies—through nutrition, exercise, rest, and recreation. Our bodies were not meant to suffer the ailments that often plague them, which often are a result of simple neglect. Dream Health is paramount, without which you cannot build any of the other five pillars of the Dream Life.

It is extremely important to realize that our health improves or deteriorates as a result of the choices WE make. Poor, aimless, or extreme choices can ruin our health. Conversely, good and intentional choices can turn the tide and lead us down a better path of good health.

Dream Health may or may not resemble the latest Mr. or Mrs. Olympia, with freakishly large and well-defined muscles. Physical perfection is a noteworthy goal; however, Dream Health realistically involves maintaining proper weight and vital signs, proper diet and nutrition, and proper activity and rest. Our physical health often determines our mental state; healthy people tend to have a more optimistic outlook on life.

Dream Health can only be created by disciplined nutrition and exercise. Rest and recreation are indispensable for the body to heal and rejuvenate. These personal practices or disciplines will create Dream Health for us. There are no shortcuts to Dream Health. We must take charge of our lives—no more excuses—and work our health plan. Dream Health is ours for the taking!

II. DREAM RELATIONSHIPS

Humans are the only species where a baby will die without contact from its mother. We are born needing relationships for our survival. We must remember, though, that a healthy self-relationship is a prerequisite to healthy relationships with others. John Maxwell reminds us that we cannot give to others what we do not have ourselves. If we love ourselves, we become more loving and lovely. On the other hand, a poor self-image often repels others, as they will not participate in our self-loathing.

Dream relationships require giving of ourselves to others. Obstacles arise in relationships when people enter them solely because they want something. "In reality, the only way a relationship will last is if you see your relationship as a place that you go to give and not a place that you go to take." ~ Anthony Robbins. Popular media today seems to promote using others for our own benefit. However, credible counselors and authors will offer an opposing view.

Our fulfillment lies in our own self-development and realization. From a healthy state of self-acceptance, we can truly give of ourselves to others to help them grow as well. A healthy relationship will bring together two healthy people who synergistically push each other to be their absolute best. Anything less is not a healthy relationship (Will Smith). We have the capacity to be our best and to push others to be their best—what are we waiting for?

III. DREAM WEALTH

Dream Wealth is the most poorly conveyed pillar in the group, as the movie and music industries have only portrayed the end result: fast cars, big houses and extravagant spending. Dream Wealth acknowledges the end result, but also addresses the strategies necessary to get there. In the process, we learn financial independence and peace, which have no price tag. Dream Wealth continues to assert the principles set forth by the previous pillars—we must invest in ourselves to gain a position of sustainability, so that then we can better help others.

A healthy understanding of money is also important to accumulate and retain Dream Wealth. No one makes money but the U.S. Mint. Everyone earns money in direct exchange for the value they create. Money is only a medium of exchange. The money you earn is directly proportional to the perceived value you create.

Dream Wealth involves four key activities:

- Spending
- Saving
- Giving
- Investing

Most people focus on spending. The result is increased debt and stress due to poor money management. People who spend beyond their paychecks to chase a false American Dream set themselves up to fail. Financial independence—the point of Dream Wealth—is about balance.

Saving, giving and investing serve as the building blocks of Dream Wealth. Financial experts use various models of planning to help us reach our goals. We must study and craft the best plan for us. Saving is a discipline that helps us focus on our future instead of only on our feelings, wants and desires in the present moment. Numerous studies have proven that the people who enjoy Dream Wealth practice delaying self-gratification, in direct contrast to financially poor people.

Investing involves putting our money into stocks, bonds, mutual funds and other outlets to create a larger return for our future using the power of compounding interest. Investing requires wisdom, and there are abundant resources to help us learn how to best invest our money. Wealth comes not by winning the lottery but by practicing sound financial habits every day.

Finally, giving is a type of investing that brings return typically in ways other than monetary. Most often, giving provides its own rewards, even if it simply involves paying it forward, or a positive "karma" (feeling good about doing something helpful for others). Giving reminds us to focus on causes other than ourselves, to positively affect others. Givers are full of life. Givers are like a lake teeming with life, where waters flow in and waters flow out. Hoarders and non-givers are like the Dead Sea. Waters flow into the Dead Sea but do not flow out. It is called the Dead Sea since it cannot sustain life.

IV. DREAM CAREER

Many people see their dream job as something where they carry their laptops to the beach, put in an hour a day and money magically rolls in. The truth is a Dream Career takes hard work and vision to generate the momentum required to be successful. Many others see their dream job as unattainable or unrealistic, so they settle for a standard 9-to-5 position, cash their checks on Friday, and spend the entire weekend dreading Monday. Meanwhile, their dreams dry up and they are miserable.

People often get sucked into life's ruts because they fall for the trap that says it is all about what they can get from a job. Jim Rohn reminds us that success in career involves whom we become at the job, not what we get from the job. We are not cogs in the corporate machine, but owners of our own companies—you are the CEO of You, Inc.

To be able to embrace this vision of You, Inc., we must have a career plan. We have to work for our dream jobs, train for them, and broaden our skillsets for them, as dream jobs most often do not magically appear in our paths. We must have discipline, vision and courage. It takes being consumed by the vision and doing whatever it takes to realize the vision. Our career plan gives us focus and the will to push through adversity. A career plan guides us toward positions we love and drives us from things we hate. Please remember at all times that the money we earn is directly proportional to the value we create. If we are wise and choose work that we love, Confucius states: "We will never work another day in our lives."

V. DREAM SPIRITUALITY

When I mention spirituality, fists tighten, jaws clench and tempers flare. Fortunately, most things that anger people about spirituality are better classified as "religion." Religion is man's way to create a feeling of spirituality, the rules to regulate morality, and the guilt and shame to punish those who fall short. Spirituality, on the other hand, reaches beyond such triviality to address two major principles: how we cope with a higher power, or something bigger than ourselves upon which we lean to gain some understanding of life; and our higher purpose, which addresses the reasons why we are on this earth.

Human beings are spiritual by nature. Buddha stated, "Just as a candle cannot burn without fire, men cannot live without a spiritual life." Science proves every day that there is more to our existence than the existential. Quantum physics studies the building blocks that make up the universe, smaller than the subatomic particle. Research shows that within each subatomic particle is what scientists have labeled "solidified light" and theorize that this is part of the God concept. Writers allude to the fact that spirituality permeates the whole of life (Alan Watts, Ralph Waldo Emerson).

Addiction counselors following the Alcoholics Anonymous (AA) format of recovery note that addicts are brought to a step that helps them realize that an outside power—whether it be God, music, the Universe, nature, or the Ideal in humanity—can help them accomplish what they felt was impossible in the past. Therefore, we must address our spirituality and develop a healthy spiritual self. We are holistic beings; each part affects the rest.

Dream Spirituality also concentrates on our higher purpose. We use our understanding of a higher power to address our higher purpose and its influence on the rest of humanity. Most people, regardless of religion, acknowledge that we must learn and embrace our purpose on this earth to experience true happiness. Purpose brings clarity, vision, determination and the focus to accomplish what is needed. It fuels our spirits when challenges and troubles arise to give us the capacity to overcome life's obstacles.

VI. DREAM GROWTH

Finally, Dream Growth helps us realize that we were meant to grow. We are all meant to embrace change, to evolve, to become better than we were yesterday (Gail Sheehy). The fullest expression of living comes from our intentional growth and change. We grow to maximize our potential to be the best version of "us." Writers and music artists throughout history have addressed the need to change not our surroundings, but ourselves (Jim Rohn, Michael Jackson). Dream Growth reminds us our life and success is a lifelong journey, not a destination.

All of us have a destiny, a purpose, a mission to fulfill. Like a toddler who is falling as he is learning to walk, we have to stumble, fumble, fall, and learn to walk toward our destiny. A pianist cannot perform well on the first day of her lessons. It takes hours of practice before she can wring out a tune from the keyboard. We have to practice and grow in our gifting. The more we practice, the more skill we have. The more skill we have, the more value we add. The more value we add, the more success will follow us. We must feed the desire to grow to fulfill our destinies. What if we all celebrated a life that fulfilled our destiny? The results would be miraculous! The more we cultivate and expand the six pillars of life, the more we increase our positive impact on the world around us.

CONCLUSION

The Dream Life will radically change the way we approach life. As we strive to be our best in all six pillars, we will find we draw more people to us, and we gain more opportunities to positively impact the lives of others. It is not about what we can get from life; it is about what we can give to this world, to this life. Who knows whom we can inspire to change their lives for the better and ultimately change the world? It has to start somewhere and sometime—why not with the person in the mirror, and why not today? Our changes can cause a chain reaction, motivating others.

I want to conclude with this powerful quote from Maryanne Williamson:

"Our deepest fear is not that we are inadequate. Our deepest fear is that we are powerful beyond measure. It is our light, not our darkness that frightens us most. We ask ourselves, who am I to be brilliant, gorgeous, talented, and famous? Actually, who are you not to be? You are a child of God. Your playing small does not serve the world. There is nothing enlightened about shrinking so that people won't feel insecure around you. We were born to make manifest the glory of God that is within us. It's not just in some of us; it's in all of us. And when we let our own light shine, we unconsciously give other people permission to do the same. As we are liberated from our own fear, our presence automatically liberates others."

ABOUT REGGIE

Dr. Reggie Chandra is an entrepreneur, husband, dad, and friend whose purpose in life is to love, to be loved and to create. He lives his purpose. He expresses his love for his family by creating magic moments for them. His love for the community is expressed through his inventions, time, and resources that he spends supporting charitable organizations and mentoring younger entrepreneurs.

In 2007, Reggie invented In|Sync, a device that synchronizes traffic signals and reduces automobile crashes by 30%. His company, Rhythm Engineering, owns 95% of the US market in this technology and has been listed in the Inc. 5000 for three years. *Inc. Magazine* listed it as the 64th fastest-growing company in the US and Deloitte Fast 500 listed Rhythm Engineering as the 43rd fastest-growing company. Rhythm Engineering holds 4 patents and continues to invent new and disruptive products that revolutionize the industry. Rhythm Engineering solutions operate in over 2,000 intersections in 31 states and positively impact over 4,000,000 motorists daily.

Dr. Chandra has invented other products/solutions and has founded six other companies besides Rhythm Engineering. He has also developed a solution to run those companies without physically spending time "in" them. He is always working "on" his businesses rather than "in" them. A self-proclaimed dreamer, Reggie leads by communicating a vision, developing a plan, and stepping back to allow his team to go to work on making the dream a reality.

Reggie's other products/solutions also include Dream Cultures, (www.dreamcultures.com) where he offers a system for employees to create and live their Dream Life. Dr. Chandra is a true visionary and believes in a team environment where each employee, as a unique, remarkable and indispensable person, has the ability to contribute brilliant ideas, passion, and feedback. In everything he does, Dr. Chandra seeks to challenge the norm, think outside the proverbial box, and identify new solutions that create value and success.

As a result of his talents, Reggie was recognized as one of the United States most inspirational CEOs by *Esquire Magazine* in 2012. Sir Richard Branson, after meeting with Reggie declared that: "You should be awarded a Nobel Prize." Governors, entrepreneurial groups, and engineering organizations have also recognized Reggie for his contribution to society.

Reggie lives in Loch Lloyd, Missouri, with his wife of over 27 years, Jenny, a board-certified physician, and their two daughters, Joan and Jubilee. Joan is a final-year medical student and Jubilee is a high school student. He continues to support the community and the advancement of new technologies to make life simpler, easier and safer.

We see our clients as invited guests to a party, and we are the hosts. It's our duty, responsibility, and obligation every day to make every important aspect of the clients' experience a little bit better.

BY RUDY LIRA KUSUMA

AN ATTITUDE OF EXCELLENCE

Building the #1 Real Estate Sales Team

Typical…this is what a majority of real estate agents are. Sure, there are efforts to market and promote yourself as distinct, but in the end, one thing remains consistent for almost every agent out there: they do everything from beginning to end with their transactions, and *I mean everything*. This includes:

- Communication with clients

- All the details of the transaction

- Negotiating the contracts

- Putting up the For Sale sign

And every one of the other steps that take a buyer or seller to their closing

I couldn't tell you how long it's been that way, exactly, but I'd venture to say that it's as close "to the beginning" as you could get. *Maybe it's time that agents consider putting their days as a one-man operation to an end for everyone's benefit.*

I instantly loved real estate when I entered into it, and found a commitment to it that I knew would last me a lifetime. Because of this, I began reflecting on how different people-oriented professions managed their business. **It's very seldom that one person wears every hat**. *Instead, they choose to focus on a specific aspect of the business and become specialized in that area.* They have a general knowledge of "the business," but specific expertise. When was the last time that anyone went to visit a doctor or lawyer and that individual managed everything by themselves? It just doesn't happen, and I saw that the real estate industry was truly doing itself a disservice by not finding the strengths in people to maximize the potential of a great consumer experience. You see, every detail is important to the "overall experience," which is the hub of my business model for the cohesive team that I'm so excited to be a part of.

AT THE HEART OF IT LIES CORE VALUES

The realization that there was a more cohesive and unified way to give people a fantastic real estate experience was brought to light from a most unexpected experience. My family and I went on a Disney cruise. I'm not certain how many of you have ever been on one or had the "Disney experience," but it is incredible. Everyone knows their role and is masterful at it, lending to a more amazing experience for the customer. So inspiring!

The feeling that my experience gave me stayed with me and in 2007, when the inspiration to be a part of a team that met this concept came, I already knew that it had to be a "clients first" experience. This sounds well enough, of course, and it is something that most every agent in the industry would likely say. I knew that doing it was different. I had to seek out people who had an instinctual understanding that:

Everyone on this team had to be really happy and enjoy what they did.

This was a profound moment for me and it quickly became the focal point of the efforts to build a team that was "the best of the best." *Having a core set of values that we all naturally gravitated toward was a criterion that could not be negotiable.* Through this, we could create a strong culture that naturally created synergy, transferring a level of excitement we had as a team to our clients' ultimate experience. If Disney could do this with thousands of employees, there was definitely a way to master this with less than twenty-five employees.

Through experiences and growth and constant re-evaluation, the business model that I've come up with consists of eight core values, all which are designed to celebrate a team that really cares about what happens to each other. This is what naturally leads to a "clients first" experience.

CORE VALUE #1: DELIVER "WOW" THROUGH SERVICE.

When I first got started in the business, I saw that there were two basic types of agents that consumers came into contact with:

- **The agent who had no time.** They're good agents but too busy, because they are a one-man show.

- **The agent who has a lot of time.** They have nothing to do and spend a lot of their time cold calling and knocking on doors, hoping they'll catch a break.

Most clients see these two types of agents and they get mixed emotions. They want the best of both worlds—the successful agent and the agent who has time to make them feel like they are their only client. Why not give clients both worlds?

"Put your money where your mouth is." is a fairly common phrase, and I'm guessing that you've heard it. We take this phrase to heart with our team, because we know that once someone hires an agent they have entered into a contract that is not easily broken. **Contracts are a much bigger risk for the client than the agent, typically, which is why we offer a few incentives that help reverse the risk and put the clients at ease.** This lends credibility to our determination to provide a "client first" experience. The three incentives that have worked particularly well for us affirming the beliefs we have about this experience are:

1. We have a performance guarantee. This states that if their home doesn't sell, we will buy it.

2. If we don't return a telephone call within 24 hours, we'll give you $500.00. Having clients know that they do come first and that we're committed to their experience with our team is imperative to our success, and it's proven to be an award winning formula.

3. Property purchase promise. If you purchase one of our listings and are not happy with that property within the next three years, we'll resell it at no cost to you.

You see, it's not good enough to just take a client from Point A to Point B. Just like on the cruise, at the end of it, you want the clients saying, "Wow! This is great and I don't want it to end." *In real estate terms, this translates into us not wanting the clients to feel that our journey is done just because they've closed on their home.* This is important because the measurement of success really comes in the clients' reviews, testimonials, and if they refer other people to us. And that is why we bring the "WOW" to service and we don't settle for just closing the deal.

CORE VALUE #2: EMBRACE CHANGE

In real estate, being stuck in a certain way will assure you of one thing—that you are going to be stuck for a long time, growing stagnant, and eventually making your relevancy in your market go extinct. There is a choice to not allow this to happen, which is why our team:

- Embraces technology, knowing that it can help us serve our clients better, and even improve how well we can do our specialties within the team.

- Gives a concerted effort to stay on top of laws and regulations, which always change on a daily basis.

We always make sure that our clients get the latest and best technology, the best experience, the best 'whatever' change the industry has. We are not staying constant. One of the best ways we've been able to create this noticeable distinction in our market is by utilizing the "talking house." This is a program where someone can tune into a radio station that, while driving by a property listed for sale, would give sale information for the driver to hear all about it. Capturing potential buyers during a moment of excitement is a strong strategy, and it would be hard to capitalized on that with an actual person, as instantaneous availability is rare. Technology is a wonderful companion to the real estate industry.

CORE VALUE #3: PURSUE GROWTH

Our team is comprised of 26 team members at this time. Something that others will frequently hear me mention is, "It seems like we are a real estate company, but in reality, at the core of it, we are a personal growth development company. We just use real estate as a vehicle to do that." It's an interesting statement, one which often draws attention. This is what it means:

Every morning we spend one hour doing training. On Saturday mornings, we hold personal goals meeting, where we dive into our mastermind and discuss books that will help us grow as individuals and within the team environment. One example of a book that we've gone through is Jack Canfield's *Success Principles*.

What we wish to achieve is about more than getting leads and referrals, it's about ensuring that we grow as individuals. That is how you make a team stronger and experience how it starts to shine, or shine brighter in this case.

CORE VALUE #4: HAVE FUN

We all enjoy what we do, which makes for such a fun work environment. This type of infectious nature carries over into what clients feel when they walk into our office. They don't need to hear us say we are a team—they feel how we are a team.

It's all about keeping it fun and interesting, as well. For example, at least once a month—most often the last Friday of the month—we have what's called a "performance club." This club is for everybody who receives at least one endorsement and referral from clients. We do something fun to celebrate this. In the past, we've gone to Las Vegas, went shooting, to Disneyland, or go a bit smaller—hanging out at the bar and having a great meal. The purpose is to celebrate, because these individual accolades are all a part of making a stronger team.

CORE VALUE #5: OPEN COMMUNICATION

Since we run our operation as a team, the clients only have one point of contact for each part of their transaction. In order to keep this flow and process running smoothly, we need to have open internal communication to have maximum effectiveness with our client communication. To do this, we:

- Make sure that clients always know what stage of their transaction they are at and everything involving it.
- Use our daily hour-meeting to address anything that may impact our operations, remaining mindful to our ultimate goals as a team.
- Operate as a "flat organization." There is no hierarchy or bureaucracy, because we don't want to focus on office politics; only what is best for the client.

Communication is an art form and together, we've found a way to ensure that we are paying attention to how we do it and always remembering why it's so important!

CORE VALUE #6: POSITIVE TEAM SPIRIT

Every person who enters our office notices a few things immediately.

- First, we have no walls, which means no private offices. Closed off spaces leads to a team that's not as cohesive as it could be.
- Second, when people walk into our office—clients especially—they are greeted with people looking at them, smiling, and showing that they are welcome, not an intrusion. It's genuine!

These steps, while unheard of in many real estate environments, are one of our strongest attributing factors for our success. *There's a sense of joy, and people reveal how appealing this is through their expressions toward us.*

CORE VALUE #7: BE PASSIONATE

Our team is about more than selling homes. From within, we truly are a personal growth company. Achieving personal and professional excellence is our mission and that's the type of people we attract to the team. Our passion is enthusiastic and we realize the purpose in everything that we do, each and every day.

Every Tuesday we hold various seminars in our office, inviting people from the community in. We are consistent and deliver great information and people know this—making it a ten-plus-year tradition. We deliver without fail and we're consistent, not growing tired of the knowledge we have to share, because we are all so passionate about it.

The people that become a part of our team have this clear understanding of the qualities that are expected from them. For some, it may be a bit too much, and that's okay. We are not for everyone—we are for those who want to find genuine satisfaction and fulfillment through using our business model—the "client first" formula.

CORE VALUE #8: GIVING BACK TO THE COMMUNITY

For every transaction our team does, a portion of the income goes to the children's hospital in our area. For one example, this year we are on a mission to raise $100,000. **Our team wants to be a part of our community, not just a stellar sales team, and giving back exemplifies how important this is to us**. It's more than words, it's actions. So, where some people will give a client a gift card, maybe, to show their appreciation, we can think of no better gift for us to give our clients or community than the gift of giving back to the community as a whole. Stronger communities make for happier residents within them, and this inspires us.

Never losing sight of where we can go...

Our desire to have a client-centric real estate team structure based on a proactive sales system that serves our VIP clients—which is every client—with less hassle, is what we are always working toward. It motivates all of us and keeps us on track.

At this time, we're not quite there, but we are the #1 team for ReMax Systems in California. We have our sights set on becoming the #1 team in the United States this year, and from there, we hope that it will continue to grow. And as it does, I'm excited to see how this business model and team that we've created is cultivating leaders to make other teams that have the same core values. Basically, through our commitment and showing the rewards of a "client first" approach, we are revamping the perception of real estate agents for consumers everywhere—and this is an exciting change!

ABOUT RUDY

Rudy L. Kusuma is an investor, best-selling author, business coach, entrepreneur, and top-producing real estate agent. He is the Founder and CEO of RE/MAX TITANIUM and the Managing Director of TEAM NUVISION, the #1 Real Estate Sales Team in San Gabriel Valley. He has been recognized as one of the Top 100 team leaders in RE/MAX Worldwide (out of 100,000 real estate agents).

Rudy and his team have sold over $500 Million in transactions. He has been awarded multiple top producers awards, including The Five Star Real Estate Professional Award as published in the *Los Angeles Magazine,* and named as one of America's Best Real Estate Agents as published in *The Wall Street Journal.*

As a philanthropist, Rudy is on a mission to raise $100,000 for the Children's Hospital in downtown Los Angeles. For every house that his team sells, Rudy and his team are donating a portion of their income to the Children's Hospital. Not only home sellers benefit from his team's award-winning service, but they donate a substantial portion of their income on every home sale to help the local children in the community.

Rudy has advised and counseled home buyers, sellers, and real estate investors from every walk of life. CEO's, executives, and business owners hire his team because their businesses are "Teams", so they understand and appreciate Rudy's Team Home Selling System. Sales Professionals and Marketing-Oriented Entrepreneurs hire Rudy's team because they quickly recognize the superiority of Rudy's sophisticated System for selling homes as quickly as possible, for top dollars. Doctors, Hospital Administrators, and Nurses hire Rudy's team because, like the executives, they are thoroughly familiar with the benefits of a Team Approach. Exceptionally busy couples hire Rudy's team because his home selling system features methods of marketing and selling homes that minimizes their involvement and inconvenience.

Rudy provides numerous public resources regarding how to buy and sell real estate in today's real estate market. In addition, as a Certified Distressed Property Expert, Rudy contributes weekly articles on foreclosure prevention options available to homeowners. His expert advice has been published by community newspapers, including: *Indonesia Media, Mid Valley News, Temple City Life, Temple City Tribune, Arcadia Weekly, Monrovia Weekly, El Monte Examiner, San Gabriel Sun, Duarte Dispatch, Rosemead Reader, Azusa Beacon,* and *Around Alhambra.*

Rudy L. Kusuma is the author of *The Ultimate NO HOLDS BARRED Guide to Selling & Buying a Home in the San Gabriel Valley* and the co-author of the book that will change the landscape of real estate industry, *Death of the Traditional Real Estate Salesperson: Rise of The Super-Profitable Real Estate Sales Team.*

Rudy L. Kusuma lives in Temple City with his wife and two sons. He can be reached online at: www.TeamNuVision.net or by telephone at 626-780-2221.

PREMIERE FASHION EXPERT LEARNS THE DEEPER MEANING OF SUCCESS

PERFORMANCE: Why did you choose fashion as a career, and how did you get started in that industry?

ULRICH: I came to it very naturally thirty-five years ago. My father's parents owned a farm south of Munich, Germany where I lived until I was four years old. Even back then, I would change clothes three times a day – and everyone thought it was unusual and wondered how I could be part of this farm family. That desire to be fashionable continued in school when I also changed three times a day – one outfit for school, another for meeting a girlfriend in the afternoon, still another hanging out later with the guys. I've always been interested in fashion, and was always attracted by the clothes worn by beautiful women in the fashion world. After attending high school in Rosenheim, I moved to a small city in France, where I got a good job for a food company. But I didn't feel comfortable with all of the ingredients they put in the items they sold. I made good money, but I didn't sleep well at night.

Everyone thought I was crazy to give up a good job and a nice apartment, but I took the risk and searched for other employment. A company called Marc O'Polo was looking for new salesmen for their Italian brand *Mason's*. I started there at age twenty and over the next fourteen years, worked my way up to Sales and Product-Manager and finally CEO and shareholder. I have just always been very strong at sales.

PERFORMANCE: Earlier in your life and career, how did you define success? How has that definition changed over the years?

ULRICH: My perspectives about life and success were shaped by many different personal experiences at an early age. When I started working for Marc O'Polo during the time many of my friends were still at University, I thought I had it all. I was driving a BMW, earned a lot of money and had many girlfriends. But the reason I couldn't go to University was pretty traumatic. When I was 15, I had acute pancreatitis and was in the hospital seven

I learned that true success results from your relationships.

times, and the following year I was in a coma and ultimately had to have a major operation. The doctors were pessimistic. They said if we do the surgery you will live till you are forty, but if not, you will only have another two years. They wanted me to take forty-five pills every day, but I refused to take their advice, believing that if there was an ultimate plan for my life I would survive.

Fortunately, I pulled through, but even while enjoying material success in the fashion industry, I had many ups and downs with the company. I made up my mind and became both a free agent salesperson and a shareholder. At one point I got married, but it didn't work out. I thought entering the distribution side of the industry would make us rich and I could slow down, but working so many hours took its toll on the relationship. The divorce was the bitter pill I had to swallow for focusing so much on having this huge career.

Later, I married Inge and we stared our own trading company, Faro Fashion, which specialized in the import of high-end Italian fashion wear. But that ultimately failed. Instead of declaring bankruptcy, I vowed to repay each of my creditors in full. From these hard experiences and our later success as distributors of the brand *CLOSED* in Bavaria, I learned that true success results from your relationships, not from just doing well in business. Life is too precious to just care about business.

PERFORMANCE: You took over the distribution of CLOSED in 1998. How did you proceed in developing your business?

ULRICH: When we started, the brand was a rock bottom, and we changed the distribution model in Bavaria. But despite previous challenges, I had always known that if I commit to the success of a company, I will follow through on that and stick with it for a long time. Slowly but surely, we built a good team and began developing the brand. Customers believed in us and our relationship was more like family and friends. In ten years we took revenues from 900 Euro to nearly 5 million. We have increased the international visibility for the brand and I'm pleased that our ethical standards ensured that customers knew we would never cheat them.

PERFORMANCE: Then, a few years ago, even as you were enjoying the success of the company, you experienced a powerful change in your personal life that sparked new passion outside the business realm.

ULRICH: Three years ago, my mother had an operation that failed and left her paralyzed. When she entered a nursing home for the first time, it led to real change in my life. While Inge, my wife, was still taking care of the distribution of *CLOSED* ladies' collection, I left my side of the business to a young man who was paid directly by the company's main office in Hamburg. I dedicated myself to taking care of my mother and volunteered to participate in many of the nursing home's events like Mardi Gras parties and Oktoberfest to spend more time with her during the phase of her adjustment. I also brought food and coffee to her elderly peers, and came up with the idea of preparing stories to read to them every Monday. Pretty soon, although my mom became a vocal critic of some of my readings, it became the favorite hour of the week for many of them.

I learned about the immense power and emotional impact of storytelling, which inspired my later writing endeavors and my ultimate goal now of succeeding in that area.

PERFORMANCE: During this time CLOSED appointed you as their official fashion broker and location scout.

ULRICH: I created a new contract with the company, dealing with the future of fashion, which is in retail stores, franchised shops and online business and other outlets. I deal with the retail people who run our shops, and choose the right franchise partners. These shops only have the *CLOSED* brand. It's more interesting work for me, and the main thing is to motivate people to form franchise partnerships. As a veteran salesperson myself, I'm aware that success in building a franchise store is based on having empathy and understanding for a customer. Thus I wanted to create these partnerships with people who will know the right way to talk to them, and understand the value of common courtesy and the fact that customers don't like pushy salespersons. That's why I prefer to work with people who will understand the deep commitment it takes to succeed.

PERFORMANCE: In line with those qualities, what are some of the keys to being successful overall in the fashion industry?

ULRICH: You have to love fashion and identify with your product. If you don't like the collections you're working with, you can't convince customers of their value. There are some brands people have a momentary interest in, but if you work with long-existing brands that succeed through many seasons, you'll be motivated to sell them, and your customers will understand that value and feel excitement. With every customer, building trust is what counts most. If people come into your showroom, the most important thing is that you create an atmosphere in which you're both the leader and team player, treating everyone with respect. My favorite saying is, "Your work time is your life time."

Further, please be more honest. Not every item is super, so don't tell your customer it is. The company wants you to sell everything they have, but your obligation is to lead the customer through the collection to find what they need. You should focus on taking care of them. If you are only aiming for the money, and your choices make them unhappy, that's not going to be good for anybody.

PERFORMANCE: Let's get back to your volunteer work with the nursing home your mother lived in. How did those experiences lead to your desire to connect with Jack Canfield of Chicken Soup for the Soul fame, who invited you to be a contributing author in his book The Soul of Success? I love the name of your chapter, "It's All About Fashion – There is no second chance for your first impression!" It connects so perfectly and metaphorically with your career in the fashion world.

ULRICH: There's a lot of irony in this. Originally I started reading at the nursing home for a selfish reason because I thought it would help my mother get the private room she wanted. When she passed away, they assumed I would stop doing charity work, but I realized that I loved reading to these folks too much to stop. I turned into a wonderful source for many of my readings: those small beautiful stories in some of Jack Canfield's *Chicken Soup for the Soul* books. I knew they wanted to hear funny, uplifting stories. Connecting with these people created a complete transformation in me. For thirty-five years, I had been making people look good on the outside. Now, all that mattered was helping people feel good on the inside. I came to Philadelphia in 2012 to attend a Bestseller Blueprint Seminar with Jack Canfield and marketing expert Steve Harrison. Jack's story really inspired me. He was refused 140 times by publishers and now he has sold over 500 million books!

When I met him for the first time, I jokingly told him I would not have come all the way to Philadelphia had I known he had just done a seminar in Heidelberg. He kindly invited me to a lunch with some very prominent people free of charge. He later told me that a single book isn't as effective as creating a series like he did.

This was the start of my book, "It's All About Fashion – There is no second chance for your first impression!" which is still a work in progress. The chapter in Jack's book with the same title is the basic text part for that project.

My goal now is to inspire and motivate people.

PERFORMANCE: What is the essential point that is communicated in the chapter – and ultimately, the book?

ULRICH: It's about the idea that there is no second chance to create that first impression. In less than one second, we decide whether we like or not. In fashion, it's all about judging by appearances and what we're wearing. But the truth of who we are goes deeper than that. Maybe those first impressions are wrong, and that guy we thought we didn't like from the start turns out to be a nice guy.

We're trained to hide behind the products we have, the cars, watches and fancy stuff, but I want people to understand that we're more than just what people see on the surface. I talk about the ways fashion can be a strong tool in our ultimate self-expression, and how to identify the type of person you are. So I talk about things on the outside and how they connect with what is on the inside – and how to find your own style.

I make some major statements at the end of the chapter: Live here and now! You can achieve anything with a pinch of humor. Those who do not live authentically as themselves will run after every trend forever. On a personal level, these writings are part of my desire to start a second life for myself with a new career beyond the fashion industry – finding new ways to help people, just as everyone can do something to make the world a better place.

For years I gave money to global organizations like Greenpeace, and that's great, but the whole nursing home experience made me realize we can accomplish a lot right in our own neighborhood. These elderly folks have given me so much just by listening. It will be my honor to tell some of their stories in my next book.

PERFORMANCE: It sounds like you are finding new ways to define success for yourself outside the industry you are best known for.

ULRICH: My goal now is to inspire and motivate people. I recently thought back to when I was sixteen and so sick from pancreatitis. I just wanted to live a normal life. I stopped writing down my dreams because I felt I might not live long enough to realize them. But that inner voice came back two years ago. It told me that I had been through so many things and I could use those experiences to help people. I was told I would not survive. All of my family members, including my brothers have passed away. Nobody on my father's side of the family ever lived longer than 54 years. There's no time like the present, and I'm on a mission to motivate people to not forget their dreams, even if they're sick or broke or facing any other sort of adversity.

I want to share my message that everyone should do something to make the world a better place. I'm so blessed with a loving wife and business partner and good friends. And embarking on these creative endeavors, I have met so many incredible people I would never have met in the fashion industry. Rather than talking over and over about the next collection in London, Paris or Milan, I'm talking about things of greater significance to me.

ABOUT ULRICH

After finishing high school, Ulrich Kellerer went to work for six months in France and travelling became his passion. Being at Fashion Fairs in Italy-Florence, France-Paris, Berlin, Dusseldorf and Munich in Germany, he got well-known in his fashion field.

Ulrich started his career in the fashion business in the early 80's, when he took a sales position at Marc O'Polo and Mason's. His strong selling skills and tenacious personality quickly made him Sales and Product Manager, and finally CEO and shareholder of the company Mason's.

He then started his own trading company called Faro Fashion together with his wife as a partner. Faro Fashion specialized in the import of high-end Italian fashion wear.

In 1998, Ulrich and his wife Inge and their Team took over the distribution of the brand CLOSED in Bavaria, Germany, which they have done for more than 17 years now.

Ulrich Kellerer advises his clients on the latest fashion styles and trends. Most recently CLOSED, a leading European fashion company for women's and men's sportswear, appointed him their official fashion broker and location scout.

American celebrities and trendsetters, such as Brad Pitt, Tom Cruise, Patrick Dempsey, Sarah Jessica Parker, Katie Holmes, Drew Barrymore, etc. have been supportive in establishing CLOSED as a recognized brand in the US.

In 2012, Ulrich came to Philadelphia to attend a seminar with Steve Harrison and met Jack Canfield for the first time. Jack recommended that he write a series of books like he did with *Chicken Soup For The Soul*. So Ulrich's first book, *It's All About Fashion*, started here.

 A media summit in New York showed Ulrich how the U.S. market worked. A further meeting with Steve Harrison and Jack Canfield in Philadelphia made his second life possible, including writing books and living for a new purpose.

Since 2013, Ulrich reads for charity every week in a nursing home, where he lost his mother seven months ago.

You can contact Ulrich at:
Ulrich.kellerer@t-online.de
www.facebook.com/ulrich.kellerer
www.twitter.com/KellererUlrich
You can find his website/blog at:
ulrich-kellerer.com or ulrich-kellerer.de

Having a World Class Mindset will directly affect how we perform, think and act.

BY HENRIK ROSVALL

A M.A.P. FOR ACHIEVING HIGH PERFORMANCE

How can you increase performance in terms of productivity? How can you make your performance more consistent? What factors influence performance? What factors can you control and what factors are not within your control?

During my keynote speeches to companies and associations, I am often asked to speak on performance success and to share my M.A.P. System for Achieving High Performance. The M.A.P. System has been developed through extensive research and coaching over the past 25 years.

After the initial keynote, I am then asked to come to the various offices and departments around the nation, as well as internationally, to conduct more in-depth programs on leadership, team-building and communication. The M.A.P. System serves as the foundation as we address specific and proven ways to:

- Increase profitability
- Lead with a World Class Mindset
- Increase sales and productivity
- Improve leadership effectiveness
- Improve employee motivation
- Increase employee satisfaction
- Improve customer service
- Increase accountability
- Increase employee retention

When I begin working with organizations, departments and teams, the starting point varies. There are some who already are doing very well and clearly understand the benefits of having a world-class coach help them get to the next level.

Other times, the starting point is very different, with some very clear challenges that need to be addressed immediately. In either scenario, the M.A.P. System is used to create a new standard, where the bar is raised and a deliberate work environment is created that feels empowering, motivating and conducive to achieve high performance on a consistent basis.

Each World Class Mindset Program is customized for the group and individuals, and the practical tools and strategies that are shared are beneficial both professionally and personally. I take great pride in providing a fun, empowering and educational learning environment where the participants feel safe expanding their existing comfort zones and make new distinctions. Because I have worked with companies from so many different industries in the past 30 years, I frequently share best practices as well as what doesn't work.

I am confident that if you apply the M.A.P. System, you too, will continue to achieve high performance results. Below you will see a description of the M.A.P. System along with a Case Study for each key point. Additionally, you will see areas where you have the opportunity to assess where you currently stand in terms of your Mindset, your Awareness, and what you Project.

I. MINDSET

In everything we do and everywhere we go, we take our Mindset with us. There are many types of mindsets such as a positive mindset, negative mindset, team-player mindset, victim mindset, raise-the-bar mindset, check-the-box mindset, possibility mindset, etc.

The type of mindset that we have will directly affect how we perform, think and act. Unfortunately, for many people, they haven't made a decision to commit to have a mindset that is positive and exceptional – a World Class Mindset. The truly exceptional high performers do not leave their mindset to chance. Instead, they have made the decision to proactively continue to condition their mindset so that it works for them in all that they do, *every single day*.

Case Study:

When Sara contacted me to start coaching her and her senior management team, they were already doing very well. The company was very profitable, the employee morale was very high and the customer satisfaction ratings were at the top in the industry. As the CEO, Sara was well-respected and perceived to be a very effective leader with a positive leadership presence. Her senior management team worked well together as a team. So why would Sara contact me to work with her and her team if things were going so well already?

Because Sara has what I call a "World-Class Mindset." With this mindset, she understood the importance of ongoing coaching to take herself, her team and the company to the next level. Continuing to learn, grow and make new distinctions has kept the motivation high and continues to be a huge competitive advantage.

With Sara's World Class Mindset, she also understood the distinction between "investing" and "spending." In my first year working with her company, a six-figure contract was signed. Because the ROI has continued to be so high, Sara has continued to renew this six-figure contract each year. By publicly holding herself accountable and introducing a company culture where self-accountability and taking 100% personal responsibility are core values, the performance, profitability and employee satisfaction has soared. Having a World Class Mindset permeate throughout the company has been transformational.

Assessment:

1. What is your current overall Mindset?

	Poor	Average	Good	Great	World Class

2. What is your Mindset as a Leader?

	Poor	Average	Good	Great	World Class

3. What is your Mindset in terms of being coachable?

	Poor	Average	Good	Great	World Class

II. AWARENESS

Having a high level of awareness directly affects how well you perform and there are numerous areas where this is beneficial, such as:

- Having a high level of awareness of your strengths so that you can use them proactively and frequently.

- Having a high level of awareness of how you are currently being perceived as a leader, team-player, communicator, listener, etc.

- Having a high level of awareness of what is the most productive use of your time, so that you can design your days and life accordingly.

In my talks, I bring up several topics where a common reflection I hear from the participants is "I have never even thought about that." Once the audience members have the awareness that certain topics are beneficial to become really aware of, they are then given a proven action plan. In the sessions conducted in-house with various teams and departments, as well as in my World Class VIP Retreats, we then make having a high level of awareness a central focus. Continuing to make distinctions and increase their awareness is something that the participants point to as being a game-changer for them, both professionally and personally. With this awareness, they then take massive proactive and consistent action upon the strategies and solutions shared with them.

Case Study:

Peter wanted results. He had no problem letting his employees know his disappointment by screaming at them when he felt they weren't performing.

I conducted an anonymous survey where 96% of the employees shared that they felt de-motivated by Peter's leadership style. Being chewed out in public and walking around on eggshells was not helping the employees perform and meet the goals that Peter had set. When I asked Peter if he was aware of how he was currently being perceived by his employees, he proudly shared that "I hope they look up to me and feel like what I say goes." When I shared the survey results with him, he wasn't surprised at all. Why not? Because he had been very deliberate about being a very authoritative leader who micro-managed and controlled as much as possible everything he could around him. He didn't seem to mind that almost everyone viewed him as a non-approachable, "my-way-or-the-highway" type of leader.

When I explained to him that such a leadership style was directly compromising results and performance – which is what he ultimately wanted – then I had his attention and he became receptive to listen to my coaching advice. Through the coaching, Peter increased his awareness of how his leadership style directly impacted the performance and productivity of his employees. With this awareness, we then worked together on a specific strategy that would transform how he interacted with the employees and how they perceived him.

I challenged Peter to be 100% committed to the steps and actions I would be recommending to him. He accepted the challenge. Six months later, when I conducted a follow-up survey with the employees, Peter's approval rating had skyrocketed. Every single employee reported that they much preferred the "new and improved" Peter, who didn't scream and yell, who didn't micro-manage, who made the employees feel valued and appreciated and who listened to their input and feedback. What happened to sales during that six-month period? A 23% increase. This was of course no surprise. Peter had increased his Awareness, and then committed to taking proactive and consistent action on it.

Assessment:

1. How would you assess your current Awareness in terms of your strengths:

| Poor | Average | Good | Great | World Class |

2. How would you assess your current Awareness in terms of how well you understand how others currently perceive you?

| Poor | Average | Good | Great | World Class |

3. How would you assess your current Awareness in terms of how to best use your time to maximize productivity and performance?

| Poor | Average | Good | Great | World Class |

III. PROJECTION

What are you projecting outward? Confidence? Positive energy? Can-do attitude? Or are you projecting negativity, stress or overwhelm? Does what you project outward affect your performance and the performance of others? Most definitely!

In my keynotes and coaching, I share the importance of being proactive and deliberate about what is projected, especially when you are in a key position in a company with the spotlight on you at all times. Others *do* notice what you project, both the good and the not so good.

As leaders, for us to get results through others while keeping them motivated and empowered, we need to make a commitment to project a confident leadership presence where others clearly understand what we stand for, what our vision is and they feel valued, appreciated and listened to.

To achieve high performance for yourself and those around you, make a commitment to focus on what you and the others are projecting. Is what is currently projected what you want projected? Or what new actions can be taken to accomplish the desired outward projection?

Steve, president of a large multi-national company, conducted a monthly all-staff meeting for all employees. The 250 or so employees at the corporate headquarters went to the large lobby area each month and attended in person, and the employees at the other locations were able to watch a video feed of the meeting.

When I started working with Steve and his senior management team, he was seriously considering doing away with the monthly all-staff meeting. He shared that he didn't feel like they were responding to what he was saying and it had become a burden for him to prepare for each monthly presentation. When I asked some of the employees what they thought of the monthly meeting, they thought it was a waste of time to see him read a power point, without any engagement with anyone. They reported that they felt he was merely "checking the box" and going through the motions at the monthly meeting. He came across as a weak leader without confidence.

I met with Steve and we focused on what he wanted to project to his employees, which was confidence, being able to make difficult decisions, and being approachable. I gave him some very specific action items for the next meeting and he did exactly what I suggested. He showed up at the meeting without a coat and tie. He sat relaxed on a raised chair in front of the room, instead of standing behind a podium. He had no power point slides. He just talked from the heart, on several occasions getting up from the chair to walk around among his employees. He followed my advice to avoid the standard "are there any questions?" at the end of his talk, and instead he invited questions *throughout* his talk.

What has resulted is a Steve that is eagerly anticipating each monthly all-staff meeting. He keeps a folder of what he will bring up in future meetings, constantly looking to take the meetings to the next level. After each meeting he writes down what worked well and what he wants to improve for future meetings. The employees are equally excited about each monthly meeting. They now feel like he genuinely cares about them and as a direct result, their motivation and productivity has soared.

Assessment:

1. Assess your current level of CONFIDENCE that you project outward:

Poor	Average	Good	Great	World Class

2. Assess your current level of POSITIVE ENERGY that you project outward:

Poor	Average	Good	Great	World Class

3. Assess your current level of being an ATTENTIVE LISTENER that you project outward:

Poor	Average	Good	Great	World Class

SUMMARY

Life can be very challenging, with countless demands and expectations - both professional and personal. The M.A.P. System will give you, your team, and your organization a solid foundation and proven strategies and solutions that are sure to help you achieve consistent high performance, profitability and positive results!

ABOUT HENRIK

Henrik Rosvall, Coach To Champions, is walking his talk – literally.

Paralyzed from the chest down in 2007, doctors informed him that he would most likely never walk again. In what became the Ultimate Case Study, Henrik used the same tools and mindset that he had used as a successful entrepreneur to defy the odds and eventually learn to walk again.

As President of **In The Zone Institute**, Henrik has over 25 years of speaking and coaching experience on such topics as mindset, leadership, teambuilding, sales success and high performance. Henrik mixes humor and enthusiasm with empowering stories to deliver a high content message that equips audiences with practical and proven tools. Participants condition their World Class Mindsets in a safe, inspirational and highly energizing learning environment.

Henrik is a highly sought-after motivational speaker, coach and best-selling author. He is frequently interviewed on topics related to mindset and how it affects behavior and performance. He shares his World Class Mindset Philosophy through:

- Keynotes
- Elite coaching
- World Class Mindset Programs
- VIP Retreats
- Home Study courses
- Breakout sessions

Three highly popular keynotes are:
- World Class Mindset for Success
- World Class Mindset for Leadership Success
- World Class Mindset for Sales Success

Thousands of people have been impacted by Henrik's mission of helping children, teenagers and adults to have a positive mindset and attitude as they go through life. Instead of living life as victims or in a constant state of stress and overwhelm, Henrik is committed to help his audiences re-claim their lives and take themselves to the next level. A certified Peak Performance Coach and graduate of Jack Canfield's *Train The Trainer* program, Henrik is committed to talking *with,* instead of *at* audiences. Messages such as *Walking The Talk, Being In The Zone On Demand, Conditioning A World Class Mindset and Overcoming Obstacles* are all in high demand. Because of his high-energy presentation style, Henrik raises the bar and equips the audiences with a positive mindset and attitude.

Credibility is essential when booking a speaker and hiring a coach. Henrik gets results, earning him extremely loyal clients who hire him time and time again.

You can connect with Henrik at:
Henrik@WorldClassMindset.com
www.WorldClassMindset.com

BY DAVID LEE

SIX THINGS KITESURFING TAUGHT ME

About Being A Successful Entrepreneur

I'm honored to share pages in this book with fellow entrepreneur, Sir Richard Branson. His passion towards business success, adventure, and living life to its fullest has been an inspiration to me throughout the years. We're also connected through a common, unique passion: kitesurfing.

I grew up in Northern California where constant exposure to high adventure sports like waterskiing, mountain biking, skiing, and windsurfing became part of who I am. I loved the freedom and the challenge found in these sports as well as being in the beautiful outdoors with family or friends.

Then, years ago while on vacation with my wife in Tahiti, I saw a guy on what looked like a wakeboard being pulled across the turquoise water by a massive, yellow, C-shaped kite. I was in awe. The Tahitians called it "Fly Surfing"… and I knew it was something I HAD to do.

Unfortunately, I wasn't able to try it out in Tahiti, but years later I finally started to take kitesurfing lessons, bought gear, and committed myself to learn. And, I thought, because of my background in high adventure sports, it would be easy. It wasn't.

Kitesurfing turned out to be one of the most difficult things I have ever learned. It was unbelievably brutal and frustrating, and I almost gave up and quit multiple times. But I pushed forward, and it has become something I love.

So why do people, myself included, find so much joy in extreme sports and activities?

Even if you don't participate in adventure sports yourself, it's hard to take your eyes off someone risking their own life in the most extreme ways possible. When you see a GoPro video of a surfer barreling down the face of a massive multi-story wave or a mountain biker racing through a

> ## It's hard to take your eyes off someone risking their own life in the most extreme ways possible.

narrow gulch...do you feel that adrenaline? How did you feel the last time you did something adventurous, thrilling or dangerous? Did you learn something? About yourself? Your relationships? Your character?

For me, my adrenaline rush comes from kitesurfing. I found that as you grow towards mastering an extreme sport like this, you gain important learning opportunities. Not just about the sport, but about who you are, how you work and what motivates you. And the best part is, you take this with you into life, business, and relationships.

THE AH-HA MOMENT

After I went through kitesurfing's steep learning curve and started to get more involved in the kitesurfing world, I started to notice something. An unusual number of kitesurfers are entrepreneurs too. Then it dawned on me. Kitesurfing and entrepreneurship share a lot of the same principals, lessons, challenges, and thrills.

As I continued to think, I started to see some of the parallels between kitesurfing and business success. And, I'd like to share six of them with you. Whether you enjoy extreme sports like kitesurfing or not, my hope is that you'll be able to relate to these parallels and the lessons learned will help you on your journey to greater success in business and life.

LESSON #1: LEARN TO NOT DIE

The first few days of learning to kitesurf, you are taught all the fundamentals, the skills, the basics, the equipment, how to set it up, take it down, and all the hazards to watch out for so you don't kill yourself or anybody else around you. It can be a very dangerous sport. The power of the kite can rip you across the ground or launch you 200 feet in the air and kill you. So, for most of the introductory lessons, you're taught to take care of yourself... otherwise serious injury or death can result.

In business, there are things that we do, or continue to do, that can kill our businesses. Common things I've seen include:

- Misguided belief that an expert 'operator' will be an expert business 'owner'
- Waiting until the product or service is perfect
- Not paying yourself first
- Lack of follow-up or lazy sales processes
- Thinking you can do it all yourself

When my business partner, Brad Martineau, and I started our first venture together, we were professionals at almost killing the business. For example, we made the huge mistake of not paying ourselves first. We went four months without pay and instead opted to pay our contractors and everyone else but us. It was a recipe for disaster. Fortunately, we turned that around and it strengthened us AND the business.

Another time, we relied too heavily on a single sales channel. A lot of our sales were generated at in-person events and conferences. We invested a lot of money into one particular conference. It was supposed to bring a couple of hundred qualified prospects into a room where we would present and sell. It was supposed to be one of our biggest moneymakers of the year. And guess what? Fewer than ten people came to our session. Zero sales. It was a complete bomb and it almost killed the business. So we had to learn to diversify how and where we sold our services.

We were scrappy, but we learned to not die. Each of these experiences... and MANY others like them, made us stronger.

To keep the business from not dying, it's important to focus on a core product or service that is well-defined and sellable. This includes everything from making sure the experience is dialed in for your customers and clients, to making sure you have ongoing sales efforts to ensure your product/service is profitable. Then, once that's solid, you can keep it running while you focus on strengthening other aspects of your business such as marketing, operations, finance, culture, vision and strategic planning.

LESSON #2: LAUNCH +1

In kitesurfing, it's MUCH safer if you have a partner or a friend to help you launch and land the kite. The kiting community is a very open community. They are there to help you because safety is in everybody's best interest. It's a great community.

Kitesurfing is quickly becoming the new "golf course" for entrepreneurs and deal-making. In 2014, I was fortunate enough to attend MaiTai's (www.maitaiglobal.org) big annual event in Maui where a unique blend of entrepreneurs, venture capitalists, and professional kiters come together for business presentations, classes, and kiting. The sessions were fantastic, but the best part of the event was just hanging out on the beach after the morning presentations and classes. Between kitesurfing, we talked about the wind, kite equipment, life stories, what we do for business, and more.

One of the guys I hung out with, Kurtis Shipcott, has become a great friend and is on a mission to keep surfers' and kitesurfers' eyes safe by designing the best surf eyewear in the world (www.kurtiseyewear.com).

Another person I met, Hans Robertson, sold his business to Cisco for $1.2 billion… in cash. I don't know many billionaires, but here he was, just another dude hanging out on the beach swapping stories and kiting together.

Kurtis, Hans, and everyone else in attendance were down-to-earth people and completely willing to give, advise, share, listen, contribute, and help anyone.

The experience reminded me of a great African proverb I once heard: "If you want to go fast, go alone. If you want to go far, go together."

If you're serious about long-term value creation or building a business that will last, having a partner, a coach, or a mentor is critical. If you look at many of the big successful brands including Apple, Intel, HP, Google, Twitter, eBay, Yahoo!, Microsoft and many others, they were started by two or more people.

So if you don't have one, go get one – a partner, advisor, mentor, or mastermind group. Don't be embarrassed to ask for help. If you're not sure where to start, the resources below have helped me in a significant way:

- Strategic Coach (www.strategiccoach.com)
- Evoking Genius (www.evokinggenius.com)
- Genius Network (www.geniusnetwork.com)
- The War Room (www.digitalmarketer.com)

And, if you're already super successful and past needing help yourself, if you see someone "new to the beach" looking around and unsure of what to do next, be the one to introduce yourself and lend a helping hand. Small businesses already face too many hazards on the road to success. Be the one to create an environment more like the kitesurfing community.

LESSON #3: JUST KEEP FLYING

A really good kitesurfer, even if they crash, will keep their kite flying in the air. Or, when the wind weakens or hits a lull, a solid kiter will "pump" the kite up and down in the sky to keep it powered up and flying.

Really successful entrepreneurs out there do the same thing when markets get weak, currents change, or the business stumbles. They make changes, shifts, and quick corrections to keep the business flying.

When Brad and I started one of our ventures, SixthDivision, it grew very quickly. In fact, we exploded past seven figures in sales within eight months. We did very well.

But, the vast majority of our revenue was processed via credit card. American Express didn't like the quick growth – it triggered risk flags on their end and they clamped down on us. It also didn't help that when they started to research us, we were a newly formed business and our office, which was in a brand new building, didn't show up as a valid address in their records. So, needless to say, they doubted our legitimacy.

They continued to process credit card transactions for us, but kept $186,000 in a reserve and wouldn't release a dime. We needed to pay rent, ourselves, employees, contractors, and continue to run the business… but our money was locked down for almost a year. It was brutal.

But, it taught us to be very frugal and manage our money with exactness. We had to learn to adjust and keep the kite flying.

LESSON #4: LET GO

In kiting, when a big gust comes, instincts tell you to grab on to the bar tighter and pull in. In reality, that powers the kite up even more and can rip you forward and drag you "over the handlebars" and wrench you, face-first, into the water… and then drag you a couple dozen yards while your eye sockets, mouth, and nose are fire-hosed with salt water. If you can't tell from the description, I've done this numerous times.

When big gusts hit, what you should do actually is sheet out…let go. That depowers the kite and it allows you to regain control so that you can continue on.

Think about the last time you experienced a big challenge or opportunity in your business. What did you do? Did you grab on tighter, pull in, and control? Or did you push out, let go, delegate, and multiply yourself through others? I'm betting you did the former. I'm guilty of it too.

At one point, Brad and I decided that in order to grow more, I should step down as CEO of SixthDivision, our primary company, so I could focus on building a new software venture we had created called PlusThis.

Up to that point, all my focus, energy, and passion had been put into SixthDivision, so as you can imagine, stepping down from something I had poured my soul into wasn't the easiest thing to do. However, the software company we created was suffering. It wasn't getting the attention it needed to thrive like SixthDivision was thriving. I needed to put all the energy I spent into SixthDivision into PlusThis, while Brad continued to drive SixthDivision forward.

So, I had to let go… to let go of my baby that I had created. And now, both organizations are more efficient, profitable, and successful. And, we're having a great time.

> # So, I had to let go... to let go of my baby that I had created.

LESSON #5: FIND THE POWER ZONE

In kiting, to have any measure of success, you've got to understand the "wind window" – where the wind is strongest, directly downwind of you. The key is to set the kite in the air somewhere in-between where the wind isn't too strong, but it also isn't too light. It's the power zone. It's where you're most efficient and balanced between power and control.

In business, it is critical to find the power zone, and avoid getting caught in the whirlwind.

When we started SixthDivision, it was very rapid-paced. We were selling, traveling all over the country, speaking at every event possible, bringing in as many clients as we could, and consulting, coaching and teaching. We were far from being in the power zone. And it was exhausting.

Being in the power zone doesn't always happen. We had to make changes to get there. And, we did this by doing two specific things for our business.

First, we decided that we would stop selling multiple products and services to fit the needs of any type of prospect and their unique needs. Instead, we would ditch everything (and all those prospects) and sell one product. One product. And, we would sell only one product until we became profitable and very efficient.

Second, instead of flying around the country to meet with clients, we made clients come to us. Every consulting client (and their team) was required to come to our office in Phoenix for their intensive consulting session. That shift dramatically changed the business… and created a much better experience for our clients. We moved the business into the power zone.

LESSON #6: ENJOY THE RIDE

When learning to kitesurf, I could have easily focused on all the times I crashed, got stuck, or was dragged across the beach or underwater.

But when I really stopped to think about what I was doing and where I was, I realized I had absolutely nothing to complain about. I was in unbelievable places, meeting new people, doing amazing new things, experiencing life, and hanging out with people I loved.

It's important to not lose sight of where you are. It's easy to get wrapped up in where you want to be, when sometimes you need to focus on the present.

Starting and growing your own company isn't easy. You have to wear a lot of hats and constantly shift them around. Payroll and bills have to be paid. Living on a razor-thin edge between success and failure can be exhausting, and the fear of failure can be paralyzing.

But, there are very few things as satisfying as creating and growing a successful small business. The freedom is intoxicating. And, despite the constant challenges, I've been able to grow my ventures while experiencing entirely new levels of involvement with my family and control of how and where I spend my time. I'm happier and healthier. I'm actively engaged and loving the creative process in business and life.

So, as you venture down the path of growing your business, please don't forget what matters most. And… enjoy the ride!

ABOUT DAVID

Dave Lee is a best-selling author, entrepreneur, and marketing automation pioneer. He was raised to believe anything is achievable; therefore, his unique ability is to help others overcome uncharted challenges and turn them into magical results.

Having driven growth and success for other organizations such as Infusionsoft and LeadMD, Dave decided in late 2011 to co-found SixthDivision (www.sixthdivision.com) and PlusThis (www.plusthis.com) alongside business partner, Brad Martineau. The companies help small businesses accelerate their growth through automated lead conversion systems. As CEO of SixthDivision, he grew the business to over $1M in sales during its first year of operation.

In March 2014, Lee stepped down as CEO of SixthDivision to focus his efforts on growing PlusThis, a software company that builds solutions to help entrepreneurs further automate their marketing and sales processes. In August, 2015, Dave co-founded another venture called PicSnippets (www.picsnippets.com), a variable image tool that helps marketers convert more leads through personalized images and pictures.

Dave graduated from the Marriott School of Management, BYU, with a Master's degree in Business Administration, emphasizing in technology marketing. In 2008, he was named a Warrillow Marketer of the Year finalist. Dave is a best-selling author (*Successonomics*, co-authored with Steve Forbes) and has been featured on NBC, ABC, CBS, and Fox television affiliates speaking on marketing automation and small business success. He was quoted in *Forbes Magazine* as one of America's PremierExperts™ and has also been featured in CNBC, Reuters, MarketWatch, and Yahoo Finance, among other notable news outlets throughout the country.

Dave has been happily married for nearly two decades and has three young boys who keep him on his toes. When he's not helping businesses succeed or spending time with family, he fills his life with service, heli-skiing, kitesurfing, wakesurfing, doing what's right, and getting things done.

You can connect with Dave at:
Dave@PlusThis.com
linkedin.com/in/davelee123

BY HARVEY MACKAY

TRUTH OR CONSEQUENCES? YOU DECIDE!

About a year ago I wrote a column on the ABCs of selling. When I came to the letter T, there was no doubt what that word would be: Trust. It's the most important word in business. Trust is central to doing business with anyone. Without it, you have another word that begins with T: Trouble.

Unfortunately, trust in business plummeted worldwide in recent years, according to an Edelman survey. The public relations firm discovered that just 38 percent of respondents aged 35 to 64 said they trusted business, down from 58 percent a year earlier – the lowest rating in the survey's 10-year history. It's interesting that U.S. respondents ranked third. People in Ireland and Japan were even more suspicious. As a life-long businessman I find this especially troubling. In my business, there is nothing more important than trust, although I would list likeability, people skills and chemistry close behind.

I've always believed that telling the truth is the best policy. In business, especially today, it's a must. A few years back, the Forum Corporation of Boston, Mass., studied 341salespeople from 11 different companies in five different industries. Their purpose was to determine what separated top producers from average producers. When the study was finished, the results were startling. It was not skill, knowledge or charisma that divided the pack. The difference came down to one trait: honesty.
When customers trust salespeople, they buy from them!

At MackayMitchell Envelope Company, we don't tolerate anything less than honest negotiations and delivery guarantees. An envelope is a very standard commodity. Sure, the paper, the glue, and the size can vary. The end product can probably be duplicated by a hundred companies. But nobody can match us day-in day-out, job after job, envelope after envelope, smile after smile. Our customers know we'll do what we promise and try to deliver even more. They've even occasionally forgiven us for an honest mistake, because they know we'll make good on our word.

When bailouts, bankruptcies, corporate scandals, and political deception erupt and occupy the front pages for months on end, people tend to mistrust all of Corporate America and Politicians. That's not fair, but something of a natural reaction.

Is this a recent development? Not exactly. Nearly one hundred years ago, President Theodore Roosevelt addressed the issue: "We demand that big business give people a square deal. In return, we must insist that when anyone engaged in big business honestly endeavors to do right, he shall himself be given a square deal."

When people get in trouble, what do they typically do? They consult someone they already know and trust. When a problem hits, it's a poor time to look for help. How can you depend on someone you have known for half an hour? I would rather rely on someone I know I can count on, even if his or her experience is limited, than start from scratch. That person can usually lead you to someone who can help you if different skills are necessary.

TRUST IS KEY

Wayne Huizenga, the only person in history to have founded three Fortune 500 companies (Blockbuster, Waste Management and AutoNation), knows plenty about building trust. He says: "I don't want to be just a voice on the phone. I have to get to know these guys face-to-face and develop a sincere relationship. That way, if we run into problems in a deal, it doesn't get adversarial. We trust each other and have the confidence we can work things out."

When trust exists in an organization or in a relationship, almost everything else is easier and more comfortable to achieve. *Trust is built and maintained by many small actions over time.*

Author Marsha Sinetar said: "Trust is not a matter of technique, but of character. We are trusted because of our way of being, not because of our polished exteriors or our expertly-crafted communications."

Trust is telling the truth, even when it is difficult, and being truthful and trustworthy in your dealings with customers and staff. People do not or cannot trust each other if they are easily suspicious of one another. Trust involves being optimistic, rather than pessimistic. When we trust people, we are optimistic that not only are they competent to do what we trust them to do, but also that they are committed to doing it.

Mackay's Moral: It takes years to build up trust, but only seconds to destroy it.

ABOUT HARVEY

Harvey Mackay has written seven *New York Times* bestselling books, two of which were named among the top 15 inspirational business books of all time – *Swim With The Sharks Without Being Eaten Alive* and *Beware The Naked Man Who Offers You His Shirt*. His latest book, *The Mackay MBA of Selling in the Real World* (November 2011) is his seventh New York Times bestseller.

Harvey is a nationally syndicated columnist and has been named one of the top five speakers in the world by Toastmasters International. He is chairman of the $100 million MackayMitchell Envelope Company, a company he started in 1960.

BY WEST SEEGMILLER, ESQ.

EMPATHY IS AN ELEMENT OF HIGH PERFORMANCE

No attorney would take the case. Or, to be more accurate, no attorney in their right mind would take the case. I am a personal injury attorney who files civil lawsuits against people and corporations that have damaged my clients. Filing a case where a criminal defendant is responsible for civil damages can be difficult if not impossible. But I took the case anyway. Here's the story.

It is 1:30 a.m. A man stands up and slides out of the booth at the restaurant after paying his tab. He is very drunk. He is thirty-three years old and wants to go home. He came to the restaurant several hours earlier with his best friend and his forty-something girlfriend. The three of them have been drinking and having a good time. About a half an hour earlier, they had been joined at the booth by the girlfriend's son and companion. The son is almost twenty-one years old. The man does not know it yet, but he is about to die.

The girlfriend's son is angry. Let's call him Mike. The man is named Orlando. Mike doesn't like the fact Orlando is dating his mother and makes some derogatory comments. As Orlando turns to leave, Mike suddenly pulls out a folding knife and stabs Orlando twice in the back. Orlando staggers and Mike stabs him again several times in the chest. There is blood everywhere. Orlando falls to the ground. Orlando's best friend cradles him in his arms as the blood drains out of Orlando's body and he dies.

The restaurant is located in the parking lot of a shopping mall. A security video high on a pole at the mall faces the entrance to the restaurant, a well-known national chain. The video shows Mike and his companion running out the front door of the restaurant into the parking lot. A few seconds later the video shows Orlando's girlfriend, the mother of the stabber, calmly walking out after them. A few more seconds pass before the video shows a police car on patrol slowly driving up to the front of the restaurant. The video shows the bartender running out the front door and frantically waving at the police car and pointing to Mike and his companion who are now a hundred feet away in the parking lot, fleeing the scene. Covered with Orlando's blood and sensing he is about to be caught, Mike throws the bloody knife under a car. The police find the knife under the car. Mike and his companion are arrested and charged with murder.

In the criminal case, the wheels of justice fell off.

A few hours after the murder when Mike's companion is questioned by police, he asks for a lawyer and refuses to talk. When the police question Mike, he tells them he didn't stab anyone. The prosecutors are in a bind because they know one of the two men in custody has stabbed the victim. Mike's companion knows he didn't stab anyone but he is still being charged with murder and that he could go to prison for life. So when the prosecutors offer Mike and the companion a plea deal to only spend four years in prison, they each take the deal. They each took the deal for different reasons.

Here is where the story takes a turn. The prosecutors did not tell Orlando's family about the plea bargains until after the deal had been finalized. Orlando's family wanted to know the results of DNA testing on the knife. But there were no results because the knife had not yet been sent out for DNA testing. Realizing their mistake, the police quickly sent the knife out for DNA analysis which revealed that Mike's blood was on the knife. This proved that Mike stabbed Orlando and that his companion did not. Mike should have gone to prison for life for murdering Orlando. Unfortunately the DNA testing came too late because the plea agreements had already been made. In the criminal case, the wheels of justice fell off.

Orlando's family was livid. They were devastated that there was no real justice for what had happened. They knew there was far more to the story than just the criminal case. The rest of the story involved the restaurant itself. Orlando's father felt that the restaurant should share some responsibility for his son's death, in part because they had served alcohol to Mike who was under age. Serving alcohol to minors in California is illegal. It was clear the police and prosecutors had botched the criminal case. Orlando's father began to look for an attorney to investigate Orlando's death and pursue a wrongful death civil case against Mike and the restaurant. The statute of limitations on filing a civil lawsuit is two years. For two years Orlando's father searched for an attorney to take the case. No lawyer would touch it. Finally, in desperation, on the day the statute of limitations was going to expire, Orlando's father went to the courthouse and hand wrote a civil complaint, preserving the case.

This was the point where I became involved in the story. I met with Orlando's father when he came to my law firm. He told me his story. He told me how much he loved his son and how much his son meant to him, his wife and his family. He told me about the restaurant and the alcohol. As I listened, I decided to take his case because I knew he had a story to tell and that if a jury heard his story, they would know and understand that the restaurant had some responsibility for his son's death. I knew the case would be difficult. It was.

> # Empathy directly results in better performance. It did in this case, it does in every case and it is applicable to every profession.

Orlando's family was close knit. They are immigrants from Puerto Rico who came to California before Orlando was born and settled in, making a life for themselves and integrating into the community. Orlando grew up in this beautiful family setting. He went to school and landed a job with a big bank as a teller. He had been employed for eleven years before he was stabbed to death in the restaurant. Orlando's family was devastated by his loss. His mother and father were distraught.

My investigation in the case revealed that the restaurant had served alcohol to Mike who was a minor. The restaurant had a reputation for serving alcohol to minors. This was because the bartenders and servers knew they could make more money and get bigger tips if they did. The restaurant management knew what was going on, but looked the other way because they wanted the extra profits from selling alcohol to minors. When Mike and his companion arrived, they were quickly served alcohol by the same bartender who later flagged down the police. The amount of alcohol served to Mike was staggering. He consumed approximately six shots within ten minutes of arriving at the restaurant. His demeanor changed as a direct result of the alcohol. He became belligerent and angry. Still, the restaurant continued to serve him alcohol. In most instances, restaurants and bars are not liable for the actions of their drunk patrons. In California, there is a very narrow exception. A bar will be held responsible if they serve alcohol to a minor that is obviously intoxicated. In this case, the restaurant didn't card anyone. They had a practice of not carding minors. The bartenders and servers knew exactly what they were doing when they served alcohol to minors and the restaurant management looked the other way because they valued profits over people.

This was not an easy case. It took over three years to work the case up. The defense fought hard. The case went to trial and the jury was shown all the evidence. When it was over, the jury awarded $40 million dollars. They found Mike and his companion 45% responsible and held the restaurant 55% responsible for the death of Orlando.

Why did I take the case when so many other attorneys would not? While I can't speak for them, I can tell you what worked for me in this case and what works for me in my professional life. I listened to my client's story and I cared. When I first met Orlando's father, I did not know all the important facts about the case. What I did know, and what I could sense, was the pain and loss that he and his family felt. I was able to understand and appreciate their pain and suffering because I was attuned to it.

We worked up the case in a way that was not only tuned in to the feelings of the victim's family, but we also conducted nine focus groups where we asked random people how they felt about the case. We wanted to know what a jury would think about the case and what happened. The focus groups told us that they were inclined to hold the restaurant partially responsible for the murder because they broke the law by serving alcohol to minors. The alcohol fueled Mike's anger and contributed to his behavior. The focus groups did not like the restaurant putting profits ahead of people. In addition to the focus groups, I spent time with the clients. I went to their home for dinner, I visited the cemetery with them and learned that they visited their son's grave twice a week without fail. The relationship with their son, and the resulting loss they felt when he was murdered, was an important story that was told to the jury who heard the case.

Listening and empathy are learned behaviors. I learned through personal experience that losing a loved one causes physical pain. I pay close attention when people tell me they are injured and in pain. Listening makes me more effective as a lawyer. Empathy directly results in better performance. It did in this case, it does in every case and it is applicable to every profession.

Was the $40 million dollar verdict a result of luck? Not a chance. Empathy was the reason I took the case, and directly responsible for the performance that lead to the large verdict against the restaurant. It helped explain the client's story to the jury. People who are injured have a unique experience. Sometimes they are helpless in bed with tubes and lines going everywhere. They are in excruciating pain. They are waiting for nurses and doctors to help with the simplest personal tasks like going to the bathroom.

They are waiting through hours, days, weeks and months of loneliness with nothing to do. They may have lost their productivity or be worrying about the uncertainty in their future. The client is trusting their future to a total stranger. They are forced by necessity to trust that their lawyer will take the time to learn their story and accurately articulate their injuries to the jury–another set of total strangers.

I have found that if I bring empathy to my clients, if I bring out the caring in my own personality and performance, this will result in others–like a jury– also caring about my client and their story. The heart of the matter is listening to and understanding your client. While a $40 million dollar verdict is clear evidence of performance, without empathy, it would never have happened. I did not take the case because I knew there would be a $40 million dollar verdict. I took the case because I cared about the client and their story. I must have been out of my mind.

ABOUT WEST

William West Seegmiller, Esq. is the founder of one of Southern California's most distinguished personal injury law firms. More than 30 years ago, Seegmiller began his practice because he wanted to help people who, like himself, had been injured in an accident.

Reputation for Doing the Right Thing:

West Seegmiller earned a stellar reputation for being a straight shooter and a zealous advocate for his injured clients. As founder of the West Seegmiller Law Firm, Mr. Seegmiller fights vigorously as he does his best to settle cases and win verdicts for each and every individual and family he represents.

Compassion for Victims:

Mr. Seegmiller knows first-hand what it is like to suffer serious injuries in a traffic accident. As a young man in his 20s, Seegmiller was in a motorcycle accident and underwent painful treatments to recover from his injuries. Indeed, he knows how important it is to treat his injured clients with first-class service. West Seegmiller is proud of the fact that he has handled thousands of cases resulting in verdicts and settlements of more than One Hundred Fifty Million Dollars ($150,000,000).

Mr. Seegmiller has the experience and confidence to stand up to the most powerful insurance companies, trucking companies, and government agencies. A warrior committed to the fight, he will not back down until his clients receive the justice they deserve from those responsible for their painful injuries.

Education:

Mr. Seegmiller earned a Bachelor's degree in Political Science at the University of California – Davis, and his Master's degree from the University of Southern California.

Additionally, Mr. Seegmiller earned his Juris Doctorate from the McGeorge School of Law University of the Pacific in Sacramento, where he was selected to compete in the highly competitive Traynor National Moot Court Team and was a member of the prestigious *Pacific Law Review*.

Since establishing his own firm in 1981, Mr. Seegmiller continues to educate himself and expand his knowledge in the legal field. He has refined his skills in the practice by attending both the Harvard Law School Program of Instruction for Lawyers, as well as The Jerry Spence Trial Lawyers College.

AN INTERVIEW WITH NICK NANTON, ESQ. & J.W. DICKS, ESQ.

EXPERTS IN SUCCESS

PERFORMANCE: How did you become experts in your industry?

Jack: I learned the importance of being an expert 44 years ago when I first started my career in real estate with my father-in-law. During that period of time, he told me the one thing I needed to learn is that "people buy people." He said, "Your job in learning how to sell real estate is to get to know people that are in your market. You need to tell your story to them so that they'll understand who you are and how they can relate to you."

I began to use what's called a farming system where you go out and you develop a certain area, and you look for people to do business with. You cultivate the area for leads. I used a newsletter format to interact with people on a regular basis and get to know them, and it worked. People got to know me through print, and relationships were forged.

I went on to different careers, but the message was always the same – I needed to get to know the people, to let them know me, and to tell my story. There would always be certain people that relate to you and your story, and this would help your business grow.

I think it is really important that the readers understand that in becoming an expert, it is not arrogant to allow your personality to show through. You should not be afraid to talk about your uniqueness, your hobbies, your talents, your gifts, and everything else to become much more interesting to people. It becomes so much easier for them to remember you, and therefore, people will remember to go to you when they need something. If your clients know a lot about you, they will look forward to seeing you in order to share their story with you. I think it's a pretty unique thing when you allow your personality to shine through based on the stuff that we do. I think that helps build expertise even more.

PERFORMANCE: Is it just the rapport you're trying to build with your audience that is important?

Nick: The way to become the best-known expert to your audience is to be the one who teaches your audience the most about the subject. Most everyone has expertise in some field. Consider my grandma. She was an expert at cooking. She had so much knowledge in her head about cooking, but she never could get it out of her head, and therefore people didn't know she was an expert cook. They'd eat her food, and the more they ate, the more they liked it, but that did not tag her as an expert to others. Having an expertise is not enough, people have to know about it, and they have to see you as the expert.

As business people and entrepreneurs, we have this knowledge in our head of all these things we studied and worked on for years and years, but if we don't get it out of our head, people will never know we're an expert.

A lot of people take on the style of doing business as, "I'm going to jockey and try to get the sale and then if I don't get it, I'll move onto the next one."

We train *our* experts to capture their prospects' information and then make an initial step toward a sale. If they're not ready, we encourage our experts to put them in their system to receive future mailings in order to maintain contact with them on an automated basis. You are continuing to educate them on that subject until they're ready to buy. If you're the one who educates them the most about what they want to know about, you become the expert.

PERFORMANCE: Do you concentrate on maintaining contact with clients on or offline?

Jack: It is very important to use both online and offline methods of contact. Today everybody thinks communicating online is the only way to go. Online is very good and there's many tools that you should use online, such as email and social media, but, offline is just as powerful.

We believe that offline marketing is much stronger than it used to be because there is less direct mail being utilized. It used to be that home mailboxes were full of advertisements, but now a direct mail piece from one of our experts may be the only piece of mail in the box. We assist our experts in creating newsletters, flyers, post cards, CDs, and small books to mail out to their prospective clients, and the returns are phenomenal.

PERFORMANCE: When you developed the Dicks + Nanton Agency, what was it that you saw was missing in people's attempts to be seen as experts?

Nick: A lot of people make the mistake of thinking it's just purely about promotion. While it is easy to talk yourself up, so many people fail to realize that it's all about a conversation with your client. Most people don't understand how to start having that conversation.

We've shown people how to start that conversation through trainings, coaching, and webinars. We strategize with them about ways they can build their position in a way that feels like conversation, that is not like lecturing as that is boring. All of our emails are personalized. I'm not sending out big mass emails, hoping the world reads them. I'm saying, "Hey John, the other day I was doing this…" so I have a conversation. This is the type of approach we teach our experts to have with their own clients.

Jack: We have clients from over 38 different countries. Nick and I started working together in our business law practice. People came in to talk about their business and they felt they were lost. It wasn't just, "Hey, I want to learn to form a business. I want to know how to build my business. I want to know how to expand it." By questioning them about what their goals and objectives were and what their specialty was, we began to use a consultation strategy to talk to them about how to grow their businesses. They had to go out in the market place and find the people that wanted their products and services based on what their niche was. They just needed to tell them their story.

Nick uses a saying so often, "Branding is simply telling your story." Story telling about what-you-do brands you as who you are and where your expertise lies.

PERFORMANCE: So what do you think is the greatest challenge people have when they're trying to establish themselves as an expert?

Jack: In some cases, it's money. In their mind, they don't have enough money to get started. We have a lot of people that come to us and say, "Hey I want to be all over the country."

We often respond, "That sounds great, but what is your budget?" You have to bring it all down to reality. I think it's about understanding where you are and where you want to go, and then using the resources that you have available to you to get started. We encourage our experts to get started in their own home area in order to see the processes and skills they will need, and then expand into one different vertical at a time. Don't try to take on the whole world at once. That's a very difficult task, especially if you can't afford it. Take on the area that you can work in and expand from there.

PERFORMANCE: Is there a certain amount of investment of time and money in order to get to where they want to go?

Nick: People always underestimate what they are going to have to invest in order to grow their business. It's not just going down and opening your doors and expecting people to come in. Today that doesn't happen. There is a definite investment of money and time.

Everybody says it's not fast enough. Well, it never goes fast enough. I don't care how big you are; it never goes fast enough. You always want to do more. But that's the whole entrepreneurial effect. I think people can absolutely start without money. You can start Word Press sites for free or find a platform where people already are, such as Facebook or YouTube, and begin by gathering an audience by talking about what you know about.

I think a lot of people are waiting for someone to come along and tap them on the head and dub them as the expert. You have to own the expertise you have and commit to learning more. Get started and start sharing, and you'll be shocked by the response you will receive, and you will also receive instant feedback thanks to this wonderful day and age of social media. A lot of people are waiting to hear about your expertise.

I had a conversation with a guy the other day who was really creative and he had some amazing ideas. He told me he has a 100 new ideas a day. While I was talking to him he continued to tell me that he really needed his business to work while at the same time telling me about all his other ideas.

> # The people that are the most successful experts are motivated to tell their story.

I told him he needed to concentrate on finishing his first idea. If that didn't work, none of the ideas were going to work. He kept moving onto the next idea instead of focusing on what he was currently working on. I think a lot of people are doing the same thing with their expertise. They have it, but they're waiting or because it's something they're uncomfortable with, they don't know how to share it. They continually find other things to do and think they don't have time for this or don't know how to do that, but they've just got to start.

You have got to be willing to share your expertise and you have to be engaging and interesting. I think the key to success today is to be interested and interesting. If you can accomplish both of those, I believe you can find success in any field.

PERFORMANCE: Do experts need to get on Oprah or be a *New York Times* Best-Seller to be considered an expert?

Jack: Just getting on Oprah is not the answer because you're on Oprah for a very short period of time. If you don't understand the process of becoming an expert and maintaining that space, being on Oprah will be fruitless in the long term.

Your day in the sun will be just a flash in the pan and you will have missed out on a great opportunity. I would rather people not appear on Oprah first, rather they should build their business so that they have the systems and processes in place, so that if they get on Oprah or if they get on some national television show, they know what to do with that.

There are very specific follow-up steps about how to tell people how to get in touch with you and where they can contact you. You have to have figured out your follow-up process because very few people will buy from you the first time. It is a constant effort to stay in touch with them to make sure they understand that you're real and that what you're saying is something that you believe in. It's not just something that you're doing to make money with.

Once they make that proven connection, that's when they start to do business with you. That's when they start referring people to you.

PERFORMANCE: What traits do you see in people who really excel at being an expert?

Nick: To be an expert, you have to have a relentless drive. Successful experts have a desire to share what they know with other people who want to tap into that knowledge. Once a potential client determines a person has passion about a subject and is knowledgeable about a particular subject, they will want to know more. They will start calling, asking questions, asking if they can do something with you as well as bring other people to you. The people that are the most successful experts are motivated to tell their story. They don't just sit at home. They want to go out and tell their story because they believe in what they do. They have it in their heart, and that's what ultimately resonates with their client.

Jack: Successful experts are people who are willing to give, not just take – those people who are willing to help other people, are willing to share.

Our next book coming out is called *Mission-Driven Business*. We've done a study on the most successful businesses today. We found that big businesses are big because there's more of a story behind them than just trying to make a lot of money. They have a specific mission in mind. Consider the business Tom's® shoes - if you buy one pair of shoes, then they donate another pair to somebody in need. There is a great backstory there.

Ben & Jerry's story about how they started off their ice cream shops, is a classic story about having a mission, and doing something for the greater good as well as to make money and support your employees. The creator of Chick-fil-A®, S. Truett Cathy, had a mission in which he wanted to help his employees, wanted them to have time off. He was a very Christian man, so he had greater ideals than just chasing dollars.

It doesn't have to be a big message, it can be just small messages, as long as you tell your story and help other people by telling you story.

PERFORMANCE: What kind of Return on Investment should people expect from their investment into their platform?

Nick: Your return on investment is what you make it. It's like building your house upon the sand or rock. You can invest in making yourself into a rock foundation upon which the rest of your platform is supported, or on sand. Which do you think is more supportive?

The return on investment is arguably very hard to measure when it comes to building your platform as an expert. My question for the reader is what do you have to lose by investing in yourself? Obviously you have to have cash flow, I get that. But if I gave you expertise and instant credibility, how many more sales might you close because you are a Best-Selling author now, or on TV.

Jack: Do you think that someone who is a Best-Selling author, is on television, or in magazines receives instant money for their efforts? Some do, but they are the exception. Experts have to be in it for the long term, to really see the returns.

When I got my law degree, I did not receive a huge ROI after graduating. Over a lifetime career of being able to be an attorney and having the experience that I gained in law school, having the contacts I gained in law school and getting to know people like Nick, those are the real returns on my education investment. Is it ROI tomorrow or over a period of time, and are you willing to use this as something to build your expertise around?

PERFORMANCE: : What are the benefits of hiring someone to you build your expert platform?

Jack: Hiring someone to help you build your platform will accelerate your time spent to become known as an expert. How does our company do that? Let me ask the reader a question. Do people pay attention to the fact that you have been on television?

People who have appeared on television are seen as celebrities and today's celebrities are the most credible people in the world according to a study published in Fortune Magazine. Celebrities are the ones that people listen to.

Hiring someone can help you become visible on television, radio and print, which will help you with speed to market. It saves time, effort and can help you avoid very expensive pitfalls.

Nick: The best way somebody can get their story together or to start sharing that story, is to start with a simple format of getting your story down somehow. I encourage you to have someone else write it unless you are a professional writer, because it is so important to project your best. I encourage experts to use a very simple format that I use for all my documentaries. Begin by answering some questions. Where did you come from? What happened in your life before now that uniquely positioned you as the most qualified person and perfect person to solve the problems of your ideal prospect? We're not going to talk about every date you had, but we're going to talk about your pivotal moments that led you to where you are now.

Move on to what you're doing now and how that's really changing people's lives. Add testimonial quotes in there for other people to tell a few stories of how you helped them. Finally, cap it off with your vision for the future. What does a bigger, better version of what you're doing now look like to you, because if you don't show that you have some vision for the future, people will not tend to want to follow you because they think you're stuck in the past.

There you have it. Very simple. Very straightforward, but _very_ effective.

ABOUT NICK

An Emmy Award-Winning Director and Producer, Nick Nanton, Esq., produces media and branded content for top thought leaders and media personalities around the world. Recognized as a leading expert on branding and storytelling, Nick has authored more than two dozen Best-Selling books (including the *Wall Street Journal* Best-Seller *StorySelling™*) and produced and directed more than 50 documentaries, earning 5 Emmy wins and 18 nominations. Nick speaks to audiences internationally on the topics of branding, entertainment, media, business and storytelling at major universities and events.

As the CEO of DNA Media, Nick oversees a portfolio of companies including: The Dicks + Nanton Agency (an international agency with more than 3000 clients in 36 countries), Dicks + Nanton Productions, Ambitious.com and DNA Films. Nick is an award-winning director, producer and songwriter who has worked on everything from large scale events to television shows with the likes of Steve Forbes, Ivanka Trump, Sir Richard Branson, Rudy Ruettiger (inspiration for the Hollywood Blockbuster *Rudy*), Brian Tracy, Jack Canfield (*The Secret*, creator of the *Chicken Soup for the Soul* Series), Michael E. Gerber, Tom Hopkins, Dan Kennedy and many more.

Nick has been seen in *USA Today, The Wall Street Journal, Newsweek, BusinessWeek, Inc. Magazine, The New York Times, Entrepreneur® Magazine, Forbes, FastCompany*, and has appeared on ABC, NBC, CBS, and FOX television affiliates across the country as well as on CNN, FOX News, CNBC, and MSNBC from coast to coast.

Nick is a member of the Florida Bar, a member of The National Academy of Television Arts & Sciences (Home to the EMMYs), Co-founder of The National Academy of Best-Selling Authors®, and serves on the Innovation Board of the XPRIZE Foundation, a non-profit organization dedicated to bringing about "radical breakthroughs for the benefit of humanity" through incentivized competition, best known for its Ansari XPRIZE which incentivized the first private space flight and was the catalyst for Richard Branson's Virgin Galactic. Nick also enjoys serving as an Elder at Orangewood Church, working with Young Life, Downtown Credo Orlando, Entrepreneurs International and rooting for the Florida Gators with his wife Kristina and their three children, Brock, Bowen and Addison.

Learn more at:

www.NickNanton.com

www.CelebrityBrandingAgency.com

ABOUT JW

JW Dicks, Esq., is a Business Development Attorney, a *Wall Street Journal* Best-Selling Author®—who has authored over 47 books—and a 2x Emmy® Award-Winning Executive Producer. JW is an XPrize Innovation Board member, Chairman of the Board of the National Academy of Best-Selling Authors®, Board Member of the National Association of Experts, Writers and Speakers® and Board Member of the International Academy of Film Makers®.

JW is the CEO of DNAgency, an Inc. 5000 Multi Media Company that represents over 2800 clients in 63 countries. He has been quoted on business and financial topics in national media such as *USA Today, The Wall Street Journal, Newsweek, Forbes,CNBC.com*, and *Fortune Magazine Small Business*.

Considered a Thoughtleader® and curator of information, JW has co-authored books with legends like Jack Canfield, Brian Tracy, Tom Hopkins, Dr. Nido Qubein, Steve Forbes, Richard Branson, Michael Gerber, Dr. Ivan Misner, and Dan Kennedy. He is the Publisher of *ThoughtLeader® Magazine*.

JW is called the "Expert to the Experts" and has appeared on business television Shows airing on ABC, NBC, CBS, and FOX affiliates around the country and coproduces and syndicates a line of franchised business television shows such as *Success Today, Wall Street Today, Hollywood Live*, and *Profiles of Success*.

JW and his wife of forty-seven years, Linda, have two daughters, four granddaughters, and two Yorkies. He is a sixth-generation Floridian and splits his time between his home in Orlando and his beach house on Florida's west coast.

BY ALAN WEISS, PhD

EXPLORATION ...

Be enchanted and unlock a new you!

My wife and I just finished walking all over Prague, which has a lot of hills. But it's a great walking city, as many cities are. I recall lovely gardens, quiet ponds, and hidden restaurants that we found by poking our noses into an alley or road that had some allure. I'm not crazy about walking, but my wife could barely keep up to me, so eager was I to follow every new path.

Years ago, in St. Thomas, we were invited into someone's home, a professional kite maker, when we thought the driveway might be a road. In Venice, we found a garden restaurant with the best salad we've ever tasted, and a 90-year-old monk walking by. In St. Maarten, we found a lovely beach with crude stone steps, supplied with barbecued chicken and cold beer by a couple of enterprising locals. In Tokyo, we found shopkeepers in the early morning cleaning fish and their streets, and in Hong Kong, a watch repairman with no shop at all, but just a lectern mounted on steps leading up a hill. In Prague, wandering off a funicular we took a mountainside path that led to a lone violinist playing Bach with no one else around, but his case open to receive the coins I proffered.

We've all had these experiences, at least those of us who are willing to take paths less traveled, to poke around where no one else is poking, and to be willing to backtrack when they reach a dead end.

I don't know many adventurous lawyers, because they are trained to within an inch of their lives to be skeptical and conservative. Unfortunately, I've met too many people who tend to act the same way, enforcing a narrowness on themselves. Performance requires fuel, and that fuel comprises experiences, exploration, and exceptions to normal habits.

> Be willing to take paths less traveled, to poke around where no one else is poking.

I believe that if we're not exploring—our surroundings, our relationships, ourselves—we're simply not growing. A balanced life requires exploration, fresh air, and new experiences. My wife and I both like to explore—the Czech Republic was my 60th country—and we feel that's one of the secrets of a 44-year marriage. (That and my telling her of course she doesn't look heavier, no matter what she tries on.)

It's tough to grow when we're "on fumes" with no fuel in the tank. It's tough to perform when we have only the limited perspectives of places we've been forced to go by business, by habit, or by others.

Is there a different route you can take to work? Is there another city in which you can have dinner? Is there a vacation destination that may be particularly appropriate for your spouse, or your kids, or your first time somewhere? (This is the disadvantage of having a "vacation home" where you feel obligated to spend discretionary time every year, delimiting your time available for other destinations.)

I've found people in their 60s and beyond exploring new places and experiences – forever young, fun and fascinating. I've found younger people so totally immersed in their work and habits that they are of no interest outside of their immediate profession. For those of us who are entrepreneurs and professional services providers, I can't think of a worse fate (or marketing position) than to be buried in your work and methodology.

Our power is in being an object of interest to others.

I met a lawyer once who asked me what was wrong with working 12 hours a day on the law, since he loved it and believed he was helping his clients. He couldn't discuss a novel with me (he didn't read for pleasure), didn't know what the latest movies were, and didn't follow sports. He was dull, and I wondered how he could fully relate to clients without understanding their lives.

"Do you have a family?" I asked.

"Yes, a wife and two daughters," he replied.

"That's what's wrong with 12 hours a day in the law," I pointed out.

Look around, venture forth, tally-ho! Take the first right. It doesn't matter where you think it leads.

ABOUT ALAN

Alan Weiss, PhD, is the author of 46 books appearing in 10 languages. The "rock star of consulting," he is the sole non-journalist in the 90-year history of the American Press Institute to receive its Lifetime Achievement Award.

Alan is a member of the National Speakers Hall of Fame® and has been named a Fellow of the Institute of Management Consultants, one of only two people in history honored with both designations.

Alan can be reached at:
alan@summitconsulting.com
http://www.contrarianconsulting.com.

OVERCOMING OBSTACLES THAT STAND IN THE WAY OF SUCCESS

PERFORMANCE: As the Founder of The Law Offices of Nick Nemeth, PLLC, you are dedicated to helping individuals and businesses resolve IRS problems. How does your work influence your personal definition of success?

NICK: Success comes to those who overcome obstacles in their personal and professional lives. As an attorney who helps clients resolve their issues with the IRS, I must maintain awareness that obstacles are merely opportunities to improve. If you let them get the better of you, you're going to have trouble achieving anything worthwhile. One of the reasons I chose to practice in this area of law is that I believe there is no bigger obstacle to financial success than ongoing IRS problems. My clients face daily, repetitive obstacles. They come to my office in tears, their marriage is on the rocks, and they haven't slept well in months. It's all from the stress associated with their IRS problems. I can see the day they hire my firm that a load has been lifted. They know they've got someone they can depend on to help them. The good news is, that while IRS problems create huge obstacles for people, they can be overcome. After meeting with me, they realize they don't have to allow IRS issues to devastate and consume their lives.

PERFORMANCE: What is the first step of your process for helping clients gain peace of mind?

NICK: First, my job is to get the IRS to tell me everything about my client's history. We compare how that matches up with the information my client provided. The IRS moves slowly, but generally I know everything they know about my client, including how much they owe, within 24 to 48 hours.

One way I help remove obstacles for my clients is by educating them about their unique situation. I help clients understand that once the IRS has issued certain notices, they have the right to garnish wages, seize retirement assets, and even seize one's home. Although the client has his or her version of the problem, I have to explain to them why they owe far more than anticipated. I've had many instances where a client thinks they owe $10,000 but really owes $100,000. My clients have been battered with so much correspondence that they're confused.

PERFORMANCE: How do you know where to start with a new client?

NICK: There are several steps I take in every case. The first step in the process is to show compliance with the filing of returns. I consider compliance a major obstacle to overcome. If any returns are missing, we get them filed. Most of my clients don't realize that the government files returns on their behalf if the taxpayer didn't submit his own. This is called a Substitute for Return. If I conclude that substitute returns were filed, I analyze them. I then make the determination to either keep the substitute or replace them with original returns. Many times when the IRS does the returns, they're not in the client's favor. I may decide to replace them, however, in some cases there is a benefit to having an overly inflated balance owed on the return. The next step is to show compliance of tax payments on current income. I look at the taxes being taken out of their current paychecks to make sure enough is deducted so nothing is owed at the end of the current year. Many of my clients are self-employed. I assess their record of quarterly payments. If it's been a problem in the past, I make sure they're paying in throughout the year. I educate my clients and help them establish good habits by making quarterly estimated payments. Analyzing the problem, educating clients, and creating good habits helps prove to the IRS that there will be no future problems and we can then concentrate on the problems from the past.

PERFORMANCE: What other obstacles are involved in resolving an IRS issue?

NICK: The last major obstacle is the financial statement. All IRS solutions are based on the client's ability to pay, and a financial statement is the basis for that determination. A financial statement is a list of all household assets, income, and expenses. Obviously, we want to prepare and analyze it before we send it to the IRS. For example, if you have no assets and no money left after expenses at the end of a month, there are ways we can make the debt to go away. Many of my clients have added difficulty because even though they feel like they're broke at the end of the month, the IRS doesn't agree. The IRS can look at your numbers for household expenses and reject some of them. They actually tell you how much you get to spend on your housing, food, insurance, and gas. For instance, you may pay $4000 a month on your mortgage, but if the IRS only allows a maximum of $1,400 per month in your county, you have to deal with it. I explain to my clients that the opponent in this instance wrote the rules and they are not stacked in our favor.

PERFORMANCE: Once you have all these "ducks in a row," so to speak, what are the specific solutions available to resolve the debt?

NICK: Once I get to this point in a case, it's time to devise a plan. There are many options we consider to resolve a client's IRS debt. Each client's case is different. I'll tell you about some of the more common options. Nobody likes the first option, which is to write a check! If the client owes $400,000 and has $800,000 available in a 401(k), sometimes it makes sense to simply pay the IRS. If borrowing the money is an option, pay them. The next options require us to roll up our sleeves and get creative, within the limits of the law. One option might be a payment plan, formally called an Installment Agreement. Negotiating a payment plan can be tricky if you aren't skilled in the practice. Often, people who owe will accept monthly payment amounts they are unable to pay. The important question is how much can my client afford to pay, versus the amount the IRS will accept? I have to remind clients that when they think they have $400 left after expenses at the end of the month, the IRS may disagree. The IRS may not allow a person to keep nearly as much to live on as they expect. Another common option we may consider is the penalty abatement process. We explore options to try to remove the penalties, whether you have full-paid the debt or are paying on an installment agreement. When a large debt exists over several years, a big portion of the debt will be comprised of penalties and interest. The interest portion will generally not go away. Depending on the circumstances of the case, we may be able to have the penalties removed, or drastically reduced. It's a long, complicated process, but well worth the effort.

PERFORMANCE: What if the client's situation is more extreme? How do you handle that?

NICK: The next option is "the hardship." It's what the IRS refers to as "Currently Non-Collectable Status." This option requires extensive work to convince the IRS that there are no assets worth seizing. We comb through financials and plead the case by trying to prove they have no discretionary income at the end of the month. IRS analysis of the same financials may be very different.

Another option is the "Offer in Compromise" or "OIC." People who see TV ads for companies that say they will settle your debt for "pennies on the dollar" may know the term. An OIC, is basically offering the IRS a severely reduced amount to settle the debt. This option is what all clients want when they come to see me. Sadly, the commercials are misleading as not every taxpayer may qualify for this program. It's a complicated process that generally takes over a year to complete. Clients have to meet very strict financial requirements to qualify. When it does work, it's a beautiful thing. They may owe $400,000 and settle for $4,000. Talk about removing an obstacle towards personal financial success!

Bankruptcy is another extreme option we can consider in some cases. Contrary to popular belief, IRS debt can be discharged in bankruptcy. Like the pennies on the dollar approach, you have to meet certain criteria. If someone meets the criteria, bankruptcy can provide tremendous relief.

The final option involves trying to get to the point where the IRS can no longer collect – the Collection Statute Expiration date. The IRS generally has ten years to collect a debt from the time it's assessed. There are several exceptions that can stop the clock from ticking. I identify these exceptions and get creative. It's important to remember that the debt is not assessed until the return is filed. People commonly come to me who haven't filed taxes in 20 years, and assume that a debt from 2002 will have expired by 2015. That's not always true. If the return has not been filed, the clock hasn't begun to tick. If a return from 2002 is filed in 2008, the debt would theoretically not expire until 2018.

My main objective is to instill a sense of confidence that they are not going to be blindsided.

PERFORMANCE It sounds like patience is an important element to success in your business. Can you describe what role having patience plays for you and your clients?

NICK: No matter which approach is best for a client, everything should be considered a work in progress. My primary focus throughout the process is to control collection activity. Cases can take from nine to twelve months to resolve. I want to make sure collection activity doesn't start in the meantime. In other words, I'm here to help decrease the likelihood of levies, garnishments and seizures. We go through the step-by-step process to determine which of the options is best. I present the pros and cons of each available option. The client is the one who ultimately decides what's best. We then spend several months pursuing that option.

PERFORMANCE: How do you define success on a day-to-day basis, as it relates to the work you do for your clients? How does helping them overcome their IRS issues translate into success?

NICK: On a daily basis, I define success as figuring out solutions to my client's IRS problems and making sure they are well taken care of. My main objective is to instill a sense of confidence that they are not going to be blindsided with a levy, garnishment or seizure of assets. The biggest fears they have are that their paycheck will be taken or bank account emptied. I give them peace of mind. I define my success and theirs when I'm able to let them know there will be a manageable solution. Many clients haven't had a peaceful night's sleep in a decade. They hear a car door slam and are constantly paranoid it's an IRS officer coming to their door. I'm here to let them know things will be okay. As long as my clients are active participants in their resolution, they feel the success of overcoming an enormous obstacle.

PERFORMANCE: Do you see wealth and success just in monetary terms, or do those concepts have meaning to you (and your clients) beyond just dollars and cents?

NICK: When a client retains us, we might be able to make their entire debt go away, or they may end up paying it in full. Either way, we have provided a valuable service and given them peace of mind that their assets won't be taken. The IRS problems that once paralyzed them begin to become manageable. We help ease their pain. People come to me scared to death that everything is at risk. They're not sure they'll be able to feed their families. Literally everything they own, including their home is at stake. Some have even developed severe ulcers and many have marital problems as a result of their issues. In an objective sense, the work I do is helping them monetarily, and hopefully opening the door to a more financially prosperous life. Beyond that, eliminating worry leads to powerful life changes, which cannot be measured in dollars and cents.

PERFORMANCE: Talk a bit about your background and what you were doing in the years before launching your firm. What led you to think you could be successful with your own firm? What did you do to ensure that would happen?

NICK: The reason I know so much about how obstacles can block a pathway to success, is because I faced so many of my own. Coming out of law school, I started working in other areas of the law. At one point I had to let my practice go because of a custody battle for my two young children. Overcoming those challenges was instrumental in my decision to focus on an area of the law that would allow me to provide the most relief to clients. Like anyone who watches late night TV, I was bombarded by tax relief commercials and began researching the companies. I knew I could do a great job for clients with problems that seem insurmountable. I made the right choice. I love this practice because, regardless of the solution we choose, we have very happy clients at the end of the process. They have finality in their lives with respect to their IRS issues. The black cloud hindering their ability to be successful in their business and personal lives is gone.

I've been a lawyer for 17 years. My practice focuses solely on IRS problems. In my mind, I knew that if I focused on my goals and could overcome every obstacle thrown at me, I could be successful. I extrapolated that concept to help my clients. In other words, I can completely identify with my clients. I know they need help overcoming issues to be successful in their lives. I'm able to provide them with support. In fact, our mission statement is: to keep the IRS as far away from our client's assets as possible until we find a manageable solution to their problem.

PERFORMANCE: What attributes drive you to be successful on your own terms and on behalf of your clients?

NICK: As a single dad of two teenage boys, my motivation is all about providing for them and allowing them opportunities to accomplish their goals. Life can throw obstacles our way. It's up to me to teach them how to overcome them and be successful.

PERFORMANCE: If you couldn't pass along anything of monetary value to your boys, only "success tips," what would they be?

NICK: I'd tell my boys to never stop fighting, never quit. One day I hope they will draw upon my ability to earn success in nearly impossible situations and know that they can do the same.

ABOUT NICK

Nick Nemeth, Esq. is a Texas attorney and best-selling author who has been in practice for over 15 years. His law practice, The Law Offices of Nick Nemeth, PLLC focuses solely on helping individuals and businesses resolve a wide range of IRS issues. Nick has been featured in *USA Today, The Wall Street Journal, Forbes Magazine, Yahoo Finance* and *Morningstar,* as well as having appeared in ABC, NBC, CBS and Fox television affiliates around the country.

As a long-time resident of Dallas, Nick possesses a unique quality only present in those who truly love their home—a complete and personal investment in the lives of the people of his community. By creating a truly local presence in the Dallas-Fort Worth Metroplex, Nick brings his 17 years of legal experience to those who truly need it . . . individuals and businesses who are being threatened by the IRS.

Nick's ultimate goal in his practice, for any of his clients, is to provide efficient, cost-effective legal representation. He firmly believes that when any taxpayer is facing an "opponent" who happens to be a branch of the federal government, one who's able to seize your property and assets without going to court, that taxpayer should arm him/herself with an aggressive, experienced law firm. Nick's staff includes attorneys, CPAs, enrolled agents and tax professionals who are dedicated to keeping ahead of an ever-changing industry: solving IRS problems. Nick is known for constantly saying, "My only job is to keep the IRS far away from my clients' assets until I negotiate an acceptable solution to their problem."

Nick was driven to become an attorney by his desire to help serve others and make a positive impact in the world. He's pleased with having found a niche in which he has been able to accomplish both these goals. He loves the satisfaction of working for a diverse clientele who are unequivocally pleased with his reputation. His dedication to his practice is a benefit to all in the area of law he's focused on—helping his clients solve their IRS problems.

Having traveled to places like Sweden, Austria, Denmark, Canada, The Philippines, Hungary and the Caribbean, Nick appreciates the ties that continue to bring him back to Dallas-Fort Worth: his law practice and two sons that keeps him a very busy man.

To learn more about Nick Nemeth and his law practice, as well as his special report, *How to End Your IRS Problems Forever,* visit: www.myIRSteam.com or call (972) 484-0829.

BY STEVE RENNER

HIGH PERFORMANCE 360

My Quest For Success

When I look back on my life over the last 17 years, it's like I have always been on this Quest. I've always been searching for something, although I may not know exactly what it will be until I get there.

I have experienced incredible success in my life. For an average hard working guy, with no formal education, no money, and nothing more than a dream; through sheer hard work, determination, and a burning desire to succeed, I have build a successful global business, and achieved personal financial success far beyond my wildest expectations.

The story began in 1998 when I started my Internet Business. At the time I had no idea what I was doing, or what my business model would be. I had never actually even used a computer, but I knew I wanted to have an Internet Business. So I registered my first domain Ezze.net, got a computer, and this was the start of my journey, my Quest.

But it all began ten years before this back in 1978, when I read an article about Bill Gates, and his vision of what this new thing called the Internet would be. Then later, in 1995, when I read about Jeff Bezos, and how he started a company to sell books on the Internet, this inspired me to start my own Internet Business.

I always knew that I would have an Internet Business, although I had no idea exactly what it would be, or how I would do it. I remember reading stories about Internet Service companies like UUNet, Prodigy, and America Online. Then I heard about a company called StarNet that was a small Internet Services company based in Chicago. I thought wow, if they can do this, I can do it too.

This is when I decided I wanted to be an Internet Service provider. I figured, if I could provide a service that people subscribe to, and paid for each month, I would surely be successful.

It wasn't so much about the money; it was about my passion to start my own business in this new thing they called the Internet. I was fascinated by it, and read everything I could get my hands on about it. At the time I worked in the construction trades as a painter, and I didn't even own a computer. I would go to the library after work to get on the Internet.

Back then computers were very expensive, costing several thousand dollars. Then one day, I met a guy that built computers, and we made a deal to paint his house, in exchange for a computer.

Now I had my computer. Next step, I got a modem and a dial up account, and I was on my way to starting my Internet business.

Fast forward to 2008, after ten years in business I learned that in Internet Time things move at an accelerated pace, and you have to be always innovating, always a step ahead or you may find yourself obsolete.

And that's exactly what happened, I woke up one day and realized that my business model was becoming outdated, and I would have to completely re-invent myself, to stay in the game.

At the time so many individuals and companies realized that they needed to get their business online, and were now trying to learn about the Internet. That's when I discovered that an entire business had evolved around Internet Marketing Training, teaching people how to market their business online.

I started going to seminars and watched many different marketing experts present their training courses, and coaching programs, and many of them had nowhere near the experience I had. People were eager to get this knowledge, and lined up to purchase their courses.

That's when I realized that with my ten years experience of successfully marketing online, I was more than qualified to teach Internet Marketing. So that's exactly what I did. I began by creating a course, "Creating A Million Dollar Online Business." It was a simple course that was basically an Interview of one of my students and a friend, a gentleman from Japan.

Then I created the cover art, burned the audio CD's and placed them in dual CD cases with custom covers, and created a transcript. I packaged it all in Priority Shipping boxes from the Post Office, with the big red, white, and blue American eagle. And went out on the Seminar Circuit.

The course was a hit, and I quickly developed a following of students. One thing I learned in teaching Internet Marketing was that once people had the knowledge, there are essential services that all online businesses need, and as an Internet Service Provider this was a natural for me to sell them my services. I discovered that the Internet Marketing courses were really a great way to attract customers to my Internet Service business.

This is when I came up with the concept of combining the Training with the Internet Services to "Provide The Tools And Training For Small Business To Be Successful Online" that has been my business model to this day.

I decided to focus on Small Business, the Small to Medium Enterprise (SME). This seemed to me to be an underserved market. SME's are the backbone of the economy, and while other companies are all out chasing the big corporations, this grass roots approach has - me to grow and prosper "Under The Radar" with little competition.

To generate traffic and business, I have successfully employed an Affiliate Sales model. I discovered long ago that money motivates people, and people are willing to work hard to make money from home working on the Internet.

In the beginning, back in 1998, I studied the concept of Affiliate Marketing. Back then the only Affiliate programs were Amazon, and a few adult sites, that offered their Affiliates a commission for referring business.

I had some exposure to the Multi-Level programs back in the 80's, and I came up with the concept of using an expanded Affiliate program that paid on more than one level. At the time I called it Hybrid-Marketing, that combined a traditional Affiliate marketing program (on the front end) with a powerful Multi-Level program on the back end. It was the first of its kind on the Internet.

Over the years, the plan has evolved and become more complex, but the concept still remains the same. Now with the focus on Retail Sales, we are on the way to building one of the retail largest sales force in the world, with thousands of happy, satisfied customers around the world, using our products and services each and every day.

Another thing that I discovered was that in addition to the Training and "Essential Services," businesses need a way to generate traffic. Traffic is the key to any successful business, and it is the fuel that powers sales. *More traffic means more customers that leads to more sales and ultimately more profits.*

Back in 2008, I came up with the idea of "Incentivized Advertising" through what I called the AdView Platform. It was a revolutionary concept at the time, and quickly became wildly successful around the world.

The concept is simple, we basically share a portion of the ad sales revenue with the people who *View* and *Rate* the ads. AdView became an overnight success, and was extremely popular with our Advertisers and Members who *View* and *Rate* the ads.

Then in 2011, we started the Acesse Search Engine. This seemed like a natural evolution for my business. This was not an easy task, but with the help of some extremely smart people, we created the search platform to attract and provide the traffic, and to provide better value to our customers to advertise. Now Acesse.Com is one of the most high-traffic web sites in the world.

Technology is advancing and changing in the Internet at a rapid pace, and the AdView Platform is not as effective as it once was. So now, nearly ten years later, I set out to reinvent my business once again.

Now we are in an amazing time of innovation and creativity.

The Internet has changed peoples' lives in a very positive way and has revolutionized the world, as we know it, creating more wealth and prosperity than in any other time in history.

Many years ago I started on this journey with a dream to improve peoples lives using the power of the Internet. I launched my Internet Service company to provide the tools and training for the *Small Business* to be successful online.

I see the future is in building platforms. We are creating platforms that provide a simple, easy way for businesses to interact and transact business with customers.

The first platform we are introducing is YouWeb, an Integrated Solutions Platform. This revolutionary new marketing platform combines web Services, mobile services and video services in one easy to use, mobile friendly platform, designed for Small Business.

There are other companies that provide these services, but we are the first to offer them in one Integrated Solutions Platform. And by Integrating or "Bundling" these services together, we are able to offer our customers a greater value and a more affordable cost. We fully expect to have well over 250,000 users of this platform in the first year.

Our research and development team is working on other new and exciting platforms that we will be introducing in the coming months ahead, including VideoMeet, our All-In-One Video Communications Platform, and AppMart Pro, our new mobile site and mobile app platform.

The world is changing at an incredibly fast speed. Most people don't understand or even want to know how the Internet works or about the technology. They only want it to work. Just like electricity, people don't want to know how electricity works, they just want to flip the switch and the light turns on.

The fact is, over the last twenty years we have evolved into an Information Technology, or IT, economy. In general terms, IT is the technology that is used to create, store, exchange, and use information in many different ways. And like the old saying "Knowledge Is Power" - Information is knowledge, and so "Information Is Power."

Now we are entering into a new era of Data Technology. Data is the new information that will drive business in the future. Data is what will drive the new economy for the next twenty years.

This is what's known as the "D" Economy. Not the Digital economy but the Data Economy. Eric Schmidt of Google has said that we now create more data in just two days, than has been created since the dawn of civilization. This is amazing!

I believe that Data is the future, and how we harness and use this Data will be key to success in the future for our world. Now "Data Is Power."

I am working with some of the most brilliant minds in the world today to create amazing new Technologies that will change peoples' lives and literally change the world.

It's hard to believe that I started back in 1998 with nothing but a dream, and now have over 200,000 customers in over 120 countries. I now have engineering teams around the world from Silicon Valley, Texas, Atlanta, India, Russia, Romania, and the Netherlands, as well as an entire team of talented people in Minneapolis in Management, Accounting, Marketing and Support, who help keep the entire operation running.

Now we are in an amazing time of innovation and creativity where anything is possible. Young people are creating new technologies that have disrupted the old traditional ways of doing business, and are changing the world. Today people have an opportunity to leverage technology to realize their dreams.

In a recent speech in Europe, Jack Ma said that "It's not the technology that will change the world, it's the dreams behind the Technology that will change the world."

We all have dreams, and you can accomplish anything you want in this world. As long as you believe and take action, you can make it happen!

Now my dream is to achieve one million members/customers, and $1 billion in sales by December 31st 2016. And I know as sure as I am standing here today, that I know that I will make this dream a reality.

Seventeen years ago, I started with a dream to help people to improve their lives with the power of the Internet. I am living proof that you achieve your dreams; and if I can do it I know that anyone can. Now the future is up to you. Follow your dreams, and never give up, and you can make your dreams a reality.

"Together We Can Change The World"

ABOUT STEVE

Steve Renner is an Internet Marketing Pioneer. He started his first Internet Service Company back in 1998, providing Internet Services for individuals and small business. Again in 2001, Steve pioneered Online Payment services with Cash Cards and V-Cash, and became a leader in this industry.

Then in 2008, Steve created *AdView*, and *incentivized online* advertising service that quickly spread around the world. In 2011, Steve started the Acesse search engine, which is now ranked as a top web destination in the world.

But it all has not been easy and Steve has had his ups and downs, but through it all he has been a survivor. He has gone on to build a successful Internet Services Company, which employs over 100 people, and provides services to small business customers around the world.

Steve is well-liked and respected in the industry, and speaks to thousands around the world at live events. His first book, *Transform*, a collaboration with well-known Sales Trainer and Motivational Speaker Brian Tracy, is an Amazon #1 Best Seller.

Steve is also a member of the National Academy Of Best Selling Authors.

Steve also writes music and is an accomplished blues guitarist. He enjoys spending time with his family, his children and especially his grandchildren.

You can connect with Steve at:
www.steverenner.com
www.facebook.com/steverenner
www.twitter.com/steverenner

THE SECRET TO BUSINESS SUCCESS

Fire Yourself Everday

FOUR KEY QUESTIONS TO ASK OURSELVES ON A DAILY BASIS TO ENSURE THE HEALTH, LONGEVITY AND PROFITABILITY OF ANY COMPANY

When Donald Trump uttered the words, "You're fired!" he not only made those two dreaded words synonymous with failure, regret, anger and frustration, he also massively engaged an audience of millions watching, as someone was heaved from *The Apprentice* every week. To the viewers, it was often obvious who would be leaving the penthouse. Poor work ethic, failure to submit to a team environment, creating confusion, ineffectiveness, and all around neglect of the task were showcased by the participants, who faced Trump's laser stare, as he guillotined his contestants, sending them humbled and degraded to face an uncertain future.

As business owners, executives and managers, we are often the boss, the receptionist, the customer service representative and more. We are inevitably wearing many hats, especially in the early stages of growth. With a 90% failure rate for most small businesses, managing to be in the rarefied air of the 10% can be tough. Growing beyond mediocrity into a great business can be even tougher. What if, instead of going through the motions of business every day, we decided to fire ourselves every night? What if every morning, and throughout the day, we had to earn the right to be at our own company? How would that change things?

The late Dr. Wayne Dyer, someone who I had the exceptional fortune of knowing personally, wrote in his book, *Wishes Fulfilled*, that we could all benefit from the dying off of the aspect of ourselves that clings to the limiting beliefs that hold us back. He urges us to make a conscious decision to literally "birth" ourselves into the man or woman that we know deep down we can be. Dr. Dyer's success was palpable, with an estimated net worth of $20 million. In his numerous works, he spoke, with great humility, about a constant shedding of the various aspects of himself that no longer served him. In business, what if we, too, made a concerted effort to jettison our arrogance, fear, cynicism and lack of focus at the end of every day, electing to start the next day from the same wide-eyed, neophytic place that caused us to be hungry enough to eschew *ordinary* and pursue *extraordinary* in the first place?

On paper I was a millionaire at age twenty-four. My then partner and I had purchased a health club with a substantial client base, a good reputation, and what we thought was a potential for growth. In our minds we had everything we reasoned would be required for success. I was a certified fitness instructor and personal trainer. I had worked in sales before and grown up in an entrepreneurial family. My partner had also been brought up in a family with a small business. He had worked with his father on everything, from the accounting, to the marketing, to the day-to-day operations. We were young, keen, energized, hungry, and possessed just enough arrogant naivety to make it work, or so we thought.

*Professional*PERFORMANCE*360* *Special Edition:* SUCCESS   89

> ## Not only are we replaceable within our own companies, we are replaceable to our clients and consumers.

Like many entrepreneurs with a great concept and a new business, we worked longer and harder, thinking that this was the solution. I recall many mornings waking up in excruciating pain from teaching over twenty high-impact fitness classes in a week and then standing for hours behind the front desk. In between, I was training clients and doing their workouts with them. My partner procrastinated on the financials and, frankly, was in over his head; we both were. We became exhausted and apathetic. The result was that we procrastinated on actually dealing with our problems, which included mounting repair bills, an expensive but necessary air-conditioning system that repeatedly stopped working, internal theft, increased competition in the market, and lack of member loyalty.

If our lives had been a reality television show, it would not have been a surprise when, on a fateful Good Friday morning, I went to our health club to teach a group cycling class and found a padlock on the door with the life-shattering news, and public humiliation, posted for all to see. We had been closed down for failure to pay taxes. I had no idea things were so grave. How would I? I had deliberately avoided the business of doing business, conveniently allowing myself to live in delusion that somehow everything was fine. In retrospect, if I had approached every day with the same enthusiasm that had been a catalyst for me to call people while in labor with my daughter to negotiate the remaining ten thousand dollars required to buy that health club in the first place, and fired myself every night, the experience most likely would have been different.

You see, I have been in the 90% failure rate, and I have also been one of the rare individuals to build a business that has surpassed the critical first five years. According to Bloomberg, 80% of new businesses fail within the first eighteen months, and having gone through it, I will tell you first-hand that arrogance was the culprit. Whether we are owners, executives, investors or someone with any form of vested interest in the company, it is imperative that we never stop earning our right to be there, and the only way to do that is to appreciate that, no matter what position we hold, we are replaceable. If you doubt that, you need only look to the late Steve Jobs and his ousting from Apple in the early years, or any other CEO or company founder who has been 'voted off the island,' to understand this concept. Not only are we replaceable within our own companies, we are replaceable to our clients and consumers. Businesses, and executives, who become complacent – think Blockbuster – end up finding out the hard way that losing our hunger, and becoming too smug, is a surefire way to hit the start button on the demise of a company.

With this in mind, there are four key questions that can help us ensure the health, longevity, sustainability and profitability of a business, and I encourage you to ask these of yourself every single day.

1. WOULD I HIRE MYSELF TODAY?

In the United States alone, there are a minimum of three applicants for every job opening, according to Gene Sperling, the Director of the National Economic Council. Essentially, the competition is fierce. Business owners and entrepreneurs do not have to compete with other candidates to walk into their own C-Suite offices everyday; however, imagine how a business could progress if every owner and executive was literally given notice at the end of the day and forced themselves to resign, thus demanding that they show up at work the next day without one hint of complacency.

From punctuality, to attitude, to willingness to grow – would you hire yourself today? If the answer is 'no,' then there are two choices: step up or step down. Our clients, customers and team members lose trust if we cannot be the person we would want to work with. Every day, make a decision to be the person you would want to hire and watch how your productivity and profits soar.

2. HOW AM I BRINGING VALUE TO MY CLIENTS TODAY?

In February of 2008, Starbucks CEO, Howard Schultz, took a risky move and shut down 7,100 retail locations in the United States to re-train his baristas in the art of espresso. What Schultz realized, especially at the peak of the recession, was that the solution to sagging revenues was to figure out how to add more value to his customers. In a memo entitled, "Howard Schultz Transformation Agenda Communication #8," Schultz wrote, "We are passionate about our coffee. And we will revisit our standards of quality that are the foundation for the trust that our customers have in our coffee and in all of us." That move, amongst others designed to heighten the 'Starbucks Experience,' were the foundation of the healthy profits Starbucks enjoyed coming out of the recession.

Every day, make a decision to add more value.

You may be having a bad day. You may feel like crawling back into bed. You may feel like the economy, the competition or even your colleagues are dragging you down, but the reality is that your clients, regardless of the business you are in, pay your bills. Adding value to clients is what keeps them working with you as opposed to your competition. Every day, make a decision to add more value. Schedule a meeting with your team and ask each one how they can serve the clients and customers to a greater level. From handwritten notes, to adding on complementary service, to authentic client care – there are always ways to add more value.

3. HOW AM I BRINGING VALUE TO MY COMPANY TODAY?

Another company CEO, Zappos founder Tony Hsieh, sent a memo to his employees in 2015. Essentially, they were to adopt 'holacracy' or leave. In this memo, Hsieh announced the removal of all 'people managers.' The employees, which in a live talk I have heard Hsieh refer to as individual entrepreneurs within the company, would strive toward self-management and self-organization. This, Hsieh feels, is the catalyst to take the company to the next level. To truly operate with holacracy, employees must aspire to add value to the company with the unique understanding that they have a vested interest in the success of the business. Other companies, such as the aforementioned Starbucks and Whole Foods, provide tangibles such as stock options and even scholarships to those employees who are loyal and have proven to add value.

Executives and employees who tend to add more value to their place of employment are often promoted and given financial rewards. Those who tend to slug through the day and are inconsiderate of adding to their workplace tend to hit the chopping block, so to speak. Ask yourself how you can add value to your company.

4. IF MY CLIENTS AND CUSTOMERS REVIEWED MY WORK AND MY PRODUCTS – WOULD THEY WANT TO DO BUSINESS WITH ME?

In 2013, Johnson and Johnson met their goal of removing two potentially harmful chemicals, formaldehyde and 1,4-dioxane, from a myriad of their products, including the much beloved 'No More Tears' baby shampoo due to consumer pressure and increasing awareness from customers in terms of what was deemed safe. Johnson and Johnson could have, like some companies, created some form of seductive public relations campaign to somehow tout 'the efficacy over safety issue' in hopes of saving the majority of loyal brand users. Instead, they spent tens of millions of dollars 'cleaning up' their soaps and lotions because after a review of their work, they were willing to take action.

Go for it and 'live' into the person you would want to hire!

Companies that fail to respond to consumer demands fail to evolve. Making a bold decision to operate with transparency as though the world is watching (and thanks to social media it is), allows us to operate at a higher standard. From how we connect with people, to what we say behind closed doors, to the integrity of our products and services – innovation and advancement come with being humble enough to make necessary changes, because our clients have called us to the carpet based on something that did not align with their demands.

I have a belief that the number of successful businesses can shift in a positive direction when we start the day from a place where we fired ourselves the night before and are earning our right to be hired. When we ask ourselves these questions, and combine them with being highly organized and efficient, our results transform dramatically. As a fellow entrepreneur, I encourage you to go for it and 'live' into the person you would want to hire!

ABOUT SUSAN

Susan Sly is a best selling author, award-winning speaker and entrepreneur. She has written, and co-written, seven books. Susan has appeared on CNN, CNBC, Fox, Lifetime Television, ABC Family, and been quoted in *Forbes Magazine* online. Susan has appeared in the highly acclaimed movie *Rise of the Entrepreneur* alongside NY Times Best Selling Authors, Robert Kiosaki, John Assaraf and others. Susan's company, Step Into Your Power™, is dedicated to providing training for entrepreneurs to become more productive in all areas so they can lead ridiculously fulfilling lives.

Susan's passion is liberating women and girls from trafficking, poverty and illness. She has collaborated with World Vision, the UNHCR, Make-A-Wish, and more.

In her spare time, Susan enjoys running and is a five-time Boston Marathon finisher. Susan is the mother of five children. She and her husband, Chris, reside in Scottsdale, Arizona.

For more about Susan, visit her website at: www.susansly.com .

SUCCESS IS HAVING THE FREEDOM TO DO WHATEVER YOU WANT IN YOUR LIFE

PERFORMANCE: At the top of your personal bio on your firm website, it says "It's not just business, It's Personal." What is the essence of that philosophy and how does it help the firm achieve success?

BRIAN: The quote speaks for itself. Everyone likes to say, 'It's just business, don't take it personally," as if their clients are just transactions and not people, but we look at things differently. The work we do is personal. I may not have a personal stake in the outcome, but we recognize that it's personal to the client. We don't look at our clients as transactions, where we just want to get the work done and move along. We want our clients to have a sense of family and partnership in the process – so they are at ease with what they're doing, and very relaxed in our warm, friendly environment. It's a team effort where they feel invested in what we are doing for them. This has allowed us to grow via friends and family referrals. My ultimate goal as an attorney is to be my clients' counselor and trusted advisor for their lifetime and, with estate planning, we strive to be their family attorney. We want to be here for their families to guide them as well.

PERFORMANCE: What were your initial goals for your firm and how did you go about achieving success with them?

BRIAN: When we started in late 2003, my goals were, like any business in its infancy, to build, run and grow a successful organization. These are the hopes of any dedicated entrepreneur. The key to achieving that is two words: customer service. It really comes down to being generous with my time and educating clients, making sure they understand the process as it goes along. Even today, I'm on the phone all the time, offering advice, not getting paid for it, not billing for it, but rather helping people simply because I feel that it is the right thing to do. If I can help someone, why wouldn't I? I would want someone helping me like this.

I am blessed with a very good sense of finding common ground with people from all walks of life and that helps me tremendously. I can intuitively see where people are coming from, what's important to them, what makes them comfortable and happy. Sometimes the things we deal with as attorneys are unpleasant situations for our clients, but we still do everything we can to achieve the best possible resolution for the client. When it comes to marketing, I'm old school, personally building relationships one at a time. I've never been into mass marketing. When we launched, the Internet wasn't the marketing force it is today. The options were TV, radio and print ads – or the old fashioned approach, which was and remains my preference.

I don't necessarily have to be the biggest legal name in Atlanta. If I was that guy that the paparazzi chased everywhere I went, the star lawyer about town, I'd have to give up the personal touch, which is the philosophy I built my business on. If you grow too big, at some point it becomes overwhelming and you start to have an automated, assembly-line feeling. So the key is showing up, remaining true to our values and belief system, putting the clients first and ensuring a great experience for them. I'm proud of what we have accomplished organically.

PERFORMANCE: Your firm has a unique array of specialties, from Real Estate and Estate Planning/Asset Protection to Corporate Law. What is your specific personal expertise and why are these the areas you choose to work in?

BRIAN: Over the years, we have delved into even more areas than those, but it made sense to hone in on the ones we focus on now for a variety of reasons. It was hard to be involved in so many other areas that might cause scheduling conflicts. Let's say you're in bankruptcy court in the morning but have a meeting scheduled for a real estate deal or estate planning strategy session. You could get stuck in court longer than you expected, and then have to disappoint your other clients. So we had to focus on the areas where we felt we could help clients the most, discovering along the way which were congruent with each other. Before we were involved in opposite types of practices, litigation vs. transactional, and it was hard to engage successfully in both. The three areas we focus on now go hand in hand. Businesses often own real estate and need estate planning and asset protection. There is often a synergy between our practice areas. Moreover, with our goal of being a client's attorney and trusted advisor, by definition we need to align our practice areas to effectively cover as many of our clients' needs as possible.

My background is in engineering and so I'm very methodical and problem-solving oriented in my approach to all things. Couple those skills with my entrepreneurial spirit and legal knowledge and you can see how I was drawn to my practice areas. Working with small businesses and companies allow me to engage the entrepreneurial side. Real estate and estate planning allows me to tap into my pragmatic problem solving/desired outcome wiring. There are always many ways to achieve the desired result, but like in the engineering world, it's about evaluating the variables and designing the best possible solution. There's no one-size-fits-all approach. Two families can appear to be similar on the surface but may have different goals, needs and concerns when it comes to family, tax and legacy issues.

PERFORMANCE: You seem proud of the fact that you have the freedom to cover more than one area of the law. Why is that important to you compared to building a practice with one specialty?

BRIAN: It's important because of our focus on lifelong relationships with the clients. I want them to think of me as a trusted advisor, not "Brian-the-DUI-Attorney" or "The Bankruptcy Guy." I want to develop relationships that are bigger than a single label. We all have people in our lives who we trust, who we call for advice when we have a problem. Oftentimes they are not able to solve the problem directly, but they will always offer sage advice to guide us toward the resolution. I want to be that attorney for my clients. I have experience and the skill set that enables me to spot issues and concerns for a lot of unique client problems. Even if some problems are outside my realm of expertise, they can still call me, and I can refer them to someone who is better suited to help. To me, those specific lawyer branding ideas are focused less on service and more on marketing concepts. But it depends what kind of firm you want to have and how you want to define your relationship with your clients. Some lawyers are less concerned with the best result than the bottom line, and that's fine for them. I think there's a way to be financially successful while serving the clients' needs in a more personal way.

PERFORMANCE: Earlier in your life and career, how did you define success? How has that definition changed over the years?

BRIAN: When you're younger, you're limited by your life experience and may fulfill that stereotype of the kid who thinks he knows everything. You think you need to make money, drive a nice car and that's all it's about. But there's a great naiveté about what really makes the world go round. From that naive standpoint, success is defined by dollar amount or tangible assets like a car or house. Those are things that define success for many, but also limit it. I now think success is having the freedom to do what you want, doing whatever it is that makes you happiest. We will all define that differently. As owner of this firm, I define it as having the freedom of being the master of my domain and creating my own destiny. There's also the notion of legacy. The amount of money I leave my family is less important than having options and the control to exercise them. Balancing my schedule to include quality family time is another way for me to measure success now. I recently read an article asking people over 65 about their greatest regrets, and many said it was the fact that they lived in fear of things that they ultimately realized they didn't have to worry about. Living life from a place of fear is never going to lead to real success.

PERFORMANCE: One of the most fascinating elements of your story is that you studied mechanical engineering, worked in manufacturing and were a business consultant before you decided to attend law school. How and why did you decide to pursue law?

BRIAN: I worked for a large Fortune 100 manufacturing company, but manufacturing is a business tied to the economy. There were also other things like labor issues to contend with, so many jobs were being outsourced based on the emerging global economy, and the industry in the late 90s was quickly changing. I am a hands-on, boots on the ground person, and my concern was that while I had a great job now, in five, ten or fifteen years, what if they shipped my position overseas? I had to make a choice. A 9 to 5 job wasn't in my DNA, and I wanted to be more purposeful and intentional in thinking of my next move. I knew it would be entrepreneurial in nature.

So, I decided to broaden my horizon and attended law school. What's interesting is that when I enrolled in law school, I didn't do so with the goal of becoming an attorney – but to gain a skillset that would help me in business negotiations no matter what I chose to do. It would give me the upper hand. I discovered that I was good at law and really enjoyed it. It involves a lot of rules, laws, rationalization, critical thinking and analytics. Engineering is about numbers, facts, and doing the math to solve things. In law you may have the same basic case a thousand times but little nuances pop in that make each case different. The law is very fluid and there are many changes regarding things like intellectual property due to emerging technologies. I loved the creative aspects of this kind of problem solving. It was second nature to me.

PERFORMANCE: Do you measure success as an attorney solely by the amount of business you take on or the relationships with and achievement on behalf of your clients?

BRIAN: It's absolutely NOT based on the business we take on, but the results I and my associates accomplish for our clients. Ironically, even though we may take a problematic situation and make it better for them, there still may be negative connotations involved and some residual pain that exists. So I have to measure success based on my ability to eliminate as much pain as possible. The good news is that there are many ways to solve an existing problem, so if one choice doesn't work, the next just might.

PERFORMANCE: You're a family man who is also passionate about animal rescue, along with all causes that help promote it. When you think in terms of achieving success in life, how important are these personal sides to your story?

BRIAN: It goes back to my earlier statement of being a young vs. older person and changes in how we look at success at different stages of life. I have a three-year-old daughter and a five-month-old baby. Having family has made me a better person, and I have learned many other skills as a result of being a husband and father. You have to treat your kids differently than you do colleagues and clients. They will challenge you in different ways. It's not just about essential tasks like feeding them or putting them to bed. Having children gives you a broader level of experience. The same goes for the charitable work I do. It's important to help people and give back – and that connects well with my desire to be generous with my professional time. When you do things in an intentional way, it changes your mindset and the way you think about things. I think it broadens my definition of success with new horizons and a unique, wider vantage point.

PERFORMANCE: What are some of the challenges you have overcome to be successful?

BRIAN: When you have your own firm, there's always the fear of the unknown, and you're only as effective as the work you did yesterday. My employees always get paid but if I don't generate enough business, I may not. Belief in myself and what I have set out to do keeps me going, but there's always that level of concern because we never know what tomorrow will bring. I'm always afraid of becoming too complacent when things are going well – because certain businesses I work with could change when the economy turns. There are no guarantees when you're self-employed. I'm from Milwaukee originally, but there's a saying here in the South: "You gotta make hay when the sun shines." Early on, people wondered why I worked six or seven days a week when things were on the upswing. But I told them that it might not always be so sunny. Success is driven by how well you adapt to the ups and downs.

PERFORMANCE: In a nutshell, define "Success."

BRIAN: For me, success is being able to have that freedom to make choices, to steer the ship in whatever direction I want, and be able to change course when necessary. What I mean by freedom of choice is that I'm not locked in to any particular mindset. If I had a certain level of success ten years ago, that may not mean much now. Say I had a good year in 2005 and bought a new BMW then. But now, ten years later, it's got four million miles on it. Maybe I measured success then by the car I drove …but that only lasts so long. Experience teaches you so many things, and you have to apply the knowledge and wisdom you gain along the way to guide those difficult but necessary changes. Estate planning is a perfect example of this. When my kids are babies, I'm going to see it differently than in 30 years when they are adults. You have to be willing to take a second look and adapt to fresh circumstances.

ABOUT BRIAN

Brian Douglas, Esq. has always been committed to the belief that a person's legal needs are personal and not just business. This is a cornerstone in Brian's approach to law and how he serves his clients. In 2003, when he founded Brian M. Douglas & Associates, LLC, his vision was to create an entire culture that embraced this same powerful concept. And he has.

Brian received his Bachelor of Science degree from Marquette University in Milwaukee, Wisconsin, where he studied Mechanical Engineering while working full time as a manufacturing supervisor for a Fortune 100 Corporation. Upon graduation, he moved to Atlanta to attend John Marshall Law School, where he graduated *cum laude* and as his class valedictorian. Brian was initially drawn from engineering to law because of his gifts for reasoning and logic—two qualities that are essential for a successful attorney. And he hasn't looked back since.

Today, Brian is a highly respected attorney with a solid reputation with his clients, colleagues, opposing counsel, and within the court system throughout the state of Georgia. Through his firm, he has taken on very diverse cases, working with bankruptcy, real estate law, civil/business litigation, foreclosure, criminal law, and what Brian is highly acclaimed for—estate planning and asset protection. According to Brian, "Establishing my own practice has allowed me the freedom to cover many areas of law. This fits my diverse range of interests and benefits the clients we serve."

A unique approach to business is a driving force behind Brian's success. Valuing the relationship with his clients and knowing that he is a trusted advisor for life's most important decisions, Brian stands out through offering concierge style services for his clients and having a no voicemail policy at the firm. When someone calls, they get a live person answering the phone and from that moment on the relationship with a potential client has begun. He is also a contributor on Fox, ABC, CBS, and NBC television affiliates as well as to *Star Tribune, Small Business Trendsetters, Worth,* and *The Miami Herald.* Recently, Brian appeared on the television show, *Times Square Today.* And now, Brian is an author, enabling him to reach out to more people about life's most important legal topics.

Brian reflects on his life's journey with genuine joy and how it brought him to Atlanta, and the practice that he loves. From day one, he's enjoyed the area for its people, the weather, and how conducive it is to some of his favorite activities, such as golf and tennis. Today, Brian is married to a wonderful woman, Tess. They have two small children who make life a daily adventure, and are passionate about animal rescue and fostering, along with all causes that help promote it. Now three Chihuahuas are also a part of the Douglas family.

According to Brian, "Life is busy, but it's never been greater. I wouldn't have it any other way."

Today's top-performing professionals must have the right skills, knowledge and attitude to compete, succeed and lead in a competitive global business environment.

SMALL WORLD, BIG SUCCESS

Performance: Brenda, you have traveled the world, experiencing more than 70 countries, and living and working on four continents. You led a global workforce development division of a Fortune 100 company and started two international companies to help people live, work and travel more effectively in diverse cultures. How does all of that come together to shape your view of today's global business environment?

Brenda: Connected. Competitive. Cross-cultural. These are three things that come to mind, whether you're living, working or traveling in this small world. From a business perspective, while organizations have the world at their doorstep and unprecedented international opportunities, it's certainly not without challenges and obstacles. If today's leader is not competent or effective at working across cultures, they will not achieve global success.

As an example, in a recent University of North Carolina Leadership Survey of 300 global human resource professionals, 94% said developing globally competitive leaders was important to their organizations' success, and nearly two-thirds said it was an urgent need. What competencies did they find most important? Multicultural sensitivity and awareness, strategic thinking, the ability to communicate effectively, and ethics and integrity.

Performance: What do global professionals need to succeed in today's competitive environment?

Brenda: Today's top-performing professionals must have the right skills, knowledge and attitude to compete, succeed and lead in a competitive global business environment. I'm often asked how people can develop these attributes. I suggest developing a global mindset by investing in training to increase cross-cultural competence, studying new languages, traveling abroad, learning about different international business practices, collaborating with a mentor, and most importantly, connecting with people who have different worldviews.

Performance: You and your team have developed thousands of global professionals in more than 50 countries. That provides a tremendous window into real-life cross-cultural experiences and challenges. What lessons can we learn from your insight?

Brenda: One of the most important lessons I've learned—the hard way—is that it isn't easy working across cultures. Early in my career, I had some difficult and humbling experiences while living and working overseas. In fact, one of the main reasons I got into cross-cultural business training and global workforce development was to help others avoid many of the cultural mistakes I unintentionally made with clients, colleagues and customers. I wanted to help others to minimize "culture shock" and be more effective whether living, working or traveling abroad.

I founded WorldWide Connect® to help people around the world bridge cultural gaps, increase cultural competence, and reach their global business goals. We provide individuals and organizations with the necessary cross-cultural skills and knowledge needed to close more deals, do more business, attract and retain clients, and open new markets in this complex global marketplace. WorldWide Connect has a team of more than 150 cross-cultural experts on six continents who are conducting global business effectiveness training and coaching for everyone from entry-level employees to CEOs, multicultural teams, expatriates and their families, international business travelers and essentially anyone else who works across cultures.

> # If you're able to follow your dreams and do what you love, that's success.

While living in Japan, I trained hundreds of Japanese business executives on how to effectively conduct business in the U.S. Meanwhile, I observed so many American business people getting off the plane in Tokyo with no idea how business was done in the Japanese culture. They didn't know what the "*meishi* exchange" was or how the Japanese sell, negotiate, conduct business meetings, and build relationships and trust. Of course, when someone "doesn't know what they don't know," it may ultimately end up negatively impacting their organization's bottom line, brand value, reputation, and long-term sustainability.

Over the past 25 years, I've learned that individuals who are the most open-minded, nonjudgmental, authentic and interested in learning about other cultures are the ones who are positioned to succeed in the global environment. Those who minimize or ignore the impact culture has on business activities may struggle to find success.

Performance: Based on your extensive international experiences, tell us more about how other cultures define success, and measure performance and leadership effectiveness.

Brenda: It might surprise people to learn that the definition of success is not universal across cultures. For example, in the U.S., we tend to focus on individual achievements, while in many Asian cultures the focus is on group accomplishments.

What defines effective leadership also differs from culture to culture. A recent research study of more than 30,000 leadership assessments from 10 countries reinforced that highly successful leadership traits vary widely from country to country. For example, in countries such as India and China, there is a strong focus on operational execution. In Nordic countries, such as those in Northern Europe, leaders focus more on planning, strategy and communication. The U.S. and the U.K. emphasize more of a hybrid leadership model. This is why it is critical for today's global business leaders to be flexible and to adapt their leadership style to the cultural context in which they are working. Of equal importance is avoiding the notion that "my way is the right way to do business," and to remember the adage: When in Rome, do as the Romans do.

Performance: So how do you define success?

Brenda: For me, success does not equal power, prestige and possessions, but rather the ability to live your purpose and develop meaningful relationships with others in this small world. We are all blessed with different skills, abilities, talents and experiences, and it's how we choose to apply them in our life and career that will determine our personal success. If you're able to follow your dreams and do what you love, that's success. When you pursue your purpose and your passion in life, chances are you'll do it very well, and other results—such as financial rewards and business accomplishments—will follow.

Performance: You went from growing up in a small town in the heart of the U.S. to being a global business leader. You've sailed around the world three times by ship, and circled it by plane many more times. You accomplished these things by the time you reached the age of 40. How did you go from a small-town girl to a successful international businesswoman?

Brenda: Growing up where I did served me well. I learned to trust others and to go out into the world with an open-minded curiosity rather than preconceived notions. I saw the world, and still do, as an extension of my community—safe and kind-hearted. The morals and values I grew up with have been and continue to be valuable building blocks of developing relationships anywhere around the globe. For me, sincerity, humility, helping people and, most importantly, being respectful are foundational components of my relationships.

As a child, I always had dreams of traveling around the world, although I didn't know anyone who had traveled overseas or even had a passport. I may as well have told those around me that I wanted to go to the moon!

Be open-minded, curious and willing to take chances.

Then one day when I was in college at Iowa State University, I saw a poster for the 'Semester at Sea' program. It was very expensive for me at the time, but I did everything I could to afford the program and participated in the 102-day academic trip sailing around the world to 12 countries. I came back home to Iowa a different person. I experienced so many things—some very pleasant and others that opened my eyes to the challenges and struggles many people face. I climbed the Great Wall of China, saw the Kirov Ballet in Russia, stayed in a remote village in India, and saw starvation in Third World countries. When you see and experience these types of things, it impacts the deepest parts of your heart and soul and forever changes your perspective of the world.

After that, I was off and running, although my path wasn't always a direct one. I sometimes joke that the song *Bless the Broken Road* is about my life. But in reality, everything I did was strategic and a building block toward my goals. I always followed my heart, trusted my gut, and listened to my inner voice even when others may have thought my plans were crazy.

Performance: For many people, it can be difficult to move from "dreaming it" to "making it happen." What drives you, and what advice do you have for others?

Brenda: Personally, I stayed faithful to my calling in life and honored my passion. I developed the appropriate education and skills, put myself into the right situations, made good choices, maintained an attitude of hard work and discipline, and didn't let fear of the unknown slow me down.

As for what drives me, I would say my curiosity and wanting to learn about the world around me! To be successful in today's world, my advice is to get out of your comfort zone, take calculated risks, and to seize opportunities for continuous learning. Take the road less traveled and blaze your own path. Over the years, I've taken some big risks which resulted in some big rewards—whether it was moving to a foreign country or leaving a comfortable corporate job to start my own business. There were times when I was all alone in a country and low on money, but I always had the perseverance to make it work. I tell those I mentor to be open-minded, curious and willing to take chances. Be willing to take that next step—even if it's on the other side of the world.

I believe that goal-setting is fundamental to success, but you also need to start with big dreams. Otherwise, what are you working toward? Don't put limits on your dreams based on your current situation, mindset and bank account. Think big. Be honest with yourself. Then, set your goals and take action so that your dreams don't sit idle. Don't wait for "someday" because that day may never come.

Performance: You're often referred to as "The Global Gal" in your efforts to help women take action on their travel dreams. Tell me more about your endeavors.

Brenda: Through my experiences, I realized that women had unique challenges when living, working and traveling overseas, so I founded Global Gals®. I knew I could help women of all ages to be more confident and savvy travelers. Whether women need help overcoming real or perceived roadblocks to travel, or are simply looking for a community of women who are interested in travel, Global Gals provides resources and support. We help women connect, learn and share through our travel seminars, retreats, cultural workshops, trips and networking opportunities. So many people tell me, "Brenda, I can't travel like you do because of my circumstances." They also tell me about their financial situation or fears of the unknown. I've had to overcome many of the same things. By using my firsthand knowledge and experiences, I help other women overcome their individual challenges so they can achieve their travel dreams and goals.

To me, Global Gals is so much more than a company. I started Global Gals as a legacy to my dad to help inspire and encourage other women to make their travel dreams a reality, just as he did for me.

Performance: Clearly your father was an inspiration to you. Tell us more.

Brenda: I have met many people that have inspired me in so many ways, and I still meet inspiring people every day. That's part of a continuing journey. But my father, Harold Hagen, was my greatest inspiration and my biggest cheerleader. Whenever I'd share my dreams, goals and career plans with him, he would say, "Just do it!" Those three simple words transformed my world and his, too. One of my father's dreams was to go on a safari in Africa. Even though the timing and the finances weren't ideal, I found myself telling Dad, "Just do it!" We ended up going together to Africa and having the time of our lives. Thank goodness we took the trip when we did. Just a few years later, he was diagnosed with Stage 4 cancer and was sent home with hospice care. We spent the 13 short days we had left together looking at our photo albums and recounting all the places and people around the world that had enriched our lives. I'm so glad he was able to share his memories of what he had done in his life instead of regretting what he hadn't done. He taught me to live life now and the importance of making my dreams a priority. His relatively sudden death was a pivotal moment for me, helping me realize the impact of his unconditional support and how it allowed me to become a confident and fearless traveler. It brings to mind a Hodding Carter quote that's one of my favorites, "Two of the greatest gifts are roots and wings." He gave me both.

Performance: I've heard you mention the phrase "small world" and have seen it in your two No. 1 best-selling books. Please elaborate on what you mean by that statement.

Brenda: Life is about relationships, and it has a way of connecting people in the most unexpected ways and places. You may encounter someone at the most unforeseen time and place, or while talking with a new friend discover that your paths crossed through a connection long before you knew each other. It's amazing how my global journey has been so full of serendipitous "small world" moments. For instance, early in my career, I moved to London without a job. As I was walking down the street, I ran into my former boss from Australia, who happened to have an opening at her international recruitment company across the street. I had a job within the hour. I even met my husband, who also is from my home state of Iowa, while we were both living in Australia.

I recently launched a website (www.smallworldstories.com) so people across the world can share their own experiences and connections. No matter how big the world seems, these moments make you realize that it truly is a small world.

Performance: Where do you go from here? What's next on your list?

Brenda: It's ironic you mention a list. I coincidentally just came across 100 goals I'd jotted down when I was 15 years old. Even then, I was a goal-setter and knew what I wanted to achieve. I've accomplished 75 of those goals so far, including being an exchange student, traveling the world, and running a business.

I'm still working on the remaining 25 on the list! Although there are some—such as Learn How to Skate Backwards or Have a Pony—which I'm not sure are ever going to happen. And, if you ask my husband about No. 24 on my list—Learn How to Cook Well—this still hasn't happened either!

On a serious note, what I'm focused on now is expanding my father's legacy and building on the momentum of what I've accomplished so far through Global Gals. I want to encourage and empower 1 million women worldwide to make their travel dreams a reality. I want to help others achieve "big success in this small world."

As my father inspired me, I want to inspire others. It's about the gift of roots and wings, and how I can use my gifts to help others.

ABOUT BRENDA

Brenda R. McGuire is an entrepreneur and a global workforce development, business and travel expert whose international career spans more than 70 countries on six continents. Brenda has more than 25 years of professional experience in the corporate, academic, non-profit and government sectors. She has lived and worked in Japan, Australia, the United Kingdom, Ireland, the United States and Switzerland.

Brenda is the Founder, President and CEO of WorldWide Connect®. With an extensive global network of more than 150 consultants on six continents, they deliver cross-cultural training, global business and leadership effectiveness programs, and expatriate support to international companies. Brenda also founded and is the Chief Global Gal of the company Global Gals®, which empowers and educates women of all ages and backgrounds to reach their travel dreams through workshops, retreats, cultural training and networking events.

During Brenda's global career, she served as the Director of Global Workforce Development for Prudential Financial in New York City. While there, she worked with Fortune 500 companies around the world to deliver customized intercultural business training and consulting solutions. She also managed a multicultural/virtual team, expanded Prudential Intercultural's global presence, and oversaw a trainer network of more than 500 cross-cultural trainers and consultants. In addition, she has worked professionally in the fields of international recruitment and human resources in London, England; Sydney, Australia; and Des Moines, Iowa. She also gained valuable cross-cultural business experience living in Osaka, Japan, for two years training and coaching global business executives.

An internationally-recognized speaker, she won the acclaimed Speakers EXPY® Award and is a frequent international speaker at conferences, corporate meetings and industry events. She has served as a guest lecturer aboard the Celebrity and Royal Caribbean cruise lines in North America, Asia, Australia and Europe. Sharing her expansive experience and knowledge, she gives audiences the tools to succeed in business, travel and cross-cultural understanding.

Due to her international travel and business expertise, Brenda has won many awards and was selected as one of America's PremierExperts®. Brenda is a No. 1 best-selling author and recently co-authored *The Soul of Success* with Jack Canfield (originator of the *Chicken Soup for the Soul* series) and *Answering The Call: Entrepreneurs and Professionals Reveal How They Said Yes to Success and You Can Too,* which both immediately hit No.1 best-seller lists. Brenda has been featured in more than 350 media outlets, including CNBC and *The New York Times,* as well as on ABC, CBS and NBC affiliates for receiving the Best-Selling Author Quilly® Awards. In addition, she was invited to share her expertise on a US Airways in-flight video, which appeared on 1,700 flights.

She has an MA in International Communication from Macquarie University in Australia, and a BS in Psychology and International Relations (with Distinction) from Iowa State University.

Connect with Brenda:
brenda@worldwideconnect.com
www.globalgals.com
www.worldwideconnect.com
www.facebook/globalgals
www.twitter.com/theglobalgals
Share your Connections:
Along Brenda's journey, she has connected with fascinating people whose own stories broadened the depths of her cultural awareness. She created *www.smallworldstories.com* for people to share the kind-hearted and coincidental "small world" stories they've experienced.

From that vantage point of experience with over 3,500 family-owned companies, I discovered their formulas for success as well as minefields of pitfalls.

BY BETSI BIXBY

TEN STEPS TO MOVE THE FAMILY COMPANY FROM BUSINESS TO LEGACY

Whether you are a first generation family business, a second or even later, or maybe just starting a business now, my guess is you have a deep longing for your business to survive you, to provide income and fulfillment to the next generation and generations beyond in a true family legacy. You are not alone.

Did you know that family businesses account for a full two-thirds of all economic commerce? That they are 90% of all the businesses in America and provide 62% of American employment according to the Small Business Administration?

But here is the problem. The odds of sustaining your business over time to the next generation are very much against you. Only about 30% of family businesses survive to second generation, 12% are still viable into third generation, and a miniscule 3% of all family businesses operate into fourth generation or beyond.

Luckily, the first three decades of my career was spent working with third, fourth and even fifth generation owners who had beaten the odds. And from that vantage point of experience with over 3,500 family-owned companies, I discovered their formulas for success as well as minefields of pitfalls that can derail intergenerational transfers—like the heartbreak of a third/fourth generation business being sold because no one really liked the business anymore.

I remember the shock of discovering two brothers that had come to physical blows in their monthly board meeting right in their own conference room. Bloody noses, chairs flying, one hitting the floor, the whole bar room brawl scene right smack in the middle of the family business. . . . And the heartache of an owner who discovered his drug addict sibling was siphoning off funds. . . . And the frustration of a daughter being excluded from family talks because she had chosen to have a baby. . . . And the horror of a family who suddenly lost the patriarch and no survivors knew how he ran the family empire and creditors wanted payment.

You can avoid all those pitfalls. However, it takes work. Just like all success, creating a family business that sustains generations and weathers all economies takes diligence and a plan. Here is your step-by-step foundation formula to create legacy success.

STEP ONE
DEVELOP COMMUNICATION SKILLS

Most families are tempted to think that legacy starts with a common vision and purpose. But agreeing on vision actually can't happen without something more important – great communication skills.

Hearing about the aftermath of a proverbial annual strategic planning meeting that turned into an all-out war between seven family members right before I wrote this chapter put a punctuation mark on this first step. Going straight to vision and planning is like trying to build a skyscraper on a bed of shifting sand.

Family legacy must be built on solid ground – which is the ability to openly communicate, addressing the most sensitive issues without anger, hostility, resentment or greed. Globally, education systems are severely lacking in communication teaching, so the first place a family must start to build legacy is by learning how to talk to each other, understand personality style differences, and ways to honor and stay engaged with differing opinions. That solid ground prepares the family for vision.

STEP TWO
AGREE ON PURPOSE

With good communication skills under your belt, now is the time to decide a clear purpose that connects the family powerfully. Do not confuse purpose with product or service! If you think your family purpose is to make widgets, and despite no fault of your own those widgets become obsolete, you've lost your purpose. So Purpose must be bigger than product.

For my core company Meridian Associates, Inc., we originally defined our purpose as blessing family-owned petroleum companies. But as I began listening to family business owners outside the petro industry, I realized their issues and opportunities were much the same as the petro industry. Based on that awareness, we expanded our purpose to blessing all family-owned businesses.

As we clearly defined our purpose beyond petro, that purpose led to developing tools and resources you get to now enjoy for family companies operating in all industries, including this book chapter you are reading!

STEP THREE
CREATE AN ENVIRONMENT WHERE CASH IS KING

The biggest killer of family companies is lack of cash. And once a business reaches critical momentum, cash is significantly different than profit. A company can be highly profitable and encounter severe cash crunches.

For a family business to survive, all owners must be in alignment regarding desired cash position including sources and uses of cash. This also takes agreement on risk and target rates of return. (Now are you seeing why Step One is communication?)

Again, we have developed a website for terrific tools you can use to get your family aligned on cash, as well as our 7 Quick Cash Fixes if your cash isn't exactly where you want it to be.

STEP FOUR
RECRUIT NON-FAMILY, OUTSIDE LEADERSHIP

Just because your family business is family doesn't mean there are family members with the skills, talents and propensities to excel in all needed positions to run your company with excellence.

So a success key is to strengthen your family business with outside leadership at both the board and operational level. Companies that bring in stellar outsiders to fill in the gaps for their weaknesses grow stronger faster than those that stick to family only.

I was reminded of this when reviewing our Outstanding Petroleum Woman Award recipients. I was struck by the scores of empire-building women who went to the marketplace for key leadership positions catapulting their company growth trajectory. Non-family experts bring critically-important strength and perspective.

Outsiders can be used to mentor 'up and coming' family without the stresses and strains of the family relationship. I know one CEO who specifically hired an outside General Manager and then made the manager's number one goal to ready his two children to take over the reins. This general manager came to the table with very strong coaching skills, something the autocratic CEO lacked, and he was highly successful in preparing the next generation of owners.

STEP FIVE
PUT PEOPLE BEFORE PROFITS

This is the place where family business can and does whip corporate America. You genuinely care about your team and it shows. Whether it's being flexible for time off when needed, doing little things to make people feel appreciated or recognizing when someone goes the extra mile, family companies shine!

When I was talking with a CEO of a major airline whose stock price had taken it on the chin and now recovered, he said he learned this *people before profits* principle the hard way. With his Wall Street background, he was so focused on the numbers that he lost sight of the people, his most important asset, and that is when the company tanked. When he set his focus on people, they did an enormous turn around.

In the family business, making people equal to, or even more important than profits, pays dividends. When you treat your team like gold, they will in turn treat your customers like gold. Doing the right thing over and over again, valuing your team, rewarding your team, always pays off.

STEP SIX
REQUIRE ACCOUNTABILITY

Family business owners are typically too nice and because of that, they are too lax. They don't make sure everyone has measurable results criteria and they don't hold people (including themselves) accountable to those results.

Luckily, accountability is a skill that's easy to learn. And it goes hand in hand with open communication. Simply set expectations, check buy-in, provide all resources needed for success, and set consequences for lack of success. Sounds simple and it is. But, the consequences part is where family companies fall down.

So what do you do with Uncle Harold if he doesn't do what he says he will do? That answer becomes exactly what you would do with any non-family member – you ask why. You see if there is a process or training issue, a time problem, a knowledge problem, or a motivation problem and handle it accordingly. The one thing you don't do is ignore it! Accountability must be applied regardless of family status.

STEP SEVEN
DEFINE POSITIONS

There is nothing more frustrating to the next generation than having no clue of expectations. Too often family members are thrown into the family business with a sink-or-swim mentality and no clear position benchmarks or authorities. They are told to go shadow someone or learn each position for a few weeks and report back for the next assignment.

This treatment creates a dynamic where the younger family member constantly feels incompetent, the other team members see or sense that incompetence, and therefore when that young person finally gets into a supervisory position, they are disrespected at best and maligned at worst.

So what's better? Bring them into a project where they can experience success because the project matches one of their God-given strengths! Let them shine. Let your team see them shine. They'll gain the necessary confidence to progress smoothly to other tasks.

I have seen even CEOs who can't define their position or tell me the results expected of them. Defining ALL positions in your company provides clarity and drives performance.

STEP EIGHT
CREATE A DECISION MODEL

The nature of family business is that not everyone agrees with everyone else – even when communication skills are spectacular. So that brings me to the more complex step of decision models.

A decision model is what helps govern a family company and allows good strategic decisions. It takes decisions out of the emotional tug of war and what people feel in their gut is their "right" decision into a more empirical and statistical model.

Not all decision models are optimal. For instance, should a crucial decision simply go to a vote? That can and does get ugly, pitting siblings against each other or parents. Should decisions be based on risk/return formulas, Internal Rate of Return or Net Present Cash Value types of analysis? Maybe. And who and how should decisions be vetoed even if most of the family wants to charge forward?

If this is sounding a little like America's balance of powers constitution, it's because family business is a delicate balance of power. But with family, the rules often aren't written or shared. Writing and sharing the decision-making rules gives clarity.

STEP NINE
ENCOURAGE MENTORING AND MODELING AT ALL LEVELS

Businesses successfully pass the baton between generations smoothly when the outgoing generation mentors and models well. We are finding that the more formal mentoring and modeling systems are documented and followed, the more profitable the company.

People learn the most from what others do, far more than what they say. My Dad used to tell me,
"Sweetie, always do what I say, not what I do" as his play on words and humbly realizing he didn't always walk his talk.

The next generation learns far more from observing than written or verbal instruction. Ideally, combining instruction with mentoring provides a fail proof method to fast track your incoming generation with congruency.

STEP TEN
DRIVE CULTURE THROUGH CORE VALUES

Businesses fail unnecessarily during leadership transition due to clashes in cultural core values. I say unnecessarily because it is SO EASY not to fail! All it takes is writing out the core values, living the core values daily, modeling the core values daily, hiring to core values, firing to core values and insisting that core values are lived out by every team member—family or non-family.

If you've never tackled written core values, I've made a super simple process available to you on my www.FamilyBizExperts.com resource website.

Follow these ten steps, and you'll be well on your way to creating a legacy business that will outlive you. Can you imagine your great-grandchildren talking about how smart you were long after your demise?

ABOUT BETSI

Betsi Bixby and her company Meridian Associates, Inc. currently assist over 3,500 of this country's privately held, family-led petroleum companies increase cash flow and profits through education, strategic planning facilitation, merger mediation, business valuation and brokerage services. Her message is one of executable steps and core competencies that every business owner or manager needs to know.

Betsi has been the most widely-read cash flow expert in the petroleum industry, where pennies not dollars, have dictated success for over two decades. Through her *Money Matters* column published by the Petroleum Marketers Association of America (PMAA) and many state and regional petroleum, convenience store, and propane associations, years of publishing her newsletter *The Meridian Financial Advantage,* and now her PetroAnswers membership website, Betsi clarifies and simplifies complicated subjects into concrete step-by-step processes that dramatically impact company performance and profits.

A financial sharp shooter, Betsi is well known for the value she brings to businesses and the families that own them. By customer demand, Betsi began Meridian's highly-acclaimed Valuation and Brokerage Division in late 1999. Betsi and Meridian quickly earned a reputation for accurate market valuations and have continued to achieve great success facilitating highly confidential sales of family-owned companies.

Betsi Bixby is also well-known by major refiners, conducting training each year for the major gasoline brands. Betsi's background includes an MBA in Finance and serving as Vice President of Commercial Lending for a regional bank before founding Meridian. She captivates convention audiences throughout the U.S. with her hard-hitting, practical key note addresses and workshops.

In 2011, Betsi became a founding member of the John Maxwell Team, intensely studying John C. Maxwell and his leadership principles based on his premise that "Everything rises and falls on leadership." Betsi and her team coach family business CEOs and their executive teams to new levels of personal and professional success.

With Christ-centered personal ethics, Betsi strives to be a blessing to her customers, her employees and the family businesses she loves. Betsi resides in Weatherford, Texas where she enjoys a ranching lifestyle, complete with cattle and horses. Betsi's equestrian pursuits include a Top-Three national ranking by The American Competitive Trail Horse Association. In 2011, Betsi co-founded Freedom Horses, a non-profit
501(c)(3) organization that links survivors of domestic violence with volunteer horse owners to build courage, compassion and confidence.

Betsi is former Chairman of the Tucson YMCA, former President of Greater Tucson Leadership, and former President of Soroptimist International of Tucson. Betsi considers her greatest accomplishment to be her daughter Sheila, who achieved a Masters in Behavioral Health Counseling and now resides in California.

If you have questions or comments, please email them to her at:
betsi@askmeridian.com

Resource website:
www.FamilyBizExperts.com

BY DAVID A. HOINES, ESQ

PLATFORM FOR SUCCESS

Woody Allen once said, "Money is better than poverty if only for financial reasons."

What follows is a reflection aided by mirrors: that is, what I have learned with the benefit of hindsight through tears and laughter as I have navigated through this life.

The following is in no particular order of importance, but are observations and thoughts of living a worthwhile existence in our go-around of life, short as it is.

As such, a brief description of my background and experience is in order so you, the reader, will understand my vantage point:

I am an American baby boomer with many years experience as a practicing lawyer with my own firm: however, I am an anomaly of sorts in that about half of my practice takes me in to the courtroom and juries, while the other half keeps me in the office addressing business, tax, and estate matters; thus, a division of my time and focus is comprised of two entirely different disciplines. This leads me to my first point:

STRANGE AND UNFORESEEN TRAILS

Be open and on the lookout for new opportunities, which arise from time to time, as you interact with others.

For example, years ago a brother and sister consulted me as I had written a Will for their father. Dad was suffering a terminal illness with certain death not far off. His physicians had hooked him up to a breathing machine through a tube inserted in his throat by way of a tracheotomy.

The problem was that Dad did not want his life to be artificially sustained by a machine - he either lived on his own or passed on. After all, no one gets out alive. Dad was mentally competent with a good brain and a seriously failing body. However, the treating physicians and hospital personnel would not accede to his wishes, as to do so meant certain death. So, he was physically restrained in the hospital from himself or his children removing the breathing apparatus.

It is important to remember that in those days, there were no Living Wills, Health Care Surrogates, etc., so what to do? If the children assisted him in his desires, they might be charged with a felony crime of aiding another in their suicide. The only realistic alternative was to go to Court - but I had never been to Court in any real way. My education was an undergraduate degree necessary to attend law school, a law degree, and a second law degree so I could specialize in tax law, which I had been practicing for the previous six years or so.

However, despite what would seem to others as road blocks, I decided to get out of my box, take the plunge and jump in even though it required tons of work, and the new experience of trial. The result, after a trial and appeals to the District Court of Appeal and Supreme Court of Florida was: (1) my client established for himself and all others the constitutional right of self-determination and choice as to his fate; (2) the Legislature,

A new trail that has taken me into many Courthouses around the United States.

at the beckoning of the Superior Court, authorized by law what we now commonly call a Living Will, so that a Court determination was not necessary for the future, but rather the properly written expression of each person; and (3) I ended up, due perhaps at least partly to the publicity, on a new trail that has taken me into many Courthouses around the United States, and a few foreign countries. In short, it changed my career and life experience, mostly in a positive way.

However, successful navigation of the trial required:

(A) <u>Perseverance</u>: It has been said that success is 80% showing up: lots of truth here, if you add the necessity of showing up on time (lots of people don't get it).

I had to persevere learning an entirely different discipline. I knew tax and business concerns, but not how to persuade a jury of people I had never seen before and would most likely never see again, as to the justice of my client's cause. That required hundreds of hours of training from more experienced lawyers in every facet of trial work, including day and weekly seminars all around the county.

One great trial advocacy instructor often remarked that you haven't tried a jury case until you have tried at least 25 jury trials - not a lot of lawyers have this experience.

Reminds me of my martial arts instructor who preached that you have not practiced a move unless you have done it at least 10,000 times.

(B) <u>Homework and Dedication</u>: You can never get it perfect, but you can get it very good or excellent. But it takes hard and dedicated work. I remember the observation of the great trial lawyer, Gerry Spence, who said in no uncertain terms to a large audience of lawyers that every hour in a courtroom requires no less than 15 hours of preparation, and if you are not prepared to make the effort, don't do it. Of course, he was right.

(C) <u>Know What You Are Not Good At</u>: It goes without saying that knowing your skills and aptitude is required for any successful career choice: You can't be much of a mathematician if the ability to add or subtract escapes you.

However, not learning what you are not good at can derail the most promising of futures, and is primarily issues of the ego, such as self-importance and arrogance.

Learn to let those with real aptitudes and skills that aren't your forte do what they do best - this is the real test of leadership: recognizing and enlisting the best people to do the task.

Perhaps no one better illustrates this leadership quality and inherent truism than Franklin Roosevelt, whose skill and expertise in selecting the right person for whatever formidable task was at hand, successfully guided the United States through the Great Depression and World War II. He was Commander in Chief, but no one expected him to lead the Crusade in Europe. Rather, he picked a lesser-ranked officer, one Dwight Eisenhower, for the job. History knows the rest, as General Eisenhower not only accomplished the task but later served two terms as U.S. President, showcasing one of the many examples of Franklin D. Roosevelt's ability to pick the correct person for the job at hand.

THINGS TO AVOID: AT ALL COSTS, DO NOT:

1. <u>Compromise Your Integrity</u>: This applies in all walks of life. Ben Franklin observed that a reputation is like final crystal; once cracked, it is never

the same. If what you say and do is not trusted, you are cooked. Period. Thus, mean and do what you say. Even if, it results in personal sacrifice. I have represented hundreds of successful businesses and business persons: if they give a warranty, a guarantee, a promise, they do it, and see to it their employees do as well. And the answer is usually right.

2. <u>Know It All</u>: This is really stupid and a prescription not only for disaster but great losses: You don't know it all. You can't know it all. Open your mind to the experience, knowledge and talents of others who just might make things better. Leave your ego at the door.

   Suppose I put my open hand, fingers pointed up, in your direction. You see my palm and the inside of my fingers. I, on the other hand, see the outside of my fingers, the nails and knuckles. What we each see is entirely different.

3. <u>Violating the Risk/Reward Analysis</u>: Everything we do has a risk/reward analysis. There is a risk walking across the street to be hit by a car; the reward is purchasing the food from the store across the street.

Suppose you live in New York, you booked an expensive cruise to the Caribbean, but you must arrive by 11:00 a.m. to catch the cruise on a certain date from Miami. Do you book your flight to arrive in Miami the day your cruise to the Caribbean Island leaves, and count on the connections working without a hitch, or do something else? Maybe book your flight to arrive in Miami the day before? Depends. How important is it that you make the flight to Miami to board your cruise? What is the risk that something might happen, (e.g., maybe a mechanical problem with your airplane, or an incident that otherwise disrupts the system of air transportation, like a plane crash or a flight control problem) to delay your arrival in Miami and cause you to miss your expensive voyage on the cruise ship, which will not wait for you?

Similar decisions are made every day. The outcomes can be the reward of success or the consequence of the risk. A successful life, whether personal, business, professional - whatever - is dependent on coming to grips with how to make every decision so the outcome is satisfactory.

You get the drift and it is <u>NOT</u>: be true to yourself. Contrarily, it is (1) open your eyes and mind; (2) weigh the risks against the rewards; (3) select the persons capable of best performing the task and (4) realize you don't know it all - learn from and take advantage of the knowledge and experience of others – including your significant other, fellow employees, as well as adversaries. In the end, it is the wisdom of judgment.

ABOUT DAVID

The Law Offices of David A. Hoines, Esq. has consistently delivered results in the areas of the law which he practices. David is respected by his clients and peers alike.

Most of us, at some point during our lives, need legal advice. Unfortunately, the legal system can be extremely difficult, intimidating, and frustrating to many individuals; but it doesn't have to be that way. The right attorney is the best cure for these trying situations.

David Hoines has the education and the experience. He has been practicing law for decades and has handled all types of cases in many State and Federal courts and jurisdictions. It is his constant goal to bring a fair and equitable conclusion in all matters in which he is involved. In addition to a Bachelor of Arts degree and a Law degree (Juris Doctor), David also attained his Master of Laws (L.L.M.).

David has been certified by the Florida Bar Association as a Specialist in Civil Litigation for each and every year since 1991 to 2011. He is a member of the AARP (American Association of Retired Persons) Legal Services Network. He was recently nominated for and became a fellow of the American Bar Association Foundation, joining a mere 1/3 of 1% of all lawyers in the U.S. In addition to membership in the Florida Bar, he is also a member in good standing of the California Bar and the State Bar of New York. He has been admitted to practice before the U.S. Supreme Court, U.S. Court of Claims, U.S. Tax Court, the U.S. Circuit Courts of Appeal for the 11th, 9th, 5th, 4th and Federal Circuits, and the U.S. District Court for the Northern and Central Districts of California, and the Southern and Middle Districts of Florida.

David will be happy to help you find the right solution for your situation or problem. And he promises that if for some reason he cannot be of assistance, he will point you in the direction of someone who might be able to help.

You can access his website: Hoineslaw.com, for more detailed information concerning his practice, background and experience.

You're not effective or efficient without process, and you will not be able to provide the client with consistent results.

AN INTERVIEW WITH MARIA QUATTRONE

SECRETS OF SUCCESS

Performance: What are the best indicators of the success of a company?

Maria: People, processes, systems and culture are the ways that a company can scale and grow. The processes I am referring to are the internal and external ones in order to run a business. It is not enough to develop those processes; you need to constantly fine-tune them. These processes are repeated many times and are duplicable. They become the systems within a business.

Performance: How do processes work within your company?

Maria: We have processes for everything. We even have processes for how to develop a new process.

You're not effective or efficient without process, and you will not be able to provide the client with consistent results. Clients expect a process to either be the same or be better than they expected or have experienced in the past.

For example, I love my hair salon. When I go in, the normal process is they greet me, check me in and give me a smock, then ask if I would like a glass of water, tea or coffee. I take my drink and am able to sit down, relax and wait for my stylist. If I go to the salon and they skip a step, it is upsetting because I'm not getting the consistent experience I've come to expect as a repeat customer.

Repeat customers want consistency, that's why you go back. You know the results will be just as good or better than before. Your favorite restaurant prepares your favorite dish exactly the same way, your salon does a fabulous job with your hair. It's the same in real estate. For many people, purchasing and selling real estate is the largest financial decision they will make and their biggest asset. We take the trust our clients place in us very seriously and know our processes are able to help them make the best decisions, as well as give us the information we need to help them.

Businesses that have been around for decades are consistent. Don't change the recipe and you have a loyal customer forever.

The development and adherence to a process or system depends largely on the owner or leadership within a company. When someone thinks, "Maybe I'll add a little more cheese to the meatballs today, or maybe I'll leave it out." - this lack of a "recipe" means the customer won't know what they are going to get.

Our business is the exact same thing. We deliver world class results by having processes and systems that clients can depend on. At the same time, the business owner must stay on the forefront of new trends with technology and in the industry, and constantly be refining best practices in a systematic way.

Performance: Have Processes been important in the growth of your company?

Maria: When a person refers someone because of the experience they had with us, it is important that we repeat or exceed that experience with the referral. If we do not provide them a similar experience it can be frustrating for the clients, and we will not have done the right thing for the referral.

For example, suppose we have a new potential client we're working with, a customer who's looking to buy a house. Our process is that we make sure they are preapproved through the lender. They come to our office for a buyer consult, and we go through all their wants, needs, desires, and answer any questions they have, and then explain the process to them as a buyer client. Our agents and support staff are all thoroughly trained in these processes, so the experience is the same for all clients. We all talk the same language. Staff are always prepared and confident because they know what to do and how to do it.

Failing to complete a buyer consult could result in buyers and staff wasting a lot of time looking at the wrong properties, the wrong areas or even losing out on a property they love because they weren't ready to write a strong offer. Our consult addresses all these things so the Buyer is in the best position to find what they want and write an offer that will be accepted.

We have developed a process for signing a new client, how we deliver marketing materials, how we get our listings maximum exposure in the marketplace, how we provide customer feedback, how we send out contracts and there is a process of writing contracts. There's a process and system for everything we do for sellers and buyers in every department within our company. We're not just going to show up at your house without being prepared. We have a process that we go through before we list anybody's home. This has been our key to success and our numbers have shown it. Processes are a key to consistency, efficiency, success and repeat clients.

Performance: How do you develop a new process or system and put it into action?

Maria: We are updating our processes daily. We constantly evaluate, add to and refine our systems. Technology changes. A new system is developed often because something happened which warranted us to learn from the incident and create a new system that would work to prevent it from happening in the future. The incidents are not always bad. For instance, I have a contract manager who writes the offers. We were sending her an email that says, here's the offer. She put together a process where we now have a form that needs to be filled out. We found that sending an email with the information isn't sufficient because there's always something that was missed. And then we would have to go back and forth. Now we get it right the first time because every single thing she needs to know is on that form.

Another example of a process change we have made concerned working with banks. We noticed that the banks decided that they wanted to write "as is" in the agreements we sent. I said, "Why aren't we writing 'as is' in all of the agreements?"

Now, we're writing it in all of our bank-owned properties that the buyers are buying "as is". It's just standard language we use in offers. Again, saving time and unnecessary steps.

We have a production meeting every single day.

Performance: How do you record the processes for employees, both old and new, to refer to?

Maria: We have a company manual. We are constantly updating the manual, and it has become rather large. Our first manual took about a year and a half to get done, but it is not complete, because it is constantly being updated.

All our resources are also cloud-based, so staff can access them at any time. We aren't constantly printing and reprinting documents, or having multiple versions floating around.

Recently, we added to our system a production meeting. We have a production meeting every single day. We review what new appointments were set, and what appointments occurred since the last production meeting 24 hours ago and this production meeting. This keeps everyone current and accountable.

In the production meeting we will review-What's in process? What listings are in pre-listing mode? What listings are active right now and where are those? What offers have been written and those we are waiting to hear from, or have received, from other brokers? What listings are pending?

It's usually only 30 minutes so not disruptive to the day, but it allows employees the chance to offer advice, support each other, and problem solve. We also encourage staff to share something they are grateful for or thank a co-worker during this time to promote our office culture and build the team.

We repeat this process every single day, because for our company it works. We used production meetings years ago, and for a number of reasons, we just stopped doing them, and we noticed quickly that things weren't the same. I questioned why we had stopped the meetings and whether we should include them as a process once again. When we implemented them as a new system, we started to see an upswing in our numbers. Absolutely hands down, we're killing it.

Performance: Has it been easy to implement processes and make it work?

Maria: I worked with another real estate company and I ran a team for a number of years and then I decided to start my own company. The first year and a half were tough. Even though I had enough clients and I had steady business, the transition took a toll on me personally, mentally, professionally and financially. I was down in the dumps.

People become scared because they're afraid of failure. Some people are afraid of success. I have found the only way to be successful is to sail your way forward. Sail right through it. I don't know any other way to reach success. When I was first getting started, I knew I wanted to work with developers, but I didn't know any developers. So I went to a job site, walked up and introduced myself and said, I can sell these for you. And I did. You can't let fear of failure hold you back from success.

It's rare that somebody is just automatically successful. Of all the great innovators and business people in the world, I don't know of anyone who was just automatically successful. I have heard and believe that an overnight success takes about 10,000 hours to achieve. You see all the glory, but you don't know the story.

It's sailing through, keeping going with that persistence and determination and grit that separates those who do and those who don't. At the end of the day, my goal is to be the very best me. I have a motto: *I always say progress not perfection.* Do your best every day. Get a little bit better. And that's why I work as much or more on myself right now mentally and physically than I do on my business.

The best 'Maria' is going to be the best business person for my company and for our clients. And it took me a while to figure out that my wellbeing came first. My health comes first. My personal development comes first. Because if you work more on you, your attractor factor changes, and it is your attractor factor that changes the outcome of your efforts. It's all about mindset.

Performance: How does mindset drive your business?

Maria: Our company believes in having a mission-driven business, and therefore we are tying what we do to giving back. We donate a portion of our net proceeds back into the community through the charity of the client's choice. We volunteer together as a team.

We have adopted several local charities we position as options for people if the client doesn't have a particular charity in mind. Specifically, we invest in the local Philadelphia schools to make them a better place for our children can have a better education.

Employees love the concept. They are excited to be part of the philanthropic effort. We also believe that having a mission-driven company attracts better clients. I know it attracts better employees, and has helped us build a better culture. So it is a win-win for everybody.

Performance: Why is it important to set the right goals in order to achieve the results you truly want?

When you have passion about what you do, people see that.

Maria: What I realized a couple years back, I had a financial goal to be at, and a goal for production units. I made the goal, but after achieving it, I felt a little hollow. Is this all there is? Is this it? And what I learned from that, is that success is the journey not the destination.

We never achieve our final destination because we're are constantly continuing on our journey. It's constantly evolving, and there's nothing magical that happens once you reach a particular goal. The magic happens in between.

I work on improving myself and further myself on my personal journey every day. I listen to podcasts about business stories, and transformations, and read as many books as I can. There are so many great books, and you can read stuff right online now. I read when I have insomnia at 3 a.m., and find all sorts of interesting articles and books online. I can't sleep because my mind is racing, and I actually want to get up and go to work. I read, and I research, and I get a lot done at that time.

Performance: What is the secret sauce in your companies and your personal success?

Maria: Our goal is to turn the ordinary into extraordinary. Because there's a lot of people that do what we do, we strive for excellence as out most driving principle. It is the thing other companies don't do, and we have not only created an extraordinary company, but it has led to our steady and consistent growth.

Our systems and processes are no good without the right people. We recruit intentionally instead of collecting agents. In any business, people who don't buy into the bigger picture rob you of time and energy that could be better spent on client relationships or business development. We advertise, interview and onboard very intentionally, to make sure we are bringing on similarly driven individuals – not just warm bodies.

All of these elements together create the culture – one in which people feel valued, both employees and clients. Employees are trained and empowered to deliver a superior experience for our clients. Our clients then become raving fans, providing repeat business and referrals.

It's all really about attitude, a company's attitude. A company's attitude is going to determine their altitude. If we can offer more value, even through the lulls we can continue to thrive. We receive so much back from our clients and community because of the value we provide to them. I believe that the company's revenue determines how many people we serve. And how well we serve them. We influence others by placing other people interest before ours, and by being authentic.

It's a simple recipe but it is one that works today, tomorrow and in twenty years.

ABOUT MARIA

"Maria Quattrone is a proven leader in the Philadelphia Real Estate Market and CEO of RE/MAX @ HOME."

Maria had a vision – to change the way a real estate brokerage functioned – and after ten years with a successful career in the real estate industry, she launched RE/MAX @ HOME in January, 2014. RE/MAX @ HOME's mission is to offer a futuristic approach to real estate sales. The brokerage model is a hybrid, combining several business models with technology at the forefront.

RE/MAX @ HOME provides a team environment where everyone is on the same playing field. They have created a proprietary system that generates opportunities for real estate agents from click to close, to the next time their client buys or sell a home. The end result is a higher level of service, a more educated consumer, and the ultimate client experience.

The brand new flagship location opened in December of 2014 in the heart of Center City, Philadelphia with just over 7500 square feet. The environment is very Google-esque for both the work place and client experience. It's modern and edgy, and includes cafe/lounge areas, collaborative space, a design center, a high tech training center, and private touchdown rooms.

Maria says, "It's all about creating a place you can call home – We invite you to Experience the Difference at RE/MAX @ HOME."

For more information, please visit: LiveLiveatHome.com or call: 800.651.0800

FINDING PURPOSE AND SIGNIFICANCE BY PUTTING PEOPLE OVER PROFIT

PERFORMANCE: Your skills as an entrepreneur have led you to successful ventures with several companies, including the property development and real estate investment firm Trisnadi Capital Partners and now the growing IT and cybersecurity firm Intelecis. Where do you think your entrepreneurial drive comes from?

FRANS: My drive has always been in my blood since childhood and I was able to develop it over the years. I always had a fascination for business. Back in second grade, I thought it would be exciting to create an exclusive club based on my passion for airplanes. Only a few kids joined the Aspiring Pilots Club, but I charged membership fees! I also had a knack for trading baseball cards, not for collecting purposes but to buy and sell and make a profit. While growing up, my parents let me explore and encouraged me to find my passion. They allowed me to dream and seek entrepreneurship, but insisted that I get a college degree to fall back on. Before my family moved to the U.S., my father was an entrepreneur who had a promotional printing business. In addition, my grandfather on my mom's side retired young due to his success in monopolizing the tobacco business in Indonesia.

PERFORMANCE: When you started Trisnadi Capital Partners, what were your initial goals for your firm and how did you go about achieving success with them?

FRANS: I didn't start with a big vision. I wanted to start building passive rental income. I remember developing an eye for identifying and acquiring underperforming investment properties that had low rents because these apartment buildings were unattractive or slightly run down. My company began to buy those and fix them up, improving the quality of life for tenants while also allowing us to increase the rents to current market rents. Building value in those properties, or "repositioning underperforming properties" as I like to call it, allowed me several options: increase net income while ensuring that the buildings would appreciate so we could sell them at a higher price for a profit. Through time, I know that these rental properties would increase in cash flow and build equity. But I soon realized that while investing in apartment buildings could build long term wealth, it wasn't going to generate any significant short term cash flow to support a family. Therefore, I needed to figure out another way to generate a sizeable monthly income. This led me to property development.

PERFORMANCE: Did you put the same principles in place years later when you launched Intelecis?

FRANS: I figured out that property development was a highly speculative business. Later when I transitioned to Intelecis, I realized I would be better

Now, success is about serving people, having the heart to help others.

off if I could continue to build a recurring income via monthly contracts from clients. This is in contrast to some IT companies that sign a large upfront transactional contract – which to me is a lot like developing properties. You're developing properties hoping you can sell for a big profit down the road, but if the market goes down, you're left holding the bag. So the lesson I applied to Intelecis was the recurring income model. It made more sense to me than bidding on large projects, building teams to work on them and then worrying about the next big deal or having to disband them when the contracts were over. I realize that this was a more calculated approach, and that recurring monthly revenue would equal a slower growing company. But to me it was more manageable growth.

PERFORMANCE: You experienced financial and personal setbacks between these two prominent ventures. What kinds of lessons did you learn during the challenging times that play a role in the success you are achieving now?

FRANS: One big takeaway was that now when I make a decision I'm a lot more patient and I determine what my potential loss might be. Anything I decide on the marketing and investment side of the business, or related to expansion, is done with a calculated and more cautious approach. I make sure that I have certain strategies in place that allows me to determine what my potential loss might be up front. I don't pursue opportunities that are purely speculative, and make sure to limit my downside risk. True, my gains are capped by this sort of approach, but at the same time so are my losses. The goal is to grow in a systematic fashion and know that I limited my potential loss.

PERFORMANCE: It's inspiring that you've now decided to do personal development and leadership coaching. What made you decide to take what you've learned and start sharing it with others?

FRANS: I have a passion for helping and serving others. Informally, I enjoy thinking about how I can help clients and other people. Sometimes I end up helping my peers who are not clients or even prospective clients. I believe what goes around, comes around, and when you have a certain energy you attract people who have that same energy and passion. Nothing for me may come out of helping that specific person, but perhaps someone else may come along with similar values and bring something positive into my life. My decision to go into personal development professionally grew out of simply talking a lot with entrepreneurs and realizing they appreciate the opportunity to share things with me and them feeling I am transparent as I share my own story with them. I don't preach to people or tell them what to do, but find that they're intrigued with my story and experiences. I've been told that my message is inspiring, genuine and real and I simply want to create more opportunities to share it. Everyone will relate to it in a different way. Some might identify with my challenging times like meeting payroll, while others can relate to the business growing pains I've gone through, yet others relate with my ability to identify and package the next investment.

PERFORMANCE: What would you say the core message you want to share?

FRANS: I want to influence people to be purposeful about their success. Success is a journey and you have to figure out how you're going to achieve your goals, with purpose. It's not just about money but about the people you touch along your journey. I like to call this a focus on "people over profit." Making money in business is great, but you can use people to make money or you can use money to serve and help people. That's the choice people have and I like to steer them in the better, more fulfilling direction.

PERFORMANCE: Earlier in your life and career, how did you define success? How has that definition changed over the years?

FRANS: Like a lot of young, ambitious guys, I used to think that success was about mass accumulation of wealth. It didn't matter who I was becoming as long as I got there. And having this narcissistic attitude, I pissed off a lot of people, investors and employees because I just looked at them like they were just there to help me get to my goal – a means to an end. I did a lot of soul searching between my real estate and IT ventures, and when I launched Intelecis, I was at the other side of the spectrum. My question to myself was, "How can I help others along my journey?" During that two-year period, I was in and out of court with lawsuits due to all the personal guarantees I made with my real estate investments and I realized that that downfall was God's way of reminding me that life is not all about me and mass accumulation. Now, success is about serving people, having the heart to help others. If you are blessed with owning a business, being an employer or investor, those positions come with great responsibility and influence. You can use it to be a jerk or to bless and serve others. If you choose the latter, you're choosing to leave a memorable legacy. To me, that's when you cross over from living a successful life to living a life of real significance.

> # They sacrificed for me so I can be a difference maker.

PERFORMANCE: You are very focused on those key words, Purpose and Significance? How do you personally define those concepts?

FRANS: To me, purpose is about looking at a greater force outside yourself. Using Legos as an example, I watch my sons use the manuals to construct great creations that the inventor had intended these Legos to be. To quote the opening to Rick Warren's bestseller The Purpose Driven Life, it's not about you. He says that the best way to discover purpose is to ask the creator. On a spiritual level, that means asking God what He intended for my life. The idea of loving others means serving others, giving as much as I can with my gifts, intellect, finances, time and experiences. To me that is purpose. Significance is similar. Looking back on the era when I was a financially successful but egocentric property developer, I realize I did nothing of any significance because I only cared about serving myself. Living with purpose and helping others creates significance. I like to use the metaphor of bread crumbs that you leave along your journey. I want people to look at the trail I've left and say that I helped them unselfishly when they needed that encouragement, or shared my experiences with them when they were experiencing similar situations. At the end of my life I want to be able to say I was more successful serving others than myself.

PERFORMANCE: You have a provocative question that you ask those you work with: "Now that you've done all this, what is your Version 2.0?" Explain what that means.

FRANS: The logical idea behind it would be what people will do with their life after they've sold their business or achieved a certain amount of success. But I get even more specific. Now that I've shared my life experience and the importance of putting people over profit, what is the new version of your life starting now? That question is my call-to-action. Are you going to start treating your employees differently? Start being more intentional about helping others? How will these ideas manifest in your life?

PERFORMANCE: What is your Version 2.0 and how have you made it a successful version?

FRANS: I challenge myself daily to live up to my goal of helping others. When I wake up, I need to re-center myself so that instead of being fixated on the deals I'm going to close, I think about how I'm going to help my clients, colleagues, friends and family and truly put people over profit. Trust me, it is a daily challenge. But, I have made it a successful version by making a habit of being aware of my impact on others, and that extends to my family and creating a business model that allows me to prepare breakfast for my family, take my young sons to school, and be there for them when they come home. By the world's standards, Intelecis is not quite as successful as it could be, but the fact that I have this balance is me defining success on my own terms. Family has always been important to me. I wouldn't be where I am today if my parents didn't leave everything behind in Indonesia to move here. That drives my passion even more. They didn't escape from a life of persecution so that I could just be average and blend in and have a comfortable middle class life. They sacrificed for me so I can be a difference maker and have the opportunity to influence others.

PERFORMANCE: Tell me about some of your own mentors and what key things you learned from them.

FRANS: Two very successful tech industry executives had a great impact on me early in my life. Dan was an IBM executive who took me under his wing when I was 18 and Henry was VP of a top Silicon Valley firm whom I met at 16. They both taught me about leadership. I looked up to them from a worldly standpoint, but they were also spiritual guys who encouraged me to focus on helping others. During that adolescent season of my life, I wasn't ready to hear it, but now I realize the wisdom of what they imparted. They helped me shape my life in terms of career choices and encouraged me to transcend the self-limiting "head trash" and doubts that I had. They gave me a new perspective that I should get out there and not be afraid to take risks. But more importantly to make and learn from mistakes.

PERFORMANCE: With the help of your family, you have created a unique charity geared towards helping the temporary homeless called We Care America. What is the focus of it?

FRANS: I've involved my entire family so that my sons become aware of how blessed and fortunate they are in a world where not everyone has the same advantages. I want to instill the values of serving others in them the same way I do with entrepreneurs. We Care America allows our volunteers to serve others, to give back. That ties in with my overall goal of putting people first. I lived in Indonesia till I was four, and remember the poverty. I never want to lose that perspective. My children never had to experience that, but this charity shows them that not all people have roofs over their heads. Every time we're putting together a new package to give to a homeless person is a chance to remind my boys and explain to them the things that really matter in life – which is showing your love for people by serving others.

PERFORMANCE: What would you say are the biggest challenges you have overcome to be successful?

FRANS: The biggest challenge is quite ongoing. It's the "head trash" I mentioned, those self-destructive, negative thoughts that grow out of low self-esteem or believing the negative stuff people say that later become self-fulfilling prophecies. As a young immigrant with very limited resources, I wore mismatched hand-me-downs and was laughed at for that and my unruly hair. Being picked on as a kid plants seeds of low self-worth. When I thought about going to college, I didn't think I could get in or make the grades. When I became an entrepreneur, those doubts continued to creep in. No matter how much success I have achieved in my life, I still struggle with "head trash," which are nothing more than self-limiting beliefs. But my mentors reminded me and encouraged me to believe in myself, and told me if I failed, all I had to do is get up and try again. Those words still resonate.

PERFORMANCE: In a nutshell, define "Success."

FRANS: Success is about how many people I can help along my journey. To me, that's when you cross over from living a successful life to living a life of significance.

ABOUT FRANS

Frans Trisnadi is President and CEO of Intelecis, a thriving, proactive and business tech-focused IT firm located in Southern California, where he grew up after his family fled from Indonesia when he was four. In this capacity, he is frequently invited to share his expertise on IT and Cybersecurity to large groups of professionals in the escrow, healthcare insurance and financial services industries. The multi-faceted speaker, mentor, investor, and philanthropist is now also a rising force in personal development and leadership coaching. Helping his peers and clients envision a bigger picture for themselves, the provocative question he challenges them to explore is: "Now that you've done all this, what is your Version 2.0?"

One of the key components of Frans' mission and branding as a multi-faceted thought leader, coach and success influencer is his ability to connect with entrepreneurs and CEOs, who, like himself, have experienced waves of great economic triumphs and downturns – and emerged from the downswings stronger and more determined to succeed than ever. He currently takes an active part and leadership role on the board for Entrepreneur Organization's Accelerator Program, seeking the counsel of other successful entrepreneurs as he shares his experiences with them.

Before entering the IT world in 2010, Frans was a prominent property developer, real estate investor and Founder and President of Trisnadi Capital Partners. His personal comeback story includes the hard-won wisdom he gained from the dark period of his career between this venture and the founding of Intelecis. And then, due in part to the Great Recession on top of speculative investments in destination rentals, the bottom fell out – leaving him and his partners with millions of dollars in personal guarantees.

During the years when Trisnadi Capital Partners was growing, Trisnadi recognized the need for more computers, servers, information security and phone systems. He knew they needed to leverage technology to make his team more efficient while he was traveling around the country looking for investment opportunities. But he wasn't able to find an IT company that offered a flat-rate monthly fee, or one that would act as his IT department and have full accountability for its services. Those firms he hired were more interested in finger-pointing and "putting out fires" than taking a proactive approach that helps avoid breakdowns, promote smooth business operations and ultimately, turn technology into a competitive advantage instead of a drain on his time, money and resources – all of which became hallmarks of Intelecis.

With the initial inspiration and support of his wife Jenny, Frans Trisnadi recently launched We Care America, a group of volunteers raising funds, awareness and creating "ready to go" packages for America's homeless. Trisnadi loves involving his two young sons in the creation and distribution of these packages so that they become aware of how blessed and fortunate they are. Trisnadi's family usually keeps their cars stocked with We Care America packages. He believes that with the help of corporate sponsors, generous donations by fellow Americans, volunteers and paid staff, We Care America has the potential to impact the homeless across the country.

I believe today will be the
day I will say the
 best words I
have ever
said.

BY KEN NUNN, ESQ.

TWENTY-FIVE REASONS WHY MY LAW OFFICE IS SUCCESSFUL

Please let me introduce myself. My name is Ken Nunn. I have been an injury attorney for 48 years. I came from a very poor family. I was a high school drop-out for one year. I finally graduated from high school at the age of 19. I graduated from Indiana University School of Business when I was 24. I graduated from Indiana University Law School when I was 27. By the way, I graduated from law school near the bottom of my class. I passed the bar exam on the first try and I was sworn in as an attorney before the Indiana Supreme Court when I was 27 years old. At last . . . I was an attorney!

When I passed the bar exam, I decided to open my own law office. I was flat-broke and had student loans to pay. I was married and had two children. I did <u>not</u> take a vacation for the first eight years after I opened my law firm. During those first eight years, I learned a lot about myself and about being an attorney. I started my law office all by myself with just a card table and four chairs, no other furniture. I made a bookcase out of cement blocks. I had absolutely nowhere to go . . . except up!

REASON #1

My first week in my law office was spent writing a training manual for my Secretary . . . who I had yet to hire. Writing that training manual was for me as much as it was for my future Secretary. I could barely afford to pay my secretary minimum wage, thus I knew my Secretary would have no experience. It was an important step in my success to write that first training manual. The manual helped me understand what I needed to do to run my law office. This manual was written before I had any clients whatsoever.

REASON #2

Another reason for my success was that I was determined to succeed. I also knew that I had a lot to learn about how to run a law office. It was truly exciting and exhilarating. My home town of Bloomington, Indiana had lots of very talented attorneys. I had to go up against those attorneys on behalf of my clients. Those attorneys taught me a lot because they beat me a lot. Each time I lost a case, I learned a little more about myself and how to be a better attorney.

REASON #3

I spent those first eight years trying to figure out how to "catch up" with the rest of the attorneys in town. I also spent those eight years trying to figure out how to do things more quickly and more efficiently. I had a rule in the office that if we were going to prepare a document (and there are a lot of documents in the legal world), that I would type the document once and then go to the local print shop and have it printed for future cases. I soon became the *King of Legal Forms* in Bloomington, Indiana. That saved me an enormous amount of time.

This was before computers. I did <u>not</u> copyright my forms. Some of my forms appeared in national sales catalogs designed to help other attorneys be more efficient. I didn't care that they copied and sold my forms. It was a compliment to me.

REASON #4

Another reason for my success is that I created a whole series of systems. I have great admiration for Dave Thomas, Colonel Sanders, Sam Walton and, of course, the King of all systems . . . McDonalds. I read all the books I could get my hands on to learn more about how to be successful and how to utilize systems in my law firm. Throughout the years I have developed more than 200 very sophisticated sets of systems that have enabled me to duplicate myself, using both non- attorneys and attorneys. I constantly update those systems. In addition, I get sixty different reports on a monthly basis. Some of the reports are daily. These systems and reports increased the efficiency of my office a hundred times over.

Today, as I am writing this chapter, I have ninety-two employees, including sixteen attorneys. I am absolutely blessed to have such a talented group of staff and attorneys. Our attorneys are fantastic. Many of them have received multiple national awards and recognition.

REASON #5

Another reason for our success is that I decided to pay my staff and attorneys as much money as possible. I did not want to make money by underpaying my staff and attorneys. My income came from fighting insurance companies on behalf of my clients. As a result, our staff and attorneys are among the highest paid in the state of Indiana. I am grateful to have such a fantastic group of non-attorneys and attorneys. I own approximately 42 cars. I assign those cars to attorneys and senior non-attorneys. We have Lexuses, Escalades, BMWs, Cadillacs and Infinitis.

REASON #6

Each day I drive toward the office from home and I always have the same attitude. I believe today will be the day I will say the best words I have ever said. Today I will write the best letter I have ever written.

Today I will create a phenomenal new system or I will tweak an old system to make the system work better. I have learned long ago . . . never be satisfied with where I am. Every day is an opportunity to outperform myself. I realize my real competition is myself. I do not compete with other attorneys or law firms. I compete against myself every day.

REASON #7

I love my law career because I fight for the little guy against big, rich insurance companies and businesses. I love helping my clients and I love the competition between our law firm and the insurance companies and their attorneys. Like all attorneys . . . I hate to lose and . . . I love to win. Winning happens when we are prepared. Winning happens when we put our heart and soul into the case. It is our office policy to "<u>never give up</u>."

REASON #8

Fifteen years ago, I made a very important decision. As a result of that decision, our income and success has skyrocketed. My decision was simply to say "no" to all the tiny checks insurance companies were offering our clients. Our new office policy would be to file more lawsuits, fight the insurance companies to "make them pay" and, if necessary, take every case, big or little, all the way to a jury. I am proud to say that our law firm is ranked #1 in the State of Indiana for doing the most injury jury trials for the past fourteen years. The total number of jury trials for our law firm during the past fourteen years is way ahead of the other law firms. Way ahead! We now have a reputation for fighting for our clients. Of course . . . we lose some cases . . . but we win a lot more cases than we lose. This decision has brought millions more dollars into our office for our clients and for our law firm.

During the past 48 years, our law office has represented more than 25,000 clients, and those clients have been paid more than $600 million dollars in settlements.

Our top jury verdict in our hometown is $15 million dollars. Our top jury verdict in the State of Indiana is $157 million dollars. My decision to stop taking tiny checks and start filing lawsuits and fighting insurance companies all the way to a jury trial not only increased our pride, it increased our confidence, it increased our income and it gave our clients justice.

My decision to fight, which was made fifteen years ago, has produced tremendous results for our law office and for our clients. I commonly refer to this program as . . . "Justice is hiding at the courthouse."

Here are some more examples:

$5,000 offer	Jury awarded $3.9 million dollars and ultimately paid $4.3 million dollars
$180,000 offer	Jury awarded $8 million dollars
$1.2 million dollars offered	Jury awarded $5.2 million dollars
$1 million dollars offered	Insurance company eventually paid $16.5 million dollars
$13,000 offer	Insurance company eventually paid $674,000
$7,000 offer	Insurance company eventually paid $325,000
$4,000 offer	Insurance company eventually paid $220,000

And there are thousands more examples.

It is important to note that this information is not designed to brag, but is designed to share the office-wide level of determination to get more money in our clients' pockets.

REASON #9

Another idea I had was also very successful. When we learn that an experienced insurance adjuster is retiring, I routinely contact that retiring adjuster and pay him for his time to talk about the insurance company's strategies for settlement of cases. The information I gained from these interviews proved to be very valuable. I shared the information with my clients to help my clients understand the insurance company strategies. It really helps us too! When I share this information with my clients, I give the material the title of *Confessions of Ex-Insurance-Adjusters*. Clients really like that. By the way, some of the strategies are brutal. Offering tiny checks to single moms and minorities; stalling cases on clients who are elderly . . . secretly wishing the client would die. It truly is a heartless business. Insurance companies will do anything and say anything to save money.

REASON #10

My next reason for my success may be looked upon as being insignificant, however, I place high significance on this. Our law office occupies a beautiful building that is 30,000 square feet and is spotlessly clean. We have two full-time building managers who do nothing except look for dirt. Daily cleaning is very important. Dusting everything, even the walls, is done on a regular basis. Our bathrooms are spotless. Our windows are professionally cleaned every 2 weeks.

Once a year we have a team of architects, painters and carpenters come into our office and make the necessary inspections and repairs to keep our building looking brand new. The exterior landscaping is meticulous. We have an outdoor lighting system that stays on all night, thus making our building very visible. In addition, it's great advertising . . . and . . . it works! I've gotten lots of great cases because of our building.

REASON #11

It's interesting to note that I have gotten this deep into this chapter and I finally mention the word advertising. Our law firm is ranked #1 in the State of Indiana for spending the most money on advertising. Our TV commercials are on the air over 400 times per day. We understand that if we ran one or two different commercials that many times a day, the public would soon become bored. To solve that problem, we have a rotation of 57 different commercials on TV each day. The public's chance of seeing the same commercial twice in one day is very low.

We like the variety. We are breaking records this year for the number of new client calls and the number of new clients who retain our office.

REASON #12

We have a policy in our office to return phone calls immediately when clients call. In addition, our Client Service Department makes regular phone calls to our clients asking the clients how they are doing and if they have any questions. Even though I am the founder of this law firm, I still work in the office between 50 and 60 hours per week. I sometimes will return phone calls late at night or on weekends. I love calling clients at those times because they are surprised that the founder of our law firm is actually making the phone calls. Some of my clients ask, "Is this really Ken Nunn who is on TV?"

I am the luckiest man in the world for doing what I love, with people I love, in a town that I love.

Here are more reasons for my success:

REASON #13

Helping injured people with difficult cases that other attorneys wouldn't take.

REASON #14

Being highly organized.

REASON #15

Teaching our staff about Indiana's new laws and how to fight for our clients. Updating the staff regularly.

REASON #16

About 10 years ago, I wrote a book about how law firms can increase their income. The book was titled *How to Double or Triple Your Income in the Next Three Years*. I never published the book, but I did apply its principles to the operation of our office. We did triple our income in five years. We didn't hit our mark in three years, but I'm happy with the results after five years. Maybe I need to publish the book. The principles work.

REASON #17

I have also written an unpublished book entitled *Secrets Insurance Companies Do Not Want You to Know* and a sequel entitled *Don't Get Ripped Off by the Insurance Companies*. I plan to publish these books as they have become a road map and guiding light for our law office.

REASON #18

Staying focused and reminding myself on a daily basis what I want. There was a time when I wanted a big, new house. So I cut out a picture of a house that I liked, and I taped it on the mirror in my bathroom so that I could see that picture every day. I saw the picture as I shaved, as I brushed my teeth, as I combed my hair. It was a daily reminder. I worked hard every day. Now I have that big house. I did the same thing with my law office building. Today, I have a new, and very large, office building. Set goals and focus on the goal until you succeed. [By the way, I put a picture of a new Rolls Royce on my mirror . . . and today I have two Rolls Royces. One is a convertible and one is a 4-door sedan.]

REASON #19

Return phone calls to clients…this shows respect.

REASON #20

Don't keep a client waiting in the outer office longer than two minutes.

REASON #21

Don't let a client on the telephone be on hold for longer than one minute.

REASON #22

At the end of every conversation with a client, either in person or over the phone, always end the conversation with, "Do you have any other questions?"

REASON #23

Believe in your client. Don't spend too much time on negative thinking. Instead focus on how their case can be won. Believing you can win is the key to winning. The attorney must put his heart and soul in the case. When that happens in our office . . . we win big.

REASON #24

I have never forgotten my roots. You can't teach hungry.

REASON #25

We believe in the Golden Rule.

ABOUT KEN

Ken Nunn, Esq. is the owner of the Ken Nunn Law Office, located in Bloomington, Indiana, which limits its practice exclusively to personal injury and wrongful death cases. For more than 45 years, the firm has built a strong reputation as a defender of victims' rights, having represented over 25,000 injury and wrongful death clients over the past four and a half decades. The law office currently consists of 91 staff, including 15 attorneys, as well as six retired state troopers who serve as investigators for the firm.

The Ken Nunn Law Office has been ranked No. 1 by the Jury Verdict Reporter for the past 12 years for doing the most jury trials in Indiana for injured plaintiffs. In 2009, the firm obtained a $157 million judgment for a wrongful death case, the largest jury verdict in the history of Indiana and the sixth largest nationally that year. That firm also obtained $15 million on behalf of an injured child, the largest jury verdict in Monroe County, Indiana.

Ken received his Bachelor of Science degree in Business in 1964 from the Indiana University School of Business, and he received his Juris Doctor degree in 1967 from the Indiana University School of Law. At that time, he was admitted to practice law in all state and federal courts in Indiana.

Ken is a member of the Million Dollar Advocates Forum, the Multi-Million Dollar Advocates Forum, and is listed in the Top Trial Lawyers in America®. He has been listed as an Indiana Super Lawyer, and is a member of the American Association for Justice, the Indiana State Bar Association, and the Indiana Trial Lawyers Association. He has been a guest lecturer at Indiana University, both to undergraduates as well as students at the I.U. School of Law. Ken is one of Indiana's Top-Rated Lawyers, rated AV Pre-eminent in Martindale-Hubbell, a rating system established in 1887. His rating is the "highest possible rating both in legal ability and ethical standards."

Married for 50 years, Ken and his wife, Leah, have two children, Vicky and David, and two grandchildren. Vicky currently serves as a litigation attorney in the Ken Nunn Law Office. Ken was listed in the 2012 edition of Who's Who of America, and was also commissioned a Kentucky Colonel by the Governor of the State of Kentucky.

BY JOHN P. NICHOLLS

THE HAPPY WORKPLACE BLUEPRINT

Often our assumptions go unquestioned, even on complex issues that should be examined more thoroughly. Sometimes, it is only when our expectations are turned upside down that we start to make a more considered diagnosis of these assumptions.

One of these moments occurred for me on a dark, wet winter evening in a remote part of eastern England. I was travelling to a school to deliver a glowingly good employee survey report, one which cited high staff wellbeing, motivation, recognition and contentment. Instead of a shiny new building in a leafy suburban setting, why had I driven through a residential area characterised with vandalised cars, graffiti and damaged street lights? Driving through the school gates, I saw barbed wires on the walls, CCTV cameras everywhere and a dark unapproachable building. Surely, I'd come to the wrong place!

After being warmly greeted at the reception area, I met the staff committee to feed back the good news and discuss the findings. Still, my expectations were challenged. Instead of the warm, fuzzy atmosphere I imagined, I was told that this was a workplace based on professional, respectful relationships ruthlessly focused on making things better for the students. The school leadership had created a genuine mission mentality which was supplemented with challenging, supporting relationships. And it worked not just for the students, but the whole school community.

The events of that evening led me to undertake a long-term investigation into what makes the perfect blueprint for a happy workplace. I have worked with over six hundred schools and also around a hundred other profit and non-profit organisations. These have ranged from workplaces with over twenty-five thousand employees to businesses with just six staff. From analysing thousands of questions and working with many employees and leaders, I have documented the eight elements that need to be considered to create a happy workplace.

1. RELATIONSHIPS

The biggest indicator for a happy workplace comes down to the quality of the relationships within it. Within teams, across teams, between different types of staff and with management - all these relationships can make or break a great working environment. People are employed for a variety of different skill and behaviour sets, so it would be unrealistic to expect everyone to get on like a house on fire. However, the organisation can expect that all dealings with others are characterised by respect, fairness, honesty and sensitivity to age, gender, ethnic and religious differences. This must be modelled by those in senior positions in the organisation.

In studies asking why people leave their present jobs, the most common reason is to get away from their current line manager. This suggests that line managers must be hired, trained and held accountable for their interactions with others. As well as encouraging managers to have real human dialogue with their staff, they need to be supported to be able to admit to their mistakes and show the considerate side of their nature.

All staff must be held to high standards of behaviour. This must be given value in the hiring criteria and backed up by robust HR procedures to tackle any bullying and harassment behaviour. Destructive relationships are costly. By creating a harmonious environment, not only is this great for staff morale but also for the effectiveness of the organisation.

2. COMMUNICATION

Communication is always a hot topic. I have run hundreds of communication workshops and this topic is always a lively affair. Some people prefer "high tech" solutions, others more "face-to-face" interaction, and almost always the solutions are expected to be carried out by someone else!

However, for communication to be effective, two rules need to be established:

Firstly, communication is everyone's responsibility.

Secondly, everyone has an obligation to use the means of communication available.

Communication is often seen as from management to staff, but it needs to go both ways. Also, communication is both talking and listening. Sitting in a room nodding is not the same as attentive listening. I learnt this from my wife as apparently my communication skills are lacking when football is on TV!

Listening not only means hearing what has been said, but summarising back to show you've heard and understand. Also, an organisation shows true communication skills through timely follow-up and delivery on promises made.

People need to feel kept in the communication loop. An easy way to do this is to list the types of communication needed in your company and ask two questions:

    1: What communication channels are effective now?

    2: What could be improved?

Other things to consider are the consistency of communication throughout the business and also the tone of message, especially from senior management. As always, trust, consideration and respect should be at the forefront.

One last thought - Email is the communication of choice by many people, yet also the biggest cause of complaint. Perhaps some time could be given to find consensus when face-to-face, telephone or a group newsletter would be more appropriate for certain types of communication.

3. RECOGNITION AND PRAISE

When looking at employee morale, pay and benefits are often glossed over, as the perceived wisdom is that other factors are more important. However, if pay is seen as unfair for whatever reason, then it does become a big issue. If your business pays less than competitors or there are differing pay scales for different employment contracts, this will cause friction. If there are large gaps in pay and conditions of leadership and other staff, this will cause resentment too.

Recognition of good work needs to be carried out consistently and appropriately. I had a boss who used to insist on naming publicly all those who did good work. However, he would always forget someone. As his deputy, I spent a lot of time salving the hurt of this unfortunate habit.

Some managers praise so much that the impact is watered down. It is important that the praise is for meaningful good performance and is timely, specific and genuine. Also, praise should be encouraged amongst all staff, not just top down. I remember complimenting my boss once, only for them to burst into tears. They'd never been praised by their staff before!

Unexpected appreciation is often more effective than a seasonal gift. One school principal used to occasionally leave cakes in the staff common room and this proved to be a powerful morale booster. This always sticks in my mind when I hear people complain about the quality of their holiday gifts. Expected gifts and bonuses often are taken for granted, whereas unexpected appreciation can really make an impact.

Recognition of consistent good work should lead to development opportunities and promotion. A lack of these options in a company will cause the high performers to look elsewhere.

4. EMPOWERED TO DO THE WORK

We all want to do a great job, so it becomes frustrating when things get in the way. Poor processes, lack of information, high workloads, time pressures, lack of equipment or poor working conditions are just some of the things that cause problems.

Staff thrive when they are trusted to do their jobs and are not micromanaged. If they are given decision-making authority, however small, this can be a huge motivator.

To be empowered to do their work, people need access to great training. Training courses, peer mentoring, coaching, job swaps, discussion groups and professional learning communities are powerful ways to help people grow in their present and future roles.

> **To be effective, the mission must be followed through in actions as well as words.**

---

5. PLAY AT WORK

Encouraging social events and playfulness at work can create high morale. Just remember, a night of salsa dancing may be your idea of paradise, but may have others escaping out of the window (no matter how high the building!). Social committees need to offer a broad range of activities and people should not be forced to have fun.

Working at a food bank can be as powerful for team building as paint balling. Initiatives for encouraging healthy lifestyles and new things to learn are great ways to improve staff wellbeing. Happy workplaces are characterised by good-humoured exchanges and a spirit of playfulness. Ask staff how this can be encouraged.

6. ON A MISSION

In the school I mentioned earlier, staff morale was driven by a powerful vision to improve the results and outcome of the students. As well as being articulated passionately by the school leadership team, all decisions were made with this in mind. Any successes were publicly celebrated and the school wrote to local celebrities and officials for endorsements, which were framed and placed in prominent positions in the building. All staff, from cleaners to librarians, felt "we are the difference to these children's lives."

I've seen similar mentalities in for-profit organisations, using similar techniques as well as taking pride in the reputation of the company. For this to be effective, the mission must be followed through in actions as well as words. Policies and practices must align with this and the vision and direction must be consistently upheld throughout the organisation, especially amongst the leadership team.

7. CLARITY

Lack of clarity of job role can cause considerable frustration, as much time is wasted working out what is in your scope and what isn't. The unexciting pieces of work are passed around as everyone feels it isn't in their set of responsibilities. Whoever gets the job feels justifiably aggrieved!

Clarity also ensures consistent behaviour across the organisation, so departments work effectively together. Alignment of goals and processes across teams will make staff happier and the business more effective. To ensure certainty and transparency are sustained, people must feel they are accountable for this clarity and any lack in this area must be challenged.

8. CHALLENGING, SUPPORTIVE FEEDBACK

Giving feedback can be scary and uncomfortable. That's why so many managers sit back and wait for the annual performance review to assess people's work. However, giving feedback shows you care about your employee's success. Setting high expectations shows you trust your colleague.

As long as the feedback is given in this spirit and is regular, clear-cut, behaviourally focused and focused on future performance, it can be a highly effective motivational tool.

Organisations where challenge and support are lacking are characterised by apathy – as no one is seen to care about the work done, or the people doing the work. Too much challenge/too little support can lead to burn-out whilst the opposite can lead to complacency. High performance and morale happens with the potent ingredients of high challenge and support through strong relationship-based feedback.

Employee's will often go the extra mile for their company to ensure they do a great job. This needs to be reciprocated. Life does throw all sorts of challenges and these will impact on work. For high morale to flourish, staff need to be confident with support when tough personal things happen. Some flexibility in short-term working arrangements goes a long way.

Larger companies may be in a position to offer an Employee Assistance Programme, offering advice and counselling on a whole range of life circumstances. The programmes I've been involved in actually saved the organisation money by reducing staff absences. In addition, it showed the company cared.

Smaller organisations could replicate this by looking at local social programmes that offer similar services for free. Staff in distress are more likely to use counselling and advice services if pointed in the right direction.

More than anything, showing care and understanding as a line manager or an organisation during difficult times makes for a happier, more humane workplace.

THE BLUEPRINT

I have detailed the main areas to consider to create a happy workplace. Remember all groups of staff are different and will continue to change as new people come and others leave. Solutions must be generated by all the staff and the responsibility must be shared by all. Leadership should champion and enable changes to be made, but the wellbeing and morale of all staff belongs to everyone.

Working in a role that is fulfilling and challenging, alongside supportive, caring workmates is a blessing. I wish that gift for you and all your colleagues.

ABOUT JOHN

John P. Nicholls is an internationally-known trainer and coach, specialising in resilience, staff wellbeing and leadership development. His extraordinary talent for establishing rapport has helped John support thousands of teachers around the world, who value his common sense, caring guidance and good-humoured approach to their professional and personal development.

John first came to public prominence when, as a school principal facing significant budget shortfalls, he took a pay cut, worked a four-day week and saved the jobs of class assistants in his school. This considerate act was broadcast on the BBC, Sky and ITV news and widely reported in the UK newspapers. Receiving letters from around the world, he was congratulated on his actions.

This steadfast focus on supporting staff morale and his ability to create positive environments for students, parents, teachers, board members and the local community, led to new opportunities. John succeeded in running the award-winning "Norfolk Wellbeing Programme" – working with nearly one thousand volunteers to improve the morale and subjective wellbeing of over 28,000 employees in 400 schools. A large part of his success was due to his talent to encourage dialogue and create consensus across various interest groups.

John's professional development work with teachers crosses four continents with workshops in eighteen countries. His coaching skills training is highly regarded and his resilience and stress management work has improved the professional and personal lives of hundreds of school leaders.

The Resilient Leader Programme, developed and run by John, is a two-day training on building healthy habits to support resilience, dealing with people we find difficult, and practical problem solving. It is supported by nine confidential monthly coaching sessions.

As well as helping schools build coaching schemes and capacity in their organizations, John advises schools on staff morale and relationship issues. His TEDx Reykjavik talk on "How To Create A Fantastic Working Environment In Your School." has won him new fans around the world.

Holding a Masters degree in Coaching and Mentoring Practice, John has given coaching skills training in places as far afield as Singapore, the United States, Slovakia, and The Netherlands. Currently, he is the Assistant Director for Nord Anglia University (Asia) in Hong Kong, responsible for training local and international teachers in the Asia region.

You can connect with John at:
https://hk.linkedin.com/in/johnpatricknicholls
www.teachersandschool.com

THE HAPPY WORKPLACE BLUEPRINT

Identifying Long-Term Investment Demand Trends

PERFORMANCE: The branding concept and mission of your firm KAMSouth is: "We Build Wealth." How did you come up with that and what does it mean for you and your clients on a day-to-day basis?

CHRISTIAN: What I do as an independent private wealth advisor runs counterintuitive to everything I learned in business school about modern portfolio theory, which tells you to be diversified. We do the opposite, running concentrated portfolios. A traditional equity mutual fund company may own 300 stocks in a diversified portfolio, but if 100 go up and 100 go down and 100 do nothing, you haven't moved the needle. The way I invest for my clients provides a true alternative to mutual funds. I may own only 30 stocks, which I feel over time is the best way to build wealth – less diversification and more concentration.

In the traditional investment management business, there are two distinct camps. The first is the mutual fund industry, which is kind of a Big Brother, managing all the money for 401(k)'s and pension plans. The other side is the financial planning industry, where planners help individuals plan for retirement but don't actively manage their money. They usually outsource that decision to a third party. My business strategy is focused in the middle of these two camps that usually don't communicate with each other. I'm rendering value by actively managing concentrated portfolios and also helping individuals make optimal decisions on their retirement. Working from that sweet spot in the middle can really improve a client's financial situation because I can offer both investment management and planning.

> ## 90 percent of financial planners are generalists, meaning they do it all.

PERFORMANCE: Do you see wealth and success just in monetary terms, or do those concepts have meaning to you (and your clients) beyond just dollars and cents?

CHRISTIAN: What I've found in my practice is that one of the most powerful motivational factors in people's lives is not money, but the opportunity to learn more, taking on more responsibilities, contributing to the lives of others and being recognized for their achievements. That's more important than the total in our bank accounts. For me personally, I think true wealth comes from having a clear purpose in life, and getting that vision right. If you have the right purpose and vision, financial wealth will follow. A lot of people come into my office without a clear vision of what they want, just some sound bites they heard on CNBC from Suze Orman or a book they have read. They've implemented a little of this and that but are left with a mess – no strategy or consistency. It's important to have a plan and consciously stick with it, because there's a lot of uncertainty in life. My role is to help people see clearly, using financial instruments to navigate through the fog. In the chapter I wrote for the book *Soul of Success, Vol. 1* called "Five Simple Rules To Sharpen Your Thinking," I discuss my unique retirement planning process:

1) Develop a Retirement Vision.

2) Build the Optimal Retirement Portfolio.

3) Focus on Retirement Distribution Strategies.

4) Estate and Wealth Transfer Planning.

That's the framework that helps people think about key financial decisions and the various dimensions of retirement planning.

PERFORMANCE: Tell me about your background and what you were doing in the years before launching KAMSouth in 2011? What led you to think you could be successful with your own firm? What did you do to ensure that would happen?

CHRISTIAN: I started my career as a security analyst with Lindner Funds, a large mutual fund company in St. Louis, researching companies to purchase for the portfolios in the areas of technology, energy and banking. I later took a position as managing director for Trusco Capital Management, where I was in charge of technology research. I went on to Harvard Business School – but even before that, I had always had an interest in starting my own firm. The simple answer to why I thought I could be successful is that I don't know how to do anything else! My experience at Harvard gave me the toolbox to implement a lot of strategies involved in setting up a business. One of the things I learned from my professor Clay Christensen, who wrote *The Innovator's Dilemma*, was that if you want to be successful, you need to start by attacking the lowest end of the market. Atlanta is a very competitive market for financial services. Taking Christensen's ideas to heart, I started teaching retirement classes in Athens and Newnan, Georgia, which are smaller cities east and west of Atlanta. My strategy was not to go head to head with large firms in Atlanta, but to begin in smaller areas where I built a solid clientele. Then I started "attacking" Atlanta, and I've been very successful.

I think my confidence comes from beginning my career in the equity research area which is the intellectual property of the investment management business. While most advisors start as brokers or insurance salesmen, I learned how to understand what a good investment was, without ever having to learn or undo bad habits. What I've seen in the last 20 years I could dovetail into a specialization based on understanding and identifying long term investment trends. I ask myself, "What are some large macro trends that are good for investments in the coming years?" As an example, ten years ago, I researched power management semiconductor chips, which became the cornerstone for laptops and cell phone batteries. A lot of the companies I identified as being great long term investments were so successful that they were later acquired by larger companies. This means increased wealth for my client portfolios.

PERFORMANCE: Why did you decide to focus on retirees and pre-retirees? What is it about their unique needs which meshed with your evolving life purpose?

CHRISTIAN: They're at the intersection, five or ten years from retirement, where they're seeking out wise counsel and guidance and realizing that they're going to need a strong financial plan for when the time comes. During pre-retirement, my goal is to get them to make choices in resource allocation while helping them reduce their tax liability. Most people don't understand, for instance, that 401(k)'s are joint bank accounts with the government. This is the perfect age to start planning flexibility and opening doors so when the time comes they can execute what we implemented back in their early 50s. On a personal level, I really enjoy teaching individuals how to think and helping them navigate the process, taking the proper actions now and charting the right course for the future.

PERFORMANCE: Tell me about your focus – and the conscious decision you made not to be a generalist?

CHRISTIAN: Within the financial planning industry, I would say that 90 percent of financial planners are generalists, meaning they do it all – financial planning, planning for college education, budgeting and investments, insurance, estate planning, etc. I think trying to do everything is an ineffective strategy. I realized early on that if I could focus on the sectors I knew better than most, which were banking, energy and technology, and could offer a total return investment strategy tied to helping individuals with retirement – that focus was my best bet.

PERFORMANCE: Let's talk about Specialization. You use a two-part strategy that involves:

1) understanding long term investment demand trends and

2) unique retirement planning, helping others with tax-efficient withdrawal strategies for retirement.

CHRISTIAN: I manage $50 million of assets, so I'm on the line and responsible for these individuals and families. What I try to do is think about long term trends I can take advantage of – not the short term "hot stock" of the day. I map that out and invest accordingly. Right now, I'm looking at Brazil. In the short term, even with the Summer Olympics in 2016, there are a lot of negative issues and a declining economy. But over the next ten years, I see Brazil's economy as a huge growth engine and driver for the world. I'm researching what companies look attractive and what investments are available. I just started researching Embraer SA, a small jet manufacturer. The company appears to have a sustainable competitive advantage because there are only a few companies in the world that can manufacture commercial jet aircraft. This goes back to the confidence it took to starting my firm.

I've always been comfortable having a unique perspective, and enjoy explaining to people why investments out of favor now may be part of an upward trend ten years out. I put people's capital to work not based on this year or next year, but what the growth outlook should be in ten years. I put the macro ten year trends together with the micro, which is the client coming to me before retirement age and helping them with their present investment allocations. I work with various dimensions of their micro details, helping them improve their financial position. I realize that I have an interesting opportunity to offer both macro and micro services to clients so they can benefit from that powerful combination and perspective. As for intangibles, good old fashioned Southern hospitality comes naturally to me, and it helps my clients feel at home very quickly. In the Deep South, that goes a long way towards building relationships with them.

PERFORMANCE: Let's get back to the concept of Rendering Value, i.e., offering a service of value or adding value.

CHRISTIAN: My goal is to meet the client where they are in that moment and help them understand everything from, say Roth IRA conversions to positioning their retirement portfolio for long-term wealth creation by focusing on risk-adjusted returns. Value comes from building a relationship, and over time moving them into the most optimal retirement position. A lot of that involves baby steps. Year One could be a small Roth conversion or a modest retirement portfolio re-allocation. Year Two, we can be bolder. It's about walking them through the process over time. I feel I render value based on very personalized service.

Most financial planners give you a 30-page report with pretty charts and graphs, without realizing that as soon as that planning report is complete it is outdated. I don't do those, but I am committed to the process, helping them ask penetrating questions and think about various dimensions of their retirement – and to genuinely move the needle and set them up for success. One way I am hoping to render value beyond my practice is authoring chapters in business books. My first was in, *Get In The Game* (2015), with a chapter I titled, "Follow The Leader: The Ideal Investment Strategy."

PERFORMANCE: What was a defining moment to you when you realized that KAM South was a success?

CHRISTIAN: I see my own success as a direct extension of my clients' success. I genuinely like every single one of them and love to see them fulfilled from a financial and gratitude standpoint. These deep personal relationships I have are very fulfilling. I started this business from my home, so the defining moment for me was when I leased my office space in this Class A building in Atlanta right near the new Braves baseball stadium. Having the confidence to sign that five-year lease was a huge step. I've tried to create a peaceful, quite research type of environment.

PERFORMANCE: When people talk about success, they usually don't mention the word "Failure." But you've said that it's a critical element on the road to success.

CHRISTIAN: I think failure is the single most important element to achieving success. To become a Certified Financial Planner, you have to pass a grueling ten-hour exam. The first time I took it in 2009, I failed. It was one of the hardest things I ever had to do, redoubling my studying efforts and dedicating another 200 hours so that I could pass it in 2011. Failing it was a galvanizing factor, and ensured that I knew the details of retirement planning better than most that pass on the first try. That's what comes from a total of 500 hours of total studying. That contributed to the confidence in the financial planning strategies I could help create with clients. All that information became a solidified database in my mind. This also became a stepping stone for three other financial designations, Certified Private Wealth Advisor®, Certified Divorce Financial Analyst™ and Retirement Income Certified Professional® which I completed.

So, out of failure comes great success. Out of failure comes the realization of your purpose and a new vision. Then it's up to you – and only you – to implement it and find the character to move forward towards success.

PERFORMANCE: What about that other "F" word, Fear?

CHRISTIAN: From an investment perspective, I love fear and uncertainty. They create opportunity and entry points to invest. Fear equals uncertainty in the market. If I'm using my financial tools to navigate…in terms of building portfolios, that translates to being able to buy a stock at a lower price when everything is going down. I like to use a San Francisco metaphor. Whether you're dealing with a clear day or a foggy day, nothing has changed except that you have to navigate through the fog. Uncertainty creates opportunity for investment.

PERFORMANCE: To what do you attribute your drive and ambition to be successful on your own terms?

CHRISTIAN: I think I am genuinely a student of the game. I love the world of investing and work tirelessly to identify these ten-year trends. If a certain company fits my profile and hits all the things I'm looking for, I get excited because I know that will help me grow and progress while helping my clients do the same.

PERFORMANCE: If you couldn't pass along anything of monetary value to your wife and five children, but only "success tips," what would they be?

CHRISTIAN: Find your passion in life, but more importantly, find your purpose. Don't be afraid to choose a path that is currently out of favor but will pay dividends in the long-term. For example, during the banking crisis in 2011, I started offering an investment strategy focused only on financial stocks that took advantage of the dislocation in prices. That strategy has done quite well for my clients and is paying great dividends now. I struggle all the time with the best way to pass along my values to my children. I've accumulated all this knowledge, but how do you pass on the values to your heirs? My biggest concern is about ensuring that my guidance can help them find their purpose in life. My recommendation would be to take the road less traveled. This makes life's journey all the more rewarding and progressive.

ABOUT CHRISTIAN

Best-Selling Author, Christian Koch, CFP®, CPWA®, CDFA™, RICP®, is recognized as one of the top thought-leaders and private wealth experts in the money management industry. He has co-authored the book, *Get in the Game,* which describes his unique four step investment process and five principles that can help individuals in the journey to be successful long-term investors.

When it comes to the investment consulting process and creating portfolios for retirement, you need an experienced wealth management professional. Christian Koch's expert knowledge and approach to traditional investments, individual security selection, retirement income distribution planning and more, can help you face the future and the intricacies of your investment portfolio with a fresh new outlook.

Christian has a unique investment process and a retirement planning system that has served clients for years: develop the vision, build the optimal portfolio, focus on distribution strategies and then evaluate wealth and estate transfer planning. He says asset location is extremely critical to maximizing efficiencies, especially during a slow-growth economy, and minimizing taxes are a significant component of success.

Christian is a Harvard Business School AMP graduate and former investment research analyst. He also holds the prestigious Certified Financial Planner™ professional, Certified Divorce Financial Analyst™, Certified Private Wealth Advisor® and Retirement Income Certified Professional ® designation, placing him in a select group of financial professionals.

In 2013, 2014 and 2015, Christian's credentials and work was rigorously examined after which he was honored with a coveted Five Star Wealth Manager Award.

Christian is on the Board of Directors of Rotary Club of Buckhead, and is involved in the Harvard Business School Club of Atlanta.

You can connect with Christian at:
Christian@kamsouth.com
www.kamsouth.com

I have always been fascinated with businesses and how they operated, and I have always enjoyed hearing stories about successful entrepreneurs.

AN INTERVIEW WITH DAVID AUER, ESQ.

VETERAN TAX ATTORNEY STRESSES LIFETIME LEARNING AS A KEY COMPONENT TO A JOURNEY OF SUCCESS

PERFORMANCE: After launching your career as a CPA with Arthur Anderson and later working as a tax attorney for a large firm in Tulsa, how and why did you decide to go the entrepreneurial route and launch your own firm?

DAVID: I have always been fascinated with businesses and how they operated, and I have always enjoyed hearing stories about successful entrepreneurs. Because I loved hearing about their journeys, I was attracted to working with them as clients. I felt like part of some fascinating learning experiences, and the journey I was on as a CPA and tax attorney involved not only helping them save taxes and protect their wealth, but learning everything I could from fellow business owners. They didn't realize it, but they were helping me become a better business owner myself! Some of the challenges I faced when I started my law practice arose from not having anyone in my family who had ever owned their own business. Other business owners have the benefit of other family members who have been in business before. The first lesson I learned from clients that were successful was that they were doing things they loved to do and they figured out a way to make a living doing it. Entrepreneurial achievement is so much easier if you're passionate about your work. Considering that it's never going to be a 9 to 5 job and you have to be 100 percent committed to it, it better be something you love. Successful entrepreneurs tell me they wake up and go to sleep thinking about their business, as if it had become like another child in their family.

PERFORMANCE: What were your initial goals for your firm and how did you go about achieving success with them?

DAVID: I think at the beginning, I thought I could grow my business into a large multi-specialty law firm with lots of partners and associates, but as I got older and more experienced and specialized, I realized that I am more effective staying small and having a specialized niche of saving taxes for my clients. As I like to tell others, it's not what you make but what you keep after taxes that is important. For most successful business owners, professionals, and investors, income taxes can erode more than 50% of their income, and income taxes are a pure expense that generates no return on their investment. Today, I spend almost all of my time helping clients from wasting their money by unnecessarily paying too much income tax.

PERFORMANCE: Earlier in your life and career, how did you define success? How has that definition changed over the years?

DAVID: When I was younger, I defined success as getting as much education as I could and continuing to learn until I knew on what I wanted to focus my career. I viewed every level of education as opening greater and greater opportunities. I realized that the more I knew, the more I realized how much I didn't know. I also felt a key component of success was all about being willing to work harder than anyone else. As I matured, the combination of education and hard work has been expanded in a more practical classroom where I continue to serve my clients. I learned the difference between working harder and working smarter.

When I was younger, I chose to defer the opportunity to make a living to pursue my education. Looking back, the cumulative effect of my extensive education most certainly better prepared me to make a stronger impact and create more value for my clients than if I had not received all of the education I obtained. As a tax adviser, I continue to spend hundreds of hours per year staying current on our ever-changing tax laws. Without the strong foundation that my graduate and law school training provided, I would have spent a number of additional years catching up to where I am today.

PERFORMANCE: How is your recently-launched Auer Tax Group unique from your previous firm?

DAVID: It's concentrated on creating personalized income tax and business strategies for my clients. Being both a lawyer and CPA, I can think about my clients' tax situation both qualitatively and quantitatively; in other words, I analyze the legal issues and identify the problem and solutions as a tax lawyer, then envision and describe the tax effect on the bottom line to my client. I recently rebranded the Auer Tax Group as America's Premiere Tax Expert. I'm listed on the Premiere Experts website, www.americaspremiereexperts.com, as well as on: www.premieretaxexpert.com, and www.assetprotectiontraining.com

PERFORMANCE: You're dedicated to providing advanced income tax and asset protection planning solutions to high income individuals, professionals and business owners. How do you measure success in serving the needs of these people and organizations?

DAVID: From a tax planning standpoint, I can measure success in terms of ensuring that they have a significant return on their investment in the form of tax savings. I know I'm successful if I can create and implement a proven income tax strategy that creates anywhere from a 2,000 to 3,000 percent return on their investments. A good measure of client success is finding ways to help clients save taxes in the form of getting a deduction for saving money and turning that money into tax free income in the future. A lot of other CPAs help their clients get the deduction today, but that forces them to report it as income in the future. Most experts would agree that income tax rates for high income individuals will be going up with increased government spending, so that doesn't make sense when you do the math. Why would you want to put money away today at 35 percent if ten years from now it would be subject to a 50 percent tax? Yet that's what most people consider "tax planning."

From an asset protection planning standpoint, I consider success as creating a bullet-proof plan and structure to protect my client through unwanted creditors and predators. With over 90% of the world's lawsuits filed in the U.S., most successful professionals and business owners walk around every day with a giant bullseye on their chest and can be a target of a lawsuit and any moment. Plus, the concept of "a jury of your peers" doesn't usually apply to these people. As a result, most clients are left taking matters into their own hands rather than leaving it up to our judicial system to protect them.

PERFORMANCE: You've recently expanded your scope to include education and training of financial advisors and CPAs on how to better serve tax clients. What prompted the move into teaching?

DAVID: I realized that I can impact the lives and finances of more people by working with other successful financial advisors and their clients. If they bring me on their team as a tax planning expert, they end up being able to provide a broader range of services to their existing clients. I think I reached the point in my career where I felt it was time to make the most of the years I have left…if that's five, ten, fifteen or 30 years, I would rather spend the rest of my life doing what I feel I'm called to do. And everything I have done as a CPA and tax attorney has prepared me for this moment.

PERFORMANCE: Many members of your family were educators. What did you learn from them regarding how to measure success?

DAVID: My grandmother was a high school teacher, my mom taught elementary and junior high, my wife is an elementary school teacher and my daughter is pursuing her degree in elementary education. Whew! Being around teachers all my life, I essentially learned that learning never ends. Most people who are successful are always learning new things and how to be better at what they do. There's a well-known phrase I heard a long time ago that I believe: When the student is ready, the teacher will appear. I feel that part of my own legacy must be giving back in the form of teaching others what I have learned. Teachers outside my home had a big impact too, particularly my eighth grade Economics teacher Mrs. Sorge, and then my scoutmaster, Bill Shaffer. Boy Scouts was learning about life in the great outdoors. There are so many ways…

> # The greatest thing in my business is when you're able to work with a client who has fear and concerns about their future.

PERFORMANCE: The financial world has bestowed various honors and designations on you over the years. Are those true measures of achievement or is true success something more personal for you?

DAVID: Before I had a degree or an honor and I was pursuing my education, those were goals or indications of success. But when I got out and started working, my reward came in the form of clients being extremely happy and satisfied with what I had helped them save in taxes. The accolades are a result of achieving that. The greatest thing in my business is when you're able to work with a client who has fear and concerns about their future. There are many risks and dangers they worry about. My job is to help them gain clarity, confidence and peace of mind by creating a plan with them, then helping them accomplish it.

PERFORMANCE: What are some of the challenges you have overcome to be successful? Are they unique to you or do you think everyone who wants to achieve great things goes through them?

DAVID: Every time I have hit a brick wall or something didn't work out the way I wanted to, I chose to respond a certain way. Rather than feel defeated and give up, I learned from that experience and got back up and tried it a different way until I made it work. There was a lot of trial and error along the way because I didn't have any family or friends in this business who could guide me, but the upside of that is feeling that I was a pioneer of sorts, blazing a path that ended up being unique.

PERFORMANCE: What are the keys to being successful in your chosen industry?

DAVID: Always try to become more knowledgeable in the area you want to work. If you're a tax attorney, don't just settle for a minimum amount of education. In most industries today, because of our rapidly changing society, information and knowledge doubles every eighteen months; common wisdom is that the shelf life of knowledge reduces in half during that period. In my business, the original Internal Revenue code was only 400 pages long. When I was in college it was a few thousand pages, and now it's over 70,000 pages. On the personal side, finding several mentors who you look up to and respect is important. They might not have been successful in your same business, but they've lived through life's struggles and challenges and can help you with your own. Another thing that has become more important to me in dealing with clients is the ability to communicate and being compassionate. Those personal qualities matter more to me than they did when I was younger.

PERFORMANCE: As a successful entrepreneur and educator, do you have advice for budding entrepreneurs who want to follow a similar path – going from working for others to launching their own firms?

DAVID: Always evaluate risks before you jump into anything, including the costs of whatever endeavor you're pursuing. Surround yourself with a team of trusted friends or advisors, and make sure they stay informed on what you're doing. Reach out to them and entrust them to hold you accountable for what you're doing. Even if you fail at something the first time, always get up and try a different way, and learn from your mistakes. If you're successful, don't take for granted that you always will be. Maintain your humility, because at some point that success may turn into failure and disappointment. One of my greatest regrets is depending on people who disappointed me because they were looking out for their own interests. People will often take advantage of you if you let them. Maybe a fifth component of success is something I paid for dearly: look for every way possible not to have a business partner, and if you're not ready to launch an enterprise by yourself, you're not ready to be in business. Research shows that most business partnerships fail, and not because of a bad idea.

PERFORMANCE: In a nutshell, define "Success."

DAVID: Success is a journey, not a destination. The secret of success is being a good steward of what you've been entrusted with. Another secret is being content with whatever you have, whether that's a lot or very little. It's more important to have progress than perfection.

ABOUT DAVID

David Auer, Esq. is the **CEO and Founder** of: (1) the **Auer Tax Group** – a national tax planning firm; (2) **Blue Ocean Strategies** – a business strategic planning firm; and (3) the **Advanced Planning Group** – a collaborative organization of multi-disciplinary legal, accounting, and financial professionals focused on tax, estate, asset protection, retirement and business succession planning strategies for successful business owners, professionals, and high net worth investors.

David has over 30 years of experience as a CPA and Attorney, earned his BSBA and MS in Accounting from Oklahoma State University, his JD with honors from Oklahoma University, and his LLM in Taxation from New York University. He has the Personal Financial Specialist ("PFS") and Chartered Global Management Accountant ("CGMA") designations from the American Institute of CPAs. David is a Fellow with the Esperti Peterson Institute and a member of the Order of the Coif, Wealth Counsel, and the American Association of Attorneys-CPAs.

BY DAROLD OPP, DDS

TRANSFORMING THE FACE OF HONDURAS, ONE CHILD AT A TIME

I want you to close your eyes and imagine you're on a mountain. But this isn't a normal mountain like Mount Everest or Pike's Peak. This is a mountain…made entirely…out of garbage.

Look around. In every direction, all you see are piles and piles of trash. Take a few steps. You can feel cans and broken glass crunching under your feet as you walk.

Stop and listen. You can hear the cry of the vultures circling overhead, looking for their next meal. Take a deep breath. Whew—that garbage smell is strong. It is so strong you can actually taste it.

Now I want you to imagine that this mountain of garbage isn't just a bad dream. It isn't going to go away when you open your eyes. Because this mountain of garbage is where you live. This is your home.

Oh! and also…you are just four years old.

They call this Trash Mountain—and it's all too real to those who have to live there.

Hundreds of children and their families make their homes in and around this mountain. How could such a horrible thing happen? Why would these families have to call a giant pile of garbage their home?

Well, back in 1998, Hurricane Mitch devastated the country of Honduras. It was already one of the poorest countries in Central America, but the hurricane set them back another 50 years economically. It also left tens of thousands of orphaned children to roam the streets of Tegucigalpa—the capital city.

Since the country was so poor, there were no resources to help these children. The kids had no opportunity for education. Many of them had no families and nowhere to turn for help. Many lived on the street. Some resorted to making Trash Mountain their home. Years later, hundreds of kids—and their families—still work and live there today.

Now, as you might imagine, if you're living on a mountain made out of garbage, you have to deal with a lot of dirt, diseases, and horribly unpleasant conditions. Circling Trash Mountain are those vultures I mentioned before, because it is not unusual for a dead body or body parts to wind up in the dump. There also packs of wild dogs roaming around, and cows who graze on what they find in the trash.

But that's only part of the hardship these families face. Historically, the dump has been the place where "bad" people live and work. Well, they still do—these children are growing up surrounded by drug dealers, addicts, alcoholics, and gangs. Some parents force their daughters into prostitution just to make another 50 cents a day so the family can eat. 50 cents! Most of us consider that worthless change. Not enough for a drink at Starbucks. And yet, on Trash Mountain, parents will sell out their children for that price.

Most of the kids also have to work in the dump—as soon as they are old enough to sift through trash and find things to sell, they join their parents on the mountain. But even if the kids are too young to work they still stay on the mountain. Their parents put them in cardboard boxes next to where they work. It is not unusual to see a two-year-old taking care of an infant, both of them in a box, while their parents and older siblings rummage through the garbage, trying to survive.

It is a brutal, brutal life for everyone, especially the children. There was a boy named Kevin. When Kevin was five, he had already learned how to hitch rides on the back of the garbage trucks—that's the way to make sure you get the best, newest stuff from the truck. But one day, Kevin slipped and fell, and the truck killed him instantly.

And the adults all around him just kept working.

That sounds like an awful, cold reaction—but the hard truth is those adults could not afford to stop. And honestly, the death of a five-year-old boy is not really unusual on Trash Mountain. The response to Kevin's tragedy simply signifies how low the value of life had become there.

So, yes, Trash Mountain can truly be Hell on Earth. But…the human spirit can never be completely snuffed out. Which is why, every so often, even in the middle of this Hell on Earth, a miracle can sneak through.

And one has.

In 2001, Pastor Jeony Ordonez and his 5-year-old daughter went on a serendipitous life-changing mission. He had some medical waste to get rid of, and he brought it to Trash Mountain. That is where he saw the children working in the dump for the first time, and it broke his heart.

Pastor Jeony's daughter was even more deeply affected. She saw kids even younger than herself living and working in the horrible conditions I described to you. With kid-like determination, she made her father promise that he would do something to help them.

Well, to this man of God, that job made any one of Tom Cruise's so-called impossible missions sound like a walk in the park. But, for his daughter's sake, and for the sake of all those trapped in this harsh reality, the Pastor tried. It wasn't going to be easy.

First of all, the people of Trash Mountain were suspicious—they had been let down before. Ministers and other people from the outside world would show up, promise to help, and never be seen again, because they were overwhelmed by the magnitude of what had to be done. So the people didn't really trust outsiders. And, despite their surroundings, they were also proud. They were poor and uneducated, but they didn't want pity. They weren't looking for a handout. They wanted a hand up.

> ## The school has become such a huge success story that it has captured the attention of the Mayor of Tegucigalpa and the President of Honduras.

But how could you help them when the whole country was struggling financially? There didn't seem to be a viable way out. Pastor Jeony decided he wouldn't give up. He felt these people were his mission. So he spent months bringing food and water to Trash Mountain. And slowly, they began to trust him. Slowly, they allowed him to part of their community.

They invited him to join him for meals—which often meant cooked garbage. He ate things like chicken insides and other dishes that no sane person would ever consider eating. And since it is an insult in Honduras to be invited to dinner and not partake, Pastor Jeony felt he had to eat whatever he was served—on several occasions, the meal made him so sick he thought he would die.

But he kept coming back—out of love. Pastor Jeony wasn't just a man of God, he also was trained as an educator, and his wife as well. Together, they came up with the idea to start a school for the children of Trash Mountain, to give them a chance at an education and perhaps a way out.

But how do you start a school in a garbage dump, with no supplies?

They soon found out how resourceful these people could be. They scrounged through the trash and found pencils and paper that others had thrown away. They used old tires to make desks for the students. Because they knew how to utilize the little that Trash Mountain had to offer, a school was born—and class was in session.

They called the school Amor, Fe y Esperanza. In English that means Love, Faith, and Hope. The first year, there were 30 students. The second, there were 50. The third year, there were 80. There, in the middle of the vultures, and the wild dogs, and the cattle and the continuous noise of the garbage trucks and the smell—that horrible garbage smell—these kids were determined to learn no matter what.

And it worked. In 2011, the first class ever—a class of nine students—graduated from AFE. One of those students Rene, was the first child Pastor Jeony befriended on Trash Mountain. Rene, at the age of four, was already working at the dump to help support his family. Four years old! He had no choice because his father was a struggling alcoholic and Rene being the oldest child, assumed his familial responsibility! Today Rene is attending the university. He no longer lives nor works at the dump and he remains a positive role model not only for his six siblings but other students at AFE.

AFE kept growing and people started to notice. The government found out and decided the school needed to move to a better location! Pastor Jeony was able to find a soccer field near the dump where they could hold classes, but there were still no buildings to hold them in.

One day, he pointed over at the soccer field and told me how he ran a school with no structures…

"Do you see that tree? That was first grade. The tree next to it? That was second grade. When the rain came, we all huddled under that big tree. When the rain stopped, classes began again."

Well, you can only run a school for so long with only trees for shelter. Five years after the first class was held on Trash Mountain, ground was broken on the first classroom at AFE. Since then, five more buildings have been added. The school has become such a huge success story that it has captured the attention of the Mayor of Tegucigalpa and the President of Honduras.

That success is the result of AFE's curriculum—it goes beyond reading, writing and arithmetic to important life lessons. Yes, they have all the normal academic classes. Yes, they learn everything from computer skills to spiritual religious education. But because of the way they have grown up, without the things most of our kids take for granted, they are taught other basic things too. Their education included how to use a toilet, and what running water is, and what a normal family looks like.

TO THESE CHILDREN, THIS SCHOOL IS A MIRACLE

Around 200 students currently attend AFE. They have started an after-school program to help adults who work at the dump all day, to improve their education and better their lives. And since the high school opened its doors in 2009, 18 students have graduated and 9 have gone on to the university. Eidy, Christian, and Stefny were the 2014 high school graduates. Words cannot express the emotion I felt as I listened to each one share their story of triumph. All three of them echoed the same sentiment, that they never dreamed of going to school. In Honduras, almost 75% of the population is illiterate, and they beat not only the odds of finishing high school, but being part of the fortunate 4% that continue on to the university. Three Trash Mountain kids with a once-thought hopeless future, now will pursue degrees in international business, agricultural engineering, and international languages. Wow!

As I re-visited the elementary school, I was so impressed by the excitement and hope in the children's voices. In every classroom, these kids are excited about their future. As I left the classroom, the teacher implored me to say to the students, "Te veo en la universidad!" In English, "See you at the university!" What a battle cry!

2014 ushered in a new medical clinic that served over 8500 patients with some incredible, miraculous outcomes. Let me share with you one of those miracles, his name is Franklin. This young man has worked in the trash dump most of his life. He is married with a young daughter. During a time of increased gang violence in the garbage dump, Franklin was shot in the leg at close range trying to escape a gang riot. He received poor, inadequate treatment at a public hospital and within two days, his leg was red, swollen, and pus was oozing from the stitches. His wife approached the medical clinic at AFE pleading for help to save her husband's life.

When AFE's medical personnel visited Franklin, gangrene was ready to set in and his life was in the balance. Dr. Marvin and Hollie, the AFE doctor and nurse respectively, rendered care and within days his leg was healing nicely and within a month he was back at work supporting his family. Not only was Franklin's life spared, but a husband and father was restored to his family! For my wife and I, this financial donation has become priceless!

AFE introduced in 2015 a revolutionary aquaponics project. What is aquaponics? Aquaponics is the combination of aquaculture (raising fish for food) and hydroponics (growing plants in water rather than soil) in a recirculating system. Waste from the fish supplies the nutrients used by the plants providing a natural filter for water cycled back to the fish. One of the greatest challenges in third world countries is an adequate food source. Though this project remains small in its early stages, the hope is to expand its capacity in the near future whereby it will yield 40 tons of fish and 400 tons of vegetables annually! This food source alone would be large enough to feed the 1000+ people who surround Trash Mountain.

As I told you earlier, Honduras is one of the poorest countries in Central America. It has no social safety net, no government programs to help the less fortunate. There are still children working on Trash Mountain who are unable to attend school, still families without homes, still people without hope. That is the worst tragedy of all.

It has been said that man can live weeks without food, days without water, minutes without oxygen, but only seconds without hope. Amor, Fe y Esperanza—Love, Faith, and Hope—has been a lifeline, not only to these kids, but to the entire community. Adults are showing up at the school, so that they too can benefit from the education that their kids are getting.

For the first time ever, people are finding a way off of Trash Mountain, and into education and real homes and better jobs. But for Pastor Jeony and his team, every day has been an uphill struggle. Their budget is meager and their challenges feel endless.

But we have the power to change that. And that is why I have told you the story of these incredible people and their struggle today. I ask that you help continue to bring these brave, noble people the hope they so desperately need. I ask that you help them escape the violence, the abuse and the horror of their everyday lives. I ask that you donate so that we can bring all the children—as well as the adults—off of Trash Mountain and to a safe and secure home. I ask that you grant these people the basic dignity that all of us take for granted.

I hope you will join me in supporting this incredibly worthy cause. This is one mountain these children shouldn't have to climb. This is one mountain they should never have to see again.

ABOUT DR. DAROLD

Darold D. Opp, DDS is a general dentist in Aberdeen, South Dakota. He received his dental degree from the University of Nebraska. In 2015 he was the recipient of the Alumni Achievement Award from the UNMC College of Dentistry. He is a guest faculty member of the school teaching senior dental students on various topics including entrepreneurship, celebrity branding, marketing, authorship, and how to be an out-of-the-box thinker.

In 2008 he created a free, fun-filled, kids' community event called SmilePalooza. In 7 years he has entertained over 30,000 attendees and now teaches business owners from across the United States, Canada, and Australia this #1 client attraction event. In addition, 786k, a business coaching program for dentists, had its premier in Scottsdale, Arizona in April of 2014. 786k teaches dentists how they can net a 7 figure annual income by focusing on moms and the #1 fascination in life, their children.

Dr. Opp is co-author with the University of Nebraska College of Dentistry faculty on *Dental Practice Transitions: A Practical Guide to Management.* In addition, he is co-author with Jerry Jones in *The Definitive Guide to Dental Success* and co-author with Brian Tracy in *Transform: How the World's Leading Entrepreneurs and Professionals Transform Your Life, Business, and Health*. He was inducted into The National Academy of Best Selling Authors in 2014.

He was selected as one of America's Premier Experts and was featured in a documentary on America's Best Dentists. In addition, he has been interviewed for *The Wall Street Journal* and *USA Today* along with being featured on Fox, CBS, NBC, Yahoo Finance, and The Street.

In 2014, he was one of three finalists for the prestigious GKIC International Marketer of the Year Award. That same year, he was also the key contributor to Dan Kennedy's "The Ultimate NO B.S. Referral Machine" information product.

Dr. Opp and his wife Pamela are most proud of their son Brian and his wife Courtney (fellow entrepreneurs) along with their philanthropic endeavors. They live by the belief that "to whom much has been given, much is required." Since making a humanitarian trip to Russia in 1993, they have worked with projects across the world such as Samaritans Purse, World Vision, World Help, Trash Mountain, and Operation Smile.

You can connect with Darold at: daroldopp@gmail.com

Find out more about Amor, Fe y Esperanza at: www.afehonduras.org

The beauty of success
is that anyone
can have it.

BY JANICE L. QUIGG

DECIDE YOUR WAY TO SUCCESS

7 Decisions

Always bear in mind that your own resolution to succeed is more important than any other one thing.

~ Benjamin Franklin

No one in my family had ever attended university, let alone law school. Yet, when I was just twelve years old, I decided that I wanted to be a lawyer. I had grown up watching television shows like Perry Mason and honing my cross-examination skills on family and friends, and thought it would be a fun way to make a living. I never wavered in my dream to become a lawyer and have thoroughly enjoyed twenty years of successful practice.

The beauty of success is that anyone can have it. It's not reserved for a select group. It's not reserved for the lucky ones, the rich ones or the most innately talented ones. Success is available to those who decide they want to be successful. In this chapter, I would like to share seven decisions that are key to achieving success.

1. DECIDE YOUR GOAL

In order to get what you want, you must first decide what you want. Most people really foul up at this crucial first step because they simply can't see how it's possible to get what they want, so they don't even let themselves want it.

~ Jack Canfield

You must first decide which goal it is that you would like to achieve. It should be your goal. If you are pursuing a goal that you are not really passionate about, it will be more difficult to achieve because your heart isn't in it. Your passion is what fuels your ability to persevere when the going gets tough. I can tell you that it would not have been possible for me to spend as many hours as I did studying in university and law school had I not had such a burning desire to become a lawyer!

2. DECIDE YOUR GOAL IS POSSIBLE

Whatever the mind can conceive and believe, it can achieve.

~ Napoleon Hill

The goal to become a lawyer was a constant and vivid one. In fact, during high school and university, I never considered any other career path. It did not matter to me that there were usually about 3000 students applying for 250 seats; it did not matter that one of my high school teachers took me aside and gently reminded me that there weren't that many women in law school, and that the students usually came from wealthy families. The only thing that mattered to me was that I wanted to be a lawyer. I could visualize it as though it were already true. The only thing that I couldn't visualize was me wearing a white powdered wig like the barristers in the United Kingdom, and thanked my lucky stars that Canadian lawyers were not required to wear them!

By visualizing my goal so clearly, I was able to overcome any obstacles that came along the way. I decided that my goal was possible no matter what!

Many top athletes use the technique of visualization – using vivid, mental images to rehearse their complete performance before a competition. World Champion Golfer, Jack Nicklaus has said: "I never hit a shot, not even in practice, without having a very sharp in-focus picture of it in my head."

At the 1984 Olympic Games in Los Angeles, 16-year old Mary Lou Retton won the all-around gold medal by just 0.05 points, becoming the first American woman to win this event. Just weeks before the Olympics, Mary Lou would often lay in her bed, visualizing herself on each piece of equipment, performing her routines perfectly. She even imagined herself receiving the gold medal.

3. DECIDE TO BE COURAGEOUS

Everything you want is on the other side of fear.

~ Jack Canfield

Whenever you try something new, you are likely to experience some level of fear; fear of the unknown is natural. As Susan Jeffers says in her book, *Feel the Fear and Do It Anyway*, underlying all our fears is a lack of trust in ourselves. If you let fear stop you from taking on new challenges, you will miss out on some pretty awesome dreams! If you feel the fear and take on the new challenge, you will develop more confidence knowing that you can handle new situations.

Instead of letting fear stop me from taking the necessary steps to achieve success, I use it as a motivator to ensure success. For example, when preparing for the Law School Admission Test (LSAT), I was terrified of failing because it would have ended my dream of becoming a lawyer. However, instead of letting fear prevent me from writing the LSAT, I used it as a motivator; fear ensured that I studied that much more to ensure that I scored in the top three percentile.

A few years ago, I was asked to speak at an important legal conference on a topic in which I had no real practical experience. My initial reaction was to decline the invitation. However, I gave it some more thought and decided to accept the invitation. The fear of having the audience ask me a question that I could not answer motivated me to read everything I could on the topic. When it came time to deliver my presentation, not only did I receive exceptionally positive feedback from the audience, but my presentation was covered in the major industry newspaper!

4. DECIDE TO TAKE ACTION

Action is the foundational key to all success.

~ Pablo Picasso

Without action, you cannot achieve success. If you decide on a goal to pursue and decide that the goal is possible, you must then decide to take action or it won't happen! I had a running joke with an old friend about the fact that by the time he finished analyzing and planning to complete a task, I would have it done already!

When Michael Jordan tried out for his High School basketball team, he was rejected. Instead of giving up his goal of making the team, he sprung into action perfecting his game.

Jack Canfield had the goal of having his *Chicken Soup for the Soul* books reach the top of the *New York Times* bestsellers list. To that end, Jack developed the *"Rule of 5"* which means that he would take five specific actions each day to further his goal of reaching the top of the list.

5. DECIDE TO BREAK IT DOWN

First, write down your goal; your second job is to break down your goal into a series of steps, beginning with steps that are absurdly easy.

~ Fitzhugh Dodson

One of the things that I hear over and over again from people is that they have not achieved the level of success they desire because they don't know where to start; they lack an actionable plan. They get overwhelmed by looking at the entire goal, instead of breaking it down into a series of smaller steps. The result is that they fail to succeed in reaching their goals.

To achieve success, you must make the decision to break down the goal into bite-sized pieces so that it is palatable. Accordingly, I suggest the following:

(a) make a to-do-list with each task forming part of the larger goal

(b) prioritize the to-do-list

(c) ensure that the first items on the list are absurdly easy so that it encourages immediate action

(d) make the list as concise as possible

(e) ensure that the tasks are completed in a timely fashion

6. DECIDE TO PERSEVERE

The will to persevere is often the difference between failure and success.

~ David Sarnoff

Persistence is an extremely important factor in success. Often what distinguishes those who succeed from those who don't is the ability to keep going long after the rest have dropped out. Significant success requires a great deal of effort and a stubborn refusal to quit in the face of repeated failures.

Michael Jordan, the greatest basketball player of all time, admitted that he had missed more than 9,000 shots in his career, had lost almost 300 games and had been trusted to take the game winning shot 26 times and missed. Michael admits, "I've failed over and over and over again in my life. And that is why I succeed...I can accept failure, but I can't accept not trying."

Thomas Edison is a perfect example of a person who exhibited a great deal of persistence and tenacity. Although we don't know for certain how many times he failed before inventing the first long-lasting light bulb, we do know that he tried thousands of times before finally succeeding. As a night owl who does much of her work during the "wee" hours of the morning, I am eternally grateful for Mr. Edison's perseverance!

7. DECIDE TO EXCEED EXPECTATIONS

It's never crowded along the extra mile.

~ Wayne Dyer

Highly successful people simply decide to do more. They not only consistently meet expectations but exceed expectations. Some examples include the following:

(a) Make them feel special. This means customers/clients, employees and partners. Remember birthdays and send them a card or present. Send them something to make them remember you. I am a big believer in gift giving and often send clients flowers, candy or cards to show how much I appreciate them. They are always very pleasantly surprised and also very grateful!

(b) Ask your customers for feedback at every opportunity. Most people will not tell you how you can improve unless you ask. You cannot correct problems that you are not aware of. Offer them a little perk for taking the time to provide you with valuable feedback.

(c) Understand the power of saying thank you. Thank your customers/clients andyour team. Too many times people forget to say a proper thank you and it builds resentment and/or results in lost customers.

(d) Under promise and over deliver. If a job is going to take one week then allow some extra time in your estimate and then surprise your customer by completing it early. I recently had a website created for another book I co-authored. The agency advised that it would be online in two weeks and had it up in one day. I was super excited to see it online so quickly and will definitely do more business with the agency.

(e) Give your staff regular praise and recognition. A few kind words of recognition goes a long way to build trust and loyalty.

(f) Add the "wow factor." I read a story awhile back exemplifying excellent customer service a guest experienced at the Ritz-Carlton. The writer's wife and two kids had spent a few days at the Ritz-Carlton in Florida when, upon their return home, they discovered that their son's beloved stuffed giraffe named Joshie, had gone missing. The child was extremely fond of his Joshie, and was absolutely distraught when faced with the idea of going to sleep without him. So the writer told a white lie to his son: "He's just taking an extra long vacation at the resort." That night, the Ritz-Carlton called to tell the writer that they had found Joshie. The writer came clean to the staff about the story he told his son and asked if they would mind taking a picture of Joshie on a lounge chair by the pool to substantiate his fabricated story. The Loss Prevention Team said they'd do it and a couple of days later they received a package from the hotel. It was the son's Joshie, along with some Ritz-Carlton-branded "goodies" (a frisbee, football, etc.). Also included in the package was a binder that documented Joshie's extended stay at the Ritz. It showed Joshie wearing shades by the pool, driving a golf cart on the beach. Joshie was even issued a Ritz-Carlton ID badge, made an honorary member of the Loss Prevention Team, and was allowed to help by taking a shift in front of the security monitors. This certainly wowed the writer and his wife and made their son very happy indeed.

CONCLUSION

In the end, it's not the years in your life that count. It's the life in your years.

~ Abraham Lincoln

No one knows how many years they have to live their life, so it is important to pack as much life into them as you can. You can sit on the sidelines and let life pass you by because you are afraid to reach for your dreams, or you can decide your way to success one decision at a time!

ABOUT JANICE

Janice is a member of the firm Glaholt LLP, practicing exclusively in commercial litigation with specific concentration in the construction law field. She has represented suppliers of construction-related materials, contractors, developers and surety companies in the construction industry.

Janice frequently speaks to the legal community and industry groups on construction law issues. She has been a member of the Ontario Bar Association Construction Law Executive since 2001 and is currently Past Chair. Janice is a Trustee of the OBA Foundation and Council Member of the Ontario Bar Association and the Canadian Bar Association. Janice has been part-time Professor at George Brown College.

Previous authorships for Janice include a chapter in Jack Canfield's best-selling book, *The Soul of Success*. Janice was awarded the Editor's Choice Award for her contribution.

Janice obtained her B.A. (Hons.) from the University of Toronto and her LL.B. from Osgoode Hall Law School.

You can connect with Janice at:
janicequigg@me.com
Twitter: @quiggphotos

Today, there are more opportunities for entrepreneurs and business startups than ever before in history. There's more money in circulation and more demand for products and services than ever.

BY JIM COLLYER

LESSONS FROM THE MASTERS

No One Makes it to the Top Alone

Believe it or not, most people are convinced that *"luck"* is the key factor in determining success. Urban legends about successful people support this nonsense. I'm sure you've heard plenty of success stories where someone just got lucky, was in the right place at the right time, or how they just accidentally stumbled and fell into success.

The thing about all urban legends is, they are completely false. Success doesn't occur through happenstance. A lot of things have to come together in a short period of time for success to occur. Luck has little to do with it. *Success isn't a gimme, you've got to put in the work.*

Today, there are more opportunities for entrepreneurs and business startups than ever before in history. There's more money in circulation and more demand for products and services than ever. And with today's technology, it's never been easier to reach the market. There's never been a better time to make money.

The problem is, even with all this opportunity, it's never been harder to make a living.

I cringe every time someone asks me for advice on "how to make it" in the business world. When it comes to success, there are two things I know for sure. No one ever falls to the top of a mountain and no one ever got there alone. I can only offer one suggestion: find a mentor.

On May 29, 1953, Edwin Hillary became the first man to reach the summit of Mount Everest. It was one of the great human achievements of the 20th century along with Adm. Robert Peary reaching the North Pole and Neil Armstrong's walking on the moon.

> ## While asking for advice can be difficult or even scary, in the end it's your best chance for improvement.

There's a lot more to the story than reaching the top of highest peak on earth. Hillary would have never made it to the top of Everest without the help of Sherpa guide Tenzing Norgay and the expedition support staff, numbering nearly 400.

Early in the expedition, Tenzing's quick work with a rope and an ice ax prevented Hillary from falling to his death in a large crevasse. During the final ascent to the summit, Tenzing led most of the way, stepping aside just a few feet from the summit to allow Hillary to be the first man to reach the top of the world.

Edmund Hillary was a master at mountaineering, but Tenzing Norgay was better. At the time, Tenzing had more experience on Everest than any man alive, including three expeditions in the 1930's and a world high altitude climbing record set the previous year. When all the fanfare started after the climb, Hillary repeated emphasized the important part Tenzing played in reaching the top of the mountain.

When Hillary was knighted by Queen Elizabeth he told the Queen, "I could have never made it without Tenzing, no man gets to the top alone."

It doesn't matter if you're climbing a mountain or climbing the success ladder, no one gets to the top alone.

What do George Washington, Pablo Picasso, and Steve Jobs have in common? All of them had something mutual between them – they sought the advice and expertise of masters to help them along the way. None of them tried to make it alone. Studies show that nearly every successful person has followed the advice and mentorship of a master.

The rapid pace of change in today's market is only increasing. We are quickly changing from a product-based to a service-based economy. The security once offered by big industry is fading. Self-employment is on the increase, more by necessity than choice.

There are over one million new business startups every year. The failure rate for business startups is staggering with 32 percent of businesses failing within the first two years. A lot of this failure is attributed to people thinking they have all the answers and not seeking advice from those who have already succeeded.

It is so important to seek the advice of people who have already achieved success. Regardless of which genre your business fits in, chances are, your product or services are not unique. Someone else is already producing a similar product or service somewhere. Someone has already succeeded in what you are trying to do. These people have a wealth of knowledge that is easily tapped into. Why reinvent the wheel? Someone's already achieved the goal you are seeking. Mentors are like guides who tell us how to climb the mountain. If we follow them, we will be able to surmount that mountain ourselves quicker than we imagined.

It's true, people who seek the advice of mentors achieve their goals faster and their lifetime earnings will average $750,000 more than the person who tries to make it alone. Experienced and educated mentors are the golden geese of the new economy.

Ask yourself this simple question, "Could I achieve my goal faster with the advice of someone who has already achieved this same goal?" I think you'll agree that a good mentor can help you succeed at a faster pace. Not only will you learn new things from a mentor, but you will also be able to take better advantage of what you already know.

The old saying "every master starts out a disaster" is quite true. In the beginning of my sales career, I was a disaster. In fact, I had a hard time selling anything. I knew very little about business and even less about what made people buy. I was working harder than ever and getting nowhere fast.

I wanted to know why some people appear to be naturally successful? Year after year, they seem to stumble into opportunities while others who work just as hard had nothing to show for their efforts.

I started reading every book I could get my hands on concerning business and success. I listened to countless webinars and began attending success seminars all across the country. While my business was improving, I still wasn't getting the rapid results I want. Finally, I gave in and started asking successful people to mentor me and tell me how they did it.

Asking people for their advice kept me from wasting a lot of energy on ideas that didn't work. Their suggestions not only gave me important insight, but also reinforced the success patterns I already possessed. I began to see positive results immediately. Over the next few months, my persistence in asking questions brought me a lifetime of business knowledge.

What I discovered was success in business isn't magic; it's based on knowledge and skills that can be learned by anyone.

I've found if you want to have a mentor, all you have to do is ask. Go to the people you admire and tell them that you admire their success and would like to be successful like them someday. Ask if you can learn from them. Ask them if they would mind answering a few questions you have. I've never had anyone turn me down when I asked for advice with politeness and sincerity.

Asking questions is difficult because many of us look at it as a weakness. It's hard to act macho when you're begging for advice. But don't be afraid to ask questions, no matter how good at business you've become. I've asked them all—the up, down, and sideways questions. While asking for advice can be difficult or even scary, in the end it's your best chance for improvement. Having a mentor is a good idea, but having multiple mentors is even better. A mentor is someone whose hindsight can become your foresight. Usually it's never one piece of advice that propels us to a higher level of success, but rather a combination of information from several mentors.

Learning from someone with more experience than you will allow you to access their accumulated wisdom and learn from their mistakes. But don't expect mentors to be able to solve all of your problems. They can't. Every problem is unique and the solution to that problem is also unique.

The purpose of mentoring isn't to have someone tell you which products and services to sell. No one can teach you which products and services will sell and which ones won't, because no one knows. However, we can teach you how to present, promote, and sell your products with the highest probability of success.

The role of mentoring is to help you make sense of your own experiences and to apply the knowledge gained from those experiences to find a solution to your current problem.

Choosing a good mentor is not an easy task. I've been fortunate to have had several good mentors in my life. Not all of my mentors have been success gurus. Some of the best mentors I've had were little more than successful small business owners. All good mentors have similar characteristics.

- They are experts in your field or a similar field.
- They have a willingness to share their wisdom and expertise.
- They have a positive outlook on life. They look for opportunities in difficult times.
- They believe in continued personal growth and are constantly learning.
- They seek the opinions of others.
- They tell the truth, even when it hurts, without criticizing.

Where do you find good mentors? Just look around you. There are plenty of good mentors everywhere. Who do you know who's already living the life style you would like to have? Watch them, see what they do, and do the same. People can be your mentors without even realizing they are doing so. It can be as simple as observing and emulating the people you admire. I've had a lot of mentors who never realized they were mentoring me.

While it's always best to have face-to-face mentoring, you no longer have to limit yourself to mentors who live in the same city as you. More and more people are using the Internet for mentoring. Not only is it cost-effective, the Internet allows access to mentors and coaches worldwide. Oftentimes talking to someone who you don't have a personal relationship with, but who's been through a similar experience, can be more constructive than with someone you know. Yes, there are a lot of great mentors on the Internet, but there are just as many whose advice isn't worth following even if it's for free. If you're seeking mentorship on the Internet, make sure your mentor is offering substance and not merely inspiration and enthusiasm. Don't misunderstand me. Enthusiasm is great if you're a cheerleader, but business is a little more complicated than that.

We live in a society that seeks instant gratification in all aspects of life. We don't want to work for anything. The Internet feeds on this desire for instant success and is packed with risk-free, guaranteed opportunities.

Not all of these opportunities are bad, some of these programs offer a good product for a reasonable price. Most of them, however, have little or no value at all. Even though it's generally understood that these systems don't help much, people still flock to buy them like lemmings following each other over a cliff. It's much easier to sell the idea of easy success than the reality of the hard work and patience required to succeed.

A mentor is not a system or a blueprint purchased on the Internet. A good mentor is someone you can connect with, who knows you and your personal struggles for success. Make sure your mentor's experience is congruent with the goals you wish to achieve. For example, if you want advice on how to run a successful restaurant, I wouldn't seek advice from a long-haul trucker. Trucking is too far removed from restaurant ownership to be of any value.

Mentorship can only help when you listen to your mentors and implement the strategies you are taught However, the truth is, people rarely do what they are told nor do they always do what they know is the best practice. Instead, most people will hang on to their old, ineffective methods of trying to achieve success. Albert Einstein said, "Insanity is doing the same thing over and over again and expecting different results." If you're not satisfied with your current results, find yourself a mentor. Remember, it's okay to communicate to your mentor what you need for your success. (So long as you still listen to your mentor!)

A lot of people hesitate to get a mentor because they're waiting for the perfect mentor to arrive. But sadly, the perfect teacher never arrives. Even a less than perfect mentor is better than no mentor at all. Just a reminder, regardless of which mentor or master you follow, in the end the only person really invested in your success is you. So, quit waiting. After all, it's always too late to wait and never too late to start winning.

ABOUT JIM

Jim Collyer is a sales executive, trainer, and bestselling author living in Nevada. Collyer has received the "Editors Choice" award, the "Pinnacle" award, and the "Moving America Forward" award.

Growing-up in the small logging and mining towns of Idaho, Collyer began his long, successful career in business at the age of ten, mowing lawns and delivering newspapers. Even at that early age, Jim had a talent for recognizing opportunities, implementing strategies, and making money.

Collyer's career includes numerous business start-ups, wholesale and retail, business consulting and coaching, contracting, logging, mining, writing, and publishing.

Jim Collyer has presented seminars and spoken in front of thousands of people. He writes articles, blogs, and books on success and business, all based on his own personal, hands-on experience. His writings are "specific" methods, techniques and approaches to doing business that anyone can use to start a business or expand their current sales.

For more information, visit http://jccollyer.com, and learn how Jim Collyer can help you and your team get trained, motivated and on your way towards meeting your sales goals.

BY PATRICIA E. TAKACS, DMD

THE EARLY BIRD CATCHES THE WORM

I have been frequently asked how I have been able to be successful in dentistry in light of the change in the economy since 2008. In addition to my main dental practice, established in 1984, we have recently opened two additional satellite offices, one in 2011 and the second in 2013, and currently employ 49 exceptional team members. I really cannot give a succinct answer because I don't really know. I had no business background in undergraduate school, except for Accounting I, which I despised. And dental school definitely does not prepare you to open up your own business, yet we are encouraged to do so. Perhaps it was the nine months of working for a dentist after graduation that gave me the impetus to open up my own office. I found myself being his dentist assistant as he would fall behind every day because he literally could not quit talking. Plus, his wife was the office manager and that was a nightmare. Whatever pushed me out the door of comfort into the world of the unknown, I can with honesty say that the ups and the downs of owning your own business are worth it.

I was extremely fortunate to have had the support of a local bank VP whose father owned the bank. He encouraged me to venture on my own, with the bank's backing, instead of buying in to the previously-mentioned dentist practice. Starting out with only one employee, "my girl Friday", we answered phones, greeted patients, walked the streets and hung pamphlets on neighborhood doors, and worked from sun-up to past sundown. Slowly we were able to build up our reputation as being accommodating, young, enthusiastic, and painless. I will give credit when credit is due to my former dentist boss— who taught me that the single most important procedure you can do to be successful in dentistry is give a painless injection. Those words ring so true today, as they have all of my career. I have taught my hygienists and my associate doctors the importance of this and believe we do make it easier for patients to accept treatment, because they do not fear the "needle."

There were times in this thirty-two-year journey that I thought we were not going to make it. Despite having plenty of patients and a good dental team, I failed to be fiscally responsible to the business, allowing patients to pay when they wanted or what they could, instead of having strong financial arrangements. It was at this time that I hired a "coach", a former dentist who had been in the trenches and was successful, as he was able to pull himself out of bankruptcy by employing the principles he taught. Education has always been a very important part of my life in dentistry, and I still recall going to LaJolla, California, and being mesmerized by the words of Dr. Dick Barnes. I consider him the first of my several mentors who was responsible for our philosophy of continuing to treat patients as you would expect to be treated, no exceptions. And I believe that bringing team members is imperative, as well, so that they can also hear the messages that are being espoused. Education is key, for front office team, to hygienists and to assistants, as dentistry has evolved and changed dramatically over the years.

Continuing education that is mandatory has the positive affect of bringing team members together outside regular hours and in fun and exciting places, such as San Francisco, Destin, FL, and Phoenix. Some may argue about the cost of this, but the intangibles of confidence, trust and self esteem, are priceless.

I remember in my early years of working in dentistry, that dental meetings and study clubs were actually bitch sessions for dentists, ranting about how 'unbusy' they were, or that the patient would not do the treatment that the dentist had recommended, or that their "staff" was ungrateful. I would sit and be silent because I loved my job, my team and my patients. It was our responsibility to educate our patients as to the best dentistry for them and allow them options to care. I never was one to tell the patient what they had to do, but rather what they could do.

We must take care of our patients and listen to them. Relationship development is so very important and is the crux of our success. Our goal is to provide a comfortable environment and excellent dentistry that is affordable. We provide hot coffee and tea, bottled water, and fresh baked cookies to our patients every day. The smells associated with a dental office are masked by scented candles and fresh flowers. Warm blankets, hot paraffin, and gentle hand massages are also part of the amenities that make us stand out from others. There is a reason why we have been in the top three for the past five years for Best Dentist Office, and these last two years being named Number One.

All dentists are not created equal. We may all attend accredited dental colleges but once you leave the confines of a university and start your own business, the dentists that succeed are the ones that never stop learning. I had a former associate who joined my practice immediately out of dental school and believed that his dental education was complete. I coaxed and cajoled him to take continuing education in any of the array of new technologies and was refused. Over time I realized that being mediocre was not going to work in my practice. Just in the past 15 years we have witnessed digital dentistry taking over. 3-D imaging and the ability to fabricate crowns chairside is but one of the many new procedures being done in our office. CT scans, digital x-rays and paperless offices add to the fray. Providing various modes of sedation dentistry is a boon to patients that have lived their life in fear of going to even get their teeth cleaned. Being trained to place implants to replace missing teeth, rotary endodontics or root canals that can be finished in one appointment and invisible braces, these are just a few of the many services that we provide that were not available 20 years ago. Yet dentists who do not learn will still be doing the dentistry that they were doing 20 years ago, and they will be the ones that are complaining because they are not busy.

Our office is a comprehensive dental office and it has been since Day 1. Not only do we look at the teeth and the gums, but we look at all aspects of the mouth, the tonsils, the tongue and the cheeks. There are so many clues that are hidden in the mouth that can lead to, or be responsible for, diseases of the body. We have all heard or read of the relationship between gum disease and heart disease and stroke. It comes down to the inflammation that is persistent in our bodies. The mouth is the gateway to our overall physical and emotional self. I have been asked why I have all of our patients, even children, fill out a sleep questionnaire. Simple. Sleep apnea, if undiagnosed, will lead to increased chances for heart attacks, stroke, diabetes, GERD and dementia, to name a few. And sleep apnea in children is often misdiagnosed as ADHD and consequently the inappropriate use of medications.

Children who snore is not a normal. It is the responsibility of dentists to evaluate children at a young age and check the position and size of the jaws, the height of the palate (roof of the mouth), tonsils and a history of tubes in the ears. Referrals to ENT and orthodontists at a young age is imperative. So what in the world does the mouth have to do with sleep apnea? The answer is airway, airway and airway. We check the size of the tonsils and the uvula, the appearance of the tongue, i.e., large, scalloped, etc., size and position of the jaws, worn-down teeth, and abfractions at the gumline on the teeth. All are indicative of potential sleep disturbance breathing. We also thoroughly review the health history, particularly paying close attention to the above diseases and the medicines that they are taking. Chances of sleep apnea being present increase as the number of medications being taken increases.

Let's take the case of my associate dentist, Jill, and her three-year-old daughter, Riley. After presenting the signs, symptoms and consequences of sleep apnea, Jill took her daughter to an ENT to evaluate her tonsils and adenoids, Tubes were to be placed in her ears, again, and Jill wanted to be sure that this was appropriate. She felt that Riley potentially had sleep apnea. After the removal of her tonsils and adenoids, which the ENT had never seen ones so large in a child her age, Riley was able to sleep through the night, her attitude during the day improved, and she no longer needed tubes in her ears. Jill and I are convinced that Riley may have been misdiagnosed and incorrectly treated if I had not gotten involved in sleep.

Take the case of Barbara, to whom I recommended a home sleep study after her questionnaire had several positive remarks. She also admitted to feeling tired throughout the day, but thought she slept well. Her home study indicated the tendency for sleep apnea so she was referred to a sleep center. Long story short, she has never slept better in her oral appliance, feels great, and thanks our office for saving her life!

John was a different story altogether. Despite all indicators including being overweight and on several blood pressure medicines, he refused to even consider that he could have sleep apnea. Yet he never felt rested. Finally, after a year he returned and agreed to a home study. It was positive, of course, so he was referred to a sleep center. The sleep physician took one look at his score after his sleep test at the center and told him, "I'm surprised that you're even alive." His index was 189 which basically means that 189 times/hour he would quit breathing for a short to a significant length of time. He now wears a CPAP and I recently saw him for his hygiene visit and he remarked to me that he has never felt better and thanks us for saving his life. These patients are why I am passionate about dentistry. We not only can give a patient a beautiful smile, healthy gums and white teeth, but are also instrumental in saving lives.

So, as a comprehensive dental office, blood pressures are regularly taken. There have been several occasions that we have needed to send the patient to their doctor after discovery of unexpected high blood pressure. There have also been refusals to take blood pressure. Not sure what they are trying to hide unless they don't want to face the facts.

We also routinely perform oral cancer screening exams, both visually, with palpation, and with the use of a Velscope. The velscope will illuminate suspected areas of pre-cancer or cancer and help us either refer for a biopsy or re-evaluate in two weeks. A staggering statistic is that oral cancer will kill one person every 24 hours. The five-year survival probability is roughly half of those diagnosed. And HPV16 is one of the main reasons for oral cancers and it is imperative that children are vaccinated at the appropriate age.

As you can now see, not all dentists are equal. I have been fortunate to have been trained with some of the best in our profession and there is still so much more to learn. I will continue to encourage my doctors that work with me to never quit learning. And I will continue to encourage all of my team members to stay abreast of all the changes going on in our profession.

Fast forward to the present and I am happy to say that both of our satellite offices are far exceeding expectations, and are attracting a large number of new patients monthly as well as producing beyond the national average. Both offices were furnished on a shoe string budget especially in light of the state of our economy. We have maintained that conservatism as the offices grow and are fortunate to be in the positive position that we are.

One story is worth relating that pertains to the second satellite office. I received a phone call out of the blue, at my office, and was urged to go see a potential new office building in the fastest growing area of Lexington. We were just in our first full year at the first satellite and I had no intentions of expanding beyond the two offices. Yet, when I entered the office space, I was literally blown away. It was a former dental office spa, nicely appointed and only used for one month. All of the dental plumbing was done so I virtually just needed dental equipment and furniture. That area of the city was the fastest growing and I was afraid that another dentist would come in and take it. So, on a verbal agreement and a handshake, I agreed to a 15-year lease in June of 2012, when the economy was terrible. Risky? Yes. But I felt the investment would be most profitable if we engineered it like our other two offices.

We are doing very well, thanks to the efforts of my amazing dental team of doctors, front office ladies, assistants and hygienists. And I must also thank the dental supply company for working with me to build our vision, along with my new friends at our local bank.

What makes success? Education. Never stop learning so that you will not lose your passion. Work well with your team because together everyone achieves more. Surround yourself with those who share and believe in your vision and your core values. Success breeds success and learning from the best and being mentored and coached by the experts in their field leads to personal, professional, and business growth.

Don't be afraid to take a risk as usually there will be a net to catch you if you fall. Be cognizant that you cannot do it alone, and reward those who have helped you and been beside you along the way. Great teams share their experiences with their patients and provide compassion and competency, and most importantly, trust.

I am blessed to be able to work beside both my son and daughter as they enter the profession of dentistry. I also share my days with my mom, who is "the cookie lady" to our patients, as well as the after-treatment care caller. And as my dad once said as he got me up before the crack of dawn when I was six to find earthworms for our fishing trip, "Trish, plan your work and work your plan. And, remember, the early bird catches the worm."

RIP, Dad...and thank you.

ABOUT PATRICIA

Dr. Trish Takacs is a 1983 graduate from the University of Kentucky College of Dentistry and maintains a private practice in cosmetic and general dentistry - Beaumont Family Dentistry, in Lexington, KY. Her interests lie in reconstruction for patients with worn-down dentition, chronic head and neck pain, and sleep apnea. The primary focus of Beaumont Family Dentistry is to provide comprehensive care for each patient, not limited to oral care needs, but including the overall physical health of each patient.

She and her husband have been married for 33 years and have a son and daughter. Her son is a 2012 graduate of UK College of Dentistry and is an associate at Beaumont Family Dentistry and her daughter will be graduating from the Dental College in 2015. Her outside interests include golf and reading, and hanging out with the family dogs.

BY LINDSAY DICKS

REACHING BILLIONS:

Finding Online Success with Your Business Platform

Imagine you're a store in a shopping mall.

Go a step further – and imagine that you were told with all the certainty in the world that this mall was about to experience traffic of over three billion potential customers – and that they'd all be walking right past your store entrance. Surely you'd be flooded with excitement – especially after you stopped worrying about where all these people were going to park.

More importantly, you'd be thinking about everything you could possibly do to make your store entrance enticing to all those people. What kind of special offer could you make? How could you "dress up" your store to attract their attention (in a good way of course)? What would be the best way to prepare your salespeople to engage this massive horde of people and convert them to paying customers so you could take full advantage of this once-in-a-lifetime opportunity? How could you guarantee that at least one percent of the people coming through the mall would come inside to peruse your wares? After all, one percent would still be *thirty million people.*

Clearly, you would do everything you could to take advantage of this amazing break. Over three billion people? If all of them only spent one dollar with you…you could not only buy that new super-sized television set you've had your eye on, you could buy the factory that made it!

Okay, it's time to stop the imagining. Because the thing is…you don't have to imagine. The shocking fact is that this is a reality *every single day of the year* every day when you're marketing yourself on the Internet, the biggest mall ever made – even if it is only a virtual one.

According to the latest figures from the International Telecomms Union (TCU), 43% of the world's population, over three billion people as I said, are using the Internet in 2015. That figure has increased seven times over since the year 2000, when TCU first began studying the Internet numbers. In America alone, there are 280 million Internet users – an increase of over 17 million from 2014. In other words, massive online growth is still happening, even though most of us think it can't get any bigger. All of this means that, at the very least, you continually have hundreds of millions of people out there available to potentially buy your products or services. And a lot more than that if you're selling to the entire world.

So – like our storekeeper at our imaginary mall - why shouldn't you be incredibly motivated to do everything in your power to get their attention? Unfortunately, hard as it is to believe in this day and age, many marketers, retailers and business leaders still don't understand why it's important to create a viable, vibrant and versatile online strategy that will continually add value to your business and branding.

Although pretty much every company worth its salt has some kind of online presence these days (including even smaller local businesses), most still understand they need to go far beyond the basics to really enjoy Internet marketing success. You can't just create a picture-perfect website with nothing but your basic information on it, and sit back and wait for the online traffic to come your way. Most are not going to be instantly interested in what you have to say – or go out of their way to find you. That's why you have to create a business platform that reaches out through multiple Internet channels and engages the audience you want to reach. Because that is exactly how entrepreneurs and professionals thrive in today's increasingly competitive business environment.

THE FOUNDATION OF YOUR BUSINESS PLATFORM

Why do you need a business platform? Well, in the words of the Harvard Business Review, "Build a better platform, and you will have a decided advantage over the competition. In construction, a platform is something that lifts you up and on which others can stand. The same is true in business."

A business platform is simply a comprehensive plan to promote yourself and what you do in a way that engages those who would be most inclined to buy from you and convert that interest into sales. In a way, it's the same process used when a potential customer wanders onto a car lot. The car salesperson understands this person is already interested in buying a vehicle, and that it's his or her job to engage that person in a conversation ("Can I help you?" "What are you looking for?") that ultimately leads to that person driving one of the vehicles for sale off the lot.

Of course, it's not quite as simple as that. The art of Internet marketing has grown to such an enormous extent that it can often seem like a baffling and bewildering world to master, especially if you're a relative novice to doing anything beyond creating your own website. It's way too easy to get lost in a sea of jargon and the overwhelming number of options.

When you're building your business platform, the important thing to remember is that the basics of salesmanship that are practiced on that car lot still hold true - and that you must build on those basics as you begin to create your own online platform.

For instance, you should be able to easily and quickly answer these questions before you even think about building a business platform:

• Who am I?

Before you pull out your driver's license to answer this simple-sounding question, let me clarify – you want to know who you are in terms of marketing yourself. Are you the friendly, understanding expert who wants to help? Are you a Master of the Universe who attracts disciples with your powerful message? Are you a funny eccentric who entertains but still has impeccable credentials? Personality is key to connecting with people on a human level – and you should use an authentic side of yourself to project a winning one.

• What am I trying to accomplish?

Some build a business platform to sell a product such as a book or promote an event, others build one for the purpose of building prestige and influence. In most cases, it's a combination of both. The more you establish yourself as an expert in your specific industry, the more you are seen as a thought leader and a credible source, and the more people are willing to trust you and take that extra step and buy from you.

• Who is my target audience?

The more accurately you can zero in on the specific demographic who would be most likely to respond to what you do, the more you can customize your messaging to that demographic. And the more specific you can be in your messaging, the better. With everyone out there selling, you want to avoid getting lost in the crowd. You do that by defining the specific type of consumer you're looking to reach and determining what message will best resonate with them, rather than trying to reach everyone at once with a generic message that doesn't engage anyone.

Your business platform's foundation should be built on the answers to those above three questions, as they will inform everything you do from the get-go. When you have all of that in your mind as you move forward, you can ensure that your messaging is consistent and has integrity. You may want to make adjustments along the way, but always remember that what makes a business platform the most effective is the same thing that works for any kind of marketing campaign, on or off the grid: a constant and appealing message that continues to reinforce itself whenever a potential customer encounters it.

That's how companies like Apple and Google built themselves into branding superstars over the years – and how you can do it too.

YOUR PLATFORM'S BUILDING BLOCKS

Once you know what your focus will be for your business platform, it's time to go to work! In this section, we'll discuss the various components that will should go into creating the most powerful platform possible.

• Website

Your website should represent the heart and soul of your business platform – and communicate effectively why you're the person a visitor to your site should buy from. To accomplish all that, you need to have the right *kind* of website, one specifically created to draw in visitors and make them a part of your marketing machine! It should be what we call a Marketing Website™.

Most people like to measure their marketing success by how many prospects click on a link, either through social media, a Google AdWords campaign or a blog perhaps, to their website. That's absolutely important – but what's just as important is if they actually stick around to look at anything! According to Chartbeat, a company that helps companies like *Time* magazine create online content, over half of the visitors to a website spend *less than 15 seconds* on a webpage. You can drive people to a website by using so-called "Clickbait" (a provocative headline that gets people to click on a link), but that actually performs the worst in terms of actually engaging Internet users once they get there.

Again, the more *specific* you can be in terms of who you are and what you have to offer on your website, the more likely visitors will be to check out who you are and what you do. You may not get as much quantity, but you will get a far better level of quality in terms of actually nabbing potential customers. It also helps to have a picture of yourself, professionally taken, on your home page to provide a human connection to your business.

Of course, you want to provide credentials, testimonials and so forth elsewhere on your website, to provide proof of your expertise and authority. But, when it comes to your homepage, the most important thing you can do, in terms of expanding your platform, is *nab the contact information of those who come to visit*.

The best way to do this is not by simply asking people to sign up for updates or a newsletter. No, the most effective way is to offer a free content-driven giveaway (a PDF Special Report, instructional video, etc.) related to your business that offers real, valuable information. When you make this offer, make it a requirement that the person enters his or her first and last name as well as email address. Don't ask for the phone number, as most find that to be too invasive and you'll lose out on a lot of valuable contacts for your marketing list.

While your website is important, its real value, besides selling you and your offerings, is in gathering that marketing list through your giveaway. When implemented correctly, this system should give you an ongoing stream of new contacts who are directly interested in what you're all about – the best kinds of leads to have!

As I mentioned, your Marketing Website™ should be the hub of your business platform.

The following platform components I'm about to mention should all be aimed at driving leads to your website, which is designed to convert those leads to paying customers!

• Content

Another important building block of your business platform is original content that's relevant to your business and newsworthy to the outside world. The fresher the content, the more likely the public is going to be interested in it – the Internet moves fast these days and anything that seems old and generic is quickly bypassed.

This content can take the form of blogs, articles or even videos – and all that content can be used not only on your website, but can be syndicated throughout the Internet, a service we provide for our clients. This is an excellent way to promote your brand and your business across the virtual universe, as long as your content avoids direct selling and, instead, focuses on providing real and useful information. And always, always, *always* provide a link back to your Marketing Website™ in whatever content you generate and place on other sites (where permitted). Again, remember – that website is your platform hub!

• Press Releases

Online press releases are an often overlooked marketing tool – but they can be very effective. And like the content we discussed above, it can be distributed to many other sites at a very affordable cost. Press releases can be created for a myriad of reasons; for example, if you release a book, open a new location, offer a new product or service, etc., you have a perfect opportunity to do a press release.

Press releases add more prestige to your brand; they cement you in the mind of the public as a top-flight business leader; they also help expand your platform to other areas of the Internet, especially in one very significant way that we'll discuss a little later.

• Social Media

The lasting value of social media is that millions of people are already there on the sites and are actively looking for engagement. And it's an incredibly powerful marketing tool: A Brandpoint study found that 68 percent of consumers check out companies on social networking sites before buying.

The problem these days is that there are so many different social media sites that it can be difficult to know where to focus your efforts. Recently, Hootsuite, an application that helps you put out your message simultaneously on various social media accounts, broke down the types of social media sites that are out there and their specific benefits for business marketing. Here are a few of the categories you should be aware of:

- o **Relationship Networks**, such as Facebook, Twitter or LinkedIn (which are all pretty much necessities these days), help you reach those in your network on a more one-on-one level,

- o **Media Sharing Networks**, such as Instagram, Vimeo and YouTube allow you to market with visuals and share content that can reach prospects on an entirely different level,

- o **Review Sites**, such as Yelp and Urbanspoon, are incredibly important for local businesses to leverage good ratings,

- o **Social Publishing** platforms such as Wordpress, Tumblr, Blogger and Medium can provide excellent foundations to post blogs and other content, and finally,

- o **Interest-Based Networks**, such as GoodReads (for book readers), Pinterest (for avid hobbyists of all sorts), and Last.fm (for music lovers) all provide access to powerful niches that may match up with your target audience.

Again, you want to use all these different channels to drive people back to your website.

· Email Marketing

If you've been wondering what to do with those email addresses I suggested you gather with your website, here's your answer. Email marketing campaigns can be amazingly effective in terms of creating relationships with those who have provided you with their contact information. Again, they've already displayed an interest in what you do, which makes them the perfect crowd to communicate with.

Of course, you can use these kinds of emails for direct selling, but I'd advise you only to do that occasionally and only with a special offer or a completely new product or service you're offering – in other words, something they didn't already know about. Ideally, you're providing valuable information along with your marketing, so your recipients think they're getting something out of the deal.

Use this exceptional marketing opportunity to establish a direct relationship. Be personal about yourself, how you're trying to help them and even solicit their opinions on what you should do next. These people have the potential to be your best customers, so you want to make them feel valued – and you also want to pick your brains to find out how you can serve them best.

· Google Search Results

Here's our big finish and the answer to the question, "Why is all of the above online activity so important?" One word: Google. The more content you have out there, the more press releases you syndicate, the more social media activity you engage in, the more engaging and interesting your website is, the higher you will rank in the Google search results (and the results of other search engines such as Bing and Yahoo! as well).

How crucial is that to your business platform? Well, according to the Fleishman-Hillard 2012 Digital Influence Index, a staggering 89% of consumers use online search engines to make their buying selections.

And ultimately, ranking on the first page, if not the first spot, of those search results is what your business platform should be aimed towards. There are, of course, other tricks and tips to make sure your ranking is high – but that's a whole other chapter (if not a book!).

One final word – for you to experience true success with your business platform, you cannot forget mobile. According to Global Web Index, 80% of Internet users now own and use a smartphone to both search on and check out businesses. That means you must build a mobile-friendly website and you should also consider creating a phone app for your business if it's suited to one.

We've covered a lot in this chapter – because there's a great deal to consider when creating a business platform that delivers for you and your business. Remember, however, that millions, if not billions, of potential customers are "walking by" your store in the giant virtual mall called the Internet. Give it your best – and you'll experience more than enough success to have made it all worthwhile!

ABOUT LINDSAY

Lindsay Dicks helps her clients tell their stories in the online world. Being brought up around a family of marketers, but a product of Generation Y, Lindsay naturally gravitated to the new world of on-line marketing. Lindsay began freelance writing in 2000 and soon after launched her own PR firm that thrived by offering an in-your-face "Guaranteed PR" that was one of the first of its type in the nation.

Lindsay's new media career is centered on her philosophy that "people buy people." Her goal is to help her clients build a relationship with their prospects and customers. Once that relationship is built and they learn to trust them as the expert in their field, then they will do business with them. Lindsay also built a proprietary process that utilizes social media marketing, content marketing and search engine optimization to create online "buzz" for her clients that helps them to convey their business and personal story. Lindsay's clientele spans the entire business map and ranges from doctors and small business owners to Inc. 500 CEOs.

Lindsay is a graduate of the University of Florida. She is the CEO of CelebritySites™ an online marketing company specializing in social media and online personal branding. Lindsay is recognized as one of the top online marketing experts in the world and has co-authored more than 25 bestselling books alongside authors such as Steve Forbes, Richard Branson, Brian Tracy, Jack Canfield (creator of the *Chicken Soup for the Soul* series), Dan Kennedy, Robert Allen, Dr. Ivan Misner (founder of BNI), Jay Conrad Levinson (author of the *Guerilla Marketing* series), Leigh Steinberg and many others, including the breakthrough hit *Celebrity Branding You!*

She has also been selected as one of America's PremierExperts™ and has been quoted in *Forbes, Newsweek, The Wall Street Journal, USA Today*, and *Inc. magazine* as well as featured on NBC, ABC, and CBS television affiliates – speaking on social media, search engine optimization and making more money online. Lindsay was also recently brought on FOX 35 News as their Online Marketing Expert.

Lindsay, a national speaker, has shared the stage with some of the top speakers in the world, including Brian Tracy, Lee Milteer, Ron LeGrand, Arielle Ford, Leigh Steinberg, Dr. Nido Qubein, Dan Sullivan, David Bullock, Peter Shankman and many others. Lindsay was also a Producer on the Emmy-winning film, *Jacob's Turn*, and sits on the advisory board for the Global Economic Initiative.

You can connect with Lindsay at:

Lindsay@CelebritySites.com

www.twitter.com/LindsayMDicks

www.facebook.com/LindsayDicks

BY JAMES DICKS

BUILD A BIGGER, BETTER BUSINESS WITH FACEBOOK!

Anyone can do it! Build a Bigger, Better Business with Facebook!

If you are not advertising on Facebook, you should be!

The number one thing I discuss with all my business-consulting clients is the most important. People buy people, unless you are a Fortune 500 company (and you have deep pockets to build a brand), then your personality is key.

You will want to make sure that you are utilizing your brand (you) on your Facebook page. The number one thing I see businesses doing wrong with their Facebook pages is the easiest thing to fix. Make sure you complete your profile 100%. Fill out all of the information that you can. Nothing should be blank: include your address, business hours, contact information, phone number, website, and a description – both long and short.

After completing your profile, you'll want to create a custom web address for your company's page. You can only make this change one time, so be sure to select a URL that will always represent your business. For example, my business page's web address looked like the following before I updated it: https://www.Facebook.com/Dnapulse-575685459252191/.

When I changed it on Facebook, it now looks like: https://www.Facebook.com/Dnapulse.

Let's talk about the two pictures you see on the top of every Facebook page. Those are your profile picture and cover photo. Be sure to use a cover photo (the larger image displayed on the page) that is formatted correctly and uses the right dimensions. Also, keep in mind that your profile photo will cover the bottom left hand side of the cover photo. Many businesses use a cover photo that has text in the lower left corner that ends up being covered by the profile photo.

I have seen some unique cover photos that use a profile picture that has graphics that make it look integrated into the cover photo, essentially creating one large seamless photo. My suggestion to most of my clients is to use a profile photo that has you in it (people buy people), and then your cover photo can be something that creates a call to action (CTA). You would be surprised at how many businesses miss the fact that the cover photo takes up 25% of the fold (the page), so use the cover photo to drive home your offer or list building opportunity. Use the CTA button in the cover photo.

Page admins can select from a group of call-to-action buttons — like Shop Now or Sign Up — to add to the top of their page. The calls to action available are:

- Book Now
- Call Now
- Contact Us
- Send Message
- Use App
- Play Game
- Shop Now
- Sign Up
- Watch Video
- Send Email
- Learn More

If you want to be creative and use something else you can create a custom tab directly under this CTA button and then use your cover photo to drive attention. For example, one of my clients gives away a free demo of their software. They have an arrow in the cover photo that points directly to the tab that says free demo. The cover photo says 1-click, 2-download, 3-free, with a big red arrow pointing to the button to click. It's a great way to use the majority of what people see (cover photo) when they first hit your Facebook page.

When selecting a cover photo, make sure to use the right size and more importantly the right format, so that you end up with a very clear high res image. Below is recommended specifications from Facebook:

PROFILE PICTURE:

- Must be at least 180x180 pixels.
- Will be cropped to fit a square.

COVER PHOTO:

- Must be at least 399 pixels wide and 150 pixels tall.
- Loads fastest as an sRGB JPEG file that's 851 pixels wide, 315 pixels tall and less than 100 kilobytes.

For profile pictures and cover photos with your logo or text, you may get a better result using a PNG file.

Facebook automatically resizes and formats your photos when you upload them. To help make sure your photos appear in the highest possible quality, try these tips:

- Resize your photo to one of the following supported sizes:

Regular photos:	720px, 960px, 2048px (width)
Cover photos:	851px by 315px

- If you use a 2048px photo, make sure to select the **High Quality** option when you upload it.
- To avoid compression when you upload your cover photo, make sure the file size is less than 100KB.
- Save your image as a JPEG with an sRGB color profile.

Next on our to-do list is to make sure your page is verified. When you browse around Facebook you will notice that some of the pages you visit have a blue check mark next to the title inside the cover photo. The blue check mark was originally reserved for celebrities, etc., but is much more widely used now. Sometimes the check mark will be grayed out or gray instead of blue, but they both mean the page is verified. By doing this you automatically show people visiting your site that you've been verified. It's a very easy process that you can do by:

1. Click Settings at the top of your page.

2. From General, click Page Verification.

3. Click Verify this Page, then click Get Started.

4. Enter a publicly listed phone number for your business, your country and language.

5. Click Call Me Now to allow Facebook to call you with a verification code.

Done! It's that simple. The deliverability of your content will also increase slightly through organic reach when you do this. We'll talk about paid and organic reach in more detail shortly. Once you have completed the above you have now taken care of the basics, I certainly do more for my clients, but I wanted to make sure I hit all the high points for you as a beginner's road map of what you need to be accomplishing on Facebook.

Now that you have a Facebook presence, you need to make sure that it is very easy to see and navigate from your web page. I was on a call with a client recently that had no access to his Facebook from his web site. I looked everywhere, worse yet I had no idea he even had a Facebook for his business until we talked. Even then, we both had a hard time finding it. Be sure that you have it linked along with your other social media channels on your web site.

We are now ready to talk about content for your Facebook. You can utilize your existing content and start breaking that up and sharing that on Facebook. Facebook generally shares less than 1% of your content to those that like your page. Facebook wants you to boost your content (paid) and enables you to choose followers or to create a new custom audience to deliver your content to. When you are posting content be sure to utilize the linking strategy! If you like a page, you can link that page in your posts. For example, DNAPulse likes Harley Davidson (one of my clients). So, when I post on DNAPulse's Facebook and want to mention Harley I would use the @ sign (@harleydavidson). When I do that, I get a pop up of Facebook pages that I can link to. This will help in organic deliverability of your content.

You will also want to use a # (hashtag). I advise using only one, no need to use more, the # is really more a twitter thing. Facebook users do use them, but you'll be penalized for using too many.

I am a big fan of testing as many variables in a controlled environment as I can. Once I do that it's all about scalability.

Let me give you an example. One of my clients was spending the majority of their budget on traditional media outlets, primarily print media, magazines, etc. We started them on Facebook and immediately started to generate leads. The client started at an average of $1,000 per lead generated, and a 3.2:1 return on investment. Now they have shifted almost all of the marketing budget to Facebook and are at about $16-$18 per lead acquisition and doing 6.2:1 return on investment. It's not hard to see where the company should continue to focus its marketing efforts.

The real question comes in whether they see an increase in sales conversion and value. I am a huge proponent of spending your marketing dollars to a diminishing point of return. There are only a few reasons to test and spend marketing dollars across other mediums if you have not spent to a diminishing point of return on the current channels that are producing a great return. One of those reasons is that you want a better sales conversion number, not lead conversion number.

But let's focus on lead conversion first, because if you don't get the leads you have no one to sell to anyway. Taking the above example, say you go from $1,000 per lead conversion to $20 and you are happy with that result, who wouldn't be? Then, why go anywhere else? I suggest get as many of the $20 lead conversions as you can while you are able to. Spend until you see the number become unacceptable, then pull back and look toward other media channels.

If you want to sell on Facebook, the best way to do that is by delivering a solution to a known problem that your client or ideal customer is having. Help educate them on how to solve it, and then train and support them on that solution. This type of engagement will not only foster a sale, but also help maintain loyalty. The true measure of a successful business is the success of its customers. It is the longevity and relationship with that customer that will create that extended customer lifetime value.

The last thing I want to share with you is what I use to create more organic engagement: Video. Why video? Video gives us motion, which catches our attention—the video brings a message to life.

Facebook wanted to become the leader in video views. On Facebook, prior to last year, YouTube was still the leader of video views on Facebook. Facebook set out to become the leader in that space. The first thing they did was spend 100 million dollars on compression technology. They wanted to not only surpass YouTube, but they wanted to deliver high quality, high definition video without the hassle and frustration of buffering. It worked.

Last year they surpassed YouTube's close to a billion views daily. Facebook has more than 8 billion views daily on Facebook now. So what's next for Facebook Video? Facebook wants to be the leader in video views across all channels, like YouTube used to be.

The reason I like using video is simple, Facebook will deliver my video content to more people that like my page organically. Whereas written posted content may be delivered organically to less than 1% of the people who like my page, Facebook will deliver my video content to upwards of 30% of the people that like my page organically. That creates more engagement and will ultimately foster sales and growth.

What type of things do I use in my videos for my clients and myself? Anything, but remember, "people buy people." So, that should give you the first clue: be in the video. Make sure the videos are less than 30 seconds—20 to 25 seconds are better. No text in first 3 seconds, after that your web site or a CTA is fine; make sure that the first 3 seconds are engaging. I have clients use a newer smart phone; take the video in landscape (camera sideways), and have customers talk about their experiences. Show your business off inside and out, talk with employees, the sky's the limit and so is the engagement, especially if you hit a home run and score a viral video post.

ABOUT JAMES

James Dicks has spent more than 25 years building business through marketing practices and experience only garnered through real world application. James is a McGraw-Hill international best selling author and has been seen on all major affiliates around the country including ABC, NBC, CBS, FOX, and CNBC.

As a consultant/contractor and owner operator, James' forte is in marketing and creating brand awareness. As an entrepreneur, he has managed all aspects of business growth, from working with nearly a thousand people to running a business with more than one hundred and fifty employees.

James is a strong believer in the longevity of a customer. It's not just customer acquisition but customer loyalty, that creates winning combinations which will ultimately prove positive for a company's bottom line growth.

James brings his technology background to DNA Pulse where he serves as CEO. He specializes in "out of the box" thinking to successfully integrate the latest technology with business sales and marketing goals. James specializes in using this technology background and experience to help businesses bridge the gap of traditional advertising and social media advertising. To do this, DNA Pulse focuses its core competencies on new media technologies such as mobile media advertising and marketing, as well as near horizon media opportunities – such as location-based advertising.

James is a member of a national Information Technology subcommittee for an office of the Department of Defense, where he collaborates with other technology industry leaders that collectively foster technology advancements and integration.

As both a former Marine and dedicated family man, James strives to make a positive difference in the lives of every person he meets.

BY LEASHA WEST, MSFS, CHFC®, CASL®, NSSA®, CLTC, MDRT

HAVE YOUR CAKE AND RETIRE TOO!

If you're like most, you've made plans to get you TO retirement, but what plans have you made to get you THROUGH retirement? If you're retired or retiring soon, keep reading…. by carefully planning in key areas of retirement, your standard of living can be maintained to support your lifestyle. Yes, really.

You may be wondering how you can uphold your monthly income in retirement, avoid going broke if you become frail, secure an emergency fund, not to mention select the best Medicare plan and maximize your Social Security.

Chances are also good that your taxable accounts [i.e., IRA, annuities, 401(k), etc.] are likely to pass as fully taxable to your beneficiaries. With a little planning, these taxable accounts can be inherited tax-free and the IRS will be paid the legal minimum requirement – no more, no less.

THE SACRED 7 OF RETIREMENT

Planning in the key areas which I call the 'Sacred 7 of Retirement', ensures your golden years will be free from worry and unnecessary financial stress.

The Sacred 7 are: Monthly Income, Medicare, Social Security, Investments, Long Term Care, Estate Planning and Taxes. These are the main categories and several have subcategories.

Sacred 7 of Retirement
1. Monthly income
2. Medicare
3. Social Security
4. Investments
5. Long Term Care
6. Estate Planning
7. Taxes

#1: MONTHLY INCOME

Monthly income usually does not continue upon retiring. Surprisingly, most folks don't have a clearly defined income plan much less know what a monthly income plan is!

A monthly income plan involves synthesizing all of your retirement accounts, and addresses the following points:

- Protection from market volatility

- Keeps pace with inflation

- Guarantees against outliving income

- Accessibility for unforeseen expenses

- Eliminate risks from lawsuits / creditors

A solid monthly income plan will provide you and your spouse an income stream for life that you can count on in any economy.

#2: MEDICARE

DO NOT EVER, EVER, EVER DO ANYTHING MEDICARE RELATED BY PHONE, MAIL OR ONLINE - EVER.

Medicare is a beast, it's just that simple. You cannot and should not try to do this on your own. I've seen tremendous mistakes and witnessed retirees overpaying for Medicare Supplements and prescriptions because they enrolled over the phone, corresponded via mail or signed up online without understanding all of their options. I've also watched retirees nearly go bankrupt over medical bills because they were not set up on Medicare properly. This is serious business folks!

It's critical that you meet IN PERSON with an independent Medicare specialist that will take the time to explain all of your options and help you select the plan that's most appropriate for your situation – every person is different.

In addition, there are many complicated rules and regulations imposed by the Centers of Medicare and Medicaid (CMS) that only an experienced, independent Medicare specialist will know. For example, if you turn 65 and DO NOT sign up for a prescription plan (PART D), regardless of whether you are taking prescriptions or not – you will be fined for NOT signing up, which is a lifetime penalty. I'm serious. You must meet with an independent Medicare specialist.

#3: SOCIAL SECURITY

One of the most important financial decisions for a retiree is when to begin taking Social Security. Did you know there are 8000+ unique Social Security claiming strategies that exist? Those who are aware consult exclusively with a certified National Social Security Advisor® (NSSA®) and are handsomely rewarded with additional retirement income over their lifetime.

The majority of retirees treat Social Security like a "land grab" and take it as soon as they are eligible at age 62; however, failure to collaborate with a certified NSSA®, and "run the numbers" can result in a serious loss of monthly and lifetime income. Planning and implementing the right Social Security strategy is one of the cornerstones in facilitating a successful retirement and harnessing as much monthly income as possible. You've only got one shot to get it right –

A Word on Local Social Security Offices

> Be very cautious of financial professionals
> hosting local Social Security seminars
> or workshops; this is the latest craze
> for annuity hunters.
>
> To locate an NSSA® in your area visit:
> www.nationalsocialsecurityassociation.com

Local Social Security offices help file and service routine claims, and process information requests. They are not going to review and build out a lifetime income plan for you. Essentially, they are "order-takers",

NOT moneymakers or wealth-protectors. The Social Security staff is typically not allowed to tailor customized claiming strategies, or to offer Social Security recommendations to single, widowed, divorced or married couples.

WORK ONLY WITH A CERTIFIED NATIONAL SOCIAL SECURITY ADVISOR®

#4: INVESTMENTS

Prior to retirement, most folks are working feverishly to save money, reduce debt, mitigate risks and hope they have enough money to live on when they stop working. Is this you?

Ideally, once you retire, you should not be taking ANY risks with your money. You heard it right, NO risk after retiring or preferably sooner – there are many alternative investments that are safe and provide a respectable growth rate and NO, the bank is NOT one of them.

There are two life phases in which your money should be placed appropriately depending on what phase of life you're in. The two life phases are: Working Years and Retirement Years (presumably not working).

Phase 1: Working Years – Accumulation and Growth

This phase includes all years prior to retiring; during this time you are working to ACCUMULATE for retirement, pay for mortgages, student loans, saving for your kid's college and pretty heavy on debt. Most workers have an employer-sponsored retirement plan like a 401(k), 403(b), or some similar pre-tax vehicle in which a portion of your paycheck is allocated; several employers match a portion of your contribution to the retirement plan.

NOTE: NEVER contribute any more to your employer-sponsored plan than what your company matches. EVER!

For example, if your company matches 100% for the first 3% contributed and 50% for contributions up to 6%, only contribute up to 6%, nothing more.

An employer-sponsored plan is a great start; however, it's fully taxable and won't be adequate to sustain your standard of living in retirement. There are tax-free alternatives to provide income streams to fill the gap.

Phase 2: Retirement Years – Protection and Preservation

Ah, at last… you've put in your time and finally ready to retire. You've spent your Working Years growing and ACCUMULATING your nest egg and have hopefully reduced or eliminated your debt. Once you stop working – it's time to transition from the ACCUMULATION phase to the PROTECTION and PRESERVATION phase. This means working with a retirement specialist and rolling your employer-sponsored plan into a safe vehicle without market volatility that contractually guarantees a lifetime income while preserving your savings and providing protection from a market downturn.

The guaranteed lifetime income is established through a legal reserve life insurance company; the remainder will pass to your beneficiaries upon your death.

Your Social Security and guaranteed income stream(s) coupled with a tax-free alternative will replace or come very close to replacing your income in retirement.

NOTE: It is imperative that you work with a retirement specialist that can guide you through each component of the *Sacred 7*; the professional whom you worked with in the ACCUMULATION phase to get you TO retirement is not qualified or trained to get you THROUGH retirement.

#5: LONG TERM CARE

No one likes to think about growing old, becoming frail, and certainly not going to a nursing home, I get it. However, a little planning in advance can help you age in the comfort of your home and avoid your life savings going to the state. Do you have any idea how much a nursing home costs? For starters, the cost of a nursing home is currently between $6000 - $8500 per month ($72,000-$102,000 annually) depending on where you live. At-home care is around $40,000 per year. So how long will your money last when you're burning through thousands every year? How will that affect your spouse? And no, Medicare doesn't pay for nursing homes. This is definitely NOT an area where you want to take the risk and self-insure!

To protect yourself and your spouse in the event one of you become frail or need skilled or custodial care, I advise the following in this order:

1.a. Long term care rider on annuity

1.b. Long term care rider on life insurance

2. Traditional long term care policy

Tied for first place are the annuity and life insurance options; both are the absolute best choices for long term care planning. And if you never have to use it, the money passes to your beneficiaries. With traditional long term care, the premiums are lost if you don't use it; the exception is that some policies have a Return of Premium provision in which you may recover your premium in certain circumstances.

I recommend working exclusively with an experienced long term care professional that holds the Certified Long Term Care (CLTC) designation and has been licensed and practicing for a minimum of 10 years.

To locate a CLTC graduate, visit: http://www.ltc-cltc.com

NOTE: ALWAYS select a policy which DOES NOT restrict your care to a licensed medical professional. Many times, a healthy family member or friend can perform custodial care in which your policy can compensate them.

#6: ESTATE PLANNING

Gone are the days of the typical estate plan where the surviving spouse gets everything; then after both spouses are gone, everything is divided amongst the kids. Sound familiar? Nowadays, multiple marriages are commonplace, more families are blended, and people become downright unrecognizable when the "who gets what" discussion is raised. So not only should there be clear instructions as to who gets what, you must also plan to pass your assets in the most tax-efficient manner.

Depending on how you manage your assets makes a huge difference between creating and possibly eliminating thousands of dollars in taxes.

One strategy that can help is called a "Protected Retirement Trust" (PRT). A PRT is designed to transfer assets to your beneficiaries tax-free under IRS Publication 525. Here's how it works: you transfer between 2% - 5% annually to the trust depending on your goals. A small amount of tax is paid as funds are transferred. Once the transfer is complete, the money is tax-free forever. PRT's are set up by an experienced estate planning attorney who works WITH your retirement specialist. Believe me; the preservation of your legacy is well worth the planning involved.

#7: TAXES

You must have a tax strategy, period. Every transaction can have an impact on your taxes. It's important to strategize your daily transactions in a way that permanently reduces your taxes.

So what's a tax strategy?

Let's start with what a tax strategy is NOT. A tax strategy is NOT about loopholes. Loopholes are **unintended** consequences of laws that were enacted. A tax strategy is about the consequences that lawmakers *intended*, which is a systematic plan of action to help you take advantage of these **intended** tax benefits. Your tax strategy is designed so you know exactly what you need to do to maximize these benefits.

Remember, the tax laws are written to encourage certain activities that benefit the economy and promote social policy. It's our job to understand and take advantage of the tax laws as they are written. Put your time and talents into activities that help you realize the most tax benefits.

This doesn't take hours every day in order to reap results; instead, your tax strategy becomes a part of your daily routine. Your retirement specialist should have a tax team that collaborates with you to develop your tax strategy.

SUMMARY

Each of these areas in the *Sacred 7* require their own individualized attention in order to put the overall plan in motion. Once the planning process starts, you will understand many areas overlap and each part of the plan works with intentional congruency. By working with a retirement specialist and forming a battle plan for the Sacred 7, you can rest easy, have your cake and retire too!

The earlier the planning begins, the easier it will be to correct course along the way, leaving nothing to chance and giving you and your family peace of mind throughout your retirement and for many years thereafter.

ABOUT LEASHA

Leasha West, MSFS, ChFC®, CLTC, NSSA®, CASL®, MDRT, known as America's Retirement Authority, is a highly decorated Marine Corps veteran and respected community leader. With the explosive success of her firm West Financial Group, Inc., she is now recognized as one of the nation's leading experts in retirement planning.

As an award-winning and multiple best-selling author, Leasha was selected as one of America's PremierExperts® and is frequently quoted in the *Wall Street Journal, USA Today, New York Times,* and *Inc. Magazine,* as well as featured in several publications and news outlets commenting on retirement issues. She has shared the stage at distinguished conferences across the country with legends of business, Hollywood, politics and sports – such as Steve Wozniak, co-founder of Apple, Eric Trump, NFL Hall of Famer and 3-time Super Bowl Champion Michael Irvin, Fashion Mogul Donna Karan, Oprah's life partner Stedman Graham, Supermodel turned Supermogul Kathy Ireland, George Ross of the Donald Trump Organization and Celebrity Apprentice, NY Times #1 Best-Selling Author Dr. John Gray, the lingerie tycoon of Europe Michelle Mone, Arnold Schwarzenegger and the World's #1 Wealth Coach, JT Foxx.

Leasha's combined knowledge and celebrity status has solidified her as a retirement planning guru, as she is frequently called on by local and national media for her ability to communicate, teach and transfer her innovative and rarefied financial skills.

Leasha's leadership skills have made her a powerful force in her community; she serves on the Boards of Directors for numerous non-profit and for-profit organizations. As a result of Leasha's outstanding volunteerism, she was awarded the President's Volunteer Service Award by President Barack Obama.

In addition to her community involvement, she is a multi-year member of the Million Dollar Round Table, was named to the Circle of Excellence by the Women in Insurance and Financial Services (WIFS), is a member of the National Ethics Association and was chosen as one of the Elite Women in Insurance by *Insurance Business America Magazine.*

Educationally, Leasha holds a Masters of Science in Financial Services (MSFS) and the prestigious designations of Chartered Financial Consultant® (ChFC®), Certified Long Term Care (CLTC), National Social Security Advisor® (NSSA®) and Chartered Advisor for Senior Living® (CASL®). She is the official spokeswoman for The American College.

Leasha has intensity, contagious enthusiasm and amazing passion for helping baby boomers, seniors, and retirees preserve and protect their portfolios, maximize their Social Security income, make sense of Medicare, generate income through solid cashflow and use growth to offset inflation.

Through Leasha's strategies and inspiration, retirees are likely to avoid probate court and protect their assets, investments and savings from losses due to volatile markets, needless taxation or an extended illness. She has personally helped thousands of clients retire in the comfort of their homes rather than being cared for in a nursing home.

If you are retired or retiring soon, and would like to learn more about securing your retirement in any economy, visit Leasha's websites to read articles, watch videos and receive special reports: www.westfinancialgroup.com or www.americasretirementauthority.com

You can connect with Leasha at:

leasha@westfinancialgroup.com
www.twitter.com/LeashaWest
www.facebook.com/LeashaWest
https://www.linkedin.com/in/leashawest
https://plus.google.com/+LeashaWest

BY DR. DIYARI ABDAH

THINK IT, INK IT, AND ACT ON IT

The Power of FAST Implementation

Have you ever had an idea for a service, product or an invention but didn't follow it through? Then one beautiful day, you were minding your own business and were happy admiring the world, or maybe you were on a flight to your dream destination and, while trying to enjoy the flight magazine... THERE IT IS!...your idea or invention is in a catalogue or on store shelves somewhere.

Of course the first reaction we usually have is; " That was my idea. Someone stole my idea!" and after few seconds you realize how ridiculous that may sound, you start blaming yourself for not taking action fast enough.

Or someone is doing a unique marketing piece and attracts flocks of clients, and only weeks before that you were thinking of setting that unique marketing idea in action.

How do I know this to the sharpest details? Well, I have been there myself several times in the past and it's painful, especially to the creative mind.

You feel you have been robbed of your idea. But the truth is you probably robbed yourself of the joy of seeing your idea come to life.

Most of us have been in that situation once or more than once in our lifetime, and it is not a very happy place to be, and usually we are sad not just because we lost a business opportunity or something like that, but it is usually because of pride and the intellectual property we think is ours (or was ours), hence people say: "They stole my idea!" or "That was my idea."

This problem will continue to exist until we take action, and by action I mean immediate FAST implementation of the ideas, projects, inventions – whatever you may think that will serve others and answer or serve their needs. If it can serve people and improve their lives and yours or your business in the process, then it is definitely worth pursuing. Even if it is not perfect at the start.

Anything worth doing is worth doing poorly - until you can learn to do it well.

~ Zig Ziglar

With this in mind, Let's talk about a few ways that can improve your implementation speed:

First try to visualize your idea or product or the outcome and think how others may benefit from it, then dramatize it in your mind to an extent that it is a 'must have' for anyone who may need one, they must obtain it and think of the scale of the production and delivery, in other words, DREAM BIG. As long as there is some basic truth to your idea, nothing should stop you from dreaming big.

Now imagine if that service, product or invention that people will talk about and need has your name associated with it, or even better, is named after YOU.

Most successful people are FAST implementers.

Don't you think that is a dream and a legacy worth pursuing?

Most successful people are FAST implementers. Once they believe in an idea that may serve others and fill a gap in the market, they start a process of implementation as soon as possible. This is after planning the various stages of the process, of course.

There is a difference between having an idea and parking it in your own mind forever – being a Dreamer – or an idea whose implementation has been delayed because of market research or other logistics. One is in the process of making, which is better than nothing or a stagnant idea, and the other is being parked and probably will never see daylight. In my experience, while you hold the idea in your mind for a suitable time to show up later, it will never come out and take action by itself. You have to take action, and F A S T!

In this technologically advanced and super-fast world, most things "worth doing" need to be done fast otherwise someone else is probably doing it right now.

This will turn into a very bitter experience if that someone else is your competitor with a limited creative mind compared to yours, but who is taking action faster than you are. Who do you think will win and whose efforts will show, the guy who has been dreaming, or the guy who has been taking actions?

This will apply not only to inventions or first time ideas, but also to routine business ideas such as marketing and advertising, and finding new ways to serve your people.

If You Think it, Ink it and Act on it.

~ D. Abdah

I have personally wasted many first time genuine creative ideas and opportunities by not acting fast enough or worse even, by not acting at all! Usually there are many reasons for this and I categorize them into 3 classifications, and once you realize your creativity and implementation enemies, you can eliminate them one by one:

1. Fear of the process

This happens when you think the process is too difficult and labor intensive or the investment is too much and it will drain your bank account.

Although these are all legitimate reasons, successful people think differently. Everything is an opportunity to learn or a challenge to overcome, instead of a permanently paralyzing obstacle.

2. Being Unproductive

This is because you allow trivial activity to take over your dayswork instead of delegating it to someone else and focusing on what matters most.

Or, letting frequent excessive entertainment with no real creative value take over a part of your day where you could have accomplished something more meaningful.

Re-inventing the wheel is another problem some people have. Everything they do has to be done from scratch, but that's what mentors, coaches and mastermind groups are for – to eliminate or decrease the learning curve.

3. Counter-productive activities

Once you have an idea worth implementing, no matter how small, it is important that you keep it "in the flow".

Do not permit interruptions or disruptions. Give it your full 100% attention. You will be surprised how FAST things can move in your favour. Once you do this and get into a routine of no interruptions and disruptions, you will find it easy to implement future thoughts and ideas at a faster and more productive rate.

Successful people usually have many projects going at the same time parallel to one other because they give each one of them the attention and time they need without wasting time on meaningless tasks and trivial activities which are nothing but robbing you of your creativity.

You can only prioritize, when you know your priorities.

~ D. Abdah

Most people want to succeed in life and business, but few know how successful people think and behave. Sometimes people label themselves successful, but their actions speak otherwise. To succeed, you need to think how successful people think in relation to FAST implementation and action taking. Here is a short list to show the differences:

- Successful people think of the solution and not the problem.

- Successful people have an abundance of creative ideas compared to other less successful people who have an abundance of excuses.

- Successful people help others, whereas less successful people expect help.

- Successful people see a solution in every problem; the less successful see a problem in every solution.

- Successful people say the solution is hard but possible; the less successful say the solution is not only hard, but impossible.

- Successful people think success is a must and not an option; less successful people think success is an option and not a must.

- Successful people have dreams to achieve, others have illusions.

- Successful people usually say: treat people the way you want to be treated, others say cheat people and deceive them before they deceive and cheat you.

- Successful people see hope in what they do, less successful people see pain in what they do.

- Successful people look into the possibilities of the future; others look into the impossibilities from their past.

- Successful people think before they talk, others talk before they think.

- Successful people make the news, for others the news makes them.

It has been noted that successful people leave clues behind, and smart people study these clues and model what they admire and resonate with.

Looking back ten years ago when I started my second business, in only a few short years we quadrupled the value of the business and tripled the gross income. This obviously was done through multiple intelligent decisions, excellent marketing and exceptional service to our clients. However, when asked by others how we managed to achieve that level of success in only a few short years, and when looking back at the dynamics and the mechanics of the process, we found that at the heart of everything was passion and speed of implementation. This was the key in many aspects of our success.

Not many businesses can survive without real passion for the initial idea that ignited the business in the first place, then passion for serving others and making a difference in the world.

In his book *The Virgin Way*, my co-author Sir Richard Branson whom I admire for being one of the coolest and most intelligent entrepreneurs of his time said, *"I have always had one paramount philosophy: if a new project or business opportunity doesn't excite me and get my entrepreneurial and innovative juices flowing, if it's not something with which I sense I can make a difference while having a lot of seriously creative fun, then I'd far rather pass on it and move right along to something else that does excite me."*

These words are so true for every business; small and large, local and global as passion and creativity are key ingredients in the success of any endeavor, and be adding speed of implementation, you got yourself a WINNER!

By creating and establishing a culture of FAST implementation, every decision can be made through that lens. This is how entrepreneurs and their companies succeed in the long term. Successful people do what it takes to make an idea come to life and make it a passion to succeed in a consistent manner.

Making FAST implementation of ideas a part of a company mission can remind you and everyone else *how important it is not to park ideas and innovations for later*, but instead taking calculated but RAPID ACTION can only lead to greater satisfaction and speedier results. Even if it means you have to master it later or tweak it for better results and perfection, you rather know it sooner than later.

RAPID ACTION can only lead to greater satisfaction and speedier results.

Make it part of your mission statement to do everything with enough great passion that makes you jump out of bed in the morning to implement it, and let it grow into something bigger and better in serving others. There is no greater satisfaction for a creative entrepreneur than seeing how people benefit from his or her ideas.

So what is the ultimate roadmap for FAST Implementation, and how can we make it part of our business culture? Not always, but most of the time, being connected to the relevant and right people in any industry means you can get things done in less time and sometimes with less costs.

Imagine if most of your ideas and innovations need trademarking as a first step in implementation. It will make more sense and things can move much faster if you know the right people in this field who can help secure your ideas at first.

Never think that certain people have no place in your business or in your future plans. Everyone can play a small or a large role when the day comes and it may be very rewarding that you took the time and made that connection while on that conference, meeting or even on holiday.

I recently met a gentleman while on a short break at a spa, and after exchanging a few words, I found out that he was a Continental Airlines Captain for many years, and is now flying private jets, and one of his passions was to encourage young Americans from the Hispanic community to get involved in shaping their future through education and becoming valuable members of their society. I, on the other hand, was looking for co-authors for my next book who shaped their own success in life despite adversity, with inspiring stories that can move people's hearts and minds and there was the synergy and we acted upon it straight away.

He always wanted to empower these ideas and maybe write something, since his story is very encouraging for many. He went from working on a tomato farm to becoming a successful airline captain, and I was looking for people with great stories. As a result of FAST implementation from both sides, he will be in my next book, and hopefully inspiring thousands with his story how he made it from a farmer to a Continental airlines captain. So connecting with the right people moves "Things" faster, whatever that may be.

Don't restrict your imagination to your business only. As a creative person you may sometimes have ideas that may apply to other industries, and choosing to do something about it can be very satisfying and rewarding. One example I come across time after time is that people sometimes change direction or branch out into new business territories and become global after being local.

One such an example is someone who has a small local business and in search of better ways of marketing. I have come across many people who were in search of better ways to market their business and as a result they repackage their knowledge and help others by applying their knowledge to other industries and this can be done on a global scale too.

Another element, besides knowing the right people in creating a FAST implementation culture, is how to get the idea, product, and service across in the quickest possible time and present it to as many clients, customers and businesses in a rapid way. This happens by mastering the art of PR (both online and offline) and knowing and creating the right channels for this purpose.

These methods can be print advertising, direct mail, trade associations, webinars and seminars, speaking engagements, social media, campaigns, events, writing books, reports and magazines, radio, TV, strategic alliances, partnerships and affiliations, fan base associations, web-marketing, Telemarketing and many more.

It's useful to master as many of these as you can, but you need to be at least familiar with all of these methods in order to have the maximum impact.

One last word, **DON'T WAIT AND MISS OUT**, engage and take action and create change. The moment you take action and create change, you become unstoppable.

Enjoy the journey.

ABOUT DR. DIYARI

Dr. Diyari Abdah is a Cosmetic and Implant Dentist, International Speaker, Author, Educator, Life and Business Coach.

Dr. Diyari Abdah holds two dental degrees. In addition, in 2006 he was awarded a Master of Science Degree – M.Sc. – in the field of Implant Dentistry (UK). He is a member of several international Dental and Scientific Associations. He is also a member of the American Academy of Anti-Ageing medicine. In 2013, he was awarded the prestigious America's PremierExperts® status. He is a visiting academic at two universities and on the editorial board of several publications.

Dr. Diyari Abdah is passionate about helping others achieve their goals in balancing life and business or career. He currently practices dentistry three days a week in his office in Cambridge, UK and spends the rest of the time writing, teaching and coaching other dentists to achieve success by utilizing his business and marketing blueprints. In 2014, Dr. Diyari Abdah hit three Amazon.com best-seller lists for the new book, *The Winning Way: The World's Leading Entrepreneurs and Professionals Share How They Are Winning in Life and Business and You Can Too!*

He continues travelling the world, especially the USA, sharing his knowledge with other colleagues through his teaching programs. Currently he is working on an MBA degree (in Cambridge). He resides in Hertfordshire, UK.

On the instructional side, his brotherhood, friendship and collaborations in recent years with the legendary Zig Ziglar's son Tom Ziglar, CEO of the Ziglar Corporation, and the intense immersion into the legendary speaker's timeless teachings and philosophies of personal development and motivation success has led Dr. Abdah to become the UK's first Zig Ziglar Certified Legacy Trainer. While devoting his ideal of three days to his Dentastique practice and serving as an Ambassador for Ziglar, Dr. Abdah has also tapped into his powerful entrepreneurial and personal development skills, he became a much sought after personal and business mentor.

Dr. Abdah joined The Emmy Award winning team at CelebrityFilms as an Executive Producer and an Ambassador of Hope on the documentary film, *Armonia*, in partnership with Armonia U.S. Inc., a non-profit 501(c)(3) corporation in the United States designed to support programs abroad committed to working with the poor for empowerment and a better life. The documentary will chronicle the journeys of several *Armonia* Indigenous Mexican Scholars (AIMS) students in Oaxaca, Mexico. The AIMS program provides an opportunity for poor Indian (indigenous Mexican) teenagers in the Sierra Madre mountains of Southern Mexico to obtain a High School education, and a chance for a University education in Mexico City.

He has also been seen in major online publications such as CNBC.com, *Yahoo! Finance, New York Business Journal, Business Investment UK* and *MarketWatch*, among many others.

Dr. Abdah can be reached at: DiyariAbdah@Yahoo.com

Everyday I saw myself playing baseball in the majors. I was going to stand in that diamond and hit home runs alongside the greats, there was no doubt about it.

BY GREG ROLLETT

THE FUTURE BELONGS TO THE YOUNG...

and Ambitious

I'm very optimistic about young people. I'm optimistic about what young people are doing today, and what they will continue to do in the future. However, with all the advancement and good being done across the world, I see young people heading in two very different directions—two very clear, distinct directions.

Moving in one direction is the young person who is glued to their phone. They are literally watching the world pass them by. They're looking at other people's Facebook and Instagram feeds and saying, "That looks fun. That looks like a great dinner. That's a great vacation." They're living through the lives of others and having none of the adventures themselves.

Moving in the opposite direction is the person who is creating their present and their future. They are taking a hands-on approach to their life. . . they're living! These are the ones traveling. . . exploring. They're creating families, businesses and jobs. They are leveraging and using technology to change their world, and ultimately the world everyone else will live in. These young people are taking an active approach in shaping the future that they want to live in.

These are two very distinct groups that young people are merging into. It is the second group that we need to pay extra-special attention to. We need to foster, coach, mentor, market to and watch this group carefully.

How do I know? I'm part of this group.

One of the earliest memories I have of myself with grand and ambitious dreams was sitting in my bedroom at 8 or 9 years old. I remember the bed was to one side of the room and my makeshift posters, which I ripped out of Sports Illustrated, lined the walls. I also had a huge, full-length mirror in my room. Every single day I would grab my mini baseball bat, which I got at a Florida Marlin's game, and stand in front of my mirror poised and ready to swing.

I would hold my bat and I'd pretend it was the bottom of the ninth, World Series, Game 7, two outs. Everyday I visualized hitting home runs. Everyday I saw myself playing baseball in the majors. I was going to stand in that diamond and hit home runs alongside the greats, there was no doubt about it.

In high school though, I decided to be a rapper. It was obviously a great career choice for a little, skinny white kid. But, you know, I had big dreams and ambitions. This might sound strange, but at the time I was modeling my rapping career after, and trying to emulate the business model of, New Orleans rapper and record label head, Master P.

Master P, whose real name is Percy Miller, was a guy living in an innercity, a troubled area in New Orleans, Louisiana. At the time, it was the murder capital of the world. It was in this environment that Master P started his record label, No Limit Records. He took everyone from his neighborhood and essentially said to them, "You are going to put out an album, and so is everyone on our block. We're all going to come out of

I never wanted to just work at McDonald's. I wanted to own thirty McDonald's.

this bad situation and get ourselves out of the hood. We're going to create lives for ourselves."

I thought that was incredibly ambitious. Using this formula, No Limit Records released 23 albums in 2008, collectively selling millions of copies in the process.

Taking this model, I used a loophole in the senior program at my high school to start my own record label. During my senior year, I was released from school at noon everyday to start a senior project. It was during this time that I signed my first artist, myself, along with my best friend at the time. Late in our senior year, we released a self-funded, self-produced and self-published album, Ballin On 82, under the moniker of The Burglazz. The title paid homage to the street we were both born and raised on in South Florida. (The real ironic part of the story is my old friend is now a SWAT team member of a south Florida police unit.)

With my newfound ambitions to be a world famous rapper, I set the bar high for what I wanted to accomplish, much like playing in Game 7 of the World Series. Dreaming should never get smaller, only larger as you continue on in life.

In the early 2000's, the pinnacle of the music industry was being on featured on TRL, in Time Square, or getting interviewed by Carson Daly. That was the big dream and the big ambition. It gave me something to strive for, something to continually work toward. Having a big dream also helped me make decisions. I had to consciously decide whether the choices I was making were moving me closer or further away from my goal.

Now, sad to say, I wasn't able to get on TRL. However, I was able to perform at Madison Square Garden at the New York Music Festival back in 2003. Performing inside that iconic arena – walking down the same hallway where the Knicks walk in, where all the great players look to shine, and all the great musicians hope to get their names in bright lights – was incredible.

I got to walk onto that stage and perform a couple songs in front of fans, industry professionals and other artists as part of the festival. It was amazing. It was as cool as you could imagine and then some.

I always had ambitions to do something grander. I never wanted to just work at McDonalds. I wanted to own thirty McDonalds. I wanted to skip the lines and the red tape and get there as fast as I possibly could.

If you listen to mainstream media, you frequently hear stories about companies speaking about their Millennial employees and their ambition like it's a bad thing. You hear things like, "He's worked here for two weeks and he thinks he owns this place."

Why is this a bad thing? Why can't we look at this as a positive character trait versus a negative one? Why don't you want employees who want to take ownership in your company working for you? Why not encourage Millennials who want to help your company grow? Why not give them the tools, guidance, and nurturing required to help them grow and get into a position where they can run the company someday?

Not every young person has these ambitions. In fact, I see a big gap between the ambitious and the un-ambitious. I believe those with drive, motivation and ambition should be celebrated, and I'm not the only one. Every year, there are magazine covers that tout the "30 Under 30," or the "40 Under 40," lists. From Inc. Magazine to Forbes to Fortune, these young and ambitious leaders are being recognized, and they help to sell a lot of magazines. You see young guys like Zuckerberg, gracing magazine covers and mainstream media, who have rapidly amassed billions of dollars.

Then, on the other end of the spectrum, you have student loan debts that outnumber credit card debts in the United States. The student loan debt has grown to more than $1.2 trillion. How can you inspire a generation to be ambitious when they can't even afford the cost of living on their own? They can't afford food or gas.

These young adults are sitting in their parent's homes with the most expensive pieces of paper they've ever owned, and receiving none of the benefits their college education promised them. Since the age of twelve, they've been hearing from parents, grandparents, teachers, coaches, and everyone else willing to offer them opinions, that the key to a good life was working hard and getting a college degree. Yet, there they sit, disheartened that all the doors are still apparently locked before them. No job. No budding, prosperous career.

So, I ask again: How can these young people be inspired to become ambitious? The short answer: technology!

Someone with whom I've been able to spend a lot of time with recently, New York Times Best-Selling Author, Peter Diamandis, says that technology will be the X-factor in many aspects of the future. Technology is the force that will continue to give us abundance, because it allows us to do so many incredible things. Technology allows the millennial generation to have multiple passions. Millennials will not be defined by one thing.

My good friend, Best-Selling Author, and International Speaker, Pa Joof, talks a lot about the concept of identity. Gen X and Boomers typically self-identify by what they do, not who they are. You commonly hear them say, "I'm a dentist. I'm a real estate agent. I'm a financial advisor. I'm a teacher."

For Millenials: That is not who we are. That is what we do.

This young group doesn't identify themselves as being one thing. They have multiple interests and multiple things that define them.

When I look at myself, I do not just see a writer, marketer, or a business owner. I'm also a dad. I'm into fitness and being healthy, I'm a CrossFitter. I live in the music world, in the marketing world, in the nonprofit world, in the media world, and in the fashion world. I do adventure races. I like food. I like cooking. My job does not define who I am.

This young group doesn't define themselves solely by the actions they partake in at the office between the hours of nine to five, or any other hours or situations for that matter. These young kids are doing some really, really cool things. They're starting companies. They are creating unicorn companies – a term venture capitalists use to describe startups that are valued at more than $1billion.

For example, Evan Spiegel, the 25 year-old founder of SnapChat, has one of these unicorn companies. SnapChat is now worth billions. All Evan did was simply take advantage of the technology and communication trends of the young and ambitious.

Then you have an entire group that creates what I call the side hustle.

You have the guy working nine to five as an insurance adjuster. However, when he goes home, he's creating statues and comic book figures that he sells on Etsy. He's potentially making just as much money selling these little statues and figurines on Etsy as he is at his nine to five. He doesn't define himself by his nine to five. He has passions. He has outside interests. He's willing to pursue multiple options for income, and not afraid to think outside the standard box.

There's an entire industry emerging where young, stay-at-home moms have created second incomes for their family by blogging about the products that they use, and getting paid by the companies to do so. They write about what they do with their kids and the different products they use to help with the laundry, among other things. This ambitious group has gone from single income families to double income families with only one parent leaving the house out of thin air, and technology. It's incredible the opportunities they have created for themselves.

Then, you have things like Kickstarter. Literally all you need is an idea, and you can have the world fund it's creation before you ever have to manufacture a product. Now, young people can be encouraged to dream big, and then sell that dream and vision to others. They can test their ideas in the real world by having real people pony up the money with less personal risk to make it a reality. This can equate to raising millions of dollars without pitching investors, or giving up large sums of their company in equity shares.

There are young people climbing the corporate ladder faster than ever. Young people are not just at a desk in a newsroom, they are either

We're really trying to create a young generation that lives a life full of ambitions.

becoming the newsroom or taking over the anchor positions themselves. These are people like Nicole Lapin, who was the youngest anchor ever at CNN and CNBC before leaving big media to publish her New York Times Best-Selling book, Rich Bitch. These are all really great examples of this generation making money, though, as we've already discussed, this group values so much more.

You have young people who are taking care of their bodies more than ever. There's a sport called CrossFit, and more than 209,000 people competed in the CrossFit Invitational in order to compete at the CrossFit Games. There are also wildly popular races and adventures that speak to Millennials. For example, the Spartan Race, an obstacle course race where you pay upwards of $100 to jump over and climb through barbed wire and hop over fences and cars. The Spartan Race alone had over 650,000 participants last year. This year they expect over 1 million people to participate in the Spartan Race, most of them under the age of 30.

You can't go from a nine to five with a side hustle, and multiple CrossFit classes each week, if you're not taking care of yourself. That extends to more than physical health too. These kids are trying to live healthy lives that feed who they are at their core. They want a full life, not just a full checking account.

Millennials are doing things differently on their vacations. They are going to see the world now! They are not waiting until their "golden years" to explore the vast cultures the world has to offer. They're not waiting until retirement to go take the two-week trip to Bali; they're going now while they still want to jump off cliffs or surf the world over. They're walking 10 miles a day seeing the sites, sleeping in hostels, and taking planes, trains, and automobiles all over the continent. They are running with the Bulls in Spain and Shark Diving in Scotland while it's still exciting and cool, they're not waiting until these things become reckless and foolhardy in their minds.

These young adults are forming groups like the Summit Series, a private mastermind group made up of some of the most impressive entrepreneurs in the world. The founders were in their mid-20s when they started the series that would allow them to connect and network with the likes of the Bill Clintons, the Steve Forbes', the Tim Ferriss', and the Arianna Huffingtons of the world. This whole movement started by inviting these types of people on ski trips. They said, "Hey, Bill Clinton, can I just take you on a ski trip?" He agreed. Five years later they bought a mountain right outside of Park City, Utah to hold these gatherings. In the process they have raised millions of dollars for charity. Instead of going on vacation, they own the vacation destination and have the best party guests you could imagine

This is a generation of people who are looking for more out of life. They're looking for better. They want a career – they just might not want to define it in the same terms as their parents. They are taking care of themselves, physically and mentally. They are doing things that their grandparents never dreamed of as possible. They want to have families and to see the world. They want it all.

Quite frankly, the ambitious ones, the kids who believe in the power of their dreams and continue to create goals that get bigger and bigger, are going to have it. So, what does that mean to you, my Baby Boomers and Gen X's? Well, my challenge to you is to look at these young people in a different light. Do not write this group off. They need your mentoring and they need your guidance.

Whether you like it or not, they're going to be the leaders of this world quicker than you can imagine. They're going to be the bosses someday, whether you like it or not. We, the Millennials, are the ones who are going to take over and control this world.

Knowing this, over the past few months, my team and I have decided to give a new voice to this generation. We've created a brand new media network called The Ambitious Network at ambitious.com.

We're going to give young people a place where they can not only see other young people doing these things, but we are going to give them the path, the blueprint, and the resources they need to actually live these lives. When they want to go take that vacation they'll know where to go, how to book it, and what is out there to discover. They're going to know how to invest. They'll know how to go out and get that first mortgage. They'll know how to go out and find the ambitious careers that are available to them.

We're really trying to create a young generation that lives a life full of ambitions, not regrets. There are a lot of people who lie on their deathbed with regrets. But, the thing is, it's always the things they didn't do they regret way more than the things they actually did.

What I want to do is help that person who is sitting at home on a Friday night binge watching House of Cards on Netflix. I want to help that person get up off the couch and start living their life.

Ambitious.com will inspire that person to want to be Kevin Spacey, not just watch Kevin Spacey. That is what we're trying to do, and it's what I think will shrink the gap between the ambitious and the un-ambitious. It's my contribution toward a better future for my generation, a future filled with potential, dreams, and a life that's completely and utterly full.

[This article has been adapted from Greg Rollett's speech at the UN Headquarters as part of the Global Economic Initiative.]

ABOUT GREG

Greg Rollett, @gregrollett, is a Best-Selling Author and Marketing Expert who works with experts, authors and entrepreneurs all over the world. He utilizes the power of new media, direct response and personality-driven marketing to attract more clients and to create more freedom in the businesses and lives of his clients.

After creating a successful string of his own educational products and businesses, Greg began helping others in the production and marketing of their own products and services. He now helps his clients through two distinct companies, Celebrity Expert Marketing and the ProductPros.

Greg has written for *Mashable, Fast Company, Inc.com, the Huffington Post, AOL, AMEX's Open Forum* and others, and continues to share his message helping experts and entrepreneurs grow their business through marketing.

Greg's client list includes Michael Gerber, Brian Tracy, Tom Hopkins, Coca-Cola, Miller Lite and Warner Brothers, along with thousands of entrepreneurs and small-business owners across the world. Greg's work has been featured on FOX News, ABC, NBC, CBS, CNN, *USA Today, Inc Magazine, The Wall Street Journal,* the *Daily Buzz* and more.

Greg loves to challenge the current business environment that constrains people to working 12-hour days during the best portions of their lives. By teaching them to leverage marketing and the power of information, Greg loves to help others create freedom in their businesses that allow them to generate income, make the world a better place, and live a radically-ambitious lifestyle in the process.

A former touring musician, Greg is highly sought after as a speaker, who has spoken all over the world on the subjects of marketing and business building.

If you would like to learn more about Greg and how he can help your business, please contact him directly at: greg@dnagency.com or by calling his office at 877.897.4611.

BEING A BEACON OF LIGHT FOR THOSE IN HIS CIRCLE OF INFLUENCE

PERFORMANCE: You've been a sales professional for over twenty years and have worked as the relationship manager for the Hooven-Dayton Corp. for nearly fourteen. How and why did you choose a career in sales?

TROY: I got into sales because one of my mentors out of school told me that if you want to be an entrepreneur, the best thing you can do is get in on the sales side of a business. Business always needs to generate revenue and if you're good at that, you'll be successful and never hurt for a job. I got into the printing and packaging world in 1995, but before that I worked in sales in coffee and vending and then sold cell phones when they first came out, and were ridiculously huge and looked like bananas! I was recruited to work for a printing company that sold customized carbon forms and envelopes by one of my cell phone customers. Since then, I have been in the printing industry. In 2003, I started working for the Hooven-Dayton Corporation, which is a premier narrow web converter and specialty printer. My role there is to manage and grow their relationship with Procter & Gamble and other strategic companies and customers.

When I was younger, everyone would tell me that I'm a people person, so I should be in sales. But as I found out, sales and strategic relationship managing involves much more than being a people person, and having a knack for developing strategies is an equal part of the process. Working with a company like P&G, there are between 400 and 500 decision makers I have to work with in any given year. As different projects evolve through various stages, there are different stakeholders we have to interact with, who have their own mini-agendas - and we have to help them meet those to bring projects to fruition.

> ## Once my business objectives are met, am I living and leading a life I truly enjoy?

PERFORMANCE: What does Hooven-Dayton do, and what is your essential role as relationship manager to their single largest customer?

TROY: It's a privately-owned label and flexible packaging manufacturer located in Southwest Ohio, and we serve both medium to larger companies that utilize a lot of labeling – mostly in consumer product marketing and pharmaceuticals. I came on as an account representative, but as our relationship with P&G - their largest customer - grew, it became apparent that they needed one person to be in charge of the relationship between them and our company. I have two major responsibilities. First is making sure that P&G's expectations are met when it comes to receiving products from us, that they're on time, at the right quality level and accurate in every way. And making sure they're satisfied overall with the services we provide. We ship to about 17 plants and contract manufacturers and everything has to get there on their desired schedule. We have to perform an ongoing conversation with all of these plants regarding what they need, and that can change on an hourly basis. We're talking massive volumes. When I first started with Hooven-Dayton, we did around $600,000 in business with P&G, and I was able to grow that to a peak of $10 million in 2011.

That's part of my second responsibility, business development. This aspect is relationship oriented, relying on constant communications with their purchasing and marketing departments. We have to make sure we're staying in front of new projects coming down the pike, making sure to get feedback on what we can execute easily and also riskier ventures that might enter us into a "Watch Out!" kind of scenario. Everything I do is part of an ongoing managed process.

PERFORMANCE: How do you measure success in your career with the company? Is it all about the bottom line or do personal relationships play a part in that?

TROY: The broad answer is that Hooven-Dayton measures success via the bottom line that is connected both to our ability to increase sales from one year to the next and also how we rank on scorecards that P&G give us, based on our pricing competitiveness in the market. Another important factor is the quality, making sure there are very few quality complaints. They also grade us on our ability to deliver products on time and on our innovations – i.e., what are we bringing to them to save time and money or help them differentiate them from their competition? The company I work for has a lot at stake in receiving strong scorecards. From the other end, P&G uses them to determine if Hooven-Dayton is successful for them. Success is determined by how well those two goals are being met, both from the perspective of my company and also P&G.

As I get older, and after having years of success with the company, I think of success in more personal terms. The questions I ask myself are, "Am I living in alignment with my personal goals, living my life true to the core of who I am?" and "Once my business objectives are met, am I living and leading a life I truly enjoy?" My personal definition of success is identifying what's important to me, and then challenging myself to live closely to that standard or vision.

PERFORMANCE: What do you feel makes you successful as a salesperson and relationship manager? Do you set goals for yourself?

TROY: Sales is a little more than 50% of my job, but the most important role I serve as a strategic account manager is making sure my company's relationship is tight with them. Once you grow that relationship, it must be nurtured, maintained and monitored. I think I have always had an inner desire to overachieve, plus it's natural for me to be in a service role. When you work with the largest consumer product corporation in the world, 90% of how you do business with them is dictated by them, so the way I differentiate myself is in how I respond back to them, the passion and innovation I bring to the table. You have to do things to create a feeling in their minds that they can't do without you in their business.

I do set goals. There are smaller goals aligned with tasks and objectives on an hourly and daily level – but then overall, too, I have goals of making sure I'm generating a certain level of money and making a certain level of outbound sales calls. On a personal level, I have goals centered around maintaining relationships, and I make sure to reach out to one or two friends a day, both those outside my business circle and those with whom I have both a business and personal relationship. My worlds often intermingle.

PERFORMANCE 360 Earlier in your life and career, how did you define success? How has that definition changed over the years?

TROY: It's easy to track how that changes. When I was young and seduced by what society deemed successful, I wanted to be that guy who wore cool suits, drove that big car, was a jet set executive and either worked for the coolest company or had his own business. Now that I realize there are many more years behind me than in front of me, and also since I have had the pleasure and honor of achieving some of that status I once deemed so important, my perspective has shifted. What's important now is feeling good about who I am and what I do on a day to day basis. Even though I don't think we ever achieve ultimate peace of mind, we can sense life coming full circle when we have a gut feeling of who we are or what makes us happy on a day-to-day basis and the values we are aligned with. When I'm in that place, with an overall feeling of happiness and achievement, I feel I'm successful.

PERFORMANCE 360 You've been involved in Real Estate investing since 2007. How did you get into that world, and what are some of the accomplishments you are most proud of?

TROY: I have always had a natural curiosity and attraction to real estate, but earlier in my life it was always from a perspective of being in awe of its gurus and moguls and not feeling it was a world I could participate in. I considered getting into it years ago, but low self esteem kept me from thinking success was achievable. Once I got older and entered into it, I realized there was nothing to fear and that I should have followed my passion a long time ago. I did research into it for a few years and was impressed by what I learned about one of the great gurus, Ron LeGrand, aka "The Millionaire Maker." I got to meet him in 2007 and since then, while I have stayed mainly within the wholesaling side of the business, working in Dayton, Columbus and Cincinnati, I have also enjoyed some success in the retail flipping of houses. Wholesale is where you purchase a property and sell it to someone who does the actual rehabbing and reselling. In 2010, I had the opportunity to co-author a book with Ron called *The New Masters of Real Estate.*

To this point, it's been a part time and business venture, but I am currently transitioning to make it a full time. Once I do this, I believe it's something I will do for the rest of my life and that I will be successful because it's such a natural passion for me. Because of that, I think I will be doing it until I can no longer physically, meaning I don't think there will be any formal retirement!

> # I realized there was nothing to fear and that I should have followed my passion a long time ago.

PERFORMANCE: You've been heavily involved for many years with Dayton United Way and Habitat For Humanity? What have been your specific roles with those organizations?

TROY: For United Way, I was the Chair of the Young Leaders Circle, which was part of the organization's drive to capture young execs under 40 to get them up to the leadership level of giving to United Way. Their goal in working with us was to spark the passion of bands of young leaders so that we could in turn inspire others to join and be part of their family. I was also the Chair of the board of Habitat for Humanity of Greater Dayton, which provided financial and strategic guidance for its affiliates that covered Montgomery and Green Counties. We would build and rehab anywhere from 9 to 15 houses each year for low income families to help lift them up from poverty and start creating a legacy for their family that home ownership provides. We accomplished this by volunteerism and offering interest-free loans. I am finishing up my 9th year of Board Membership there, and that is the maximum anyone can serve.

PERFORMANCE: When you think in terms of achieving success in life, how important are these charitable activities?

TROY: I think it's very important to be involved in my community. When we think of our communities, we usually think we take a lot from it, but it's so important to give back – which for me now also includes being a mentor to young people, both formally and informally. I am always seeking new opportunities to make a difference. One of my missions is to become a true beacon of light for my circle of influence. That's one of the personal affirmations I say on a daily basis. What's fascinating is, we don't always know the extent of that circle because there could be people you're not interacting with who are observing your behavior. As long as I can be an example to others and shine a light for them to see further than they can presently imagine and follow a greater path, I'm fulfilled.

PERFORMANCE: That's so inspiring that you're mentoring. Who were some of your mentors and what are some key things you learned from them?

TROY: First let me say that I don't believe any one of us can achieve success purely by ourselves. Whether we acknowledge them or not, we all have people in our lives that we admire or want to emulate. So why not strive to become affiliated with them? Like any relationship, it's give and take. Some of the greatest joys and most heartfelt lessons I have learned have come from my affiliation with the two young men I mentor the most. In my own youth, my uncle Enos Singer was a mentor to me and a lot of other people. He died much earlier than any of us expected, but the greatest compliment someone can pay me is to say that 'Enos would be so proud of you' or 'What you did reminds me of what Enos would have done.' That is also a sign of success to me.

Enos gave me a lot of formal advice when I asked for it, and some unsolicited advice as I needed it. Honestly, though, I learned the most by just observing him and how he differentiated himself from others – and how people reacted to and gravitated towards him. I could tell he was successful by his mannerisms and habits and the way he led his life.

PERFORMANCE: What would you say are the biggest challenges you have overcome to be successful?

TROY: My biggest challenge by far was overcoming my low esteem and self-limiting beliefs from early in my life. For many reasons, I didn't see myself as the kind of person I ended up being. In my early 20s, I experienced a big mind shift where I practically re-birthed myself and it became apparent to me that we can be what we want to be if we think we can. My thoughts that I wasn't qualified to work in real estate, or that I was limited because of my race, were wrong thoughts. I owe so much to Brian Tracy, whose self-empowerment works *The Psychology of Selling* and *The Psychology of Success* played a huge role in my personal reinvention. I'd listen to these cassette tapes when I got up in the morning, when I was driving around in my early days as a salesman and before I would go to bed.

Years later, I had the opportunity to hear Brian speak live at an event, and it gave me chills just to be there with this man whose encouragement had meant so much. He had been this faraway teacher, mentor, and father who helped me overcome my negative "Woe is Me" attitude and depression – and I got a chance to tell him what he had meant to me! Now thanks in part to him, I am living the life I never thought I would lead – maybe not the level of success that others enjoy, but to where I am very pleased with and closely aligned with what I deem successful.

ABOUT TROY

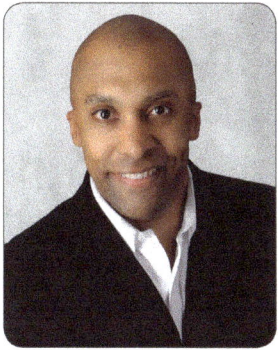

Troy Singer is a native Ohioan who loves living in Dayton Ohio. His true passions are Real Estate investing, golf, traveling, running and CrossFit. Troy also enjoys serving on committees for the Dayton United Way and the board of the Dayton Habitat for Humanity.

Troy co-authored the Best-selling "The New Masters or Real Estate" with Ron Le- Grand after meeting him in 2007. Since then, Troy has enthusiastically stayed within the wholesaling side of the business as a part-time investment and business venture.

In addition to Real Estate Investing, Troy is a trained sales professional with over 19 years experience in print and packaging sales. He currently works for the Hooven- Dayton Corp in a relationship manager role to the company's single largest customer. The Hooven-Dayton Corp is a label and flexible packaging printer in Dayton, Ohio.

You can contact Troy, visit: www.TroySinger.com

Or call him at: (937) 609-9792

BY JOSIE TYTUS, CPC

A LASTING IMPRESSION

Your Life, Your Legacy

I wonder if they can see me?

There I was, my four-year-old self in the back of my parents textile shop peering out at the customers through the rolls of fabrics. I loved this moment. I loved the store. I loved the fabrics. I loved seeing happy customers. I loved spending all day with both my parents. I loved my life.

So, when did things change?

Life takes us on an unknown journey with many ups and downs and the occasional spiral. What might seem obvious on the outside isn't always the way things are. Having grown up with entrepreneurial parents presented a set of challenges for me that I didn't know I signed up for.

Mine was a journey that took fifty years to create (so far); time well invested because of where I am today. Often, it wasn't very pretty. Sometimes it was very confusing. But without the struggles, I wouldn't be writing this for you today.

I'm going to share with you what I've come to understand about success and it's role in your life. You'll explore the most powerful thing that's going to get you the success you desire. You're going to understand the difference between being successful and living a legacy. You'll see what it takes to ignite wealth creation so you don't have to work so hard at it.

Once I discovered the formula for Success, my life took a new direction. I was empowered to lead my life. I had a newfound direction that was so clear. I knew what I had to do and couldn't wait to get going every day. I didn't have to explain or excuse myself about what I do. And that gave me the freedom I had always longed for.

Today, I have the freedom to:

➢ Create my work

➢ Choose how I deliver my work

➢ Meet and work with incredible people from all over the world

➢ Work from anywhere

➢ Work when it suits me

➢ Create as much income as I desire

In today's economy, you have the most favorable opportunity in history to make a huge impact by sharing what you know. We have so much information coming at us. People are starved for help and simplification from someone they can trust. They want to learn from you, to have you narrow down their options, to have you show them a new way – the best way of giving them some perspective.

You have something very special about you that provides tremendous value. What you have to offer matters. Your life has provided you everything you need to get clear about your work in the world. Your real work is to figure out what that is and get in alignment with it so that you can lead your life successfully.

The problem is most people don't do this. Most people don't see themselves as valuable enough to make it. You may fantasize about it, but that's where it lives, as a fantasy. You go out looking for an answer to that prayer, but never gather enough evidence to know you are the messenger, the leader, the Expert.

Two major factors are at play here. Doubt and Resistance. When you don't understand the value of what you offer, you act from hesitancy. If your internal belief system doesn't agree with your aspirations, you are going to face resistance. These two forces will keep you from reaching success.

In my case, I had parents that created success with very little. I had a huge desire to develop my own success. Except, I could never figure out what that was. So, I did a lot of things. In fact, I took a new job about every three years. I knew how to make money, I had a beautiful family, but I never landed on that 'thing' I yearned to discover about myself or my place in the world. I was starved in this area.

It took me a while and cost me lot, but the effort was worth it.

Today, I'm a #1 Best Selling Author, make a difference with what I do, get to travel to places that inspire me, am surrounded by people I adore who lift me higher, and get to do the work of my life developing the messages and legacy of Experts.

Getting there wasn't easy.

Success entrusts seeing what is not yet visible

I was born to immigrant parents who arrived in Canada with two suitcases in hand, my brother, four at the time, in the other. Out of desperation to find work they opened a retail business that provided our family a lovely life.

Everything about that life was good. Everything except me. I was different than they were. I was first born in this country. I was the girl. I had different tastes. I had different desires. I had different beliefs of what was possible. But I had no one to share them with. I was the outsider in my own family. My life took a different direction.

The family business went to my brother. My bosses took credit for my accomplishments. My final breaking point was the abrupt ending to my twenty-year marriage. I had given myself to the marriage, relinquishing career aspirations to support his. When that marriage dissolved, I was once again on the outside. No career, no income, no life. I was speechless and lost.

What I realized is that even though I had been living a 'nice family life', I seemed to be missing from it. That experience provided the perfect opportunity for me to step into a bigger role in my life. I surrendered myself to exploration and discovery.

Once I committed to figuring 'this thing' out, I was open to learning what was possible for me. The very first thing I did was take a public speaking course, even though I had no idea what I would be speaking about. It terrified me. From this small start I put everything I had into my personal and professional growth until I developed a powerful system I call SUCCESS ALIGNMENT™.

The model depicts a transition of life before and after implementing Success Alignment™.

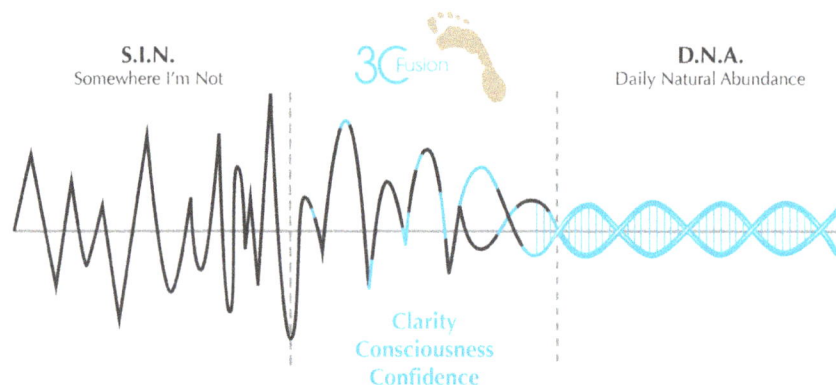

S.I.N.
Somewhere I'm Not

3C Fusion

D.N.A.
Daily Natural Abundance

Clarity
Consciousness
Confidence

On the left, the lines are jagged, up and down – severe. In this space you try to fix problems. You push for success. You want to control the outcome. Efforts from this space are strained and stressful. From this side of the fence, you are living in S.I.N. – trying to affect your life by being **S**omewhere **I**'m **N**ot.

When you cross the fence over into your D.N.A., you know your purpose, you are clear about the life you want, you have a Vision that pulls you forward, you experience meaningful success in all you do. In this space, you live in **D**aily **N**atural **A**bundance.

In discovering the realities of success, I came across a lot of bad advice like this:

1. You're supposed to have it all figured out by now. When you don't have it all figured out, especially having successful parents like I did, you walk around burdened with shame for not being just like them or better. After all, you had privileges and opportunities they never had. You suffer in silence while the hunt for answers continues relentlessly.

Reality: You do have the answers in you. You just may be in a temporary amnesia trying to figure it out. The good news is you can recover.

2. The success you generate is directly proportionate to your level of education. For years I walked around feeling inadequate because I went to college for something that did not reflect my gifts.

Reality: Your greatest education is when you're out in the world. The real world is nothing like what they teach you in school.

3. Or how about the 'fake it till you make it' path to success. It's so far off base. You cannot deceive anyone, especially yourself, pretending to be something you're not.

Reality: Success Alignment™ is the embodiment of success. Understanding what you are uniquely designed for is the only way to create sustainable, joyful and meaningful success to last a lifetime. Success Alignment™ is a way of life, not a goal. It's the conscious effort applied to develop your legacy in order to leave a lasting imprint.

You want to be accomplished. You want to be well rewarded. You want what you do to be meaningful. You want to be recognized as a leading Expert. Success Alignment™ provides all that and includes consciously creating success in every aspect of your life.

Success Alignment™ happens when what you do and who you are being matches who you are at your essence. You have the capacity to have that. You hunger for it, because it's in you. It's not a pipe dream. It's a realistic opportunity available to you.

There are stages to Success Alignment™. How you navigate them varies from person to person. How quickly you get results depends on how willing you are, how developed you are and how committed you are to having success.

DESIRE IT

Success begins with desire. Desire might show up as a yearning, a nudge, a thought, an inner calling, a feeling that something's missing or there's something more. Mastery begins with a desire to be more, do more and have more.

- o What's calling for your attention?
- o What's missing in your world?
- o What do you yearn for?

DEFINE IT

This piece had me perplexed for years. By defining success, you begin formulating a Vision. Most adults have a difficult time answering these questions,

- o What is success?
- o What do you really want?
- o What is your BIG VISION for your life?

DISCOVER IT

Your highest value is hidden in your personal genius. This is an area to be explored and excavated. Your life has taken you through circumstances both good and bad. This is where your gold is.

    o What has your life shown you about you so far?

    o What triggers you? What brings you ecstatic joy?

    o What do you know to be special about you?

ALIGN WITH SUCCESS

Get in agreement with success. Prepare yourself and your surroundings to reflect and support your vision.

    o What do you already have that's working?

    o What needs to be re-arranged in your world - relationships, time, space?

    o Who will stand with you for your success?

EMBODY SUCCESS

Take yourself from wanting to become to BEING SUCCESS-ful. This is high-level work that requires regular, purposeful attention. Success Alignment™ goes beyond having tools and strategies to achieve success. It's a philosophy about life and your work in it. The majority of your work to affect change and how you do success is in this stage.

    o Who are you if you are success?

    o What's different in your world when you are successful?

    o If you are success, how do you show up?

VOLUNTARY EVOLUTION

You're changing whether you choose to or not. Success Alignment™ puts you in the driver's seat to affect the change you want. By taking the first step you shift all universal energies to support you in generating that success.

    o What do you stand for?

    o Where will you put your stake in the ground?

    o What business / work will you create to support the life of your choosing?

When you match the inner expression of who you are, plus the gifts you are steward of, with an outer expression of how you utilize those gifts to serve others, you have Success Alignment™.

What it looks like is being on purpose, creating wealth, achieving great results. What it feels like is joy, pleasure, confidence, fulfillment.

Those who judge your VISION don't understand what you're capable of

Each of us has something unique about us that when activated, becomes so valuable it is recognized as a contribution to the world. That is life satisfaction; being on purpose with your work, being aligned with what you were created for and actually doing it.

This is the imprint you leave in the world. It's how you create your legacy – with *Clarity, Consciousness and Confidence* - the 3C FUSION SUCCESS FORMULA.

The model shows how your efforts aligned with Success affect your results. You are at the centre. The lower energies feel like an attack. The higher energies move you in the direction of your Vision affecting Success.

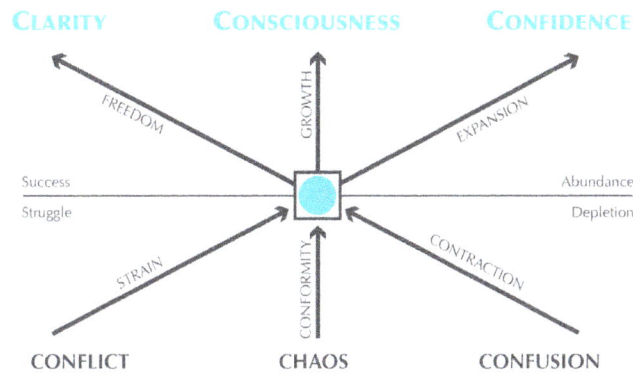

Here are three things you can do to begin aligning with success.

I. NOTICE YOUR NIGGLING

It's the part of you calling out for a bigger life. Do something to address it. Capture ideas and thoughts that bubble up for you. You'll soon begin to see a bigger picture forming. I began with a public speaking class, not knowing where it would take me.

The opportunity here is to do your inner work to discover what it wants you to know about yourself. Your life provides you with everything you need to know to get into Success Alignment™.

II. CREATE SPACE

This is the most important work you will ever do. Make room for it. Put it in your calendar and guard it as though your life depends on it – it does.

Do something everyday to develop your Self. It could be reading, learning, writing, or getting into a great conversation where you are seen and heard.

III. ENGAGE A MASTER TEACHER

The right support will make all the difference to your effectiveness and achievement. Find someone who is a little further down the road than you are, someone you connect with that can see you for your potential and hire them. Otherwise, you're building on quicksand. As the Master Teacher of Success Alignment™, I facilitate my students' transformation into the Experts they are destined to be.

Progress requires action. Start with this assignment.

For the next thirty days, set aside twenty uninterrupted minutes to answer the following questions. Use a new page for each. Daily, return to these questions with fresh eyes, adding to what you wrote. At the end of thirty days, read it through. Pull out the pieces that are most meaningful to you. Make a decision to do something new, something different with what you learned about yourself.

- What do you want to be known for?
- What have you been missing?
- What difference do you want to make?
- Who do you want to impact?
- Who are you being in this new bigger, bolder Vision?
- Why is that important to you?

Living in Success Alignment™ creates distinction. With distinction you have greater value. People pay a premium for that. Your competition disappears. No one has what you have. That puts you in high demand. This is your footprint.

Success Alignment™ is a way of life. Your success starts at the beginning. Your starting line is exactly where you are.

Placing your footprint in the sand is the path to independent wealth, making your impact in the world and living your legacy.

Walk with purpose …

ABOUT JOSIE

Josie Tytus is founder of 3C FUSION where Experts develop their Legacy.

Josie was raised in a Family Business. Entrepreneurship was in her bones, but it would take her half a lifetime to come to terms with it.

Pushed out of the family business she had to find her own way. She spent the next 25+ years in the Corporate world in Management exploring the Retail, Publishing, Entertainment and the Meeting industries. In her continual search to find her life's work, she gave herself promotions every three years and discovered a knack for finding or creating jobs to suit her lifestyle, not the other way around. She experienced the many intricacies and inner workings of different business models including two business start ups along the way – one providing services to the Interior Design Industry, the other a Speakers Bureau getting speakers booked for Corporate Events.

But life had bigger plans for her. She left the corporate world for the most important job ever, being a mom. All was good until her twenty-year marriage abruptly ended taking with it the life she had known. She lost family, friends, income and most significantly, herself. In two short years, she lost three of the most significant men in her life; her husband due to divorce, her father who passed away and her only child, 13 at the time, to Parental Alienation. Shrouded in confusion, she would spend the next five years in seclusion searching, learning, questioning and finally discovering how to be independently successful. It was during this process that her trademark system Success Alignment™ emerged and 3C FUSION was born.

 Success Alignment™ gives people access to having joyful, relevant and meaningful lives by elevating themselves to their highest potential. Josie went from living a life of trying to do the right thing to a life of doing the things that matter. These two worlds are polar opposites. One ignites success; the other stifles it.

Josie has lived her processes and today shares them to generate success in others. She has found her life's work - to help aspiring Experts live their legacy by uncovering their Genius and turning it into a life that matters by leaving their mark on the world.

All coaching, mentorship and programs at 3C FUSION are designed to help the emerging Expert by creating a life of significance using your unique Genius, making the Money you want in a way that's fun and impactful, and making a Difference by leaving your Footprint in the world.

Josie loves to turn Entrepreneurs, Speakers, Authors, Coaches, adult children of successful parents (this comes with it's own set of challenges), those challenged by finding their life's path and those with a burning desire to create their own success, into Experts.

Josie Tytus is a Success Alignment™ Expert, Speaker, Certified Professional Coach, NLP Master Practitioner and #1 Best Selling Author.

Website: www.3CFusion.com
Blog: www.3cfusion.com/blog
Facebook: www.facebook.com/3CFusion
LinkedIn: www.linkedin.com/in/josietytus
Twitter: @JosieTytus

AN INTERVIEW WITH ANELIA SUTTON

DEVELOPMENT OF A SERIAL ENTREPRENEUR

Performance: What was your previous career and how long did you work for someone else before going into business for yourself?

Anelia: I'm proud to be a military veteran with eleven years in the United States Navy Reserves, still serving. My job title was Information Technology Specialist, so gravitating to a business using my technical skill was natural.

Performance: What ignited the spark in you to start a new business venture or to make significant changes in an existing business? How did the idea for your business come about?

Anelia: I've always wanted to work for myself from a very young age. I can remember as far back as nine-years-old dreaming of opening my own business. When I wanted to go into real estate I wasn't permitted, due to age limitations. I was thirteen years old. I would play with baby dolls for sure, but I also read business books and magazines.

Performance: What do you feel is the major difference between entrepreneurs and those who work for someone else?

Anelia: Probably the major difference is the values that they were brought up with and the influences that surrounded them. If one had the blessing of being around positive and supportive people that encouraged one to reach beyond their temporary and perceived limitations, there would be more entrepreneurs. I believe that we all have a genius inside, that we are all creative and that we all have tremendous potential. The question is...will we take the time to discover, explore and develop our potential and other blessings?

Using the metaphor of the elephant, if when young, the elephant is tied up to a pole, it will struggle to break free. After several unsuccessful attempts to free itself, it finally settles down to accept its fate and doesn't try to escape anymore. Therefore, when it is older and bigger and even though it is stronger, it still perceives that it can't master the pole and break free. So, it becomes docile and gives up the pursuit of freedom.

If when young, human beings are told that they can't do this and that, they must get a JOB (Just Over Broke) for a living and that is the only way to make money and create wealth, then they might believe that and work at something they may not be happy with for the rest of their lives, and consequently grow to feel resentful or unfulfilled. This can also result in depression and other feelings of gloom that captivate them and continue to work against them.

Of course, with all due respect for people who are working for others, if you are clear on who you are, your values and you share a vision with others, you may join them on a mission to accomplish great things. That is not necessarily working *for* someone, but rather with someone to realize a mutual dream. There are great intra-prenueurs too, who are entrepreneurs that work within large corporations or organizations.

I, personally, value freedom highly. The freedom to work wherever I want, whenever I want and with whomever I want. That also led me towards the type of work that I chose to do. I would free all the elephants and retrain them into their "natural" environments.

There is a great sense of self-worth and self-efficacy that comes from being an entrepreneur. I want everyone to feel and experience that. One of my missions is to free cubicle workers by empowering them with the IT skills they need to create wealth on the Internet.

Performance: What do you typically tell people when they ask you what you do now?

Anelia: It depends on the situation. If I have time, I'll say I'm an entrepreneur which is often greeted with a puzzled stare. I should be more specific I guess, and simply tell them what I actually do. I build websites, empower people to create their own income sources or businesses on the web, and I am a writer and author of books. The next one to come out is Tiny Little Empires.

Performance: What do you enjoy most about what you do?

Anelia: Being the master and ruler of my own schedule, having the freedom to travel and spend quality time with family. Engaging and communicating with people in all walks of life. Seeing people become highly successful as a result of my work and their input. Seeing people come into their own by becoming empowered in every great, productive and contributive way. Seeing smiles on people's faces. It's the fruit of my labour. :)

Performance: What are your hobbies? What do you do for fun in your non-work time?

Anelia: This may come across a bit strange, but I love treasure hunting for miniature chairs in vintage and thrift shops. I have a few adorable mini chairs in my collection now! Other than that, my hobby is health. To research the best foods and nutrients available and to look after myself well and others too. I intend to open up a vegan restaurant in the near future.

Performance: What does a day-in-your-life consist of?

Anelia: I read and respond to emails, write, and conduct exciting learning meetings with my team all day until I shut myself down. I tutor my son, go on shopping sprees with my mom and spend lots of quality time with my family and friends.

Performance: What book has inspired you the most?

Anelia: *Who Moved My Cheese* by Spencer Johnson. It's a great book if you have an entrepreneurial mindset. I use it as a reference whenever I'm faced with making a big decision.

Performance: Excluding yours, what company, or business do you admire the most?

Anelia: I don't want to name one company but in general, I admire any company with these key attributes: they have an inspirational story behind their success, they have a strong reputation for partnering with staff (i.e., team members), they give to charity, and they exercise community responsibility.

Performance: Other than deciding to work for yourself, what was the single most important decision you made that contributed to your success?

Anelia: I measure success based on time freedom – so all of my decisions are based on the high value I place on precious time rather than money, though the money does come.

The single most important decision I made was to decide to give birth to myself. . .

- To become all that I potentially am.

- To recognize who I am based on my good and healthy values.

- To create a crystal clear vision of the life I wanted to lead.

- To create an empowering role for myself to contribute to this world and humanity in every positive, meaningful and significant way.

I am on a mission to give this world the best that I have, the best way I know how and to keep experiencing, growing and developing my potential and that of others.

Performance: How does being an entrepreneur affect your relationships with your friends and family?

Anelia: In the beginning, it was awkward because friends and family wouldn't respect my work space or my work time because I work from home. Eventually, I had to set a few boundaries.

For the most part, my decision to become an entrepreneur has enhanced my relationships with my friends and my family in as much as I was living a life true to myself and as a result became a much happier, freer and more fulfilled human being. In addition, I could spend more quality time with them. This had an enormous positive impact on those in my environment. Of course, at first my friends and family were a bit challenged as it "appeared" like I was going against the grain of how things were supposed to be and "should" be. Naturally, I was. :)

Soon, however, and once they accepted my new parameters, they came to realize that this was the best thing that I ever did and continue to do.

Performance: What would you say are the top skills and attributes needed to be a successful entrepreneur?

Anelia:

- o To be curious, creative and respectful of others.
- o To enhance and expand their vision(s).
- o To create worthy missions that contribute to the greater good.
- o To be unstoppable!
- o To become great delegators.
- o To be humble and inspiring.
- o To empower others to do great things and then stay out of their way and let them do their thing.
- o To develop the ability to communicate clearly and effectively.
- o The ability to build and develop highly meaningful, significant and mutually-beneficial relationships.
- o The ability to manage priorities which include time management, self discipline, self management, project and people management.
- o To promote healthy living.
- o To make decisions based on good, great and healthy values.
- o To be values based, solution oriented and results driven.
- o To have a great sense of humour.
- o To become a great, gracious and influential leader.
- o To be socially responsible and contribute to this world making it a better place for all.

Performance: If you had one piece of advice to someone just starting out, what would it be?

Anelia: Set out and become the BEST 'you' possible. Share YOUR essence with the world in your own unique way. Take great care of yourself and others. NO matter what challenges you face, remember that the world is abundant, gracious and forgiving. All failures are great learning grounds. Learn the lessons and become the change you need, as Gandhi says. Dream, DREAM BIG, be bold and do great things. Take action and do it now. :) Move forward consciously, mindfully and graciously.

One of my favorite quotes is "I gotta be myself – Everyone else is taken." You were made unique for a reason. Discover what that is. Take the first step, then the next step, and so it goes until your destiny is revealed – only then will you achieve a deep sense of purpose. Otherwise, you're going to be chasing the next big thing and shiny objects for the rest of your life.

Performance: How would you like to be remembered?

Anelia: I was born to do great things. We all were. As a sensitive person when I see someone or something hurting people, I cannot ignore it. It will literally haunt my dreams until I do something about it. I simply must help by being of service in some significant way to make it better. One of my favorite quotes is "Hurt people hurt people. Healed people heal people." So, I would like to be remembered as someone who made a meaningful difference and inspired others to make a significant difference also.

I would also like to be remembered as being a force of nature. Unstoppable. One who was part of the solution NOT the problem. One who creatively did something about the needs she saw and helped heal the hurting in humanity. I would like to be remembered for the healing centers I helped to build to put an end to senseless suffering and give people a chance to reset and become the best possible thus contributing their whole being to make this world a better place for all.

ABOUT ANELIA

Anelia Sutton is the founder of TINYLITTLEEMPIRES.COM for investors seeking high-growth alternative investments and MAGICOFDOING.COM offering online courses for micropreneurs.

Anelia Sutton brings a fascinating resume and passion as a serial entrepreneur to the growing phenomenon of her online business development company Tiny Little Empires and its offshoot ORE (Online Real Estate), dedicated to creating blog-style websites that generate monthly passive income. Gaining a foothold in the ever-expanding content revolution, Sutton is helping clients across the world discover the bold new, Buffet-like asset class where no traditional investor has gone before.

A native of Panama City, Panama, the Maryland-based innovator founded her company in 2011 with a mission to invest in small business start ups in order to help other aspiring entrepreneurs to, like her, become "Ex-Cubicle" workers. She is the daughter of a Mestizo-Panamanian mother and Afro-Panamanian father. With over eleven years of service, Anelia is a veteran of the U.S. Navy (and a current Navy Reservist) who was activated for her skills in Information Technology during Operation Iraqi Freedom.

An MBA with a specialization in Human Resources Management from Northcentral University, her business management career has included the development of private and government organizations. She's also the author of three books and is a member of the National Association of Female Executives (NAFE). But for all of those personal and career accolades, when Anelia Sutton started her first online blog in 2008, admittedly "as a creative outlet to get rid of excess thoughts," the last thing on her mind was trumpeting them – though she was happy to mention the general fact that she was a serial entrepreneur.

She is a member of the National Association of Female Executives, recipient of America's Premier Experts award and proud to be a U.S. Navy Veteran still serving. Anelia Sutton is a vibrant, down-to-earth, engaging guest with an infectious laugh that will make you smile. Her expert advice has helped people build their business online.

Please direct all media, publicity, and spokesperson inquiries to: http://tinylittleempires.com/contact/.

BE AKUHLA YOU:

Get the energy you want!

PERFORMANCE: Tell us about "AKUHLA" and what inspired its creation.

NOSH: My work centers around helping my clients return to a state of inner harmony while discovering their natural capacity for abundant energy.

Clients come to me because they're experiencing general unease about their lives. They're stressed because of relationships, work and other things occurring on deeper levels. They often have difficulty processing the experience they're having and need support. These stressful situations hurt their performance at work and their personal relationships. They feel they're not doing as well as they can because they're not feeling as well as they could in their lives. Even when they try to get back up, they're spending a lot of energy to get well. They're tired and drained and might get sick or just lose the great enthusiasm and drive they once had. Maybe they're gaining weight and experiencing neck and body pains. They can't sleep, their sex drive goes down and they don't feel as alive as they want to, on the whole. These are all symptoms of a basic lack of wellness. After seeing these patterns coming up again and again in my one-on-one coaching work, I was inspired to create AKUHLA. The goal was to share my tools with a wider audience and make a bigger difference.

PERFORMANCE: What sets you apart as a coach? What do you hope to contribute through AKUHLA?

NOSH: As a coach I've always focused on the mind-body connection, looking at what is creating a state of stress, separation and tension in the body – as well as a state of general unease. Most of my work centers on removing blockages and obstacles and bad patterns that create a disturbance in the body's natural communication abilities.

Internal discovery, for me, means exploring and then uncovering the root causes of mental and emotional garbage, toxins, stress, pollution, old traumas and negative patterns from the past we are beholden to. We often cover up the productive, healthy elements of ourselves with an illusion of self-image, where we perceive ourselves to be something other than what we truly are.

When the things we expect from life suddenly change - from friendships and work relationships to marriage - they can alter our perception of our own reality into something we can no longer enjoy.

AKUHLA is designed to provide emotional, mental, physical and spiritual support. It is tremendously rewarding to know that we're helping someone out there to live the life they have always dreamed of, clearing blockages and problems they have lived with for years.

Engaging with the tools and information on the website can really help people overcome the stress and anxiety that has been limiting them. We hope to bring them joy, a state of total confidence, clarity and a sense of certainty, and to be a catalyst for their fresh and exciting new game plan for living. Ultimately, we want people to experience a deeply satisfying level of success through AKUHLA.

PERFORMANCE: How do you define success and how has that definition changed over the years?

NOSH: Success is wellness and wellness is success. It all boils down to that. However, it took me a while to come to this understanding. When I was younger, I thought success meant having a big house, money in the bank, being able to take nice vacations and accumulating the usual material

Many of my early clients were financially wealthy but still unhappy.

things. But life taught me that all of those things can still leave you feeling empty and unwell.

Many of my early clients were financially wealthy but still unhappy. They were successful in certain areas of their lives, but not others. This made me examine what it would take to really create the highest quality of success, which is what lead me to create AKUHLA.

Even when people have the money to do what they want to do, they also need to have the freedom of personal time, good physical health, peace of mind, loving relationships, healthy connections with their parents and children, friends, a sense of purpose, a spiritual connection to something bigger than themselves, a sense that their work is valuable and that they are happy with their career. When these areas of a person's life start going in a beneficial direction, then they feel that they're living a well-rounded, successful life. They finally feel well.

PERFORMANCE: So can you tell us a little about your personal journey?

NOSH: Well, it's ongoing!

Everything emerged from the fact that I experienced my share of pain and suffering early on. I could not do what I wanted to do or live the life I wanted to live. I could not enjoy the simple things. Unlike most other kids, I couldn't go out and have fun. I had unusual symptoms and problems doctors could not fully understand. It was never clear why my body had so many internal problems. I was sick, drained and I just didn't feel comfortable in my own skin.

Essentially, my life was out of whack and I wanted to figure out what was going on. For me, being physically healthy again would mean I could go out in the world to celebrate, play, create wealth, contribute and have strong, productive relationships – living a life with purpose and leaving a legacy! I became unwilling to suffer anymore and did everything I could to figure out what it would take to stop my state of dis-ease.

I decided that I needed to take charge and control my health and level of well-being. I started to learn about many different styles of healing and eventually I came to understand the depth of the connections between the mind and body. Once I started to get well, strong and healthy, I realized this was a field I had come to know a lot about and it was natural to believe I could go out and help others. So really, my quest began as a child. I had the experience of losing my health and in the process of having to regain health, I realized the importance of having great energy.

PERFORMANCE: And did you carry your understanding of energy into your adult years?

NOSH: Yes… but not entirely. Gaining strength and stamina propelled me to achieve high levels of money and what I perceived to be success. However, once this so-called "success" kicked in, I started to lose my good health and energy all over again.

This time it was because I was overworking myself and failing to live with inner harmony. My days were full of stress, pressure and endless distractions. I was constantly overloaded.

When I regained balance, I realized there is a profound relationship between being healthy and wealthy. Through all of these gains and losses and gains again, I came to a deep realization that true success is finding balance and harmony of health and wealth on many levels. Having lived through the ups and downs, I completely relate to the difficulties of thriving in our modern day society. This is why I'm so passionate about sharing AKUHLA. I know firsthand that it works and has the power to completely transform a life for the better.

PERFORMANCE: So have you seen many of these life transformations with clients?

NOSH: Absolutely. The truth is we are beings of infinite potential with infinite possibilities. However, without proper guidance during the process of becoming who we are meant to be, we can get confused or stuck in relationships that stunt our growth. This leads to mundane states, lacking creativity that then limit our potential to contribute. Providing emotional, mental, physical and spiritual support through Coaching makes a big difference in determining the level of success someone achieves.

Once the client discovers their capacity to be at ease, that's the first step to cultivating energy within. Then it's just a matter of accessing it, which is where AKUHLA Tools really make an impact.

PERFORMANCE: Can you tell us about these AKUHLA Tools?

NOSH: Sure, the Tools are meant to remind people that they have a reservoir of innate intelligence with the capacity to access infinite wisdom at anytime. We empower the individual to regain a sense of wholeness in body, mind and spirit by guiding them through daily personal reflection. Clients create an "Awareness Journal" and answer engaging questions to gain a deeper understanding about what makes them function best.

In our "AKUHLA Way" interviews, I discuss in depth a range of topics stemming from questions that have come up for clients. This includes coping with pain and loss, the art of relaxation, wholeness and healing and so on. Here I offer practical tips and strategies for mastering your energy.

We also offer our "AKUHLA Meditations" – a series of audio recordings that are meant to support, challenge, encourage and heal. We think that these messages can inspire and center the listener to create a better, brighter day both at work and at home. It's all meant to promote the healthy habit of choosing to be AKUHLA you everyday.

PERFORMANCE: Does AKUHLA work for everyone?

NOSH: We like to think so and to make it easier we provide our audience with different levels of engagement. This includes everything from online courses to seminars and VIP Luxury Retreats. We also offer an AKUHLA energy exercise program called the Art of AKUHLA. For a select few we even offer private coaching sessions.

PERFORMANCE: What do clients experience from diving deep into the courses, seminars and retreats?

I decided that I needed to take charge and control my health and level of well-being.

NOSH: We focus on cultivating an unconquerable spirit with the support of community to foster inner calm, acceptance, peace and overall rejuvenation. Our team consists of people who are one hundred percent committed to the process of AKUHLA energy. We help people achieve their life goals through emotional stability and mental clarity. This equips them to face life's many problems "full-out" and to achieve massive results with ease and efficiency.

AKUHLA ensures that people feel successful in life on every level. This goes beyond healthy finances and pre-programmed ideas of success. We coach people to stay happy while enjoying a harmonious relationship between heart, mind and body. In fact, people love it so much, now we have a long list of clients who want exclusive one-on-one *personal coaching*.

PERFORMANCE: Really? Is there that much demand for personal Coaching?

NOSH: Yes! And there is good reason for it. A good Coach can support you in achieving phenomenal success. However, a great coach lives the teaching. This means being open about the challenges and getting down with you on a relatable level about what it really takes to create awesome energy for life.

Through AKUHLA, we look at all aspects of what it takes to feel truly happy and be fully healthy on a day-to-day basis. We achieve things on two levels: internally, we look at the space a client is living in, the repeated patterns and thoughts that are holding them down and the ways in which stress and tension live inside their body.

Externally, we strongly believe that mental, emotional stress manifests on a physical level. We examine their routines of living and their conditioned responses to stress, pressure, pain and fear. We then pinpoint the key areas that need proper healing and integration, which manifests in making our clients strong, healthy and well on the whole.

PERFORMANCE: Sounds Awesome. When did all this start and where do you see it going in the future?

NOSH: I started out as an acupuncturist and found that the patients coming in had symptoms and problems that modern medicine failed to address. They would come to me suffering from a general unease about their lives, feeling that their energy is "just off," or they're having trouble sleeping. They were in pain on many levels, often taking pills everyday, and experiencing many unwanted side effects and that was not their idea of "feeling good or living well." They wanted something more, so I started digging deeper and found a solution. I realized that most people actually know why they are suffering. They are aware on some level about the root causes behind their pain and misery. They just don't know how to fix these areas of imbalance in their life.

In the process of helping these people, a significant pattern started to emerge. I noticed that the hidden cause for most of the pain and stress was around troubled relationships either with significant others, parents, siblings, close friends, their boss at work or with money. Sometimes it was their relationship to the physical image of their body and poor self-perception. The process of healing and supporting these clients to find freedom from pain led me to develop AKUHLA.

This has become my main focus. This involves more than treatment of pain. With AKUHLA, we offer new ways to perceive and actualize the process of having great energy. In the future, I see this method adding a lot of significant value to the field of mind-body medicine.

PERFORMANCE: That's so wonderful. Can you tell us a little about the AKUHLA approach?

NOSH: It's the process of remodeling the human being! We get down to the studs, to the very foundation of what a person believes and truly desires. After a complete understanding of the client as an individual, we design a custom plan, laying out what needs to be done. We then do everything we can to help them model the best vision of living an amazing life.

We coach them on how to maintain their mental, physical, emotional and spiritual energy in all different areas of life while staying laser-focused on creating great results. We do all this based on who they really are at the deepest level of being. This is why the process of achieving success can actually heal, because clients are now creating a life that energizes the soul and it satisfies them on the whole.

They transform to become a new individual who can show up for themselves and the world. They respond very differently to stress, pain, problems and difficulty. They see themselves in the best light and see their situation with clarity. This makes them effective when dealing with fear and trauma – the past no longer limits them.

With our help, they are able to take the necessary action required to create a massive level of internal energy. This makes them unstoppable and what's great is that they learn to enjoy both the process and the result.

PERFORMANCE: Thank you for sharing all this wonderful information. It's been a pleasure talking to you.

NOSH: Thank you for listening. This was fun and I hope we talk soon again.

AKUHLA ensures that people feel successful in life on every level.

ABOUT NOSH

Energized by all good things in life, Nosh Marzbani has a passion for the study and pursuit of cultivating great energy.

As a highly respected and sought-after Holistic Healer, Acupuncturist, Coach and Trainer based in Beverly Hills, California, Nosh focuses on addressing the whole person and is an expert at integrating the mind, body and spirit. In so doing, he guides and supports his clients to achieve deeper levels of balance, harmony, physical energy and inner peace through personal empowerment.

As an expression of his life's quest to help others gain an understanding of wellness, Nosh developed a powerful set of tools to manifest an AKUHLA you. Through his website, he connects with those seeking to fully actualize their potential while cultivating a spirit of aliveness and positivity.

In his books along with his intensive coaching retreats, online seminars and workshops, Nosh offers many opportunities for you to connect with his work and find real success through AKUHLA.

Nosh loves adventure and action sports. He travels the world, learning about human nature, music, art and culture. He is a serial entrepreneur and real estate investor who became a millionaire before the age of 30. He graduated with honors as a Master in Asian Medicine and served as the Admissions Director for SAMRA University. Nosh has also won multiple gold medals in martial arts and continues to be a devoted practitioner.

To learn more about Nosh and his work, please visit: www.akuhla.com

AN INTERVIEW WITH DR. JOSEPH MARCIUS

SMILING SUCCESS

PERFORMANCE: The word 'success' is often associated with money and productivity, but what does it mean to you? How do you define success?

DR. MARCIUS: I don't think of success in monetary terms. It's really more about doing what you love to do and being able to do what you love to do well and with passion, in both your personal and professional life.

PERFORMANCE: How does that translate to you and your profession?

DR. MARCIUS: I truly enjoy helping people, and dentistry has allowed me to do that on a daily basis for many years. When I can make someone feel good about themselves, I consider it a success.

PERFORMANCE: Tell me more about that. Is there one person you helped who really stands out?

DR. MARCIUS: There was this one patient – let's call him Jim – who always hid his smile behind his mustache. When he first came to my office, I could see his teeth were in really bad shape. He was so embarrassed that he grew his facial hair long enough so it would hang over his lips. At the time he had just been laid off and was looking for a new job, but he was having difficulty with the interviewing process. He didn't have much confidence in his appearance, and I think that really came through to prospective employers. So I examined him and then we started on a treatment plan. Within weeks Jim was a completely different person.

PERFORMANCE: How so? What kind of changes did you see in him?

DR. MARCIUS: He seemed truly happy for the first time since we met. When I wrapped up our final appointment, I handed him a mirror so that he could see his teeth for himself. At first he tried to smile, but he couldn't. It was as if his muscles were out of practice, like they hadn't moved that way in years. When he opened his mouth, he actually lifted his hand to touch his teeth, as if he didn't think they were real. Tears came to his eyes. He took my hand and we did the guy hug thing, you know, shook hands, shoulder to shoulder. He said, "I cannot believe what you did for me. Thank you so much."

PERFORMANCE: When he had that reaction, what was going through your mind? What did it mean for you to help someone in that way?

DR. MARCIUS: I was so happy that he was happy. I was thinking to myself, I hope this changes your life as much as I know it can. I want my patients to know that I think about them as people. I think about their overall health, both physically and emotionally. To help someone land a job, to help them make a connection with the love of their life, or to help them regain the use of their teeth, that means everything to me. It's why I got into this line of work.

PERFORMANCE: So how did you get into dentistry? Was this a lifelong dream or did you sort of stumble upon it?

DR. MARCIUS: I sort of stumbled upon it. There were a few career paths I thought about pursuing, but dentistry seemed like the perfect fit for what I wanted, which was to be my own boss in my own practice in an industry where I could help others. I knew a dentist who worked in the area where I grew up, and I talked to him a lot about the business. He told me that dentistry was a rewarding career, but it also allowed him to do other things he enjoyed, like cycling, and traveling. I thought, gosh, I'd love to have that kind of balance in my life.

PERFORMANCE: Was it what you expected it to be?

DR. MARCIUS: No! Not at all! It was a lot more work than I ever anticipated. But part of that has to do with who I am as a person. I always want to be the best. Not that I want to compete with anyone else, I just want to be the best version of myself and therefore the best dentist that I can be.

PERFORMANCE: You've been a dentist for more than 30 years, and I'm sure you've seen a lot of changes in the industry during that time. How have you been able to keep up with developments in the field while still running your own business

DR. MARCIUS: As with so many industries, there has been rapid growth and development when it comes to the technology and materials that we use in dentistry. I feel it is my responsibility to my patients to keep up on the latest changes so that I can give them the best choices in care available today. That has meant taking thousands of hours of continuing education courses across the country, and even abroad. I've had to carve out the time from my work schedule to make room for these courses, since many of them are several days long, not including travel time. But I choose not to look at it as a hassle or inconvenience. Instead, I see it as an opportunity to learn and better myself.

PERFORMANCE: A lot of your patients have deep-set fears of the dentist. Why did you decide to make helping these people a main focus of your practice?

DR. MARCIUS: Because I also hated going to the dentist! My dad used to have to chase me around the house and sometimes around the block just to get me there. I was afraid. It seemed like every time I went I was hollered at for something, like I didn't brush my teeth enough, or it had been too long since my last appointment. Plus the dentists I went to lived up to the stereotype – they were all old and grumpy!

PERFORMANCE: Do you remember your first trip to the dentist?

DR. MARCIUS: Not really, probably because I blocked it out! But from what I do remember, the anticipation of what was going to happen next was almost too much to handle. The machines made these noises that were enough to make me want to jump out of my skin. I was always relieved once it was over.

PERFORMANCE: So, can this kind of anxiety be crippling?

DR. MARCIUS: Absolutely. Many of our patients avoid the dentist for years because they are afraid, which can greatly impact their overall health. Sometimes, the fear intensifies when the patient is also dealing with a physical disability. This is part of the reason why I began to learn more about IV Sedation.

PERFORMANCE: What's IV Sedation? And how has it allowed you to help your patients?

DR. MARCIUS: IV Sedation stands for intravenous sedation, or sedating patients using an IV. I started learning more about this method when I began to focus my studies on implant dentistry, but I didn't realize just how helpful it would be for people with high anxiety. Some patients have emotional or physical limitations that have prevented them from seeking out dental care. Many have had a terrible past dental experience, and the sound or feeling of the metal instruments near their teeth can trigger those negative memories.

PERFORMANCE: Do you remember a particular patient with severe emotional or physical needs that was helped through IV Sedation?

DR. MARCIUS: Yes. A few years ago, a young man with Tourette Syndrome came to us, looking for help. On top of dealing with this disorder, which greatly affects his ability to communicate with others, his teeth were also in pretty bad shape. His mother explained to me that her son – I'll call him John – suffered from very quick tics that shook his head and shoulders. This made it extremely difficult for him to get something as simple as an X-ray, let alone a long dental procedure. But over time, I was able to gain his trust.

PERFORMANCE: How did you do that?

DR. MARCIUS: On the first appointment, I just talked to him. We sat down in a consultation room away from all of the instruments and other dental things that made him nervous. I sat eye to eye with him, and said John, what is it that I can do for you? He said, I'm afraid of the dentist but I want a nice smile. I said, I understand how you feel, don't be embarrassed. I told him, if you trust me, I can help you overcome this fear. He looked at me with some skepticism and said, you know, I'm really worried about having needles in my mouth, I'm worried about moving, because of the tics. I wanted to assure him with the IV Sedation, he would not have to worry about any of that. So gradually, after we got a few appointments out of the way, we built this trust, and eventually a friendship. He went on to get a girlfriend, join the marching band and study to become an airplane mechanic, and I think he would say that was in part due to a renewed sense of confidence that came from his new smile.

PERFORMANCE: Does your success as a dentist depend on this trust?

DR. MARCIUS: Yes, very much so. I cannot do the work I need to do for the people I want to help unless they let me in. When they have trust in me, that's when I can offer the best care. Dentistry is a very intimate thing because I'm in their personal space. In our culture, when you get within three feet of someone you're usually getting ready to kiss them! Patients, especially those that fear the dentist, are going to be uncomfortable with this, emotionally speaking. They know there might be some physical discomfort too, because no one has dental instruments in their mouth every day. Also, I want them to trust that I'm not judging them. I don't want them to feel bad or embarrassed about the state of their teeth. A lot of people who come to me, their teeth will be black, actually black, from decay. Some know their breath is very bad from periodontal disease. Because of all of these factors, I ask them for permission to look in their mouth. I want them to feel like they are in control of the appointment.

PERFORMANCE: What do you say to people who feel like it's too late in life to fix their teeth?

DR. MARCIUS: Recently, I had a patient who told me he was babysitting his young granddaughter when the little girl asked him, "Grandpa, what's wrong with your teeth?" He scheduled an appointment with me that day to get his smile fixed. He's 70 years old, and his teeth never bothered him before, not until his granddaughter said something. He didn't want her to think of him as the grandfather with a bad smile. Another man, also a grandfather, came to us recently with a similar problem. He hadn't worn dentures in years but his granddaughter was getting married. He told me, "Doc, I need new teeth so I can be in the family portraits." What I tell people is, if your teeth bother you, something can be done, no matter what your age. There should be nothing holding you back.

PERFORMANCE: It really seems like you've been just as affected by your patients as they are by your dentistry.

DR. MARCIUS: I know I'm greatly affected by them. Some of my patients land their dream job, or finally get the courage to ask out the guy or girl they want to date. Things also happen to them that never happened before. I've had patients tell me about standing in line at the grocery store where other shoppers went out of their way to tell them, wow, you have a beautiful smile. One person told us about her first time eating a full rack of Baby Back ribs, which was made possible because we restored her ability to chew. It gives me a lot of joy when patients return to my practice to tell me these stories. Their success becomes my success.

ABOUT DR. JOE

Patients of Dr. Joseph G. Marcius come away with a beautiful smile and renewed sense of self-worth. With more than 25 years of advanced training in both the surgical and restorative phases of implant dentistry, and thousands of hours of continuing education, Dr. Marcius brings the benefits of modern science to his daily work. As co-author of the book, *Wake Up! With a New Smile!*, a patient's guide to dentistry, he understands the importance of ensuring the best possible experience for every person he treats.

A first time visit to the office of Dr. Joe is unlike many other trips to the dentist. His friendly staff welcomes patients into an airy waiting room, where they are invited to relax before a one-on-one consultation. Many who seek the help of Dr. Marcius suffer from physical disabilities or deep-set fears of the dentist, concerns he addresses during this meeting. When appropriate, he discusses the possibility of administering Intravenous Sedation, a method to ease the patient to sleep prior to a procedure. Dr. Marcius then designs a treatment plan tailored to the specific needs of the individual. After he is finished, patients often shed tears of joy. For many of them, it is the first time they can remember truly smiling.

When he is not at his dental practice, Dr. Marcius is most likely in another part of the country honing his craft. In 2014 alone, he attended more than 300 hours of dental implant continuing education courses, which included a trip to the Dominican Republic where he performed maxillary sinus bone grafting surgery in order to place dental implants and restore a person's ability to chew. On a recent trip to New York City, Dr. Marcius gave a televised interview at The Hard Rock Cafe in Times Square to talk about his success in the field.

Dr. Marcius is a lifelong resident of Akron, Ohio. He graduated from St. Vincent High School, and attended the University of Akron before earning his Doctor of Dental Surgery degree from Case Western Reserve University. He is a member of many organizations, including the American Dental Society of Anesthesiology, the American Academy of Implant Dentistry, the American Academy of Cosmetic Dentistry, The Crown Council and others.

He has also participated in a number of postdoctoral training programs at various institutions, including The Dawson Academy, Sclar Center for Implant Dentistry, the Calderon Institute of Implant Dentistry, the Misch Implant Institute and more.

For additional information on Dr. Marcius, please visit: www.AkronDental.com

BY RICHIE JAYNES

THREE PILLARS TO HIGH PERFORMANCE AND A CHAMPION LIFE

When it comes to living, performing at a high level and being a champion, there are certain pillars that I believe need to be anchored place for them to be achieved. I have built a multi- million-dollar business with one of the largest, most successful, organizations in the direct sales industry. This is a direct reflection of my ability to establish these pillars in my life. As I look back on my life and reflect, I find that the one most important pillar is my Spiritual pillar. There have been many people who have played a significant role and influenced my life. The main characteristic that they all possessed was their spiritual life. They all had a certain calmness and peace about themselves. They were confident and how they handled all kinds of situations was evident in their actions. Your spiritual pillar, I believe, is the most important area that needs to be your foundation if you desire to succeed. Without this pillar as your foundation, all the other areas will never become aligned and in order. There have been times in my life when things didn't go the way I had wanted, and when I reflect on it, it was usually when the Spiritual Pillar was not aligned or had been compromised.

Whatever your beliefs are, it is imperative you have a strong spiritual pillar in place. The stronger the foundation the harder it will be to bring down. I would encourage you to seek out a mentor that has a strong spiritual life. This person you will seek wisdom and counsel from as you grow, and come into situations where you will require another sound viewpoint. They will hold in confidence your discussions and will be able to hold you accountable while growing and making this journey. Your spiritual life will be your compass. It will direct you and determine how you handle everyday situations and decisions with a peace you haven't ever experienced before. There is no room for compromise in this area. Be strong and stand firm within your Spirituality pillar, and it will set everything else in motion on the right course.

When I was first starting in the business and entrepreneurial world, one of the first lessons I learned was in order to be successful, I had to work on myself and Personal Growth. Personal growth is the second pillar in your quest for high performance. My very first mentor had the single greatest influence on my life. He taught me Personal Growth is a pillar of success. Always work harder on yourself than anything else. He was a strong spiritual person who helped me develop that pillar, as well. It was not a coincidence that he had both of these qualities. I would describe him as a combination of Vince Lombardi, Tom Landry, and Billy Graham all rolled into one. As you might imagine, a very strong individual. When moving towards high performance/success remember that personal growth will always come before the financial growth. It will take time to achieve personal growth so patience and hard work is a must. This pillar is something you will constantly be working on throughout your life.

Personal growth is not a one-time deal. It's an all-the-time deal. Most of your great leaders work on their personal growth till the day they die. It is a lifetime commitment. Personal growth requires you to be intentional. I want to highly encourage you to get engaged in personal growth books, tapes, seminars and whatever else that you can, that will add value to your personal growth. The level of your performance will be directly dictated and related to the books you read, the tapes/CDs/podcasts you listen to, and the people you spend time with. As you become better at these two pillars, you will find you will climb towards performing at a higher level. Your level of income will always be determined by the level of your personal growth.

A prime example of this is when athletes come into a lot of money through a professional contract worth millions; if they lack personal growth and spiritual pillars many are not able to handle what comes along with this money, and make poor decisions that have life-changing, unintended consequences. Losing it all and at the end of their careers, many end up working at a car wash, laying bricks, or getting into trouble. I could give many examples of situations that occur due to not having personal growth. This is due primarily because their personal growth has not caught up with their financial growth. You may be saying to yourself: well, I know a lot of people that do not have good personal growth and they are successful. My answer is: eventually it will come crashing down in some shape or form. It will be either in the financial area or relationally.

There are numerous examples in the world today that are seen in the newspaper or on TV. It may be a movie star, athlete, or well known business person. When you lack personal growth this is the affect. So your personal growth is an extremely important pillar if you are ever going to reach a high level of performance. There are no shortcuts or easy ways to achieve personal growth. Self reflection, time, and hard work are required to achieve this pillar. This is another area you must be intentional. Always be working on your self more than you are working on your business. When you do, this pillar will grow deep roots into the ground and when the strong winds blow you will hold steady. Strong winds are inevitable and will one day come, and if you've done the hard work on yourself you will overcome anything that comes your way.

The third pillar in your journey toward high performance is the pillar of fitness. I am extremely passionate about this pillar. Fitness runs deep in my blood and has been a part of my life for many years. As far back as I can remember, I was an athlete and embraced fitness. I am a true believer in this pillar as an important part to anyone that wants to perform at a high level. Whether it be in the boardroom, playing field, or everyday life. Most of my adult life I have taught fitness as a lifestyle. You must choose to be healthy. I have witnessed many individuals that work extremely hard in business, but most neglect their health. I like to say: What good is your wealth without your health? This is the time you are supposed to enjoy life, but you cannot if you are in poor health, right?

If you ignore your health you will find those years spent taking medications and visiting doctors. Because you have neglected your health you will most likely be in some kind of constant aches or pains. You do not want to work hard all your life and get to retirement and not be able to enjoy it, do you? Fitness has to start now. Just decide to decide. The younger you start the better, but it is never too late to start. Exercise is the best anti-aging medicine around. Exercise and fitness play a vital role in your everyday success. Take a look and study high performance individuals. Those People, whose names you would recognize and consider successful in the business world, utilize exercise/fitness as part of their regimen. Whether it be a weight lifting routine, yoga, running or some sort of functional fitness, they all have it as part of their daily routine. Success leaves clues. So does failure. If wealthy, high-performing individuals are making fitness a part of their daily routine and you want to experience success too, then you may have to do what they do. Make sense? Would it not make sense for you to incorporate some sort of daily fitness regimen in to your life?

In addition to a regular fitness routine, nutrition cannot be overlooked. Eating healthy and properly fueling your body is imperative. Successful individuals also take their nutrition seriously, as well. I want to encourage you to find a good program or plan and get your health on track. There are many programs out there to choose from. I am, personally, not a fan of fads diets that are the trend of the month. What I do promote is a plan that will help you change your habits and can be followed easily on a daily basis. What I mean is it will not require a special program to achieve good health. I like healthy eating programs that allow you to go to your local supermarket and shop and buy conveniently. I am a fan of organic, locally grown I (I like supporting local farmers), and foods that are minimally processed. This includes sustainable fish and grass-fed beef—those that are not full of hormones and steroids and other harmful medications, pesticides, etc. In addition, staying away as much as you can from GMO products is ideal. I encourage you to do the same.

As you can see nutrition plays an important role. And contrary to what you may have heard or believe, you cannot 'out exercise' a bad diet. If you don't want to be discouraged take my advice. I've been doing this a long time and know what works. Don't try to reinvent the wheel or find shortcuts. There aren't any. Remember, we are talking about High Performance and living at a level that can create greatness. Make exercise and fitness part of your life and make it a lifestyle. I am not concerned with how much you do or how many minutes you exercise. I am more concerned that you are consistent. You should commit to exercising on a regular basis. As your fitness levels get better you will start to notice how your daily performance starts to improve. Being fit takes action. It's a journey and not a destination – it's a decision. Living a fit life takes commitment. Make the decision today and start living a High Performance life.

As I look back on my career from sports up to the boardroom, there is no other way to achieve success than by establishing the pillars I have shared with you. No other way to live and be able to perform at a high level. I decided that if I am going to be on this earth, I might as well be the best Me that I can be, and perform at the highest level possible. The same can be and should be be true for you. I truly believe it takes just as much effort to live a mediocre life or an average life as it does a High Performance life. You just replace some of the other habits that are holding you back and replace them with those pillars I've discussed here. When you place these three pillars into your life, achieving and living a High Performance life is more attainable. My definition of High Performance is about performing higher than your competition. It is about dominating and playing at such a high level that your competition does not even know there is a game going on or that they are even competing. Time is going to pass whether you are performing high or not.

So why not decide today to start living the life you were meant to live and reach the destiny that's waiting for you? You may have once dreamed about living at a higher level, but didn't know how to achieve it. I have given you the tools to help. Remember, a High Performance life is a journey, not a destination. Decide to live a champion's life. Make it today. Be the champion you are meant to be!

ABOUT RICHIE

Richie Jaynes has years of business leadership and even more years of business success. Richie received an athletic scholarship to play football at Abilene Christian University, which he attended for two years before transferring to Texas A&M Commerce University, where he continued to play football and received his degree in Kinesiology and Sports Studies. Upon graduation, he received a position as an Assistant Strength and Conditioning coach at a major university in Dallas, Texas achieving one of his goals in life. After a one-year stint there, and at the early age of 23, he bought one of Dallas's top fitness centers, pursuing his life goal of owning a fitness center. There he maintained and ran a successful 12,000 square foot facility with over 3000 members before selling and opening one of Dallas's best athletic training centers.

Very shortly after opening the training facility, Richie was recruited to help build and lead a sales and marketing team for a multi-million dollar direct sales company in Dallas, TX. At the age of 27, Richie became one of the top producers in Advocare International, a nutrition company that has pioneered the world of Athletic and Well-Being supplementation. Richie has recruited and lead a team of over 8,000 people, and his team has generated sales in excess of several hundred million dollars. Richie has owned and operated his own Advocare business since 1997 and has received many awards and recognitions for his outstanding performance, and has become one of the top producers in that company along with achieving their top-level Diamond distributorship.

Richie's leadership ability and relentless work ethic has also led him to the Oil and Gas industry, where he has been involved in several multi-million dollars real estate transactions and developed several oil and gas wells. Richie has helped several investors build their portfolio to great success. Richie has been married for 23 years to his wife Cindy and has two beautiful daughters. Richie continues to pursue business endeavors and opportunities, never resting and always on the look out for that next champion to help build something great.

Richie and his family's motto is:
Live Every Day Like A Champion. Be A Champion.

To contact Richie:
972-898-3754
richie@richiejaynes.com

BY DR. IVAN MISNER

TEN WAYS TO WASTE YOUR TIME IN A NETWORKING GROUP!

Referral business from networking groups can pay off handsomely, so make the most of every meeting.

Word-of-mouth marketing is a sure-fire way to generate new business. A single referral can start a chain reaction of new business as positive word spreads. It's no wonder networking groups pay off handsomely in referral business and that membership in a good networking group can be worth a considerable amount of money; especially if you calculate the time you spend each month and the value of that time.

So make your time and efforts worthwhile. Don't squander your opportunity by doing the wrong things in those meetings.

Success in a networking group comes when the rest of the group members trust you enough to open up their best referrals to you. Unless they've seen your work, you have to earn that trust by demonstrating your professionalism to them. Since founding BNI (the World's largest networking organization) almost 25 years ago, I've seen how people truly succeeded in networks and I've seen how other people totally waste their time in them.

Here are ten mistakes to avoid if you don't want to waste your time in a networking group:

1. Go ahead, air your grievances among your fellow networkers and guests; after all, they really want to hear about your complaints.

2. Wing it in your regular presentations to fellow members—don't worry, you have a mulligan.

3. Use one-on-one meetings to talk about your networking groups' issues instead of learning more about each other.

4. Focus your efforts primarily on selling your services to members of the group.

5. Don't rush to follow up on a referral when someone gives you one. Hey, they know where to find you if they really need you.

6. While other people are doing their introductions, that's the perfect time to think about what referrals you can give that week.

7. Never invite your own guests, just focus on those who show up.

8. Don't worry if you get to the meeting late. No one will notice.

9. Absenteeism, it's no big deal. You can just call in your referrals ... right?

10. Take that phone call and check your messages during a meeting. No, no, it doesn't bother anyone; actually it's a sign of real professionalism that everyone admires.

Imagine how you'd respond if someone in your networking group continually exhibited the behaviors above. Would you be enthusiastic to pass them referrals? Of course not! You'd be hesitant, rightfully, because they've convinced you that they are unprofessional and irresponsible. Of course you'd withhold your valued connections.

We all need to beware of these common pitfalls and take great care to avoid them. They're great reminders that doing business through word-of-mouth marketing requires a special ingredient that only you can supply—commitment.

Commit to the process from the beginning. You have to be an active, responsible, professional, accountable participant and show your fellow networkers the respect, attention, and support that you want them to give you.

You see, the key concept in referral marketing is relationships, and referral relationships don't just spring up full grown—they must be nurtured. Avoid the ten mistakes on this list because they're detrimental to growing your referral relationships; they will cause the time you spend in your networking meetings to be nothing more than a waste.

Focus on growing your referral relationships by acting in ways that are exactly opposite of what's described above and concentrate on building relationships based on mutual trust and shared benefits. You'll get a lot more out of your group and so will your fellow members.

Remember, if you start putting together your network when the need arises, you're too late. The better way is to begin developing relationships now with the people whose help you will need in the future. Your networking group meetings offer the perfect opportunity and the perfect place to do this. Make the most of this opportunity because there's no room for wasted time. And if you see chronic offenders at your next meeting, print out this list and pass it along.

ABOUT DR. IVAN

Dr. Ivan Misner is the Founder and Chairman of BNI, the world's largest business networking organization. He is called the "father of modern networking" by CNN.

Dr. Misner is also the Sr. Partner for the Referral Institute, an international referral training company.

Dr. Ivan Misner is a New York Times bestselling author and writes a regular blog at: www.BusinessNetworking.com. His latest book *Business Networking and Sex* will be released in early 2012 and can be previewed at: www.BusinessNetworkingAndSex.com.

A legacy plan can meet
the needs of many
people who may
not have a lot
of wealth.

BY MARILYN GARNER, ESQ.

YOUR LEGACY PLAN:
A Building Block For Generational Success

In the Bible, Abraham is known as the "father of many nations." I also consider him to be a very wise man. Abraham created one of the earliest legacy and estate plans that we know. He shared his wisdom and wealth with his many sons, and even included plans for his burial. The benefit for Abraham's very large blended family is that the vast family wealth and spiritual heritage were passed forward for generations, with no disharmony!

In another biblical account, one of the greatest examples of legacy planning is David's provision and instructions for building a magnificent temple for the Lord. Before his death, David "prepared abundantly" his own legacy and estate plan for transferring to his son, Solomon, not only family wealth, but instructions for life and for erecting the temple. In 1 Chronicles 22, David gave Solomon specific instructions, including material, for completing the project.

What's fascinating is that in verse 5, David describes his son Solomon as 'young and tender' (inexperienced). David knew, then, that he must make extensive preparations before his death. David understood that allowing Solomon to gain access to all that was stored up for him was a recipe for disaster and not success. This is a major consideration on which I advise my clients – resist the urge to give your children too much too soon. A sudden transfer of riches into the lap of an unsuspecting, unprepared youngster (or even oldster) can be a disservice to the child and the parent.

How can an estate plan or legacy plan be incorporated into your family's success story? Advance planning for perpetuation of your family and personal goals ensures your control over decisions. This is one of the areas where we see that failure to plan is planning to fail. Most people spend their working years pursuing careers and building wealth. Everyone plans for a long life well lived. But what happens if you are sidelined by illness, injury, disability and eventual death. Who will speak for you when you cannot speak for yourself? Will your family be cared for in the manner that you intend? How will your wealth be divided? Who will care for your minor children? Success is not limited to career, business or academics. Success is an integral part of your family heritage.

An estate plan is mostly a set of documents that define: What do you have? Who gets what and when. It deals primarily with transferring material possessions. A simple estate plan may not be sufficient to transfer non-material wealth of a family to future generations. A legacy plan, on the other hand, is more about "YOU," as a person. It includes what is meaningful and important to you that you believe should be passed on to the next generation. It is not limited to transferring material wealth.

A legacy plan will include conveying to heirs your family values, history and experiences, religion and spiritual background, personal goals, medical history, intellectual property, reputation, leadership qualities and so much more. David was a man after God's own heart, and much of the legacy that David left for Solomon was a continuation of the same relationship with God that David had. Because it includes more than just fortune and wealth, a legacy plan can meet the needs of many people who may not have a lot of wealth. Preparation of either a legacy plan or estate plans is incomplete until all things necessary for completion of the plan are identified and provided. They both are built on the basis of plan and provision. Your greatest achievement depends on a good plan and sufficient provision.

Question: As a practitioner, what kinds of information should a person include in a legacy plan?

Answer: Some of the things that I recommend for preparing a legacy plan include:

- What is the family's medical history?

- What is the family structure: is it a blended family – (which affects 95,000,000 people).

- Are there former spouses or children from other relationships?

- What provisions will be made for present spouse? former spouse? minor children? adult children? Step children?

- What are the plans for rearing minor children in the event of your death or disability?

These are some of the major considerations for a good legacy plan. If these major decisions are not made in advance, a person risks having these decisions made for them by others, such as a court or guardian. Imagine the effect on your loved ones if these decisions are not made in advance.

Question: Should parents talk to their children about their legacy or estate plan's specific provisions?

Answer: I believe that not talking to your children could be a tremendous missed opportunity for most families. Children need to know that their parents have made plans for their own care in the event of illness or disability. The children also need to know that a careful plan has been prepared and that the parents have made specific provisions for the children. I do not believe that the children need to know the exact details of the plan; this may create unnecessary anxiety for the parents and children.

At the same time, it's important to remember that approximately $42 trillion will be inherited by or passed on by baby boomers. That's $12 trillion from their parents, and another $30 trillion that they will pass on to their children. This level of wealth should be discussed with family when it is appropriate. Passing on wealth is certainly important, but one of the most effective ways to teach children about your views on wealth is to let them see the parent's example of managing assets. This is another way to achieve success for your family.

Question: There will be a lot of business owners who will want to know what should be done with their businesses when they retire or die. What would you recommend?

Answer: I would like to see that family assemble a team of its most trusted advisors to devise a strategy for continuing, transferring to family, winding down, or even selling the business. The team should consist of a business advisor, CPA and tax planner, attorney, or other parties who can assist.

Question: If you were sitting across from a client, what would you specifically say concerning a leaving a legacy?

Answer: As I'm sitting across from a client, here are some questions that I would like to get the answer to:

- What are the most important non-material assets that you would like to pass on to your children?

- If you could distill all of your words of wisdom down to a single theme, what would you want your children to know?

- Does your family have a specific religious or spiritual tradition that you want your children to be raised in – in the event you are no longer around?

- What three events most shaped one's life?

- What were the three best decisions you've ever made?

- What are you most proud of about your life?

- Of all the things you've done and accomplished in your life, what has given the biggest fulfillment?

- What guiding principles do you live by?

- Who would you consider to be your most trusted advisor? What is the most valuable piece of advice they ever gave you?

- What has brought you the most joy? Sadness?

Question: What are some obstacles that might occur in building a great legacy plan?

Answer: Again, if it's not inclusive of both a plan AND provision, it can cause disasters for the surviving family members.

We'll take the example of Michael Jackson, the world-famous entertainer. Michael Jackson established the Michael Jackson Family Trust, which laid out the exact instructions for how he wanted his family to be accommodated. It was a great plan, but he skipped one very important little step. He never funded the trust. He did not take the final step to transfer his assets into the trust! Because he never gave provision, his family was forced to suffer through court hearings, legal expenses and delay that largely could have been avoided.

Question: Speaking of obstacles, what challenges should families try to avoid.

Answer: Parents know the strengths and weaknesses of their children. Decisions have to be made with these sensibilities in mind. David knew that his son Solomon was too young and inexperienced with life and business to turn everything over to him at one time. Some children may not be good money managers. Some may have substance abuse or developmental challenges. Most young children do not have the ability to manage large sums of money. (Think of professional athletes who make a lot of money and are penniless in a few years.) Third parties such as guardians or trustees can help to ensure the successful completion of the parents' plan.

Another thing that families should avoid is naming one child as trustee over another. That could lead to the kind of family legacy that you don't want, which is generational family disputes and squabbles.

If you have a plan in place – congratulations to you! If not, or if your plan has not been reviewed by your attorney in the past five years, you might want to take some time to get a makeover or checkup. October 19-25th of this year is National Estate Planning Awareness Week.

Take some time to look at what you can do to support the success of your life. A carefully constructed legacy plan will positively impact your children and generations to come. It's never too early to start planning your legacy to ensure its greatest success.

ABOUT MARILYN

Marilyn Garner, Esq. is the founder and Managing Attorney at the Law Office of Marilyn Garner, Principal Office in Arlington, Texas. Marilyn's three primary practice areas are Legacy Planning, Small Business Consulting and Bankruptcy. Marilyn represents individuals, families and small businesses in State and Federal Courts of Texas.

Marilyn's expertise includes litigation, claims, trials, and hearings in all legal proceedings involving financial distress from excessive debt and Estate Planning issues. A highly important segment of Marilyn's duties includes compassionate individual counseling regardless of client station in life.

After being mentored at a large national law firm by two attorneys who became bankruptcy judges, Marilyn sought to bring "big law firm" expertise to the individual, family and small business level. Marilyn's view is that a "small claim" is entitled to the same vigorous representation as any professional sports team, institution of higher learning, Fortune 1000 corporation or even a large hospital district.

Marilyn's favorite part of practicing law is FINDING THE SOLUTION! Often, there is no single best answer. Marilyn's joy is working through the issues, testing different options to best resolve a client's problem and to realize a great conclusion. Her clients are always provided the personal service and dedication to which they are entitled.

In 2012, Marilyn was honored as a participant in the Inaugural Class of "Who's Who in Black Dallas," Other awards and recognitions include being peer-rated AV Preeminent 5 on a 5-point scale by Martindale-Hubbell and recognized as an article presenter for the Morgan King Bankruptcy Symposium of California. Marilyn has been featured locally on KRLD-CBS radio, WFAA-ABC TV, KDFW-FOX TV and features a nationally-syndicated interview in 2014 broadcasts on FOX News, ABC, CBS and NBC television affiliates.

It was during her representation of individuals suffering through illness, unemployment, threatened loss of assets and resulting strained family relationships, that Marilyn recognized a need to help individuals define and protect their legacies. She knew that she needed to help those dear people realize and protect their true worth and how to pass on the fullness of their lives – history, experiences, heritages and family legacies - to help future generations reach their own potential and success.

Despite her busy career, Marilyn makes time to be involved with community and professional organizations. She has been a former member of the National Association of Bankruptcy Trustees, National Association of Consumer Bankruptcy Attorneys, and Dallas County and Tarrant County Bar Associations. Marilyn was past President of the Dallas Association of Black Women Attorneys. She is a current or former Board member of the following organizations: Nexus Solutions, New Beginnings of Arlington, and Medical Center of Arlington Cancer Center Advisory Board. Marilyn demonstrated her dedication to children as a Founding Board Member for Metro Christian Academy of Arlington.

Marilyn was born in Cleveland, Ohio and now resides in Arlington, Texas with her husband of 34 years. Marilyn enjoys traveling, gardening, horseback riding and spending time with her relatives and church families.

You can connect with Marilyn at:
marilyn@legacyplan.academy
facebook.com/legacyplanacademy

BY DANETTE GOSSETT

IF I BUILD IT, WILL THEY COME?

I was on a roll in my 20's and 30's with my marketing career working at some of the top advertising agencies in New York City. I was moving up the ranks quite nicely and by the time I was 32 years old, I had moved to the client side as the Director of Marketing for a large national cruise company. I thought I had arrived!!

Well, a little over two years later I was downsized quite unexpectedly. We had merged with another company but I didn't think my position was at risk. I had heard that their Marketing executive had interviewed for my job and not gotten it, so I assumed I was safe.

I was wrong.

I immediately put my name out in the community looking for consulting work while I looked for a job. I was recently divorced so had no other support and of course I had to eat! I was fortunate. I received offers for consulting as well as some interesting job positions. I didn't really enjoy the consulting work. I would work hard to develop plans and strategies for my clients and when they didn't take my advice it was very disconcerting. Why pay me if you weren't going to listen?

After a couple of months, I was offered the opportunity to set up an in-house advertising agency at a major telecommunications corporation. The challenge was very interesting to me, that is, until I walked into their lobby for my final interview. I don't know what was different that day, but as I walked up to the receptionist the hair on the back of my neck stood up. I felt uncomfortable. I tried to push aside the feeling that something was off and proceeded with the final day of introductions and negotiations. I really liked and respected the woman who would be my boss. But still, the uneasiness kept returning.

I knew I could do the job. Of course, it would be a challenge, but I was up for it. Yet, something kept haunting me in the back of mind. My new "boss" and I went to lunch and she began talking about my start date and package when I realized "I can't take this job." I told her that I thought one day I would spontaneously combust if I did. She was shocked but appreciated me figuring this out before I started. I was mortified but still walked out with a new lightness to my step.

While I waited for the plane to Miami I called my mom, her first reaction was, "Who is going to take care of you?" and with a very slight hesitation, my response was, "ME."

And I have.

I come from a very entrepreneurial family and I guess it was in my genes to ultimately start my own business. Of course, in the early years it was a challenge not having a regular paycheck. And I didn't realize until much later that my tolerance for financial uncertainty is higher than most. So, when I talk to people today about starting a business I tell them to do what I say not what I did. I just started. No research, no money, no real plan at the beginning. Just a need and the drive to take care of myself.

To me, failure was not an option. Ever. It never occurred to me that I might not succeed. Now, I've been told I probably could have been bigger, more successful. But that is their dream, not mine. I am successful. I've been able to sustain my lifestyle and provide employment for my employees for over 23 years.

So, how have I succeeded in business for more than 20 years in a very crowded marketing field?

PIG-HEADED DISCIPLINE

When I first started my business, I worked out of a corner of my garage. I set it up just like any office. And I got to my desk every day by 8:30am. I even ate lunch at my desk. Part of it was fear that if I didn't "work" I would miss something. I didn't put in a load of laundry or clean out the refrigerator even when no one was calling.

I always felt there was something I could be doing to grow my business.

Not long ago (wish I had done it sooner), I spent a weekend with a couple of friends at a Tony Robbins Business Mastery event. It was amazing to see the thousands of people being engaged, motivated and inspired. And, yes, I walked across the burning coals. He is an amazing coach.

And he talks about one of the key success elements. Discipline. He said you must get your PHD – Pig-Headed Discipline.

I've always been pretty disciplined. Some of my friends say I'm too "scheduled," but I have a lot on my plate and to get it all done I feel the need to have a plan, a schedule, and be disciplined.

Each month when I meet with my Advisory Board, I develop my list of accomplishments for the previous month, what my goals are for the next month and what I need their assistance with.

After my weekend with Business Mastery and Tony Robbins, I realized that my discipline wasn't something I should make excuses for, it was something I should embrace even more because it helped me to reach my goals and exceed them.

My Advisory Board recognized I was accomplishing even more than before and asked what was different. So, I explained about my PHD – Pig-Headed Discipline. Now, when we realize there is a particular project that's been hanging around too long, we remind each other that we need to focus our PHD and get it done. Many of my fellow Advisory Board members have taken this PHD to heart and feel that it's making a difference for them too.

I do believe it's a big part of my success.

MY TOP FIVE ELEMENTS FOR SUCCESS AS AN ENTREPRENEUR

Well, maybe it should be six. But then, I think Pig-Headed Discipline (PHD) really does stand on its own. If you don't think you have the discipline to self-motivate and work your plan every day, then maybe a different type of success is your path.

1. Ask for the Business

I was the Chairman of the Coral Gables Chamber of Commerce (an organization at the time of about 1800 members) and during our monthly breakfast meeting (with about 300 in attendance), I would impart what I hoped were words of wisdom. I started to print cards with these "tidbits" and hand them out at the end of the meetings. It would just have the simple tip. At one meeting I said don't forget to "Ask for the Business." And you know what, I got so many comments. Everyone realized that they were "networking" and not really letting people know they wanted to do business with them. People came up to me repeatedly for weeks afterwards and commented on how they had forgotten for years to ask for the business. And now they were and they were seeing positive results.

2. Be Visible

Throughout my entrepreneurial career, I have been visible in the business community. I have volunteered with non-profit organizations that were important to me and became involved in business organizations like the local Chambers of Commerce. I am still visible and involved after more than 23 years in business. I am a Trustee and Board of Directors member for the Greater Miami Chamber of Commerce and have volunteered for several of their highly visible programs. Why? Because people still like to do business with people they know and trust. And what better way to get to know me and trust me than to see me in action. Of course, I do enjoy giving back to my community. Being involved keeps me in touch with community issues and allows me to be connected to businesses and people that might not come into my sphere were I not involved. It definitely has been a significant factor of my success.

3. Be Passionate

To live a successful life at peak performance, develop a plan and set specific goals. Setting goals is like developing a business plan. When you develop a plan, you take control of your own destiny. The plan provides clear direction and focuses on the things you want to do. Your plan gives you a clear picture of the outcome you want to see at the end. Be specific; allow your plan to determine how your business should run for maximum effectiveness. The plan will keep you on track and move you forward without distractions.

4. Ask for a Referral

It's the same as asking for the business. We forget. If our clients like what we have been doing for them, then why not ask for a referral to a colleague in the same company or a different one? What holds us back? Well, my theory is that we don't ask because we don't want to bother them or we're afraid they may say no. But it's been my experience that every time I ask, I get a referral. Many times they will even say, "I can't believe I didn't suggest this sooner." I have a client who is now the CEO of a major hospital and while we used to meet quarterly, his time has become more limited as he has risen within the ranks, but we still have lunch at least twice a year. And you know what? He still comes prepared with a list of people that I should know. If you make it a part of your process, your discipline, asking regularly for referrals will pay off in your long-term success.

5. Find a Mentor

I've had mentors from basically the beginning of my career. I had a boss from one of my first jobs in New York City that I looked up to. He taught me the ropes of the advertising business. He was tough. He made sure I knew to be prepared at all times with answers to questions that might never be asked. I do believe he was a big reason for my early success in the New York Ad Agency world. We stayed in touch for more than 20 years. We didn't talk that often, but if I ever had a situation that needed an objective view, I knew I could count on his counsel. I've been fortunate that most of my past bosses have been there for me. They have offered to listen when I needed to vent about a situation or bounce off new ideas and they have even brought me business!

There have been times in my career that I wish I had asked someone other than a past boss to mentor me, but I didn't. Looking back, I realize I didn't want to bother them. I was afraid they would say no. Well, I was definitely wrong. Most successful people find the time to mentor and help. They want to. It's part of their success. And they want to help you achieve yours.

Lately, I haven't had just one mentor, I've had an advisory board of ten business people that are my collective mentors. I wish I had done it sooner. Being a small business owner sometimes you need people to hold your feet to the fire to get something done or to help you through difficult personnel and financial decisions. Even if you have PHD!

Yes, I told my mother I would take care of myself. And I have with the help of a lot of great friends, family, employees and mentors. 23 years and counting!

ABOUT DANETTE

Danette Gossett has always loved marketing and creating campaigns and promotional programs that help her clients succeed. She started her career more than 30 years ago working with some of New York City's top advertising agencies of that time including Dentsu/Y&R, Saatchi & Saatchi and Lowe Marschalk.

She moved to the corporate side of marketing as National Advertising Director for Avis Rent-a-Car Systems Inc., winning a Gold Effie for Advertising Effectiveness. Later she became the Director of Marketing Services for Royal Caribbean Cruise Line.

Danette currently resides in Coconut Grove, Florida, just south of downtown Miami. She is the President and CEO of Gossett Marketing Communications, Inc. and the co-founder of Promotions Resource LLC, and co-author of the best-selling book, *Transform*.

Her company Gossett Marketing prides itself on providing creative solutions for growing sales, building loyalty and getting results through sales promotions, products, online company stores, incentive programs and direct mail. Gossett Marketing helps a wide variety of businesses from travel, tourism and hospitality to education (Universities), healthcare and service organizations.

Promotions Resource LLC is a partnership venture with Kevin Danaher, and together they launched: www.SalesPromotions.org. They are providing a marketing and sales promotion authority website resource for businesses seeking to understand and create more effective sales promotion programs.

Danette has received a number of industry awards and recognition including: the Best-Sellers Quilly Award from the National Academy of Best Selling Authors; the EXPY Award from the National Association of Experts, Writers & Speakers; Hot Creative from Direct Magazine; Outstanding Woman Business Owner of Miami-Dade County by the National Association of Women Business Owners; Top 25 Promotional Products Industry Influencers by the Quality Certification Alliance; Top 100 Minority Business of Miami-Dade County by the Greater Miami Chamber of Commerce; Decade of Excellence from the Women's Business Development Council of Florida.

Danette is also very active in the community. She is a past Chair of the Coral Gables Chamber of Commerce, past President of the Foundation of the Coral Gables Chamber of Commerce, Mentor for the University of Miami School of Business, Member of the Board of Directors of the Greater Miami Chamber of Commerce, Trustee Member of the Greater Miami Chamber of Commerce, Chair of Business Excellence for the Greater Miami Chamber of Commerce and a Charter Member of the Ladies of PACE for the PACE Center for Girls, Miami.

For more information, visit her websites: GossettMktg.com, SalesPromotions.org and InterestingMarketingTidbits.com. Also, please follow Danette on twitter at: @ Marketngtidbits and @SalesPromoOrg

People think it is crazy for me to
do the things I dream about.
I am a big dreamer.
I always dream crazy.
Dreams motivate me.

BY PERMINDER CHOHAN

GROWTH DOES NOT JUST HAPPEN BY ACCIDENT...

You Must Work At It

When I first started out, I lived my life according to what other people wanted to see in me. I was always thinking, "If I do this, what will the other people think about me." Later on I stopped worrying about what other people thought about me and I started going after things I wanted to do in life. I no longer worried about other people's approval on the things I wanted to do.

There came a time in my life where I wanted to move up to the next level. I was not exposed to people who were in a bigger circle because I only talked to people on a smaller level. I thought if I wanted to go into a higher level or do something different, I had to come out of my comfort zone. I was afraid to approach them. I thought, "How were they going to react when I approach them to ask them something?" When I went to talk to them to get ideas, they shared all their information with me. I became so relaxed and they became the people who helped me grow in life.

People think it is crazy for me to do the things I dream about. I am a big dreamer. I always dream crazy. Dreams motivate me. When they say I'm crazy or it can't be done, I take it as a challenge and I push myself to do things better and greater each time.

While the nature of dreams needs to inspire us, you must also recognize that dreams cannot be realized in one single step. Taking a step each day will bring you closer to the things you want to see in life. To create lasting change, be specific about the things you want to do. Write down the smallest detail for each step. It is more powerful to complete ten things and achieve one single goal; especially if this goal makes a difference in all areas of your life.

Personally, I keep a notepad with me and on my night table. So many ideas go through my brain every day. Sometimes I get good ideas and bad ideas. Get into the habit of writing the good ones down to prevent you from forgetting them.

Everyone is capable of creating dreams of the life they want to live. It is impossible to fail at anything you want to do. It depends on whether you have a driving, burning desire to achieve your goals. With this burning desire, you will never fail.

NO ONE IMPROVES BY ACCIDENT AND PERSONAL GROWTH DOES NOT JUST HAPPEN ON ITS OWN

You have to work for it. Anytime you want to grow in life, it is you who needs to do it. If you want to improve your life, you must improve yourself. You need to clearly understand and know what you wish to achieve in life. Also, you will never get anything done unless you start doing it.

Several years back, I had a new advisor come to me and he expressed reservation about getting started. He did not know who he would go after once he was licensed. I told him to focus on getting licensed, and then worry about things which came later. He got his license, we worked together on our relationship, and I took him through all of the steps. He became my number one advisor in my office in the first twelve months.

RELATIONSHIPS AND BEING ACCOUNTABLE ARE VERY IMPORTANT

You have to be true to other people; be honest and put yourself in their shoes. I appreciate what others do for me. Without gratitude, happiness is rare. It's not easy to be grateful all the time. Sometimes you need to remember the people who were there in tough times for you. You need to show them gratitude and thank them for being there for you. Whatever I am today is all because of other people. Whatever I have done in life, they supported me. I have seen a tremendous growth in my business because of that.

Appreciation unlocks the fullness of life. It turns what we have into enough and more, denial into acceptance, a meal into a feast, and a stranger into a friend. Appreciation also makes sense of any past, brings happiness for today and creates the vision for tomorrow.

The other thing I do for accountability is I make my goals public. I share my goals and dreams with other people. When I tell them what I intend to do, it puts pressure on me to keep working at it. I ask them to keep asking me until I achieve my goals. It is similar to having a deadline to keep you moving. You want to be around growing people if you want to be a growing person. If you are committed, you will attract others who are committed; if you are growing in life, you will attract others who are growing in life. This puts you in a position to begin a like-minded group of people who can help each other to be successful, because they all want to grow at the same time.

Some of the goals you want to achieve cannot be done on your own, you need other people. I strongly believe in teamwork. There may be someone at hand in the same field; team up with them and take advice from them. Look at what they have done in their life and ask them how they got there – so they can guide you to go into the right direction.

Brainstorming can also help you grow. Get together as a group, and brainstorm and share ideas. Sometimes ideas from other people are ideas you would never consider yourself.

> # The people who get ahead in life are the ones who create the circumstances they want to be in.

The following ten peak performance principles also helped me to grow and succeed:

1. Focus

Clearly focus on the things you want to see, the way you want to see them in life. Then narrow your list to the things you want to focus on. Prioritize your work and assign priority to the steps.

Recognize unproductive activities and focus more on strengths to produce better results. Get excited about things you want to see happen. Believe in yourself. Visualize the life you want to live come into reality.

2. Get Rid of Past Negative Baggage

No one wants to carry old baggage. Move forward and make changes in your life. If you want to grow, overcome your fears, forget about past challenges. Do not worry about making mistakes. Every time you make a mistake, think of it as an opportunity to learn another way of doing it differently.

Failing once does not mean you are going to fail again or fail forever. Each time you face an obstacle, use that obstacle as an opportunity to learn something new. Remember your successes by calling on positive past performance. Believe you can become successful again in life, by recognizing you overcame obstacles in the past.

3. Establish Your Goals like a Business Plan - Be Very Specific

To live a successful life at peak performance, develop a plan and set specific goals. Setting goals is like developing a business plan. When you develop a plan, you take control of your own destiny. The plan provides clear direction and focuses on the things you want to do. Your plan gives you a clear picture of the outcome you want to see at the end. Be specific; allow your plan to determine how your business should run for maximum effectiveness. The plan will keep you on track and move you forward without distractions.

4. Take Responsibility for Your Actions

Be accountable for your actions. Take responsibility for all the situations and positions in your life, and positive changes can happen. Whatever the situation you create, it is your responsibility and nobody else's. If you want to see change, be ready to take the first step towards that change.

Be very specific when measuring or tracking your progress. Measuring will help you see if any improvement has taken place. Recognize the problem areas as well at the same time. If you are not achieving the results you want to see, if you do not measure the progress, then you will not see that clear picture. In measuring the progress, you see the troubling areas, and you can pay attention to the methods used and change them when necessary.

5. Discipline Yourself

Discipline yourself to enjoy your life tomorrow. If you are self-disciplined, then you are free from laziness, weakness, fear and doubt. Self-discipline also allows you to feel inner strength and individuality. Take responsibility to make changes in your life. Stay close to the people who have done great things for you.

Be aware all the time of which direction you are going in, and in which direction you want to go. If it is the wrong direction, change it.

The people who get ahead in life are the ones who create the circumstances they want to be in. They do not try to find them, they create them. Take the initiative and do something specific every day.

Be aware of your thoughts. Sometimes you may think of something positive to do, but your heart tells you to do something differently. Train your brain to think positive. Do this by staying positive; think positive and stay close to positive people as they share their positive stories with you.

6. Develop Personal Standards and Self-Awareness

Expect more from yourself than anybody else. Be an example to other people. Accept nothing less than your absolute best in all that you do. If you want to grow in life, you need to develop self-awareness. If you want to grow your potential, you need to understand your weaknesses and strengths. Focus on your strengths. Be passionate about the things you do. There is a direct connection with passion and reaching your potential. Passion gives you the energy to excel in life. Your attitude toward life makes a huge difference.

7. Make a Difference

Making a difference, for me, is not just making money. It's also making a difference in other people's life. Everybody can make money. Making a difference or making a positive change in somebody's life is unreplaceable with any money. Let someone know that you care about them or thank them for being there for you. It will surprise you how much better you feel.

8. Self-Development

Self-development is also very important. You have to upgrade your knowledge and skills on an ongoing basis. I always look up to my ideals for new ideas.

You can always learn more by reading more books, listening to audios or watching videos of every leading person that you like. You can also go to other people in the same business to learn more from their experience, and always be open minded. Sometimes we feel embarrassed to go to others, fearing what are they are going to think about us. You have to overcome those fears to excel in your life and business.

9. Maintain Good Health

Health is very important. You need enough energy to get going all the time. So you need to have enough rest. Staying balanced gives you energy and happiness to do things in life. Make sure you like the work you do. Focus on the things you like to do for yourself. Don't hold onto things which stress you out. Call upon a person who you trust. Go and see them and talk about things.

10. Recognize Barriers and Negative Self-Talk

When we look at barriers to success, sometimes we are our own enemies. You make sacrifices in life, when you have to keep learning, growing, and changing. When you do these things, you sometimes pay a price. You have to work harder and work longer. Do not let barriers stop you.

If you want to change your life, change the way you think of yourself. Change the way you talk to yourself. Encourage yourself every day with positive self-talk. Be disciplined in doing things and taking steps.

Do not compare yourself to others. Compare yourself with yourself and your past performances. Make a goal to become better. Have a desire to become better today than you were yesterday. Always look back and compare the weeks, months and years with where you are today. Be encouraged by how far you have grown.

Being truthful to yourself is a tremendous self-esteem builder. Every time you take action that builds your character, you become a stronger person. It gives you confidence and positive feelings about everything you do.

Follow these principles and barriers will be overcome, and peak performance will take place.

ABOUT PERMINDER

Perminder Chohan is a firm believer in being genuine, honest, and trustworthy. It's these three principles that have driven him his entire life. He's a veteran insurance industry leader, working as a Managing Director with Desjardins Financial Security Independent Network (DFSIN) –Richmond South office – since 2009. His efforts for authentic success has been proven, building a team of over 150 agents and focusing on helping them achieve excellence through organic, grass roots efforts in sales.

Back in 1998, Perminder started his career in the financial services industry, joining the Registered Education Savings Plan Company. Within six months, he became their number one agent nationally. From there, things began to grow at a rapid pace, one which he kept learning from in order to become a leader to others in their pursuit of financial and personal success. Then he expanded into the life insurance industry, becoming a mentor and being instructional to over 200 agents.

Perminder's success is notable, but it did not come without a lot of hard work. Having been raised in India, when Perminder moved to Canada he did not speak the English language. He didn't shy away from embracing opportunity, though. He began creating challenges for himself that he was determined to conquer. Learning the English language was one of those challenges, and he set goals for himself to make that happen! He fed off the energy that setting goals with deadlines gave him, and realized that any goals he may have could be achieved through a solid plan, a commitment to success, and, of course—much hard work!

Community involvement is another thing that Perminder is passionate about. He is a tireless supporter of many activities and events that are important to the South Asian community in the Greater Vancouver Area. His generosity and sponsorship include: fundraising for twenty different charities in the area, sponsoring sports activities and teams year after year, and even bringing fan favorite Bollywood acts to Canada to perform. He is also invited to present at awards ceremonies that honor achievement.

To his community and work environment, Perminder is definitely a valuable contributor. However, to his family he is considered a loving, caring father and husband. When asked about the factors of his success, he always expresses that none of it would be possible without the support of his loving wife, Deep, and his children, Henna and Armaan. Together, the entire Chohan family finds joy in being involved in their community and giving back.

Career Awards:
GAMA International Awards
Agency Builder Award 2013
Agency Builder Award 2014
Agency Builder Award 2015
Agency Achievement Award 2014
National Management Award 2014

Desjardins Excellence Awards:
Recruiting Award 2013 – was declared number one in Canada
Recruiting Award 2014 – was declared number one in Canada
Recruiting Award 2015 – was declared number one in Canada Business Growth 2013 – was declared number one in Canada
In-Force-Growth 2014 – was declared number 2 in Canada
In-Force-Growth 2015 – was declared number 2 in Canada
In Force Growth 2015 - Number 2 in Canada.
Excellence below 50 Associates 2013- number 2 in Canada
Excellence below 50 Associates 2014- number 1 in Canada
Excellence below 50 Associates 2015- number 1 in Canada

Last Published Book – UNCOMMON
Editor's Choice Award
Best Selling Author Award

BY RENATA ANGELO

TWELVE STEPS FOR QUANTUM HEALING

We live in an amazing time of human history. We all have capabilities far beyond our expectations. We are spiritual beings having a human experience. Imagine what would happen if you could tap into your full potential and use it all? Who could you become, what could you do or what could you have?

To find out what you are truly capable of, you have to step outside of your comfort zone into a growth zone and welcome change in your life. *Your challenges are your greatest gifts, because they are here to give you the opportunity for growth.*

Einstein said: "The problem cannot be solved with the same mindset that has created it." The key to overcoming challenges is to raise consciousness. Your outer world is just a reflection of your inner world. If you don't like what you experience on the outside, you just need to change what is going on inside.

Some people learn and grow naturally, others need a big wake up call in order to change something. The latter was my case. In my early twenties, when I lived in Australia, I got hit by a car while driving a motorbike. The person who ran me over became my spiritual teacher. My challenges became my greatest gifts. I have spent some time in a wheel chair and I have been experiencing chronic back pains 24/7 for several years. After a year of rehabilitation, doctors classified me as partially disabled and recommended me to learn to live with the pain. I didn't like that idea, so **I became determined to turn the impossible into the possible. I started the quest to find a cure for chronic pain.**

I was willing to try anything. I did all types of exercises (yoga, pillages, swimming, etc.) I even started to study nutrition to have a proper diet. I used all kinds of painkillers. I reached the point where I felt that I did everything. Looking back now, I can say I was not even halfway through the journey.

Then I got an insight – I realized that I cannot be running west, looking for a sunrise – because it won't be there. I turned to eastern medicine and I tried acupuncture, acupressure, ayurveda, homeopathy, reiki, sound healing, chakra healing, aromatherapy, etc. You name it. Unfortunately, the pain did not go away.

Then I started to discover the power of the mind. I realized that our thoughts influence our reality. I was fascinated by examples of patients with multiple or split personalities. Psychologists observed that when people switch personalities, sometime the color of their eyes change, as well as their voices. Allergies or marks on the skin can reappear or disappear. Eyesight can worsen or improve.

I found it even more fascinating that one patient had diabetes and when he switched personalities, he was diabetes-free. I wondered how was it possible that one physical body would die without a shot of insulin and the same body could live without it when the personality switches. It seemed to me that the mind was influencing the matter, so I started to experiment with it.

I used visualizations, affirmations, NLP, Ho'oponopono and other mental techniques. I started to change my attitude, I worked on forgiveness and focused on appreciation and gratitude. I was definitely feeling better and it gave me the strength to go on. However, the pain was still there.

I believe that the key to self-healing is finding the inner courage to live life.

Finally, I realized that I had to integrate all parts of my being. Not only my body and mind, but also my soul. I stop searching for answers outside and I turned within. At that moment, something started to shift. I started to practice meditations every day, and I discovered that inner voice within.

At the beginning I kept ignoring the inner voice, because I did not know what it was. Once, when I was facing a life-threatening situation, I asked for guidance in meditation and I received it. Not only did it save my life, but something more profound happened at that moment. When God / Universal Intelligence / Source / Intuition / whatever you want to call it - gave me guidance and I made a decision to follow it – I experienced quantum healing. The pain was taken away with a message that it fulfilled its purpose – and it disappeared forever.

Firstly, my mind was not capable of comprehending what just had happened. More than one thousand days in constant pain 24/7 and I was suddenly healed during meditation? It did not make any sense to me. I wanted answers.

A few years after this event I spoke to Deepak Chopra and he told me in that meditation, I most likely achieved the state of homeostasis, and then my body experienced spontaneous healing. I found it fascinating that it happened in a moment when I - atheist - for the first time in my life, consciously acknowledged God and asked Him for the answer. I received it instantly. Then I argued with Him for a few minutes that I couldn't do what He told me, but finally I surrendered and decided that I would follow the guidance. That decision changed my life. As Tony Robbins says, "Decisions shape your destiny." It was 100% true for me.

When I spoke to Dr. Amit Goswami (Professor of Quantum Physics at the University of Oregon and the author of the book, *Quantum Doctor*), he confirmed to me that what I experienced was a quantum healing. That experience gave me much more than health. I got a glimpse of what is possible. I found out that within each of us, there is potential far beyond our wildest expectations. I have realized that we all are creators of our own reality. The difference is that some of us create our reality consciously, and others do so unconsciously.

I believe that the key to self-healing is within each of you. You have to take full responsibility, raise consciousness, find courage to live the life you always wanted. Love yourself and believe in yourself. Figure out what you love to do and go for it, regardless of whether you failed or got hurt in the past. Go boldly for your dreams and never give up. Step outside of your comfort zone into the growth zone. Live here and now and appreciate little things. Serve and contribute to others. Connect with the Source. Have fun and fully participate in the dance of life. Become the best version of yourself. Leave a legacy.

I have put together steps how to self-heal:

STEP 1 – TAKE RESPONSIBILITY

An essential part of self-healing is to first take full responsibility for your own health. Don't expect that only someone or something can heal you. You can heal yourself. Take charge. Start being proactive and look for solutions. Never take the role of victim - only unsuccessful people blame others or circumstances. It is not for you.

STEP 2 – TAKE A HOLISTIC APPROACH

See health in a holistic way. I believe we have a physical body, an emotional body, a mental body and a spiritual body. If we don't take into account karma, we can say that illness is firstly created in our mental body, with our thoughts, attitudes and outlooks on life. Our subconscious beliefs influence our emotions. Our negative emotions have a huge influence on our health. If you want to change something on your physical level, start first with changes on your mental and emotional level.

STEP 3 – DEVELOP HEALTHY ATTITUDE

Attitude is altitude. Pick the right one. It helped me to believe that to every problem there is a solution. That out of everything bad, something good will come out. Be grateful, positive, optimistic, forgive yourself and others, and believe in yourself. Open yourself to change. You cannot do the same things and expect different results. Choose to believe that you are destined to succeed. Never give up.

STEP 4 – EMOTION IS ENERGY IN MOTION

We all have life energy. In India they call it Prana, in China it is called Chi. If it is not flowing properly through each organ of your body, you will develop an illness. Your mission is to take all energy blocks away and get yourself back to flow. You might not be able to control all the events in your life, but you can always control your focus and meaning you give to those events. This will influence the way you feel. That in turn will determine whether or not you will create an energy block. Positive emotions will give your body a better environment for healing.

STEP 5 – GIVE YOUR BODY THE BEST CONDITIONS FOR HEALING

Your body has a natural capacity to heal. Health is its natural state. Unfortunately, we often create interferences to our health. The main interferences could be unhealthy food and drink – causing lack of nutrition and an acid environment in your body. You could also experience mental and emotional stress, unhealthy lifestyle with bad habits, lack of sleep and lack of movement. Nourish yourself with organic foods, drink pure water and move!

STEP 6 – TAKE THE STRESS AWAY AND RELAX

You might have a lot of stressors in your current life. It is important to deal with them effectively and resolve them. Create more time for yourself. Find time to play, dance, paint, read, kiss — whatever you enjoy the most. Spend time with those you love. Serve and contribute to others. That will give you a feeling of joy and fulfillment.

STEP 7 – LAUGH YOUR WAY TO HEALTH

When you laugh, your brain secretes endorphins and you are able to deal with pain better. You can watch funny and inspiring movies and listen to jokes or hilarious stories that put a smile on your face. Read funny books. Surround yourself with people who make you laugh. Enjoy happy moments.

STEP 8 – GET OVER YOUR FEARS

Step outside of your comfort zone to a growth zone. You might experience fear from the unknown, fear of failure, fear of rejection, fear of. . . you name it. Face the fear and do it anyway. I get participants in my life seminar to walk over the fire (not just over hot coals). Your mind is like a fire—it is a good servant, but a bad master. Use your mind to support you, not to sabotage you.

STEP 9 – USE MENTAL TECHNIQUES

When you find your life purpose and set clear, compelling goals, use mental techniques to get you there faster and more effectively. My favorites are visualizations, affirmations, NLP and Ho'ponopono. Create a visionboard. When I did my first vision board, I put Brian Tracy (bestselling author and success expert) there. Now I feel blessed that Brian is my mentor and I have co-authored two books with him. Mental techniques help you to program your mind to support you, not to sabotage you.

STEP 10 – MAKE USE OF PLACEBOS

Be smart and trick yourself with placebos. For example, I have put pills full of vitamins and minerals into a bottle that previously contained painkillers and then I have swallowed them. I convinced myself that they are the strongest painkillers on the planet.

STEP 11 – PRAY SMARTLY

Lot of people pray for their pain and illness to go away. It does not make much sense, because the pain is there for a reason. I would pray for the wisdom to understand what I need to change within me (which thoughts, attitudes, feelings, actions, etc.). Then I would pray for the strengths and courage to take actions.

STEP 12 – MEDITATE

Thirty-minute daily meditations will transform your life. Get ready for miracles after half-a-year of daily practice. It is inevitable. During the meditation, you will get in touch with your higher self and also with the Universal Intelligence – with the Source. You will raise your consciousness. You will develop your intuition and if you will follow it, you will experience more "coincidences" in your life. You will happen to be in a right place at a right time, surrounded by the right people. You will have serendipitous moments.

Life will become a true adventure.

ABOUT RENATA

Renata Angelo is an inspirational speaker, coach and a bestselling author. Her life mission is to raise consciousness on this planet. She believes that within you there is an amazing potential, and she wants to support you to connect with it.

Renata feels blessed that she has cracked the code to quantum healing and she was able to self-heal. She would love to show you how to tap the power of your subconscious and superconscious mind and how to raise your vibrations so you become a vibrational match to your goals. She will teach you how to develop your intuition and she will empower you to take action steps that will turn your dreams and goals into reality.

Renata offers private coaching and she is ready to support you to take your life to the next level. She will share universal principles and techniques that you can apply to all areas of life (career, relationships, finances...). She would love to be your guide on your journey to success.

Renata has fifteen years of experience in the areas of personal, professional and spiritual development. She was teaching the subject of "Training and Development" at Griffith University, Gold Coast, Australia. In Europe, she founded three companies and she was also a co-founder of a non-profit organization, Czech Vipassana o.p.s., that holds meditation courses. Renata lived on four continents, and that gave her great opportunities to meet and understand people from different cultures.

Renata was featured on national TV and she was also invited to speak on radio shows and educational conferences. She has published articles in personal development magazines and co-authored two books with Brian Tracy – including *Pushing To The Front* which became a bestseller in the USA.

Renata is often invited as an inspirational speaker to corporate events and conferences. She leads transformational seminars and teambuilding events. Her programs are highly interactive, fun and they will challenge you to step outside of your comfort zone to a growth zone. Renata is a certified firewalking instructor from F.I.R.E. Institute in USA, where she studied under Tolly Burkan. She is famous for her transformational firewalking program where she teaches advanced mental techniques during which she safely leads participants to walk over fire (not only hot coals). Renata's clients are corporations like AEGON, ALLIANZ, American Chamber of Commerce, British Chamber of Commerce, IKEA, Mary Kay, METRO, NuSkin, O2, T-Mobil, Unicef and many others.

Renata's life passion is turning 'Impossible into Possible.' In her programs she will create a paradigm shift for you, when you break through your old limiting beliefs and create new supportive ones. You will discover the power of creative visualization, affirmations, NLP, meditation...etc. You will learn to raise your vibrations, tune into abundance frequency, connect with intuition and use the law of attraction in action.

Renata will inspire and empower you to get from where you are to where you want to be fast.

You can connect with Renata at:
www.RenataAngelo.com
info@renataangelo.com

AN INTERVIEW WITH ROD WALKER

DISCOVERING YOUR INNER MAVERICK AND NEVER TAKING NO FOR AN ANSWER

PERFORMANCE: When and how did you decide to become an entrepreneur? Talk about some of your successful ventures and why you are proud of them?

ROD: In the mid to late 90s, when I was in my mid 20s, I went through a situation where I had severe health issues. I ended up being diagnosed with vertigo, but at one point a doctor practically imposed a death sentence on me, telling me I had an incurable autoimmune disease. The emotional rollercoaster inspired me to re-evaluate my life. I was a UPS driver at the time, and while it was steady work, I knew it wasn't where I wanted to retire from someday. I couldn't impact my life the way I wanted to, working for someone else. So I quit. I got involved in a network marketing company via their CEO, and that was my first experience with some very successful multi-millionaires. Getting into their inner circle, I learned how they thought differently about work, success and money. That experience sparked my desire to be an entrepreneur and I didn't look back. I dabbled in network marketing myself for two years, but realized it was still like working for someone else. I let a new adventure begin.

I started an event planning company that turned into a high end one-stop-shop wedding business. The vision was to apply the Fred Meyer/ Walmart Supercenter concept to the wedding industry, with ten in-house services. I created various joint ventures, including promotions with Men's Wearhouse – even calling their founder George Zimmer to do a local event in Portland with them. Over the years, we did close to 400 weddings in Portland and throughout Oregon. I learned quickly that entrepreneurial success involved figuring out how to systemize, then franchise the business while taking a different approach than everyone else. Creating a successful service experience model, we became popular with people going all out, spending $40-50,000 on their events. I learned about raising capital and working with investors as well.

PERFORMANCE: But in the late 2000s, when the economy tanked, things changed. How did you get into your current ventures, including healthcare and marketing services?

ROD: To say I hit rock bottom would be accurate. The market crashed, I went bankrupt, experienced business failures, got divorced and lost my focus all at once. I took a year off before finding the fire again to start over from scratch. A buddy of mine was involved in operating a tradeschool for dental assistants and I saw he was doing well. So I entered that business by working for him. Later, I started out in senior care and ended up working more with clients with disabilities. These were small facilities where we would convert single family dwellings into repurposed residences. There were multiple approaches involved. I bumped around and found my niche there, providing treatment programs for seniors and people with disabilities. I also ended up purchasing the operating dental assistant tradeschool from my friend. Once I got rolling, fresh opportunities presented themselves. I invested in various small businesses and did some real estate investing, too. I'm currently doing all that and planning my next adventure!

People have all sorts of misconceptions when it comes to entrepreneurs and success.

PERFORMANCE: Earlier in your life and career, how did you define success? How has that definition changed over the years?

ROD: I think my definition evolved in stages. Years ago, I spent time with the organization of Robert Kiyosaki, the businessman and investor who wrote *Rich Dad, Poor Dad*, staffing some of his events and attending his various success seminars. Being in that environment while working for the network marketing company, my idea of success was just finding ways to replace my UPS income with residual income that would help me retire early someday. It was all about having enough wealth to retire and having financial freedom. But during the subsequent two-year period when I struck out on my own, I realized that my success would come through owning my own businesses. The sky could be the limit. I asked myself, "How do I create a million or billion-dollar opportunity?" My concept of success shifted from "financial independence" to, "How can I create something so unique that everyone loves it and wants a piece of it?" That became my definition of success. In finding success again after the down years, I realized that it slightly changed again. I needed to be myself and become more of who I really am, instead of suppressing myself. It was more than just setting goals. It was, "What do I really want in life?" Forget what everyone else says. What do I want? At that point I understood I'm a bit of a maverick. Most people don't think in terms of living life on their own terms.

PERFORMANCE: What are some of the challenges you have overcome to be successful? Are they unique to you or do you think everyone who wants to achieve great things goes through them?

ROD: The number one thing was self confidence, actually believing I could do it. That was the biggest hurdle. Once I got past that, everything turned around. I emerged from self-doubt to the idea of doing things to prove to myself I could, using "the doubters" as fuel to keep going. There was no single turning point. So many naysayers tell people like me who dream of creating big things that they'll fail. Some "Negative Nancies" that say they support you might turn around and judge you for taking unnecessary risks. But I learned that when someone tells you something won't work, that person's really saying that THEY can't do it. I've had many points where I felt like I was doing 90 on the freeway with a flat tire. The ride wasn't perfect but I wasn't going to pull over. The tire is going to be flat no matter what! That's what life is all about. Tough challenges will pop up regardless, but it didn't matter once I found my flow. Whatever happens, I just kept going.

Needless to say, I'm also a risk taker willing to try new experiences which flows into my personal life. I had never in my life ridden a motorcycle, and two months ago I bought a Ducati racing bike. It's one of the fastest, most dangerous models you can buy I was told! Everyone told me I was going to kill myself riding it but I told them to buzz off, don't tell me how to live my life! I've gone back East, up to Seattle and down to California doing track days on the bike, taking training classes like the pro racers do. It's been liberating and mirrors my professional life. People have all sorts of misconceptions when it comes to entrepreneurs and success. They tend to think you just got lucky. WRONG! It's about taking or being prepared for a moment when the right opportunity arises, and then taking advantage of it with everything at your disposal.

PERFORMANCE: Do you think the road is easier or harder right now for black entrepreneurs? How so?

ROD: The PC answer, for black readers who may be checking out this book, is that yes, there may be race-based challenges you have to work through to connect well with the markets you choose. But honestly, that's not been my reality. Hard is hard or easy is easy no matter what color you are, right? At the end of the day, no matter the obstacles, regardless of the nation's economy, success goes back to who you are and what you're going to do. I live in Oregon where only a small percentage of the population is African-American. It's hilarious but human nature is that people tend to want to relate to people like them, and since I've been told I "sound white" on the phone, I assume they are surprised when I show up to talk to them. At that point, it's up to me to make things happen. These stereotypes – and the experiences I have had because of them – have created an opportunity for me to talk in public about them in lighthearted, funny ways.

Stereotypes exist because there is some truth to them. All cultures have certain traits. I'm thinking there are ways I can build a brand around being honest and un-PC about these topics. For instance, if I pull up in a fancy sports car, people wonder what team I play for! A couple of fellow black entrepreneurs and I keep saying we should write a book about being the "whitest black guys you know." I would love to incorporate these ideas into talks about coming from humble beginnings and succeeding against all odds.

You have to believe in yourself. You can't take no for an answer.

PERFORMANCE: You've said that because of the way you act and talk on the phone, people assume you are white - and are later surprised to find out you're not. Is this a blessing or a burden?

ROD: I would say it's a blessing in disguise. I don't think people treat me poorly but we all have preconceived ideas about people and the way we think they should talk, act and where they should live. It's kind of funny and refreshing for me, wondering where those limiting, silly ideas come from and why they've taken hold. But like I said, at the end of the day, it doesn't really matter. The blessing is that when people compliment me, I've connected with them on some level and made a good impression. I think I'm blessed with a strong personality and ability to connect. If the whole racial sound and act issue helps disarm people and make them feel comfortable, then I will use it. That can then lead to silly small talk and then more serious, focused talk about doing business - and that's a WIN!

PERFORMANCE: You like the phrase, "discovering your inner maverick." What does that term mean to you?

ROD: You have to believe in yourself. You can't take no for an answer. You need to create your own reality. Figure out what you want and make it happen. Don't be afraid to say what you want and don't change what you want for other people. The final component of being a maverick is figuring out strategies (unconventional, if necessary) to plow through the difficulties that certainly will arise.

PERFORMANCE: I understand you are working on a new image and brand for yourself. How is that going? Can you share any details of your current plans and future ambitions?

ROD: I'm focusing on three areas which fit my personality but seem unrelated to all of the other work I've done as a business owner – speaking, a radio show and doing comedy. I want to open a dialogue about all these things we've talked about, regarding success, business, racial stereotypes, living your dream, lifestyle – you name it. We're so PC and serious all the time. Stop being so stuffy! So what if I "talk white" and am black and you're Jewish. Let the stereotypes go. We are who we are. At the end of the day, it doesn't matter. What matters is, "Are you going to get up and do the work it takes to change your life?" That's the platform I'm looking for! I want to find outlets where I can get people talking and thinking about this kind of stuff. I have a little Howard Stern in me. I'm the guy of whom my friends say, "What's he going to say next?" In other words, I have no filter. I definitely want to lead into something edgy.

I believe we're born into a situation that's handed to you, but it's up to us to break through barriers to succeed – whether you're a single mom launching a new company or want to be an executive at the company you work for. You have to ask yourself, "Can I do it regardless of my race or culture, background, lack of money, resources, etc.?" I think if I'm conducting motivational seminars or doing standup comedy, I would use the race and social class issues as humorous points. I want to talk about the stuff people think about but are sometimes afraid to express publicly!

PERFORMANCE: As a successful entrepreneur, do you have advice to budding entrepreneurs who want to follow a similar path?

ROD: I tell them they need to be a little bit of a maverick – on in my case, a lot more! Don't try to fit in and don't worry about everyone else and their opinions of what you can accomplish. You have to be yourself and do something different. Everyone else out there is doing a variation on the same old thing. It's up to you to break out of that rut and create something unique. Embrace the fact that you need to put customers first. Your thought should be, "How can I serve them differently and meet a need in the market?" – no matter what industry you choose your path in. It's not just about your needs and wants, but it's definitely all about you when it comes to using your business as a means to reaching your goals and achieving your dreams. No one else can do that for you!

PERFORMANCE: Do you have any regrets? How have you learned from your mistakes?

ROD: Of course, but those of us who want to be successful make mistakes, move on quickly and get over them. Everyone stumbles, but you should give yourself only a few days to beat yourself up – and then get on with things. My biggest regrets are looking back at those times along the road where I let people talk me out of things I really wanted to do. They would say don't try this or that, and I would give in to those doubts. That sums up most of my successes and failures. I experienced the most success when I stuck with what I set out to do and followed what was best for me. The times I didn't succeed were when I toned things down and took steps backwards – because everyone was telling me to do that.

PERFORMANCE: In a nutshell, define "Success."

ROD: It's figuring out what you want, being unapologetic about what you want and going out into the world and getting it, PERIOD! Then I would say look back at all you have accomplished and acknowledge that it's a great thing that you have done it; but then let that fuel your future success. Sometimes I look back at how far I've come and wonder if it's all real. Gratitude is also essential. Different entrepreneurs will have different answers. Some will say it's what they're able to do, and how they're able to impact people's lives and leave a legacy. Success encompasses a lot of things. For me, it's about taking stock of my journey so far and realizing I have done some amazing things and looking forward to what's next!

ABOUT ROD

Growing up, Rod Walker's family moved around so much that he joked that his parents were like "black gypsies," relocating in different cities every few years. Born in Chicago, he moved to Houston at age seven, then to the Bay Area at 13 before heading on to Sacramento for a handful of years before settling in Portland, Oregon - where Rod has now lived and worked for 20 years. Learning to adapt to change from an early age has proven to be an advantage in his adult life and career. That same type of restless spirit that inspired his parents to move so many times drives Rod's multi-faceted success as an entrepreneur.

He enrolled in college to study for an MBA but dropped out quickly, deciding that the things he learned eventually starting his own business would be his "college." While working a steady job as a UPS driver, his entrepreneurial juices started flowing – spurred along by a doctor's wrong diagnosis, telling him he had an incurable autoimmune disease. He made a clean break from his "day job" and got involved in a network marketing company that used an ecommerce platform to sell financial planning products. After learning a great deal about business, money and success from the perspective of the multi-millionaire entrepreneurs and company owners he became involved with, Rod decided he was ready to launch his own company.

Rod launched an event planning company that quickly evolved into a high end one-stop-shop wedding business, with an array of ten in-house services. Drawing on his innate marketing skills, he created many unique cross promotions, including one with Men's Wearhouse. In the six years he was in business – first with a partner and then on his own – Rod handled the details of close to 400 weddings throughout Oregon. He especially loved the start-up phase, the opportunity of creating something substantial from the ground up. He learned the importance of marketing and systems, being prepared for unexpected challenges, and that "there's not a lot of room for excuses."

The market downturn in the late 2000's, as well as personal and business failures, forced him to shift gears. Rod began working with a couple of friends who specialized in the healthcare treatment programs. At one point, he also bought a dental assistant trade school. While continuing to work in the healthcare field, he is now also engaged in outside marketing and consulting for other businesses, building his clientele via word of mouth.

I'm motivated to help because I have been in the frustrating place my clients have experienced, where I was treated like a number.

HONESTY, INTEGRITY AND A DETERMINATION TO SUCCEED

That Includes Giving Back and Helping Others

PERFORMANCE: You essentially make a branding concept out of your ability to bring honesty and integrity to what you call "the slimy world of credit card processing." Why do you think it's slimy and what is the driving force behind your more positive approach?

KEVIN: I discovered that some individuals that work in my industry are taught to just sell the product and accept a commission. They fail to understand that to be successful, it's more complex than just "sign here and move on." So they set up their customers with the ability to accept credit cards, then leave them high and dry. For the customer, it's as frustrating as buying a car from a salesman at a dealership and having to start a relationship over each time you set foot in the dealership because that salesman who knew all about you and any previous issues is gone in months.

Working with a hands-on professional service like **Swypit** involves not only setting things up, but being there through every step of the way. My team and I are available anytime assistance is needed. We become like a concierge, a personal point of reference. We have the knowledge to solve any problems that arise, so you don't have to feel like a number. We offer two key things: very competitive pricing and excellent customer service, which are actually pretty hard to find in this industry. I am also a Certified Payment Professional, a designation given to those who not only have a broad range of expertise in the industry, but also demonstrate mastery of sales, pricing and interchange, business process, operations and workflow, products and solutions, risk and regulatory compliance and security matters.

I'm motivated to help because I have been in the frustrating place my clients have experienced, where I was treated like a number. I wanted to be unique in treating them with respect – and in turn that gives me a leg up on the competition.

PERFORMANCE: How do you convince skeptics who have a generally negative opinion of this realm?

KEVIN: I think that people need to be more diligent in their research when it comes to their money. They should be thoroughly checking out organizations that are impacting their profitability. Just because someone says they'll save you money doesn't mean they will. It's easy enough to Google people and see if they are legitimate. The secret to my success is the trust factor. Most people I work with are referrals from others who have had positive experiences working with me and know what I can achieve for them. They will call me and say they were referred to me, and that I can fix their problem and make them more profitable. With a few simple questions, I can determine what is causing them the most issues and put them on the right path to managing their business the way they want it to be. They know from the start they're working with a professional who understands their pain. We don't have quotas and I don't sell equipment. I listen to their needs and provide solutions so they can do what they need to run their business.

PERFORMANCE: You were a personal chef on private yachts for dignitaries, politicians and business professionals before you entered the business world yourself. How and why did you make the transition?

KEVIN: The owners of the last yacht that I worked on, were the family of the original distributors of a major soft drink. It was clear to me that they did very well and I learned that every time someone opened a bottle or can of soda, they made money. That always stuck with me. A few years later, when I was working as a business consultant I heard something similar - that it was possible for individuals in the credit card and merchant services industry to earn a few pennies on every transaction. Working as a chef, I knew that I was on these boats trading my time for money and wondered if there might be other opportunities for me out there. Ironically, every step of the way, I always thought about that day the soda distributor told me about recurring income. While "cheffing," I thought I would rise in the food service industry and someday perhaps own some restaurants. Then, things changed when I met a wonderful woman, Sarah, on one of the yachts who eventually became my wife. About a year later, I "jumped ship" and set out to figure out the next phase of my life in some interesting ways, including riding my Harley from New Orleans to Kansas City to visit my mother. Sarah and I moved first to New York, where I worked for contract food service organizations. She was from Colorado, however, so we eventually moved there and I found an opportunity to work as a business consultant.

PERFORMANCE: You mention that being around these high level people on the yachts enabled you to develop "street smarts of business superhighways." What do you mean by this?

KEVIN: Getting to know all these multi-gazillionaires allowed me to learn more than a few tidbits of business knowledge from them. These are principles that I then mixed with my street smarts to help regular business people understand things in an effective, simplified way. Instead of sounding like a robot or script reader reeling off pearls of wisdom, I used my innate communication abilities to share what I knew with others to help them. I still do this today. I learn a lot from my customers which I can then draw from to help other people become successful and more efficient in their business. Knowledge is power and power is knowledge. The more knowledge you have the more power. This doesn't make me better, but it gives me access to a lot of important things I can share with people when the time is right.

PERFORMANCE: Tell me about your venture into business consulting? From there, what gave you the confidence that you could be successful as an entrepreneur?

KEVIN: I was working for a company that would confidentially help business owners find buyers for their businesses. I worked in five states – Colorado, Arizona, Idaho, Kansas, and Wyoming – and became one of their top salespeople. Every week, I would get a list of 20 owners and make appointments to see them, then collect a large dollar deposit to help get the ball rolling. I did well at conducting business evaluations and telling them how much their businesses were worth. Then one day I saw the company on "60 Minutes," portrayed in an unflattering, unethical light. No matter how well I was doing, I knew it was time to leave.

The confidence I have came from never taking no for an answer and completely believing that I was going to make it - then moving forward to make that happen. I was inspired by Michael Jordan's story about overcoming poverty and saying nothing was going to stand in his way. He wasn't going to just play basketball but create a brand for himself. Those kinds of success stories fueled my drive and ambition to be successful myself. I absolutely refused to give up.

PERFORMANCE: Tell me about some of the greatest challenges you had to overcome?

KEVIN: There's never been a fight that was easy to win. I'm five foot one, and when you're small, you have to pretty much fight all the way. I have faced a lot of adversity in my life. Not long after I graduated from culinary school, I scored my first food service job at an exclusive resort in Northern New Jersey. I bought a nice car, racked up credit cards and was living it up. Then I got a harsh wake-up call one day when I arrived at work and was told that they were shutting the place down. At the time, I was living on the property and had to move out. So I was homeless, but still had the nice car! I had a tough choice: go back home to live in upstate New York with no real future, or head to New York City with big dreams. I chose the latter and slept on couches until I found a job. I was living with my sister, and at one point and she kicked me out. But I took the couch with me, and slept on it another six months until I could afford a bed. Those were tough times that truly humbled me and help me remain grounded with a humble perspective even though I'm doing well now.

Working as the Assistant Director of Food Service at an exclusive all-girls private school on the Upper East Side, I really began to see wealthy individuals and what money could do for people. Students included Ivanka Trump, Estee Lauder's grandchildren, and actor Peter Boyle's daughter. Working at the school afforded me time off and connections in the yachting industry, where I started working part-time on charters. One of the yachts was the Mariner III, and I cooked for stars like Bruce Willis, Madonna and Sharon Stone. Being around many successful people really motivated me to create a successful life for myself.

PERFORMANCE: Earlier in your life and career, how did you define success? How has that definition changed over the years?

KEVIN: Considering those months when I was truly down and out in my 20s, I think success was just being able to pay my bills. These days, as a business owner, it's about being debt free and enjoying my life fully without living beyond my means. A lot of people spend every penny they earn, but to me, spending money as you're creating more wealth for yourself doesn't translate to success. I think it's a matter of being free and not feeling tied down.

PERFORMANCE: When you started Swypit over 15 years ago, what were your goals and what steps did you take to achieve them?

KEVIN: I'm a unique individual in that I don't make specific goals for myself, I just make everything happen. No one's going to stop me from getting where I want to go. I'm driven and self- motivated and refuse to quit. Putting in the hard work ensures that I will be successful without concern for reaching concrete goals. I knew I wanted to make a great living for me and my family and enjoy and live life fully. I keep moving forward and get back up when I'm knocked down. When I was a kid, I was bullied and made fun of, but I didn't care. It motivated me to be more successful than those who were hurting me. At **Swypit**, I make that happen by doing what others in my industry are not willing to do – giving merchants the service they deserve with the pricing they want. Make things easy for them so they can focus on their business. I've found that in this industry, the majority of people selling a credit card machine don't care about the customer. With me, everything I do is about the customer and taking care of them. When people realize it's not about them, but the customer, that's when real success kicks in.

PERFORMANCE: What drives you to be successful?

KEVIN: I just never wanted to give up. I knew one day I would make a difference. In first grade my principal used the expression about sticks and stones and I've always believed it. Even back then, I was smarter than the bullies and my entrepreneurial spirit kicked in. I figured out how to create alliances with them and they became my bodyguards and then my friends. Later in NYC, I learned that success was about being in charge of my own destiny and that no one would hand anything to me. When I was struggling, I would walk past the homeless on W. 23rd Street late at night after I finished work, and I felt disheartened – like I had to do something to make my life better than this. I was driven to do whatever I could to make sure I never had to live in fear again and get to a place where I didn't have to worry about having a place to live. I had to go through these hard times to get that fuel for my later success. If there is a will, there is a way.

PERFORMANCE: It's inspiring to see how heavily you are involved in local community foundations, events and charities in your home in Frisco, Texas. Discuss some of your activities and why these are important to you.

KEVIN: I like to say that in 2003, I "met" Oprah Winfrey while feeding my young daughter at 2 a.m. I turned on Oprah for the first time ever and she was talking about the importance of giving back to one's community. I realized that meant finding ways to help others. That's when I started giving back. When I am helping others, that's when real success is happening for me. As the adage goes, the more I give, the more I get back. I'm very active in my community of Frisco, Texas. I just finished my term as Planning and Zoning commissioner, and am currently on the Board of Directors for the Chamber of Commerce.

Through that organization, each year I sponsor Military Appreciation night with Donnie Nelson, General Manager of the Dallas Mavericks, and owner of The Texas Legends NBA-D League team at the Dr. Pepper Arena. On January 16, 2016, we presented a portrait to the family of "American Sniper" Chris Kyle at our annual charity event. The American Fallen Soldiers Project, in particular, is a great avenue for me to give back to. It's a way to thank the families of those who have made the ultimate sacrifice for us, to live free.

My father has said for many years that I give too much of myself, financially and personally. He feels that people will take advantage of me. Yes, that can happen. But, I genuinely like to help people gain success so they can get where they want to go in life.

PERFORMANCE: As a successful entrepreneur, do you have advice to budding entrepreneurs who want to follow a similar path?

KEVIN: I think one of the most important factors is finding a mentor who is willing to give of him or herself wholeheartedly, while not wanting anything in return. Beyond that, I truly believe that if someone is willing to take the time and energy to work hard, they will have extreme success in business. As someone who has amassed a large network of friends and key business contacts, I have learned that surrounding yourself with great people is a huge plus. And of course, figure out some way to help others.

ABOUT KEVIN

As owner and founder of Swypit, Kevin Hodes prides himself on bringing honesty and integrity to what he considers, the "slimy world of credit card processing." A former chef aboard luxury yachts, his craft brought him into contact with business professionals, dignitaries and politicians, enabling him to develop "street smarts of business super highways." Intrigued, Hodes turned from the galley to launching a business consulting firm; a move that eventually led him to the world of credit card processing.

Hodes is quoted as saying, "I got into sales, but I brought my food service savviness of making things incredibly awesome all the time," he said. "I found myself a little niche in the business—taking care of customers."

The end result has melded his expertise and personal integrity. Hodes' company, Swypit, offers next generation electronic payment processing solutions, combined with world-class service, price and leading edge technology. Swypit is the endorsed merchant services provider for the Southwest Carwash Association, Texas Tire Dealers Association and numerous nationwide franchises and Chambers of Commerce. In addition to card acceptance services, Swypit offers businesses free credit card terminals and discounted point of sale systems capable of managing inventory and payroll, gift cards as well as cash advance services. Kevin's company focuses on providing exemplary customer support in an industry that is rife with third party providers, who are often more intent upon selling equipment than providing an effective solution for businesses, small to large.

As a Certified Payment Professional, Kevin Hodes has demonstrated the necessary knowledge and skills required to perform competently in today's complex electronic payments environment. This ETA Certified Payments Professional Program (ETA CPP) recognizes that effective merchant service providers must provide not only a broad range of knowledge of the industry, but demonstrate mastery of sales, pricing and interchange, business process, operations and workflow, products and solutions, risk and regulatory compliance and security matters. The ETA is an international trade association representing more than 500 companies that offer electronic transaction processing products and services. Their mission is to advance the payments industry profession by providing leadership through education, advocacy and the exchange of information.

As an individual, Kevin served as a Planning and Zoning Commissioner in one of the fastest growing cities in America. He is a board member of the Frisco Chamber of Commerce and The American Fallen Soldiers Project. He is active in community foundations and events including the Boy Scouts of America, Eagle Gymnastics Academy, Donnie Nelson's Texas Legends Military Night Sponsor, Frisco Citizen's Fire and Police Academies, Wipe Out Kids Cancer, Young Entrepreneurs Academy and an alumni of Leadership Frisco. With regard to his impressive dedication to the community, Hodes says, "I believe that you need to give back. If you don't give to the community, then you shouldn't even be in business." Kevin's attitude has proven to be a cornerstone philosophy of his character and is ultimately responsible for the enormous success of his company.

You may obtain further information about Frisco, Texas-based Swypit by visiting the website: www.swypit.com or by calling: 1-877-379-9748.

We are all leaders of The New Era - let's commit to walking our talk at a World Class Level so that we can proudly leave a legacy of significance and success for our next generation.

BY SUSSI MATTSSON

WALK THE TALK

At a World Class Level

Imagine what the world would be like if every leader genuinely "Walked The Talk"…Now imagine if we all stepped up as leaders and walked our talk *at a World Class Level*…We would experience an environment filled with countless benefits including, but not limited to:

• Increased profitability

• Even higher level of respect

• More trustworthiness

• Greater credibility

• Increased motivation

• Sources of inspiration

• Strengthened loyalty

• Higher employee retention

• Decreased stress

• Better decision-making

• More clear and specific communication

THE "TALK"

Begin by asking yourself – "Am I a better than average leader?"

Most leaders would no doubt answer that, "yes"…they perceive themselves to be a better leader than the average leader. Yet, if you ask yourself – "Am I a leader who walks my talk *at a World Class Level*?"…your answer to this question might be different.

When I coach top-level leaders, one of the biggest challenges they face is that they don't clearly know what their "talk" actually is. Many have never taken the time to reflect upon what they stand for or what their principles are. It's natural for many leaders to have principles, but actually living by them isn't all too common. For example, you might see yourself as trustworthy, but if the world sees you otherwise, there is a disconnect. By looking at yourself from the outside in, you can improve the results and close any perception gap that exists.

Other key factors that are also instrumental in identifying the talk include having a clear understanding of one's core values, beliefs and vision. Your core values drive your day-to-day life, as well as your decisions and behaviors. Knowing that behavior follows beliefs gives you an opportunity to discard or upgrade any beliefs that can possibly limit you. By learning how to develop empowering beliefs and investing time to solidify those beliefs, you gain an incredible competitive advantage.

On the other hand, without the commitment to be consistent and conscious to live your core values, beliefs and vision, it's very hard to achieve long-term success, personally or professionally. It also becomes nearly impossible to rise to your greatest potential and your higher value.

To help identify your "talk," ask yourself:

- What do I stand for?

- What are my core values and beliefs?

- How do I integrate them into my life and the culture of my business?

- What is my bigger vision and how do I communicate that to
  my organization?

Once you clearly know your "talk" the challenge then becomes how to proactively and deliberately take action upon this knowledge. Clearly, knowing your " talk" is very important; yet having knowledge alone will not be enough.

It is only by knowing who you are at your core and staying true to yourself that you can cultivate a World Class Level of Walking Your Talk. With your newfound strong and confident leadership presence, you will have more loyal followers and customers and you will be in even higher demand - all of this because you are adding world-class value.

Intentionally acting upon your talk and what you stand for will set you apart from most leaders.

Here are some examples of helpful questions as you ponder your "talk":

- In your opinion, what is your *current* talk?

- What do you believe others perceive your current "talk" to be?

- What "evidence" do they have for those beliefs?

- What do *you want* others to perceive your "talk" to be?

- Moving forward, what *specifically can you do* to reinforce your "talk" in the eyes of others?

A common denominator among all World Class leaders is having a high level of self-awareness. Questions such as the ones above, will help further increase your self-awareness.

THE "WALK"

An additional challenge many leaders face is *how* to "walk" the talk, once that "talk" has been identified. For example, when I started working with David, one of my coaching clients, he had just learned that his employees did not believe he was walking his talk. There was a large gap in how he perceived his "walk" compared to the perception his employees had. As the CEO of a multinational company, David came to me to help him close this perception gap and learn how to walk his talk at a World Class Level.

Think of your "walk" as your habits and actions. Habits can only become habits if you repeat them often enough. The first step is of course to increase your own level of awareness of your existing habits, good or bad. By proactively creating and cultivating even more beneficial and successful habits, you will directly raise the level of your "walk" – an imperative factor for "World Class Walk."

In an early coaching session with David, I shared with him the different levels of walking the talk that exist. This was a huge eye opener and served as compelling motivation for him to raise his standard to achieve a World Class Level of walking his talk.

Through regular and deliberate actions, David developed strong and empowering habits that served him very well and relieved his pain of not being perceived as he desired. It's important to remember that with pain often comes an opportunity to grow and to rise above yourself. By being consistent, committed and doing what's right instead of what's easy, David reached the World Class level of walking his talk and not being afraid of his own greatness and success. The prior perception gap was eliminated due to David now walking his talk at a World Class level.

Here are some examples of helpful questions as you ponder your "walk":

- In your opinion, how specifically are you "walking" your talk?

- Moving forward, how specifically will you provide evidence to others that you are congruently and consistently walking your talk that you deliberately created?

- In your opinion, what are negative consequences for you if others don't perceive that you are walking your talk?

From your answers above about your core values, your "talk" and your "walk," you have a great platform to consistently "Walking Your Talk." This means that you will experience such benefits as:

- Your level of success will increase

- You will feel even more focused and motivated

- Your life will become more in alignment

- You will feel more in harmony

- You will become a better decision maker

- You will be even more respected by others

- You will gain increased trustworthiness and loyalty

- You will have clarity over your vision and goals

- Your self confidence will increase

- You will be more solutions oriented

- You will be a leader worth following

Remember, as a leader, you are always in the spotlight. Others notice what you do and don't do. They also take notice of how you do things, so pay attention to your own standards. What is your level that you have set for yourself?

WALKING THE TALK AT A WORLD CLASS LEVEL

By having the knowledge and understanding how the world sees you, hears you and responds to you, you can become even more successful in Walking Your Talk at a World Class Level.

An important distinction is that it's possible to walk the talk yet at different level – ranging from poor to World Class. From my extensive experience working with top level leaders, here are two examples where leaders were initially not walking the talk at a World Class Level.

Richard, for example, believed that being punctual for meetings was not important because he was the CEO, and the meetings couldn't start without him. His belief system translated to a talk that punctuality was not important. So was he walking his talk? Technically yes, his walk (actions) matched his talk. He walked his talk but yet showed no respect for his employees' time. From his perspective, he was doing nothing wrong, yet his employees didn't perceive him being a leader who walked his talk. They perceived him as being arrogant, unreliable and untrustworthy. This huge gap in perception needed to be eliminated.

I worked with Richard on his self-perception, his core values and his beliefs, and from that platform we then transformed current habits, deliberately created new successful habits and combined those with intentional actions. His work was phenomenal and gave him results very quickly.

In additional to working with Richard, I also worked with the whole company's Board on manifesting the company values, beliefs and culture. All leaders within the organization went through my World Class Leadership Program.

Another example is my coaching client Sofia, the CEO of a large international company; she shared she had an open door policy, yet she couldn't understand why people didn't come to talk to her. She didn't say good morning or good bye, she never had lunch or coffee with any of her colleagues or employees. It may sound absurd, but she really did not know the name of anyone except for a handful of people. Her challenge was the perception gap between her "reality" and the reality of those around her. They did not perceive Sofia as approachable and they had no confidence in her because they simply didn't know her, and felt uncomfortable sharing their challenges, concerns and thoughts with her.

In coaching Sofia, we identified what specifically would be required in order to be perceived as a leader Walking The Talk at a World Class Level. Using "The World Class Walk The Talk System" that I have developed over the past decades, Sofia got great results just in few weeks. There was a successful transformation towards the World Class Level.

DARE TO DECLARE

Leaders frequently come into my Elite Coaching Program with the belief that "actions speak louder than words." This is of course accurate to a large degree. What you do overrides what you say in terms of how you are perceived by others.

When those around you perceive that you are walking your talk, then you have their respect and loyalty. In order to maintain this perception, it becomes important to be aware of actions matching what you are saying. For example, if you tell others that "learning, growing and developing new skills is important," then they also want to see firsthand through your actions that you are committed to learning and growing.

If they don't see that from you consistently, then their perception of how well you are walking your talk will be adversely affected.

To truly demonstrate that you are Walking Your Talk at a World Class Level, I recommend that you "Dare to Declare" what you stand for and what you are committed to doing and being. When you take this action of verbally, and perhaps even in writing, share what you will be focusing on, and what others should expect from you, their respect for you will increase dramatically – if you follow through.

As part of the World Class System the participants create their Leadership Action Plan (L.A.P.). An integral part of this L.A.P. is to Dare To Declare.

I have coached senior leaders, who when I have recommended to them that they share publicly what they stand for and what they will improve moving forward, they have said "I rather not, because then they will know what my talk is and I would be held accountable, and I don't want that." Imagine how well respected a leader with such a mindset is…That's right, not at all.

The leaders who Walk The Talk at a World Class Level take pride in others knowing what their talk is. They have zero concerns about someone "finding out" their talk. Instead, they have the confidence to Dare to Declare their talk!

When we walk our talk at a World Class level, we become Difference Makers, not only in other people's lives but also in our own life. We positively impact, empower, inspire and touch the world around us and ourselves. When we make a deliberate decision to walk our talk at a World Class Level, we become leaders of the new era. It's time to step up the game and make a difference.

We are all leaders of The New Era – let's commit to walking our talk at a World Class level so that we can proudly leave a legacy of significance and success for the next generation.

ABOUT SUSSI

Sussi Mattsson, also known as "Sussi from Sweden", is an in-demand International thought leader, dynamic speaker, executive coach and best selling author. Her interviews have aired on numerous news outlets, such as CNN, Fox News, CNBC and Bravo. She has also been featured in many publications, including *Forbes Magazine*.

Sussi is a founding council member of the Global Economic Initiative Forum and has been a featured presenter at the United Nations in New York. She is personally mentored by Jack Canfield and is also a Canfield *Train The Trainer* graduate.

Losing her mother to cancer as a little girl, and having her father sell her at the age of 8, further fueled her desire to live a life of significance and authenticity.

As President of Mattsson Group, Sussi has extensive experience spanning decades, and has empowered, inspired and given hope and courage to thousands of people to reach far beyond what they themselves believed was possible. She is an expert in Executive Coaching and has developed a proven success formula for developing World Class Leaders.

All of her corporate clients, regardless of their field, have one key common denominator: They are committed to being and developing successful future World Class leaders. In her role as a speaker, coach and Board advisor, Sussi is innovative, walks her talk, and is not afraid to push the envelope and live on the cutting edge.

Keynotes such as "Walk The Talk at a World-Class Level", "Different is your New Normal", "From Wounds To Wisdom", are all in high demand as well as her exclusive World Class Retreats. All programs are customized and based upon real life examples. Sussi takes great pride in her commitment to maximizing the performance of each participant.

With her strong passion for being a true Difference Maker, she created and founded the global movement "Wounds To Wisdom". This movement was started in order to build bridges between our past wounds and future successes. By building bridges between the past, present and future, we create "New Normals".

In one of her forthcoming books, *From Wounds To Wisdom*, Sussi takes the readers on a journey of hope, courage and overcoming obstacles as she describes her compelling life story. Another of Sussi's upcoming books, *The Big 3 – How to Build Your Success Foundation*, provides the readers with practical tools and strategies for having a rock-solid foundation for success.

Prior to becoming the President of Mattsson Group, Sussi worked as an Interior Architect for thirteen years on such projects as ambassador mansions, five star hotels, office complexes, schools in third world countries, and living/working quarters for scientists worldwide. Because of her international success and commitment to achieve World Class results, Sussi was also recruited by IKEA Headquarters to be the Business Developer for IKEA, an integral position she held for five years.

You can connect with Sussi at:

Mattsson Group: 3905 State Street 7-512 | Santa Barbara, CA 93105 USA

www.mattssongroup.com

BY PA JOOF

THE CYCLE OF INFLUENCE:
7-E's" to Becoming a Master Communicator

Every day you have interactions with others, whether it be one-on-one, a small group, or a mass audience. You have a message and you want to get your message across effectively. Or you may want to persuade someone to make a decision in your favor. In the middle of the communication, you might feel that they're just not getting your point, and you're at a loss because you have such conviction about the value of your message. But you don't quite know how to access what it will take to influence them. In order to do that, you must understand what influences them.

The great leaders in history were able to move individuals and nations because they understood what the masses wanted and so they delivered their messages in ways that would grab people emotionally and move them to action. They discovered that the secret to becoming a Master Communicator was to become a Master influencer.

I invite you to join me in a journey of the "7-E's," as I share ways to influence others no matter what circumstance, no matter what size audience, and no matter where you are. These skills can be used in business, in your personal relationships, even in daily interactions with strangers.

GET TO KNOW WHO YOU WANT TO INFLUENCE

When you first embark on the journey of having an impact on peoples' lives, whether it be verbally or in writing, you must first understand who it is you are addressing. What is important to them. You can't understand what people want until you understand what they need. What's the difference? They may want what you have to offer, but what they really want is a means to fulfilling a need.

- It could be wanting to own something to feel significant.

- It could be wanting to know information so they feel certain.

- It could be wanting to hear or receive something so they feel loved.

THE JOURNEY OF THE "7-E'S"

I invite you to join me in a journey of the "7-E's," as we follow a counterintuitive path by starting with the last step, so you're clear on what it is you want to convey, also known as your End Game, which is Step #7 of the "7-E's." Then we'll follow the progression of Steps 1-6.

STEP #7: THE END GAME

What is it that you want to accomplish?

- Do you want to negotiate a price or terms of a contract?

- Do you want to sway them into aligning with your way of thinking?

- Do you want to persuade them to make a certain decision?

- Do you want to move someone to take action?

Your ultimate End Game is to serve and give people what they want, delivered in a manner in which they are open to receive the information. Here's where these Influence skills become tricky. YOU have an End Game, and you want your End Game to be THEIR End Game, but you must first identify how your End game is going to meet one or more of their needs in order to meet yours. The key is to focus on them and their needs, but always being mindful of your End Game and how you can achieve your outcome by meeting a need.

STEP #1: EXPECTATION

You want to start by managing your expectations, which will enable you to manage their expectations. Before you meet, ask yourself: what are some possible scenarios (a.k.a. objections) that could arise? The key is anticipation so you are prepared and can comfortably tackle anything that comes your way.

Then you can start by preframing what you will be sharing. By finding out first about who you will be interacting with, you can connect them at the beginning with what you are going to share or offer. And don't beat around the bush. There's nothing worse than someone taking way too long before they get to the heart of what they want.

So carefully crafting what you say in the beginning of the conversation lets them know what to expect. Pay attention to cues:

- Are they visibly engaged and want to hear more?
- Are they asking valid questions indicating they are present and assessing what you are saying?
- Or are they looking at distractions around you instead of paying attention to you?

Honor that many people have little time for idle chatter, and they want you to get to the point efficiently, so they can decide whether they want to give up some of their precious time for you or what you have to offer them.

STEP #2: EXPERTISE

You want to position yourself as the Expert, backed by experience. It will add to your credibility, which will bring them another step closer to your End Game. AND, you also want to make it Easy, so they are not overwhelmed at first base. Remember to keep it Easy, or Simple. You may be a Financial Planner or Broker meeting with someone who is investing for the first time. You don't want to go into Options, and Buy and Hold Strategies. You want to position yourself by educating them on the basics of investing first. You're giving advice based on your knowledge and experience, and that will lead them to Step #6, where they become a part of important decisions that are impacting their lives.

A key to being an expert, however, is not to share elements of your background just so you feel significant. Just share what is relevant to them or the conversation you are going to have. There is a fine line between bragging vs. adding credibility by sharing what has taken years for you to learn through formal education, or the distinctions you learned from the School of Hard Knocks.

STEP #3: ENERGY

Your Energy has the power to impact others, merely in the way that you deliver your message or just by your presence. People are forgiving if you are exuberant, use your body to express what you want to say, and if you lead the way in how they feel through your example. With the right energy and passion, and a congruent level of certainty and conviction, 80% of the job is done.

The fastest and most effective way to access Energy whenever you need it, is to move your body. Make sure you get in state before you are face-to-face, or before you pick up the phone to make a call. As they say in the Nike commercials, "Just do it!"

- Make a fist and yell, "YES!"
- Give high fives to people around you.
- Get people to clap repeatedly, engaging their entire bodies.
- If it is one-on-one, be sure you are sitting or standing with shoulders back, head up, smiling when appropriate, and natural, full breaths to keep you calm and centered.

Most important, make sure you have an abundance of energy that will impact others, and make sure it is sustained throughout the interaction. Not only does it show you are present; people tend to mirror, or match the person they are engaged with. By setting the example, they will most likely follow what you are doing.

STEP #4: ENGAGEMENT

The key is Presence. It's not just about being there physically. There is no past or future. There is only NOW. You must condition yourself to look solidly into their eyes, knowing that in your heart, at this moment in time, they are all that matters to you. And don't be afraid to share challenges you are having if it is relevant, which will lead them to feel you are authentic and not trying to hide behind a mask or a life where everything is sublime. Not only will it provide another means of connection; it will also begin to build a level of trust so they will not be reluctant to open up, because you, too, are vulnerable and will understand.

Then the Engagement begins and they participate in the conversation or the dialogue versus just passively listening. Ask questions to elicit information about themselves and to compel them to take part in meeting their needs.

People love to be entertained, and what better way to convince someone than through a story that will help them understand your point. Or it could be a metaphor, which is a comparison of two things that may be poles apart, but have some common characteristics between them. An example is, "There's no elevator to success. You have to take the stairs." With storytelling metaphors, they start feeling how authentic you are as a person. You start getting the audience on your side.

Don't hold back, and be animated and get them to laugh. Get them to laugh at you, perhaps about something silly that you did. Entertainment is just another form of Energy.

By creating this type of atmosphere, you can move people on to deeper levels.

Then if a decision has to be made, or if you are seeking alignment, they will feel they were a part of the outcome. Then it isn't all about you and your End Game.

STEP #5: EMBRACE

Through the process of using Energy, whether it be through Entertainment, or some other form of Engagement, people will begin to Embrace their emotions, allowing them a secure and safe space to open up. This process is about building trust, and at this point, people will give you permission to go even deeper. Or to be open to what it is that you are passionate about.

Your audience will never remember what you say. They'll always remember how you made them feel.

STEP #6: EMPOWER

As you go through the steps of the "7-E's," you are taking the person, the audience, or the group through a deliberate path that will enroll them in owning the decision, or the outcome.

Step #1: You managed their Expectations by letting them know up front what you will be sharing. And by being prepared, you can effectively manage your Expectations.

Step #2: You positioned yourself as the Expert who can advise based on your knowledge and experience.

Step #3: You have sustained Energy, which has the power to impact throughout the interaction.

Step #4: You have Engagement. You have engaged them in the process, so there is mutual participation.

Step #5: You have led them to Embrace their Emotions, so they are in the appropriate space and mindset to make a decision.

Which brings us to Step #6. From this place, they become part of the End Game so you are Empowering them to take ownership. Then it becomes their decision on whether or not to take action, or to align with your perspective, or whatever the End Game might be.

#7 BACK TO THE END GAME

So coming full circle, you influence others so you arrive at the same End Game. Your End Game becomes Their End Game because you took them on a journey that led them to acknowledge that by following your strategy, your offer, your perspective, their needs are being met.

THE CYCLE OF INFLUENCE

The next time you are tested during an interaction, you can tap into these "7-E's" with ease because you have developed the skills of a Master Communicator who is able to influence others. With preparation and anticipation, you will be able to effectively persuade others to understand and embrace your End Game.

ABOUT PA

Pa Joof's message of *Making It Happen Now* is a reflection of how he lives his life. He takes and embraces information and turns it into action NOW. Born to illegal immigrants in the UK, Pa's family was sent back to their country of his ancestry when he was just a child. In the tiny republic of The Gambia, he lived with little, but had a burning passion to help those around him. His humility comes from sharing the family home with 30 others, and understanding that the human condition is not permanent. As a international speaker, trainer and coach, he inspires, motivates and guides over 200,000 people worldwide to transform to a more wealthy and purposeful life. His life has been far from ordinary. He left The Gambia at the age of 17 and returned to the U.K., where he supported himself through University, earning a BA Hons. degree in Business Analysis.

He rose through the ranks in the corporate world, creating shared value for many people and leading to a position as Head of Banking for a Fortune 500 company. Pa was responsible for over $1 billion in assets. He achieved financial independence at the young age of 30 - a mere 13 years after leaving The Gambia on his own. His success speaks for itself.

Pa has created multiple businesses worldwide, creating shared value for many people and generating millions of dollars in revenue. He has guided many clients to the same ranks of success, creating multi-million dollar businesses in less than six months and taking big, established companies to the next level.

Pa Joof currently runs various companies that operate in different countries around the world. This is impressive for a man who swept floors in order to pay his way through University while supporting not only himself, but also his 12-year old brother. His background in the financial industry qualifies him to train others on the psychology of wealth and sustainable strategies to develop the right mindset. He is President of the *Wealth Institute*, which is an international platform of industry experts providing knowledge, know-how, mindset and empowerment towards high performance on a grand scale.

Pa is also a powerful leader in Personal Development, coaching individuals from CEO's, athletes, and politicians to peak performance on a personal and professional level. The wisdom he shares comes from the heart and stems from his real life experiences, and he sets the example by walking his talk. He possesses the unique ability to connect with individuals, revealing their best qualities and attributes. He discovered his calling of inspiring people and is a key visionary of the *Making it Happen Now Foundation*, working with young people and communities to give them the greatest possible opportunities.

His message of *Living Your Legacy* by *Igniting Your Power* is the foundation of seminars that he presents internationally, training and coaching tens of thousands of people. He has a unique style, engaging energy, infectious laugh, natural charisma and a larger-than-life presence that has a compelling impact. And his delivery produces results – *Making it Happen Now!* Pa was voted one of the Top 100 Business Leaders To Follow on Twitter and he has been ranked in the top 100 motivational speakers in the world.

Because most of us want happiness,
freedom, and more security in
our lives, working on our
personal growth so that
we stay successful, is
a wise investment.

BY DR. KATHLEEN ALLARD-WASAJJA

FIVE WAYS TO BETTER HANDLE THE IMPACT OF SUCCESS FOR GOOD

"I thought it would be easier."

Many successful people have shared this comment with me over the years. Sounds familiar? It's a situation we all can face. As you know, while almost everyone secretly dreams of success, it's one thing to achieve it, and another to handle its impact. Achieving success requires a great deal of work and dedication... but this is only the beginning.

High Achievers often prepare for failure but are rarely well prepared for handling the impact of success in their personal lives. Knowing how to handle success is the key to maintaining your long-term performance and success. You might think you're the type of person whom success won't affect, but whether you want it or not, success will change your life. Here's how: success increases your responsibilities, the number of decisions you make, the risks you take, and the expectations (and criticism) you receive from others. Schedules become tighter. Success also changes how people act around you and whom you can trust. Ultimately, success has both advantages and challenges.

Just like physical symptoms can be "red flags" about your health, success also has them. Treating the cause can be a game-changer because, at some point, most successful people will experience challenges in one or more areas of their lives, including: personal, professional, family, relationships, health, or finances.

There is a reason why most successful people struggle. The reality is that most people who experience success are unprepared for certain challenges because they are entering a new learning curve. I imagine you're in a similar situation in that we're all busy, and this becomes another challenge. If we don't move past the "I'm still too busy to take time to grow myself" phase, we may struggle.

Throughout my years as a medical doctor, a personal and professional coach and a hypnotherapist, I have helped dedicated and talented entrepreneurs, CEO's, personal development leaders, athletes, actors, people in the entertainment industry, and professionals such as lawyers and medical doctors, experiencing challenges in their personal lives. Using the insights from my own experiences, I felt that I needed to reach out and help more people. Why? Because successful people are typically highly successful in certain areas of their lives, but are often silently struggling in other areas, and often have very few people to confide in and help them.

This inspired me to design the Achieve Method: a practical mind, body, emotional, and spiritual program that helps successful people support success by becoming more empowered to face the reality and pressures of their public and private lives.

Planning time for personal growth is an investment. It can help you feel better by providing more insight into your life. You'll have more ideas and establish a stronger inner foundation. We all need this to better handle the challenges of the outside world, to break free of the "success trap" and ensure our ongoing success.

There's no evidence that the challenges accompanying success will decrease anytime soon. Because most of us want happiness, freedom, and more security in our lives, working on our personal growth so that we stay successful, is a wise investment.

But it gets better.

Success can be managed with simple, daily course corrections so that you can feel better.

SO, WHAT'S THE PROBLEM?

Success typically leads to too many or too few of certain behaviours, actions, and emotions. Success can easily get you off track with your top priorities in one or more areas of your life, including personal, professional, family, relationships, health, or finances.

For those in the public spotlight, adaptation can be difficult. Long-term unhandled success can sadly lead to substance or prescription abuse and death. We all have stories in mind of talented and successful people whose lives went in a downward spiral due to the impact of success.

Let's look at some effects and "red flags" of success (you might even recognize your own situation, and if you have an unstable life or health condition, please refer to your health care provider):

- chronically increased stress levels
- fatigue or exhaustion
- a feeling of being stuck
- anxiety, worry, fear, frustration, and depression
- isolation or loneliness
- mistrust
- increased expectations from others
- sleep and health issues
- relationship and emotional issues

What are you currently challenged with? How can you make your life easier right now?

"Where do I start?" . . . you might be thinking.

Great question. Keep reading because we'll look at some of the issues as well as some of the strategies and principles that I teach successful clients in the Achieve Method program – through coaching, online courses, and luxury retreats. You'll see exactly what you need to do.

WHAT ARE THE STRATEGIES?

1. BLIND SPOTS TO BREAKTHROUGHS

What's the most common blind spot we have?

It's thinking that, unlike other people, we don't have blind spots!

And guess what? We all experience blind spots, everyday, in different areas of our lives: personal, professional, family, relationships, health, or finances.

Blind spots are, for example:

- the things we don't know, but need to know

- the things we don't see, but need to see

- the things we don't hear, but need to hear

- the things we know, see or hear, but our subconscious mind ignores

Put together, you can see why these blind spots limit the quality of our thinking, our decisions, and the value we bring to others.

People in leadership positions who lead with "unmanaged" blind spots can create dysfunctional organizations and companies that go out of business by:

(a). thinking that all past strategies will work in the present

(b). treating beliefs as facts

(c). being disconnected with what's happening at the base level

(d). not inquiring in detail about peoples' true satisfaction levels

(e). not valuing employees' opinions

(f). underestimating their competitors
. . . and the list goes on and on.

Let's illustrate the concept of blind spots with an example.

Take only 15 seconds to look at the following sentence:

Count all the "F's" in this sentence:

"FINISHED FILES ARE THE RESULT OF YEARS OF SCIENTIFIC STUDY COMBINED WITH THE EXPERIENCE OF YEARS..."

How many "F's" did you see?

Many people see 3. But there are 6 F's! Surprising, don't you think? If after learning that there are 6 F's (and you're like me and still don't see them all), you've just experienced a blind spot!

So, what's happening? When reading this sentence, most people find that their minds can't seem to process the word "of" and see the "F" in "scientific."

Why? Our minds read "ov" and don't see the "of." We also tend to skim read because we quickly recognize the words after the beginning letters.

Strategies for: <u>Blind spots to breakthroughs</u>

1. A great beginning is to remember every day that you have blind spots.

2. What do you need to know, hear, or see? Ask others for their insights. If you're a leader or business owner, spend more time with your customers, your employees, and industry thought leaders to get more details/information about their opinions and ideas.

3. Everything changes. Always keep in mind, even if you have a highly successful business, there's always something more or better you can do for your clients to stay ahead of the competition. Seek detailed feedback more frequently to spot your blind spots.

4. Open your mind to stay "teachable." Be more curious to fill your gaps of knowledge and to learn about new trends.

5. Read or train to up-level your thinking and problem-solving skills.

6. Jay Abraham, a well-known business and marketing expert (the expert to the experts) has helped thousands of clients in 400 industries. He teaches us to look at what other industries are doing, so that we can learn better ways of doing things or solving challenges.

2. A NEW AND IMPROVED YOU

How many times have you promised yourself that as soon as you achieve something, you would take more time for yourself?

The majority of successful people struggle to take time for themselves even when they most desperately need it. Something always comes up! That's when you realize that if you don't make time for yourself, your priorities, and the moments in your life that never return, it won't happen. So why would you want to commit to this now? Simple, so that you don't end up missing out on your own life. I know you may be thinking "easier said than done," but it's still doable. It will not only be beneficial for your health and wellness, but also for others, and it can give you more ideas.

When we think of success, we usually think in terms of achieving goals, and acquiring titles, promotions, or material objects. While this can be a part of success, these accomplishments often leave us feeling as if something is still missing. So, instead of running uniquely after accomplishments, seek fulfillment in the things you choose to *accomplish*.

Success is not a final destination for a list of accomplishments to achieve.

It's more of an ongoing journey in which each day matters in terms of creating what you want to experience.

If you think about this for a moment, you'll notice there's a difference between:

❖ who you are
❖ who you want to be
❖ who you should be

— Who you should be (who you were meant to be) is being authentic to who you really are, as opposed to other people's expectations and who they think you should be.

— Who you should be is about freedom! It's about making choices that match how you want to feel, with what you want to experience, and doing what you're most passionate about – all while bringing value to other people's lives.

We can all get off track with some of our priorities, but the sooner you make course-corrections, the better.

Strategy for: *A new and improved you*

(i). Living in the "now". Take 5 minutes or more during the day to ask yourself:

• How am I feeling?

• What am I deeply craving to experience right now?

• What choices are supporting my health, who I should be, and what I want to experience (making my day better)?

• What choices are not supporting what I want to experience?

• Review your schedule and ask yourself: "Which course corrections can I make right now to make today a better day for myself and for others?"

• Do I need help to commit time?

• What am I learning about myself from these experiences?

(ii). Every 3 months, commit to taking more time to relax and think about your life.

If you struggle with this, have someone "send" you somewhere relaxing. You'll see more clearly, get more insights, and avoid getting completely off track with some of your priorities. Make sure you don't let other events change what you have planned.

3. WHEN LIGHTER IS BETTER

This may not sound exciting to read, but if you overcome this one obstacle, you can make your life easier.

Self-awareness doesn't automatically come with success. The reality is that, something is always limiting us from achieving the next level in our lives.

- We all "carry" unresolved feelings and emotions about challenges we experienced years ago; this silently drains our energy by creating fears and stress. We also all get stuck in maintaining things that are no longer meant to be – whether it's our habits, relationships, careers, or other circumstances.

- Midlife, which is often a "wake-up" period during one's 30's, 40's, or 50's, is a stage when these difficult emotions often resurface.

- No matter what your level of success is, you have fears, insecurities, a lack of confidence in certain areas, blockages, and difficult experiences. These influence our lives; they originate from our childhood and adult experiences.

- Difficult experiences can create too much or too little emotional reaction affecting our behaviours, actions, and decision-making in various areas of our lives. They can even impact our health.

We store both positive and difficult experiences in our subconscious minds. That's the deep part of the mind that controls our beliefs, habits, actions, memories, and personalities. While you may think that your conscious mind leads your decisions, the main influence comes from the emotions that you have stored in your subconscious mind, a part you're not consciously aware of! Your subconscious mind both helps and limits you.

Carrying a lighter emotional load promotes better thinking, problem-solving skills, leadership, and performance.

Strategies for: <u>When lighter is better</u>

a) Which situations are most affecting me?

b) What do I feel like working on?

c) Make a personal growth plan, which can include some of the following strategies: personal reflection time, mentoring, spiritual coaching, courses, or retreats.

d) Consider what many high-level athletes use: self-hypnosis and hypnosis. Contrary to what most people think, during hypnosis, you're in full control of what you do and say. Hypnosis is a safe and effective method of creating an optimal state of mind to make changes in your life. We experience a natural state of hypnosis multiple times a day, for example, when we daydream.

4. GROWING YOUR GROWTH TEAM

The higher you rise, the harder it can be to open up to the people around you. High achievers often have very few people around them that they can trust, and who will tell them what they most need to know, hear or see.

Strategy for: <u>Growing your growth team</u>

(i) Continue to grow your trusted growth team with mentors, coaches, or other professionals from different backgrounds who can support you in this challenging, yet awesome journey because as you grow, you will have new needs.

5. HOW TO STAY MORE GROUNDED

When you achieve great success, you can get "carried" away.

If success brings you fame, you'll benefit from advantages such as wealth, access to preferential treatment, and public adoration. However, it will also change your life: you'll have to manage the stress of being in the public spotlight and lacking personal privacy.

Successful people who become famous often develop two personalities: a public one and a private one. The greater the difference between the public and private lives, the more challenging it is to adapt because the "public version of you" is not the real you; inauthenticity does not create fulfillment.

Strategies for: <u>How to stay more grounded</u>

(i). Always remember who helped you become successful:

— You once hoped and worked for the things you now have. Keep your success in perspective by remembering that no great success is achieved alone.

— No matter how talented you are:
Your success = your talents + the help of other people's gifts and talents + the value you bring to other people.

— Tell the people who have helped you how grateful you are. Also, ask yourself what you're doing to show them that you value their help and dedication.

(ii). Give back:

— Success is a privilege, an opportunity to serve others by offering more value.

(iii). Stay in contact:

— Stay in contact with people you appreciated before you became successful; they can help you stay more connected.

You've finally learned some effective strategies to better handle the impact of your success in your life, business or career. It's time to use the strategies I shared with you. Choose one that you like and then build your way up to include others.

I hope these last few words will help you do what you already know you need to do:

*We have two lives, and the second begins when we realize
we only have one.* ~ Confucius

ABOUT DR. KATHLEEN

Kathleen Allard-Wasajja, MD is a Medical Doctor, a Personal and Professional Success Coach, Hypnotherapist, Speaker, Best-Selling Author, and Co-Producer.

If there's a life that you crave... Dr. Kathleen Allard's passion is to help Generation X (born in the 1960's, 1970's, and 1980's) women and men create their ideal life with actionable strategies to transform their personal life, transform their career or business, and incorporate a healthier lifestyle.

Founder of a personal and professional wellness development and training company, Vitality Leadership Group, Dr. Allard helps high achievers overcome challenges and obstacles to achieve important life goals. She believes that there's no better time, with the experience that you've gained so far in life, to learn how to move away from stress and fear. The quality of your life should be going up, not down.

Dr. Allard's focus is also on giving value to her clients by teaching them to achieve high-level mindsets, as well as thinking and problem-solving skills. She believes that, in today's economy, investing more "in yourself" to create a stronger personal foundation can bring a greater ability to adapt to changes, and more freedom to move from where you are to where you want to be. Dr. Allard brings a unique approach to personal development through her signature programs, *Achieve Method* and *Successful Life Strategies*. She offers live transformational retreats, coaching, and online courses to design and support a customized plan for each of her clients.

Dr. Allard has over 15 years of experience as a Canadian physician (MD), practicing family medicine, has a background in emergency medicine and integrative medicine (conventional and natural medicine), and holds a bachelor's degree in nursing. Dr. Allard's studies in medical school earned her the Rhône-Poulenc Award of Excellence in neurology.

In addition to her medical training, Dr. Allard is a personal and professional success coach, US-certified hypnotherapist (National Guild of Hypnotists), and also a John Maxwell Team Member, providing transformational training to organizations with her program, *Successful Leadership Strategies*. Furthermore, she is a member of the National Association of Experts, Writers, and Speakers® in the US, which recognized her in an issue of *Newsweek* magazine in "The Next Big Thing" feature. She is certified in radio and television broadcasting and is fluent in both French and English.

Dr. Allard co-authored the Best-Selling book, *Success Starts Today*, alongside Best-Selling Author Jack Canfield. Furthermore, she received an Editor's Choice Award for her contribution to the book. She has also co-authored the Best-Selling book, *The Big Question*, with legendary Radio and TV Personality Larry King and is Co-Producer of the Larry King TV special, *The Voice of a Generation: An Evening with Larry King*. She has been featured on ABC, NBC, CBS, Fox affiliates, *USA Today* and *The Wall Street Journal*.

For more information on how to bring your life to a higher quality level, contact Dr. Allard at:

www.vitalityleadershipgroup.com

BY JEFFREY MAGEE

ONE DEGREE TRAJECTORY CHANGE MAKES MONUMENTAL ROIs

To attain a higher level of ROI in everything you do, first understand the Trajectory Code Model. We all start at Point A in route to our individual and collective goals known as Point C. Far too often individuals and organizations get off track and marred in Point B dead-end behaviors.

Be deliberate and purposeful: Point C defined as Goals and Objectives, measured by objective and specific Key Performance Indicators (KPI) and B milestones, are created from one's Values that drive one's inward Vision and outward Mission Statements (MAPS). It is as one leaves Point A the Starting Points that for a short period of time actions and behaviors place you on either a trajectory towards Point C or Point B.

Recognizing what those actions or directives are as one leaves Point A and being able to extrapolate forward which trajectory pathway line you will be sent down, is critical to success, achievement and sustained performance that matters.

In reality, what most people and organizations experience is best intentions when leaving Point A (the on-boarding of a new employee, the starting of a new campaign or initiative, etc.), but unless there are mindful individuals, coaches, mentors, milestones for benchmarking or systems in place to continuously evaluate or selfevaluate where one is at all times, on trajectory pathway C or B, one can evolve off track.

Think of the KPI's that keep one on pathway line C in route to Point C goals as the GPS system for accelerated growth. As one goes off course towards trajectory pathway B if one could easily recalibrate to pathway C then success could be easily attained and more often attained.

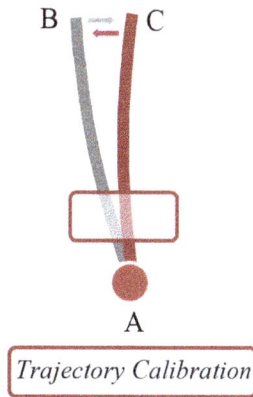

Trajectory Calibration

But once one evolves towards Point B with no accountability mechanisms in place or individuals that care for accountability, it becomes one's Behaviors that keep working in the unwittingly Point B trajectory. And over time this Behavior becomes Habit forming, and Habits becomes one's Personal SOP (Standard Operating Procedures). At this level it becomes engrained within one to operate and see things only from this dead-end trajectory, which in turn becomes your vested Emotions, and your emotions cause you to take Ownership that your way (SOP) is the only way and the best way.

When one reaches the dead-end pathway of Point B the explosion causes defensive behavior, blame, gamesmanship, the necessary change to get from Point B to Point C seems far too overwhelming for most.

Now, imagine if at the base of the Trajectory Model at Point A we had people, systems and tools in place to continuously ensure we are making the simple and easy recalibrations necessary to ensure arrival at Point C? I call these easy adjustments the 1% factors. The intersecting and progressing ROIs that can be plotted into the Pathway C Trajectory, that never ends are numerous.

When one operates from a greater understanding of the Trajectory Diagram and an understanding of the historical to present state influencers upon oneself and others within the base circular area, known as your Trajectory Code, then you can manage and forecast human behavior more accurately and facilitate simple 1% change calibrations to attain greatness. Consider the new ROI vocabulary that your Trajectory Code can drive:

1. ROIntellect – Now demand that you continuously enhance your mental DNA and draw deeply from within to always showcase the best of you and others!

2. ROIndividual Initiative – Now imagine that your Trajectory "C" line were paved with support systems and people to allow you to deliver on ROI #1, so you and others freely gave 100%, 100% of the time, and accepted nothing less from everyone in your space?

3. ROInterpersonal Relationships (leverage multiplier) – Now imagine you could have 100% presence of mind to be able to leverage 100% of the people you know and could motivate others to do the same in pursuit of Trajectory Point C.

When one has clarity of Point C with clearly defined Language that guides every action, it can become a common DNA thread that unites people of like cause, mind, or goal with one another and now the cumulative energies can be overwhelming. And that would spell real ROI (Return On Investment) of any capital you get to work within!

ABOUT JEFF

Jeff Magee (Ph.D., CMC, CBE, PDM, CSP) the "Thought Leader's Leader" ... accelerates organizations forward through his Leadership Academy of Excellence™ Series, Performance Driven Selling™ platform, Keynotes and performance-based Coaching (www.JeffreyMagee.com). Jeff is the Group Publisher & Editor-and-Chief of Professional PERFORMANCE/360 Magazine™ (www. ProfessionalPerformanceMagazine. com), Editor of Performance Execution and Performance Driven Selling™ Blogs, former nationally syndicated Radio Talk Show Host (www. CatalystBusinessRadion.com), as well as a published author of twenty-three books, translated into 21 languages, including the best sellers: *The Managerial-Leadership Bible© Revised Edition, Your Trajectory Code®, Performance Execution®* and *The Sales Training Handbook®*.

Jeff is also a columnist and highly sought motivational-leadership speaker. Jeff is also the recipient of the United States Junior Chamber's Ten Outstanding Young American's (TOYA) Award and the United States National GUARD's Total Victory Team Medal for civilian contribution to the Armed Services.

To book JEFF, contact him at DrJeffSpeaks@aol.com.

CMC – Certified Management Consultant

CBE – Certified Board Executive

CSP – Certified Speaking Professional

PDM – Certified Professional Direct Marketer

BY PATRICE TANAKA, FOUNDER & CHIEF JOY OFFICER, JOYFUL PLANET LLC

PURPOSE:

A Competitive Advantage in Business and Life

We all know that purpose is important. Living on purpose makes you feel alive, clear and authentic. Those with a sense of purpose tend to live longer and have better relationships. People with a higher purpose have a healthier outlook on life and are more resilient to stress.

Purpose is also a huge, competitive advantage in business and life.

I know. I've experienced first-hand the power of purpose in my personal life and in my business. This experience led me to exit the last of three successful PR & Marketing agencies I co-founded to start Joyful Planet, a consultancy focused on helping individuals and organizations discover and live their purpose to unleash greater success, fulfillment and joy in their personal lives, their businesses and their communities.

In 1990, after leading a group of 12 colleagues in a management buyback from Chiat/Day Advertising to co-found an employee-owned PR agency, I realized that our unknown start-up, PT&Co., would be competing against thousands of established agencies in New York City, which is home to the greatest number of PR agencies on the planet. How could we compete and win against such a huge field of competitors? I believed that our agency's greatest strength and differentiator was what our group of employee-owners was committed to doing through the vehicle of our company.

We explained that PT&Co. was committed to creating: "Great Work. Great Workplace. Great Communities that Work." Today, this would be called a "business purpose."

In 1990 no one talked about business purpose and neither did we. What we knew is that we had come up with a radical proposition for any business, much less a PR agency. Back then, PR agencies suffered from the perception of being sweat shops, willing to take on any client with a budget no matter how questionable their reputation.

Our business purpose communicated the agency's focus on creating great work, because that's what attracts and retains top clients, and creating a great workplace in order to attract and retain the top talent necessary to produce great work. Finally, we talked about our commitment to creating "great communities that work" or healthy, sustainable communities, within and beyond our workplace. Our business purpose was the reason we felt compelled to turned down four different tobacco manufacturers despite their hefty PR budgets.

THE POWER OF A BUSINESS PURPOSE

Communicating our business purpose helped attract the kind of clients we sought, including American Express, Avon, Charles Schwab & Co., Dyson, Ernst & Young, Godiva, Girl Scouts of the USA, Liz Claiborne, Mercedes-Benz USA, Microsoft, Target, Wines from Rioja, Spain and Wyndham Hotels & Resorts, among others.

Our business purpose helped us laser focus on creating a great workplace. The result was one of the industry's lowest annual employee turnover rates of 10 percent. Average employee turnover rate for PR agencies was and still is 30+ percent.

Our agency's focus on creating "great communities that work" helped us to produce award-winning PR campaigns such as Liz Claiborne's "Love is Not Abuse" program, addressing the issue of domestic violence awareness and prevention. This campaign alone garnered our agency more than 50 awards and was cited as the "best example of a public, private and non-profit partnership" and as one of the "Top 5 PR Campaigns of the Decade" by the *Holmes Report* (January 2010). Over the years, we helped many other clients address important public health and social issues, including breast cancer awareness and early detection, literacy, financial literacy, youth leadership development and hunger relief, among others.

Within eight years, PT&Co. was named the *#1 Most Creative* and *#2 Best Workplace* among all PR agencies nationwide by the *Holmes Report* (Fall 1998). Two years later, our agency was ranked *#1 for Quality Reputation* among all PR agencies in New York City (and #3 nationally) by Thomas L. Harris/Impulse Research (September 2000).

This is the power of a business purpose that resonates with all stakeholders from employees to customers to suppliers to shareholders to the community-at-large.

Increasingly today, purpose is being communicated by many innovative, forward-thinking businesses, including: Deloitte ("Make a positive, enduring impact that matters"), Google ("Organize the world's information and make it universally accessible and useful"), Patagonia ("Build the best product, cause no unnecessary harm, use business to inspire and implement solutions to the environmental crisis"), Unilever ("Make sustainable living commonplace") and Whole Foods ("Nourish the health and well-being of people and planet by being the authentic purveyor of food for the greater good").

Purpose-driven businesses like these understand that the best, long-term growth strategy is to create "value" for ALL stakeholders not just shareholders. These companies are not only focused on enhancing "profits," but on contributing to the greater good.

PURPOSE-DRIVEN BUSINESSES SIGNIFICANTLY OUTPERFORM PROFIT-ONLY FOCUSED COMPANIES

Research, in fact, reveals that "purpose-driven" companies significantly outperform "profit only" focused companies. In a 15-year study of all S&P companies, Rajendra Sisodia in his 2014 book, *Firms of Endearment, How World-Class Companies Profit from Passion and Purpose*, reveals that purpose-driven companies experienced 1,681 percent growth vs. only 118 percent growth for profit-only focused businesses.

It's not enough, however, to simply communicate your business purpose. You must "operationalize" purpose in every aspect of your business to generate the kind of results that Sisodia cites. According to the 2017 Ernst & Young Global Study, *How Purpose Can Reveal a Path Through Disruption*, 97 percent of companies that deeply integrate a broader sense of purpose into their operations report a good or great deal of incremental value from doing so, including: Greater customer loyalty (52 percent); Preserving brand value and reputation (51 percent); Attracting and retaining top talent (42 percent); and Developing innovative new products and services (40 percent).

At PT&Co., we "operationalized" purpose in every area of our agency from our hiring practices (we asked prospective hires about their life purpose), to our employee benefits and policies (we offered strong benefits, including paid maternity leave), to the way we designed our workplace (our office had a living room, eat-in kitchen/lunchroom and a meditation room for naps or quiet reflection), to the suppliers we worked with to the clients we chose to represent (those offering quality products and wanting to contribute to the greater good). Our business purpose was the North Star that guided us when we felt compelled to terminate relationships with clients – we resigned our biggest client on two separate occasions because we could no longer, in good conscience, continue to represent them.

These actions reinforced the agency's credibility to employees and clients, alike, about how seriously we lived our business purpose.

Twelve years into building our employee-owned agency, I was totally burnt out from 60-hour work weeks while caring for a sick husband, who died after valiantly battling a brain tumor for 16 years, and fulfilling endless, professional and civic obligations.

I sought help from an executive coach who reassured me that she could help me feel better, but that, first, I needed to "re-think" my purpose in life. When I heard this, I was annoyed. I had just finished telling the coach, Suzanne Levy, that I was totally out of gas. I didn't have the energy to re-think my purpose in life. Suzanne was understanding, but adamant that she couldn't help me unless I could share my new purpose and then help me feel better by living it.

Over the next two weeks before our next coaching session I considered and rejected many life purpose statements. At my next session, I shared with Suzanne that my new life purpose was informed by the nearly 3,000 people who died on 9/11, just five months earlier. I told her that I was haunted by the idea that nearly 3,000 people went to work that morning and didn't return home that evening.

I knew those people were caught short, probably not having done many of the things they most wanted to do in life because they were banking on living long enough to do all those things. I told Suzanne that I wanted to live my life in such a way that I could be "good to go" no matter how little notice I might have before my death because I would have done or would be doing what was most important to me.

I shared with Suzanne that my purpose in life was "to choose joy in my life every day, to be mindful of that joy, and to share that joy with others." I told her that if I could live my life this way every day I think I could be "good to go" whenever it was my time.

THE POWER OF A LIFE PURPOSE TO FOCUS AND DRIVE US

This simple statement of purpose resulted in me accomplishing the following things over the next 15 years: taking up ballroom dancing at age 50 (something I wanted to do since I was eight, dreaming of dancing like Ginger Rogers); becoming a ballroom champion; writing a book, *Becoming Ginger Rogers…How Ballroom Dancing Made Me a Happier Woman, a Better Partner and a Smarter CEO*; leveraging the lessons I learned from ballroom dancing by close partnering and co-founding two other, successively larger PR & Marketing agencies – CRT/tanaka and Padilla, one of the top 10 largest, independent PR agencies in the U.S. and the largest, employee-owned agency; starting my Joyful Planet consultancy; writing a best-selling book, *Beat the Curve*, with renowned management consultant and coach Brian Tracy, and sharing my joy by supporting three non-profits, including Dancing Classrooms, which uses the vehicle of ballroom dance to help children enhance their self-esteem, self-confidence and partnering skills.

All of these accomplishments resulted from the simple act of discovering and living my life purpose. I've accomplished more in the past 15 years than I had in the previous 30 years of my life. This is why I believe discovering and living our purpose is a strong, "competitive advantage" – it can focus and drive us to accomplish what is most important.

Based on my first-hand experience and subsequent research, discovering and living our purpose should be a no-brainer. Sadly, it is not.

Fewer than 20 percent of leaders have a strong sense of their individual purpose, according to the authors of "From Purpose to Impact" in the *Harvard Business Review* (May 2014), and even fewer can distill their individual life purpose into a concrete statement. The authors, Nick Craig and Scott A. Snooth, go on to say that, "the process of articulating your purpose and finding the courage to live it – what they call 'purpose to impact' – is the single, most important developmental task you can undertake as a leader."

Bottom-line: Knowing our purpose is a powerful, competitive advantage in business and life because it can focus and drive us to accomplish what is most important in a highly efficient way. Knowing our purpose is like having our own personal North Star, helping us navigate the challenges of business and life.

HERE'S HOW YOU CAN DISCOVER YOUR LIFE'S PURPOSE

- Identify your greatest talent, expertise or passion that you can leverage to help other people and our planet.

- Articulate a succinct, but galvanizing statement of purpose that communicates how you will leverage these to accomplish what is most important for you to do in life.

- Memorize, recite and share your purpose with others as often as possible. Doing this will help you "inhabit" your purpose and sharing your purpose will help you enlist support to accomplish what is most important.

- Actively live your purpose by taking action on a daily basis.

HERE'S HOW YOU CAN DISCOVER YOUR ORGANIZATION'S BUSINESS PURPOSE

- Identify your organization's greatest strength or differentiator and how you will leverage it to contribute to the greater good.

- Articulate a succinct, but galvanizing statement of purpose that communicates this and how your organization will create value for all stakeholders, not just shareholders.

- Communicate your business purpose to both internal and external stakeholders in an ongoing way.

- Operationalize your purpose in every area of the business so it becomes a living, breathing expression of your organization's values.

ABOUT PATRICE

Patrice Tanaka is a serial entrepreneur, co-founder of three award-winning, PR & Marketing firms and Joyful Planet, a Business & Life Strategy Consultancy to help individuals and organizations discover and live their purpose to unleash greater success, fulfillment and joy in their personal lives, their businesses and their communities. This is the subject of Patrice's best-selling new book, *Beat the Curve* (2016), co-authored with renowned management consultant and coach, Brian Tracy, and other business leaders. Her chapter is entitled, "Live Your Life's Purpose and Unleash Your Joy."

This book and her consultancy, Joyful Planet, is the culmination of Patrice's personal and professional journey in the wake of 9/11 when she was depressed, in a malaise and exhausted from building a business with 12 other partners and caring for a sick husband who died of a brain tumor after a valiant fight. An executive coach Patrice sought out during that time challenged her to rethink her life purpose, which, after some reflection led Patrice to say: "My purpose in life is to choose joy in my life every day; to be mindful of that joy, and to share that joy with others." Pursuing her joy led her to take up ballroom dancing, which resulted in Patrice's first book, *Becoming Ginger Rogers...How Ballroom Dancing Made Me a Happier Woman, Better Partner and Smarter CEO* (2011).

Apart from chronicling how Patrice pursued her joy of ballroom dancing, taking her first dance lesson at age 50, *Becoming Ginger Rogers* tells the story of her award-winning track record in creative problem solving for some of the most successful global brands. "The only reason I started my first PR agency, PT&Co., is that it was the best solution I could come up with to avoid having to fire four talented colleagues when we lost our biggest account," explains Patrice. She led 12 colleagues, including the four in danger of being fired, in a management buyback from advertising agency, Chiat/Day, to co-found an employee-owned PR agency in 1990. Within eight years, PT&Co. was recognized as the *"#1 Most Creative"* and the *"#2 Best Workplace"* among all PR agencies in the U.S.

Prior to starting Joyful Planet, Patrice was Co-Founder, Chief Counselor & Creative Strategist for Padilla, the largest, employee-owned PR agency in America. Previously, she was Co-Chair, Chief Creative Officer and *whatcanbe* Ambassador for CRT/tanaka, an entity she co-founded in 2005.

Patrice has been honored by many organizations, including *PRWeek* (Hall of Fame 2016), Public Relations Society of America ("Paul M. Lund Award for Public Service"), *The Holmes Report* ("Creativity All-Star"), New York Women in Communications ("Matrix"), Girl Scouts of Greater New York, *Working Mother* Magazine, Asian Women in Business, University of Hawaii ("Distinguished Alumni"), among others.

Born and raised in Hawaii, Patrice graduated from the University of Hawaii and moved to New York City, realizing a childhood dream of living in Manhattan. In 1979, she joined Jessica Dee Communications, a PR agency she helped build that was acquired by Chiat/Day Advertising in 1987.

Connect with Patrice at:

Patrice@JoyfulPlanet.com

LinkedIn/Patrice Tanaka

Twitter/Patrice Tanaka

FOLLOW YOUR PASSION

P360: When did your passion for writing begin?

SHAUNEQUA: I've always been a writer. Ever since childhood. I loved writing science fiction and fantasy. For me, it was a way for me to use my imagination and get all of my thoughts and ideas out into the world. I was born in Brooklyn, NY, and I am the youngest of four kids. So, even though I wasn't an only child, I was the baby of my family and my siblings were all 9, 10, and 11 years older than me. I ended up growing up in a situation very similar to an only child. And being that I was by myself a lot of the time, I was very introspective regarding everything around me. This actually helped me because I became very connected with my "inner voice".

P360: Did that connection with your inner voice fade over time?

SHAUNEQUA: In a manner of speaking. I held on to it as long as I could, but as you grow up you begin to drift away from it more and more. You lose that connection to yourself when you start to be around more people. As an example, you begin to attend elementary school and you start to hang around other people. In doing so, you begin to lose the attachment you have with yourself. No longer are you only thinking about who you are, what you love, what crazy ideas you're having; now you're thinking about your friends, your teachers, your clergy, etc. Then as you age, it expands on a more grandiose scale to your personal social status, the clothes you wear, professional affiliations, etc. Overwhelmingly enough, you begin to live much more connected to the voices of the people around you, rather than listening to your own. Additionally, the older you get, the more detached you become with who you are at your core because there's so many distractions pulling you from yourself.

P360: How did that detachment play itself out for you?

SHAUNEQUA: While attending college, I was offered a part time job within the cosmetics department of a major retailer. It was an odd offer, at the time, because I actually didn't wear make-up, at all. I explained this to them, thinking that this might be a problem. However, it was not. And, they said, "No, it's no issue at all." With that, my cosmetics career began. And, what I soon discovered was that I really enjoyed it, and, was actually really good at it.

After graduating college, I was offered a manager level, full-time job within the industry. Seeming like an awesome opportunity, I accepted. Enjoying all moments I've experienced while working within the cosmetics industry, I've always known it wasn't really me, you know? I mean, at my core, I was a writer. Using my days off to write religiously, as well as my lunch hours, while at work. The people I worked with within the industry knew I was a writer. My family and friends have always known that I was a writer, and deep down I knew it as well. And, it could possibly blossom into more than a hobby. But, I felt like I could finally be an adult, pay the bills, save money, have a life, until I sell that killer script, book or movie. It was a good plan and helped me not become the stereotypical starving artist. Additionally, I was gaining a lot of success, so I stuck with it.

P360: So, you had pretty good success in the cosmetics industry?

SHAUNEQUA: Yeah I did, and I really loved a lot of the industry. I worked for different department store chains, and, at one point I had over 200 people reporting to me, during the high volume holiday season. I became a highly successful cosmetics/accessories planner/buyer and I was in a lot of ways, at the top of my game. But, deep down, I knew I wasn't put here on earth to be a cosmetics planner and buyer. And it happened so quickly, you know? Once you get out of college, you start thinking, "Ok, I've graduated from college, I need to be an adult now. Let me get my life together." And you're trying to get your ducks in a row. You're trying to make your family happy, your boss happy, your friends happy, and everyone around you happy. And the more I focused on making everyone else happy, the more I lost touch with my own voice.

I started losing myself. I was focused on placating everyone around me thinking that was the best thing to do rather than being true to myself. And that gets more exhausting than you can ever imagine. There's an old saying that you can't pour from an empty cup. In other words, if all you're ever doing is trying to make people around you happy, then you're forgetting that at the end of the day you have to make yourself happy to replenish your own cup. This happens all the time with people. We get so bombarded by all of the demands around us that we forget to listen to our inner voice. And all I was doing was focusing on the needs of people and clients around me, and I wasn't listening to the needs I had within myself to create. I was burning out. And then I ended up being forced out of my job due to an injury.

P360: What happened?

SHAUNEQUA: Well, part of what made me successful was that I was involved in every minute detail of my business. I'm a control freak. Even in my four inch heels, with make up on and in a suit, I would still be in the stockroom or at the truck unloading, because that was just how I was. And one day I was moving boxes that I really had no business moving and I completely threw my back out. It put me out. And in one quick moment I went from a successful career in the cosmetic industry as an Executive to the confinement of my bed, with limited mobility due to the pain. I knew in that moment that everything had changed. I couldn't go back to my old career, it was too physically active and demanding. Suddenly, I was trapped. And, I was forced to start listening to my inner voice again.

P360: So, life forced you to listen to your inner voice again?

SHAUNEQUA: Exactly. And I really think that's it. I'm not the same person I used to be, but the beauty of it is now I'm regulated to writing. People always say, "God has a sense of humor." And I believe that's true. He was basically saying, "I made you to be a writer, and you keep doing this other thing, but I want you to be a writer. So, how about you be on bedrest for a while and be in a position where the only thing you can do is write?" And I think back over my career and can see different ways in which there were things calling me to get back on track with my writing, but I just didn't listen to them because I was going head first into my industry. And then with my injury I was finally able to stop and look at what I really believed that God put me on this earth to do.

P360: What is it like to now pursue your passion for writing?

SHAUNEQUA: Its different than with my former career, because I honestly feel like I *have* to write. I *have* stories and ideas that I have to get out onto paper, just like when I was a little girl. I'm finally in touch with who I really am and what I really think, and I have all these ideas flowing out. I think it's so critical to be honest with yourself and pursue your passions. Too many people in this world ignore the things that deep down they really want to do, and instead pursue all of the things that they believe the people around them want them to do. We sacrifice our own voice to adhere to the voices of others. And through my life I've learned that that is a huge mistake. It will lead you to exhaustion (and maybe even a severe back injury!). However, when you are operating within your passion, then it doesn't even feel like work. It feels like something that you just simply *have* to do. There is no option. And that is truly a wonderful feeling.

P360: What are you hoping to accomplish with your writing career?

SHAUNEQUA: Well, for one, the beauty of listening to your inner voice is that you don't *need* to accomplish anything anymore. You are writing purely for the joy of writing, not to make other people happy. But, I would say one of the things I'm extremely passionate about is writing about life in such a way that it gets people talking with each other. One of the biggest problems in our world today is that people have stopped actually talking about life with each other, discussing ideas. And, I want to work on projects, put out work that could possibly get people to start talking with each other about their lives again. That's my hope. But, the beautiful thing is, now that I'm finally listening to my inner voice, the only thing that really matters is that I stay true to myself.

ABOUT SHAUNEQUA

Shaunequa Jordan is a CEO who works under the company umbrella of her namesake, Shaunequa, LLC., a company formulated to protect all of her artistic endeavors, six years ago. Shaunequa is a writer and has been one for many years. Her first love is her ability to transcribe an idea, or thought, into a script instantaneously. For her to write out thoughts is synonymous with a painter utilizing a brush to start the shaping of a picture. Her first love of writing a script works because she sees her thoughts in pictures. Her thoughts are mini movies that she rushes to transcribe on a page.

Shaunequa has held few authors in high regard. But, as a child, she loved Steven King, James Baldwin, Zora Neale Hurston and Judy Blume. She connected to such a small group of writers because in her youth she had an odd quirk. When reading a novel, she needed to be able to SEE and visually picture, what the words were saying to her. If she could not mentally visualize the words on the page easily, she would quickly lose interest. She has suffered through reading many novels over the years, but has never held this inability of fluid movement within a story, against any authors. She just has always chalked it up as her own personal, odd little quirk ... And still does.

She sits on a lot of work – books, plays and scripts. She has been aggressively approached in the past by publishers, never giving in. She has always held strong to her direction for her projects. Possibly, a little stubborn? Maybe. But, she is open and flexible to work with. Additionally, in doing so, she will hold steadfast to the core meaning of a concept, and understands that there are always varied ways to showcase an idea. For her, this is the fun part, and where the games begin.

To understand the depth of her talent, here is a dialogue with her that explains her passion:

"Why do you do what you do?"   Shaunequa: "Honestly, because it is easy for me, second nature."

"What inspires you to do this work?"   Shaunequa: "An unheard thought, idea, that needs to be expressed."

"What do you believe about it?"   Shaunequa: "That books, movies and plays are an awesome way to reach and communicate with the masses. It is just an extremely difficult way to do so."

Besides being a goofy, quirky, individual who is a child at heart, Shaunequa is a Brooklyn, New York native. She is from the Bedford-Stuyvesant area, where she was a proud, active, community-driven citizen. Here she sat on her local Community Board, specifically, CB2, and the Neighborhood Advisory Board, NAB3. Her involvement within her positions touched on land use/zoning issues, transportation monitoring, and community programs that focused on the youth and the elderly. Her commitment to her community holds a special place in her heart.

Her heart still resides in Brooklyn, although her spirit has settled in Blooming Grove, New York, in the lovely Orange County of the HUDSON VALLEY.

To connect with Shaunequa, visit:

shaunequa.com

lmao@shaunequa.com

Instagram: shaunequa

Periscope: shaunequa

Facebook: theshaunequapage

Facebook: whoisshaunequa

Shaunequa LLC

BY BRENT CAMPBELL

SUCCEEDING BY HELPING OTHERS

Long before I began my business career, I listened to my father and mother teach me how they had worked together as a team to build careers and a family. I listened to them talk about the struggles of being a young couple, managing a budget and saving for a growing family. As I thought about their story, I saw the life that they worked so long to achieve become possible. As a young man, I struggled through what we used to call the "oatmeal years"—because that's all I could afford while revenue was poured back into the company—earning my first clients and expanding my business. One of the problems that I faced was how to ramp up, expand and what to do with the money we made.

For a long time, I thought the right thing to do was look for the shiny whistle—the new software program, the new theory, that new thing that a lot of people initially loved. As time went on and I gained more experience, I realized the smart thing to do was to find mentors and people who had successful business experience. Why is this important? It is important because we are more fulfilled when we help those around us achieve their dreams, and this, in turn, helps us become more successful in business and in life.

On one occasion in my early in my twenties, I'd gone home to visit my parents. While we were sitting on the back porch talking, I was reminded of the quote that is attributed to Mark Twain, "When I was a boy of 14, my father was so ignorant I could hardly stand to have the old man around. But when I got to be 21, I was astonished at how much the old man had learned in seven years". The good news for me was that I was lucky enough to realize that he had good ideas and strong life experience he was willing to share. I remember that visit as one of my most eye-opening experiences. What I realized was that by listening to my father and his peers, I could avoid some of the financial issues that most of us have experienced . If I was able to avoid just a little bit of it and convert the time that I saved to a positive experience, what would I be able to do with that time? The obvious answer was do the same thing my wife, my parents and others with different life experiences had so selflessly done for me—help others think about the problems or challenges they were facing in their own lives, help them think about how to re-order those challenges they were facing and develop a strategy to work through or around those issues that they found slowing them down.

My wife, Jennifer, is one of the kindest and most knowledgeable people I've ever been lucky enough to know. Most of us have heard the phrase *there's no need to reinvent the wheel*. It's something she reminds me of frequently, and If we think about it, she's right. We must be smart and observant enough to know that we need to find mentors in our own lives who have already faced challenges we're encountering to help us move forward.

There are several things that I work hard to share with my clients and their employees. The first of these is to *Keep It Simple*. There is no need to make things more difficult than they already are. All of us face challenges that we don't expect or are unprepared for or want to deny. It can be the death of a family member, the downturn in a business or a challenge from a competitor. Our challenge as leaders in our communities, and in the world, is to create an environment that is more productive, less stressful and more purpose-led than previous generations. If we don't learn from mistakes that we made when we were younger, and from the people who came before us, we're not doing the best that we can do and we're doing ourselves and our children a disservice.

My wife has done a wonderful job reinforcing this in our home and in her practice as one of the top Realtors in the country. I reflect on her encouragement in helping those around us, and her work with our family, the community and her business. We believe it's our job to create a better world for our children. But it's not simply to create a better world, it's also to create a world in which they can be more successful than we are. It is to help advance human knowledge, research and quality of life so that we all can do what we want, in a positive way, and in a way that helps other people in the world around us. When I was young, I thought of people who could afford anything they wanted as lucky. Those who inherit wealth may be blessed, but I think the real fortune depends on whether they use their good fortune to help others. For most of us, it's determining a goal, designing a path to get there, and then doing it. Sounds simple, but it's not.

She used to say that something could be *simple but not easy*.

My grandmother had a wonderful phrase that seemed overly simplistic to me even as a child. She used to say that something could be *simple but not easy*. I find that a resolution can be straightforward when one thinks through what both parties want out of a transaction or exchange. Getting to that resolution may not be as easy as we hope for. Daily challenges of life can interfere with what we are trying to do in moving our companies and ourselves to a better place.

When I was young, my father taught me how to play chess. It seemed like a simple game. But the more I played, the more I realized how complex the strategies could become. The longer I played the more I enjoyed it. I realized there was a higher level of thinking that was required for this game and it became a metaphor for me in my own personal and business life. What does the person on the other side of the chessboard want? It was a true lightning moment. I realized that in every transaction, every interaction with other people, we need to think about not just what we want, but what they want. What is it that we can do for them? How can we serve them? Dr. King admonished us not to judge people by what they look like, but by their character. I had the honor to speak with Mrs. King when I was young adult. It was a very brief conversation and I was struck by how calm she was and the dignified way she carried herself. She wasn't loud or abrasive, but rather, she seemed resolute in what she was doing when I met her in Washington, DC. It was a chance meeting, but it stays with me all these years later and reminds me to think about how we help and mentor those around us.

In primary school, we were living just outside Washington, DC and the riots of the late 1960s were consuming sections of the city. My mother and I talked about it and she told me that she thought society was changing. I asked her what she meant, and she said that when she and my father were married the rules were very defined. The husband's job was to go to work and provide for the family and the mother's job was to stay home and take care of the house and children. Life was changing dramatically around me and luckily, as a child, I didn't know any better. My parents were very pragmatic and told me that I needed to learn a different path—a different way. So, my mother began with small skills, and taught me how to make a bed with hospital corners. She taught me how to set a table. She taught me how to take care of my brother and sister (not a job I always enjoyed). My father taught me how to take care of the house—how to do small repairs, cut the yard, and do home maintenance. I began to think in terms of what else I could learn because I felt very comfortable with these rules that society was reshaping and redefining for my generation. A major part of this thinking was including others and how we could help them, too.

When I began expanding my business, my initial thought was to develop a financial division that would fund my client's dreams and help them begin to grow and prosper. I received a telephone call one day from a realtor that I did not know and did not know how she found me. I wasn't advertising, and my team wasn't advertising. We were simply quietly speaking to people we already knew and offering to assist. The realtor who called me told me about a client of hers who was not going to be able to reach the closing table and was supposed to close on her home in two days. The bank called her and said that they had discovered that a significant portion of her income was in cash. It made perfect sense to me because she told me she was a waitress and a lot of her income came from tips. While she was reporting her income on her mortgage application to her lender, she neglected to mention it on her taxes and if income is not claimed on your taxes, you can't use it to be qualified for a mortgage on a home. But I also learned by talking to this potential buyer that she was living in a very abusive situation and needed to be able to protect her son and herself. I sat down with her and with the realtor and we came up with a two-part strategy. The first part was how to resolve the financial

It had to do with helping someone who needed my assistance and didn't know what to do.

challenge she had put herself in by not claiming all her income on her taxes. This part made sense to me as a lender—it's what I did. However, the second part of the strategy was not something that anyone even whispered about in lending circles. It didn't have anything to do with lending. It had to do with helping someone who needed my assistance and didn't know what to do.

How many times have you had someone in your family or at your office very obviously not know what to do about a difficult situation in which they found themselves and you've watched someone else in the office not help at all—but who had the ability to help? That is a perfect opportunity to benefit both people. If we help the person who needs something, that's a good thing, but if we help the person who has the knowledge necessary to help realize that they have an obligation to help those around them, that is significantly more important. Because that person has knowledge they can use to assist others, we should actively encourage those people to engage and assist those around them.

So, what do we do with this? First, keep it simple. What is my first goal? What do I need to achieve that specific goal? Who do I need to know, who do I need to ask help from to reach that goal? Next, how do I plan to reach my goal? Do I need to speak to my mentor and how do I help others in the process? Keep the major tenets of your life and business philosophy positive and always make sure you're including others in your path forward.

ABOUT BRENT

Brent Campbell is a banker and entrepreneur who enjoys helping his clients realize their goals and become purpose-led. Whether it's purchasing a home, building a company or business, or moving up to the next level of their careers, Brent's experience is often invaluable to the people with whom he works. He has a "will do" approach of fostering and helping the creative process for his clients by listening to the clients' concerns and assisting them in overcoming their own perceived limitations. Brent feels there is always a solution or strategy to any challenge, and he works to help others see that in themselves.

Brent founded his first company in 1983 and has been creating and building businesses for himself and others ever since. Brent's focus is in helping his teams and clients determine what is best for them and what will help them move forward the fastest and while helping them remain positive and productive. His goal is to help his clients understand the challenges they face, determine a plan to meet those challenges and work toward the success they see for themselves, their families and their businesses. Brent has been continuously involved in finance, technology development and manufacturing.

He is an alumnus of Johns Hopkins University and The College of William and Mary. He is the CEO of FHG Financial, a private equity group that specializes in the mortgage, financial and technology arenas. Brent is recognized as one of the top mortgage and business enterprise experts in the world and has worked with the Executive Office of the President, multi-national corporations, regional and local companies and individuals.

Brent has 35 years of finance, business, consulting, project management and manufacturing experience, most recently with EccoStone, a manufacturer of green building products. During that time, he has headed numerous financial, development and management teams and has been directly involved in mergers, acquisitions and divestitures. He has filed and sold several patents and has helped clients around the globe, advising in diverse fields including commercial manufacturing, telecommunications, biotech, insurance, healthcare and distribution. Brent has a proven track record for building high performance teams through collaboration and strategic planning, and has fun doing it!

You can connect with Brent at:

bcampbell@fhg.com

www.twitter.com/BrentFHG

BY KWESHA DENICE NEAL

THE BLUEPRINT THAT OPENS THE DOOR TO A BETTER LIFE

Throughout our lives, we have a tendency to become entangled in troubling situations. During those times, we tend to question ourselves, "Why me?" and feel isolated and alone. The truth is, it's not just "you." In everyone's life there exists a good person, someone with a big personality who is well known in both social and workplace situations. This friend is supportive and always willing to give good advice to her family and friends. They are the type of person that, from the outside, appears to have a wonderful life. However, deep inside of them, there lives a dark cloud of unhappiness.

I have a friend like that in my life. You see, that person has been working at the same job for 15 years. The same job she promised herself she'd work for a maximum of five years. Instead, she got stuck in the motion of life and never moved forward to accomplish her dreams. She broke her promise to herself, and in the process of working countless hours in an unfulfilling career, she lost value in herself. Suddenly, she no longer recognized herself or the person she had become.

At work one day, all of her deep, emotional build-up came crashing down almost instantaneously. The immense amount of emotion caused her to breakdown and weep; weep for a change in her mindset and a change of lifestyle. When she went home that evening, my friend started to examine herself mentally and emotionally. She grabbed a piece of paper and a pen and wrote on it: "I Must Move Forward." She had come to the conclusion that she was not only unhappy with her current situation, but also her state of mind. She longed to be free from a job that had no purpose, did not add value to her life, and required her to isolate herself from the world of possibilities. She wanted to be able to live her life with no strings tying her down, but she couldn't find a realistic way to make that fantasy become a reality.

A few weeks later, she ran into Karen, who she had not seen for what seemed like decades. They both had some serious catching up to do. When she had spoken to Karen years ago their situations were very similar. Both women had felt stuck, unhappy, and lost within themselves. But, something was different about Karen this time around. Karen was friendlier and seemed genuinely happy with herself and her life, almost as though she had been reborn. There was a glow about Karen, and she had a confident smile that radiated throughout the room. During their chat, Karen shared that she had been seeing a life coach, and that it had greatly benefitted her life and her bond with her family. The life coach had helped Karen deal with life and cope with her troubling situations in different and more positive ways.

Karen went on to explain what a life coach was. A life coach provides a form of coaching someone that focuses entirely on one's self. This style of coaching aims to evaluate and assess your current strengths and weaknesses in order to improve certain aspects of your life. After their conversation, she was left aghast to see such improvement and how much happier Karen was. She was also impressed by the amount of advice and coaching that Karen was receiving.

A few days later, my friend pondered over the wonderful life Karen was living. She decided to scope out a life-coaching program for herself that would fit her lifestyle. With extensive research and adjustment, she was able to find a personal life coach that changed the way she viewed life and relationships. After she experienced drastic changes in her life due to her own personal coach, she was inspired to help others that had found themselves on the same path she had once been on. She became a certified personal development coach and began coaching clients to help them reach their goals and live a life that they love and desire. She quit her job and started living a life she loved. She was helping others to find fulfillment, which in turn was bringing fulfillment and happiness to her in the process. She wrote her first book in 2017, *REVEALING WHO YOU ARE, Seven Chapters of Happiness*. The book was first launched in Toronto, Canada on August 19, 2017, then launched in the U.S.A. on October 21, 2017. On November 9, 2017 she had her very first live television interview on *The Nikki Clarke Show*.

At this point, you're probably wondering, "How does she know this story so well?" The truth is, it is about me, Kwesha Denice Neal. I wanted to share my own story so that you would know I've been where you are. I understand the unhappiness, doubts and emptiness you may be feeling. Now, I want to offer you my own self-tested blue print for opening the door to a better life!

My best advice to my clients and friends is that you need to follow two things in your life: your heart and your subconscious mind. Those two will never cease to amaze you, and they won't ever fail you. Remember, all things are possible when you change your mindset of the world and the environment around you. Take advantage of your life. Stop waiting to grasp the abundance of happiness that you truly deserve. In this chapter, I will provide you with the strategies that you need to walk down the road of success. These strategies will help you escape the world of sameness that exists within all communities.

IT BEGINS WITH YOU

The first lesson is: Everything begins with YOU. You are the only person who has complete knowledge of your lifestyle, what goes on inside of your brain 24 hours a day, 7 days a week, and your personal development and growth. To clarify, personal development and growth is the ongoing process of understanding and developing oneself. This is a vital part in a person's growth, success, and happiness. It is the foundation of emotional, physical, intellectual, and spiritual health. By far the most challenging part is adopting a personal growth mindset. "Why?" you may ask? Because you must program your brain, and you must tell it what it's supposed to do.

Let's talk a little about our wonderful brain. The human brain weighs only three pounds, but we only use 10% of our brain. When we are awake, our brain produces enough electricity to power a small light bulb. The brain has more cell types than any other tissue in our body. The power of the right side of the brain is all visual, it sees pictures and uses imagination. For example, before you purchase something, such as a house or car, the right side of the brain creates the image you see of you with those things, like decorating a new home or driving that car. The left side of our brain is more logical. It understands reason. To continue our example, it helps us determine if those purchases are rational. Can we afford that home? Does that car have a good warranty, etc.? Our brain stores our wonder powers.

THE BEAUTY OF THE CONSCIOUS MIND

Now, let's discuss your conscious mind. Consciousness is a state of awareness; your conscious mind is aware of your surroundings ten seconds before you even realize it. The beauty of the conscious mind is that it knows each and every one of your purposes. This is where the thought process of your life begins. Your conscious mind is continually processing what is going on in the environment around you. Conscious minds function like computers. They accept and receive data, and put out information. The conscious mind communicates effectively with the outside world and the inner self through speech, pictures, writing, physical movement, and thinking.

Take a seat, close your eyes, and make a fist. Now, open your eyes, and slowly release your fist. The moment you open your eyes, your mind instantaneously becomes conscious and aware of what is happening. Why is the conscious mind so great? Because everybody's is different. Everyone's thought process is different than the person sitting left, right, in front of, or behind you, but their function is the same. We live in an era where the conscious mind is frequently changing based on society and the environment someone is living in.

YOUR PRECIOUS GEM

What if you were told that you won a contest and the prize was from the world's largest luxury jewelry brand, Tiffany's? There is no doubt that you would be excited. Your prize consists of the finest diamonds, gold, and rubies that exist on earth today. Did you know that you were born with an even greater asset? That asset is your subconscious mind. This is where your personal treasures are hidden. The conscious mind is connected to your subconscious mind. Inside of your subconscious mind is a memory bank with an unlimited supply of learning abilities.

The subconscious has all the answers you are looking for; you just need to ask it the right questions. Here are some questions that will help guide your life in the correct path:

1. Who am I?

2. What is my purpose in life?

3. What makes my life complete?

4. How can I achieve my goals?

YOU MUST CLAIM YOUR AUTHORITY

This is your power and your right. Your authority is where your core values are stored within you. If you ever lost your authority, or never used it, now is your time to take control of it and enforce those values in your life. Authority gives you opportunity, guides you, and empowers you. It is a feeling of trust, understanding, and giving opportunity to share your greatness with others and to share other's greatness. Authority is your power to show people what you are made of and let them know your importance. For example, your authority is like the 206 bones in the human body; it helps you stand up for what you believe in. Your authority also has the ability to stretch as you acquire new knowledge, like the skin that covers your entire body. Lastly, your authority is like your grip on life, it helps you hold on tight to your goals. Authority is what you and I were born equipped with.

What is required to have authority? You must have great work ethic to focus on the problem, and you must take action and be creative, outstanding, and a great leader and decision maker. Authority allows you to take one for the team when nothing is going according to plan. There will be many occurrences throughout your lifetime when your authority will be tested. When these times come up, don't let them overwhelm you. Remember that you can handle anything that life throws your way.

Just because we all have some type of authority, does not mean that it comes from a specific job title. You have to work to gain authority. It is not just handed to you when you ask for it. Authority brings great assets in leadership. True authority is like winning the Noble Peace Prize; only 127 people have ever won this high, official prize.

I hope you took some knowledge from this chapter to help you find yourself and the amazing qualities hidden deep within you. Don't be afraid to let them shine. I hope you take these tools and they help you forge a life filled with happiness, abundance and fulfillment. Once I learned to use these gifts that I possessed, I was able to find my passion in life and use them to help others. I hope you, too, can be added to the list of people I have helped over the years, who have reclaimed their lives and found the joy that's been waiting for them.

ABOUT KWESHA

Kwesha Denice Neal is a Personal Development Coach and speaker. She helps her clients to have a clear vision of themselves, to take the lid off their lives and live a life of happiness – a life they truly deserve – to pursue the things in life they want to do and manifest their greatness, and to go into their soul and find their core of joy.

She coaches them to become fearless and to truly reveal who they are? She builds a rapport with her clients, helping them to come out of their comfort zone, to give the word "NO" a new meaning, to turn their lives on and let their dreams be real to them. And she lets them know they can and they deserve it.

She teaches:

1. Shifting the mindset.

2. Why take action in your life.

3. Bet on yourself.

Kwesha has been coached by John Maxwell and she thanks others for coaching her and mentoring her. She is the Award-Winning author of the book, *REVEALING WHO YOU ARE – 7 Chapters of Complete Happiness*.

Kwesha Neal is the Founder of: Woman On The Rise in New Jersey

Contact information:

Revealingwhoyouare.com

Womanontherise.com

Kweshaneal@yahoo.com

HOORAY FOR EPIC FAILS

Dollhouses, Long–Jumping and GMAT Scores

PERFORMANCE 360: You've lived in eight countries, traveled and worked in 65, and had an adventurous 30-year global career in technology, business, and economic development – yet young people are your greatest inspiration?

ROSIE: Absolutely. They keep me guessing, imagining, and creating. They call me out on "my stuff" and never let me forget a promise (a.k.a. bribe!). In all sincerity, I'm dedicated to ensuring that they – and, perhaps, the adults in their lives (their influencers) – see that our best performances are often born from hurtful feedback, missing the mark, and humiliating moments.

PERFORMANCE 360: Intriguing! We'd like to interview you in a playfully different way than usual. Could you share three examples of failures when you were young that led to success in adulthood?

ROSIE: Absolutely, this will be fun! Going back to my first epic fail…

I'm 9-years-old (4th grade) and our immigrant family is new in the neighborhood. I can only watch selected TV shows and only on weekends. So, I'm excited to watch a special program on the Labor Day holiday – the Jerry Lewis MDA (Muscular Dystrophy) Telethon.

I watch famous people answering telephones and a big number on-screen going up really fast! Despite the excitement, I'm really sad watching all the stories of kids whose muscles aren't working well. Most can't play outside. But Jerry says I can help by donating. Thing is, he isn't specific.

Given that I can't use the phone and don't have whatever it is that people are "donating," I know I can give something else. I'll make a dollhouse – using boxes, buttons, popsicle sticks, cotton balls, clothing scraps, whatever. I'll mail it to the kids, of course.

When I finish, it's gorgeous! Until people point at it and start laughing. I'm gutted. They think it's ugly. I ask that my dollhouse be mailed to Jerry but, honestly, I don't know what's happened to it. All I know is that I'm not the artist I thought I was.

PERFORMANCE 360: Please tell us there's an upside?!

ROSIE: You bet there is! My ego is bruised, but I'm determined to make $$$ because I discover *that's* what everyone is giving. It's called a donation. Go figure.

How will I do that? I'll run a carnival-of-games in our back yard! Maybe I'll even earn "street cred" in the 'hood. Whatever it takes to make new friends, right? We kids love playing kickball in the street, catching frogs, building frog castles in sandboxes, and collecting fireflies. So, an outdoor carnival will be the ultimate fun-fest!

I pick the Saturday, ask friends to help, get "stuff," make tickets, and tell everyone. I ask our parents to donate prizes plus food and drinks for sale. I make decorations and sketch backyard blueprints.

I find everything for the games: ring toss, croquet, putt-putt golf, fishing-in-a-kiddie-pool, cards, find-the-ball-in-the-cup, hopscotch, etc. Prizes will be tons of coins, $1 and $5 bills (wow!), gum, candy, and gift vouchers like "don't have to make your bed all weekend," "watch TV on a school night," and "pizza and ice cream Monday."

On carnival day, I greet guests, handle registration (money!), lead games, give prizes, and clean up. Post-event, I count everything in the bucket. We've banked about $30! *That* we can donate – whoop!

PERFORMANCE 360: Whoop-whoop, indeed! Looking back at your 9-year-old self, do you realize anything now, as a business woman, that you didn't know then?

ROSIE: I've never thought about it through that lens. I guess I was "in business" even though at that age I didn't even know what that meant!

- Vision: A world where people didn't hurt.
- Mission: Help kids who needed help.
- Strategy: Help *Jerry's* kids.
- Objective: Run a backyard carnival to make money.
- Product Development: Offered games, food and drinks.
- Marketing: Promoted by word-of-mouth (the only way to do it back then).
- Sales: Pre-sold door-to-door and on event day.
- Customer Experience: Made it fun.
- Operations: Acquired and managed resources, designed blueprints, set up and dismantled infrastructure, and cleaned up.
- Human Resources: Recruited volunteers.
- Project Management: Did everything A-Z.
- Venture Capital: Fundraised and secured gifts-in-kind.
- Accounting/Finance: Oversaw pre-, during- and post-event.
- Corporate Social Responsibility: As a group of neighborhood kids, donated our $$$ to help Jerry's kids.

PERFORMANCE 360: That's wild! Rolling with the theme: When did you first parlay that carnival prowess into professional success?

ROSIE: I was 23 and in my first job after university. I horrified my fellow Finance graduates when I declined a banking offer and the opportunity to go to Wall Street. Instead, I joined the Peace Corps as a Volunteer in the Small Enterprise Development Program in the Dominican Republic. I swapped Masters of the Universe big bucks for no salary – and lived in an isolated mountain village hut, without electricity, running water, food store, or communications. Nirvana!

In the village, a group of illiterate, abjectly poor women showed me a crude, 3-inch-wide blob of loosely-woven fiber. They asked me, "Can we sell it?" Wanting to be culturally-sensitive, trying hard not to laugh, I asked, "What is it?" One woman replied, "We don't know, but can we sell it?!" I didn't have the heart to tell them it was a pipe-dream.

The blob was made from sisal – a cactus-looking plant. They wanted to use its stiff, prickly fiber to make sellable things to generate income for their families and community. Until then, the only cash inflow came from the men using the crude fiber to make sacks for storing tobacco leaves.

The 83-year-old village matriarch implored: "Look where we live, Rosie! The soil is useless; we can't grow anything. We have nothing, and we're too isolated for the government to care. We need to help ourselves, but we have no education, no skills, no money – nothing but this nearly useless plant. Can you teach us?!" They saw me as some sort of genie who would turn water into wine, so to speak. How could I say no? If these loving, hard-working villagers wanted my help, I would! How? Didn't have a clue!

We had challenges galore. My CV consisted of pizza, burgers and video arcade jobs – meaning no "real" business experience. I also had no weaving, dyeing, design, or artistic skills. Zilch! The women had no education, business skills, or money. They also had no self-confidence to start their own microenterprise, suffered from a crippling fear of S-E-L-L-I-N-G, and were scared to travel beyond their mountains. (Note: I've told every CEO with whom I've worked that he/she could never create a more challenging role than the one I had in that village.)

Forging ahead together, I unknowingly "ripped" a page out of my Carnival Playbook:

- Vision: A peaceful, economically equitable world.

- Mission: Help others help themselves (Peace Corps maxim).

- Strategy: Help *my villagers* help themselves.

- Objective: Teach women how to make something beautiful out of virtually nothing, manage their own micro-enterprise, and generate income.

- Product Development: Designed and created hand-made artisan goods from (free, ubiquitous) sisal fiber.

- Marketing: Word-of-mouth (the only way available).

- Sales: Four women volunteered to travel for the *first* time in their lives to *cold-sell* – walking the streets of a coastal city on their island[1], hauling prototypes in dilapidated boxes, and knocking on shop doors, telling their story.

- Customer Experience: Treated clients with respect, gratitude, and exceptional service.

- Operations: Organized and scheduled themselves into teams to: (1) acquire raw materials (sisal, leaves, roots, bark) and tools (machetes, sewing needles, pots, firewood); (2) strip, wash, dye, and distribute fiber; and (3) travel, sell, and deliver products.

- Human Resources: Each person taught, led, and inspired others.

- Project Management: Each person learned and supported everything A-Z.

- Venture Capital: Submitted successful grant proposals for funding, supplies, and design consultants from NGOs.

- Accounting/Finance: Team-elected treasurer managed the books.

- Corporate Social Responsibility: As a village, helped our village.

The women discovered not only how talented they were but also how inspirational they were for their children, husbands, and community. Their successes made them my heroes:

1. A breathtaking portfolio of hand-made baskets, coasters, bags, etc.

2. On the *first* day of cold-selling, landing their first gross order from the most respected, high-end, indigenous art and jewelry boutique.

3. Top-selling group at the National Artisan Fair in the capital city, Santo Domingo.

4. For the women themselves: New design and business skills, booming self-confidence, and even *more* respect and admiration for their courage from their own villagers and those from neighboring communities..

5. For the village: Community-generated income and artisan pride: making something beautiful and valuable out of virtually nothing!

PERFORMANCE 360: What a memorable once-in-a-lifetime experience! Do you have another childhood-to-adulthood success story?

ROSIE: Here's one for sports lovers.

I'm 12-years-old (middle school) at the district track & field championships. I'm in five events, but my favorite is the long-jump – perfect for a sprinter with natural vertical leap.

I'm in the finals with 12 girls, but I'm the shortest (4.5ft/1.37m). I'm also the last to jump, after the tallest girl (5ft/1.52m) – who is also the record-holder and most favored to win. Her first two jumps smash my lifetime bests. On my first jump, I scratch/foul. On my second, my hands drag the sand behind my body – securing my place at the bottom of the rankings.

On her final jump, Tallest Girl nails 15ft (4.57m) – the farthest jump of the day, breaking her own record. Her coach, team, and spectators

---

1. They had never been in a big city or seen the ocean before!

go crazy. The judges are stunned, and I'm in awe. And fear. Fear that I'll scratch again. Hand drag again. End with the worst performance of my career (remember, I'm 12!). It doesn't help that many teams are leaving, and others are giggling and pointing at the last, shortest, most underwhelming long-jumper.

I just want to leave. Those girls are mean, and they're mocking me. Spectators are leaving too, as if the event's over. I want to cry, but at the same time, something deep inside me stirs big time. I *know* I can jump. Far. "Please stop laughing at me," I whisper as I breathe and commit to my final jump.

I eye the sandpit and sky... and start running. Fast. Plant foot. Bicycle-kick upward. Stretch. Legs. Arms. Fly. Yes! Land. Propel forward!

Ah, the blur. The shrieks. The smiles. The hugs. I cry (the good kind). I did it! I've jumped farther than I've ever done before – 15ft 2in (4.62m) – and win first place! Gold medal in my heart.

PERFORMANCE 360: Way to go, Rocky... er, Rosie! How did that self-belief moment translate as you grew up?

ROSIE: I go for it. Run my race. Jump my jump. Silence the mean girls! Because I know and feel what's truly me. I trust my heart and gut instinct to do what I want, no matter how ridiculous I may look to others.

At 23, I declined banking, Wall Street, and big bucks. Outcome? You already know!

At 30, with a Wharton MBA in Finance, I took the path less travelled. I chose *industry* (telecommunications, mobile, and digital) – *not* investment banking or management consulting. That was 1995. If you remember, that was the beginning of massive waves of growth and innovation in those Cinderella sectors. I surfed them from the get-go!

Working in a huge corporation, I was advised to play golf, align with specific executives, and remain at U.S. headquarters. Apparently, I'd rub C-level elbows and advance faster. Instead, over the next five years, I sought out and landed opportunities to live around the world, launching multinational joint venture (JVs) and emerging technologies. Rather than do what tens of thousands of other employees did, I just did what jazzed me. I think I'm the only employee that got to do what I did, and I'm grateful.

I also declined offers from two of the most revered and adored tech companies on Earth. I'm glad I did that for two reasons: I freed up those positions for two lucky people to do what *they're* passionate about and gave myself the freedom to do the same.

PERFORMANCE 360: Always great to hear about outsiders making their mark. One more story?

ROSIE: This one is for school children, teenagers, young professionals, or even Ivy League (U.S.) / Russell Group (U.K.) hopefuls who think that if they "fail" standardized exams, they're losers.

Here's my headline to you: I spectacularly "failed" the GMAT (for MBA applications) three times! But I'm still kickin', so you can, too!

Backstory: I'm 28, with five years of work experience in international economic development. But, I've got bigger dreams, so I want to get two master's degrees: MBA (Business Administration) and MIA (International Affairs). Shooting for the stars, I apply to the top three Ivy League MBA+MIA joint degree programs plus others.

FYI: GMAT scoring is 200-800; two-thirds of test-takers score 400-600 (mba.com). My wish-list schools reject 95% of applications. I research GMAT scores for matriculants, so I know I need 700+.

I pay mega-bucks for a prep course. Why? At 17, I crashed and burned three times on my SATs (for college applications). On day 1 of the prep course, we start "cold" by taking a mock exam as a benchmark. Every week, we learn strategy and take exams. I get mega-confident as my scores significantly rise. (Note: They guarantee refunds for those who don't score higher on the real exam than on the benchmark.)

Drumroll, please. Yes, you guessed it - on the real exam day, I implode! Not only is my score not 700+, it's *lower* than my benchmark! I take the GMAT three times and produce a 3-peat failure, mimicking my SAT debacle. I'm too humiliated to share my scores or ask for a refund. For my MIA applications, I know I also need uberly-high GRE scores, but I take the completely opposite approach: *no* prep course, no money, no studying, no stress. Drumroll again. Yes, you know it – I score-to-the-moon on my one and only exam!

Knowing my GMATs stink (and the "F" in Accounting on my university transcript won't help either), I crank on all other application requirements (especially the essays). I not only get into my #1 MBA+MIA joint program, but also receive scholarships, grants, and loans for my Wharton MBA and a generous MIA fellowship from the School of Advanced International Studies (SAIS) at Johns Hopkins University!

Since then, I've had a phenomenal career, fulfilling a childhood dream of living, traveling, and working around the globe. I'm now in Act 3 (the best part yet) – passionately doing and fully living *My Why!*

PERFORMANCE 360: Another great story, indeed. What lessons learned have served you since?

ROSIE: There's a fine balance between "going for it" (with everything you've got) and letting go, relaxing, and trusting that the outcome will come at a time and in a way just right for you – often surprising you in a way you least expect!

There's no perfect score, grade or ranking that guarantees success. Deal-breakers are rarely that – if someone is creative and inspired enough to explore possibilities and make them happen.

When I served as an alumna interviewer for Wharton MBA applicants, I was often asked about "required" GMAT scores. I'd tell my story (not disclosing that I was the protagonist) and end it, saying: "With three GMAT scores in the gutter, the young woman submitted her application anyway." Dumbfounded, they would always ask: "Did she get in?" I always replied: "Yes, and she's interviewing you today!" Priceless.

PERFORMANCE 360: Thanks for the inspiring stories for young people (and adults, too!). Any last nuggets of wisdom?

ROSIE: You bet!

Did that unwanted feedback sting?

- Go to Plan B: Be bold.
- Commence Plan C: Create your own carnival-of-fun-and-impact!

Did you miss the mark?

- Well, the second, third, fourth… gazillion-th… time is the charm! So, hang in there!

Have you suffered the most humiliating moments?

- So what? Strike a pose with those badges of honor. Your own stories will inspire others!

HIP, HIP, HOORAY FOR EPIC* FAILS!

(*) "Epic" is in the eye of the beholder.

ABOUT ROSIE

Rosie Unite is the Founder and CEO of ImaginateLife™, a for-profit global social impact venture (www.imaginatelife.com).

She is passionate about the power at the nexus of neuroscience, epigenetics, quantum physics, and spirituality to heal bodies, elevate minds, and transform lives. Known as *The Possibilities Whisperer*™, Rosie shares her extraordinary experience to help others stretch beyond their perceived selves and connect with life's abundance.

ImaginateLife™ offers the knowledge, skills, and awareness that inspires and empowers others to discover their innate power, live fully, and seed a greater consciousness. Services include keynote speeches, workshops, special events, and advisory services.

Rosie is deeply grateful for the visionaries on her amazing journey.

Dr. Joe Dispenza is a renowned neuroscientist, educator, and *NY Times* best-selling author. To-date, Rosie has completed nine of his workshops globally — the majority Advanced and Advanced-Follow-Ups.

She is honored to have participated in his extensive research on meditation effects on brain and body. She's been QEEG (quantitative electroencephalography) brain mapped by U.S. and German neuroscientists, heart coherence measured by HeartMath Institute, individual energy field tested by GDV technology, and group-measured for energy in workshop environments by GDV Sputnik sensors.

She continues to support breakthroughs in *neuroplasticity* — the brain's ability to change via new neural connections — and *epigenetics* — the study of heritable changes in gene expression not involving changes to underlying DNA.

Rosie greatly appreciates the inimitable Larry King. She was not only co-author of his book *The Big Question* but also one of the Executive Producers of the groundbreaking film *The Voice of a Generation: An Evening with Larry King*. Captivated by people's lives, Rosie watched the legendary *Larry King Live* on CNN for years. She found his unique, humorous way of engaging with guests across the spectrum always edifying and entertaining.

Rosie also co-authored the book *Success Breakthroughs* with the innovative and generous Jack Canfield. She has also worked directly with Jack as a Certified Trainer in *The Success Principles*™ (one of his numerous *NY Times* best-selling books) and *Canfield Methodology*™. She is grateful for his legacy and forever inspired by his endearing guidance to share her story with the world.

Previously, in her 30-year global career, Rosie was a leader and executive in the *Fortune 500* corporate, start-up, and social impact sectors. A Wharton MBA, she helped launch and grow new companies and emerging mobile, telecommunications, and digital technologies. She began building businesses in the Peace Corps — helping community-based microenterprises.

Rosie has worked with well-known organizations including: Sprint, GTE (Verizon), DoubleClick (Google), Johnson & Johnson, France Telecom, Deutsche Telekom, Intelig Brazil (TIM Italy), World Bank, Inter-American Development Bank, Women's World Banking, Foreign Affairs, Academy for Educational Development, and Habitat for Humanity.

A globe-trotting, life-long student, Rosie is a Sivananda Hatha Yoga Certified Instructor and has completed Vipassana 10-Day Meditation and Levels 1-2-3 of EFT Universe's Certification Program (i.e. Tapping). Fulfilling a childhood dream, she has traveled in 65 countries and lived in eight: USA, Brazil, Netherlands, Hong Kong, Spain, Bulgaria, Dominican Republic, and the UK.

BY TERRY RASNER-YACENDA

OPENING THE PERFORMANCE DOOR TO BECOMING A CONSISTENT PERFORMER

Introduced as the Keynote Speaker, I thanked my host, wandered across the stage in my typical peripatetic speaking style, adjusting my lapel microphone on the way. I stopped, planted my heels, looked at the audience, and began:

"I am woman, hear me roar (!) because I am too big to ignore; – plus I'm strong, sure and successful, with just a bit of sass. Oh yes, share with me the simple pleasures in life!"

. . .THUD!

It was not that I had nothing to say, but no one beyond the first few rows could hear my voice; the microphone that had been sound tested minutes earlier was stone dead. Fortunately, it was nothing more than a mechanical battery pack issue that was quickly resolved.

I had rehearsed these opening lines many times before because they were the condensed version of WHO I BECAME as a woman who OVERCAME six life-changing episodes of adversity (a seventh is yet ongoing):

- **a young mother**, who held my eight-month old baby son (Brandon) as he died in my arms.

- **a young mother**, who was counseled by doctors and geneticists and told point-blank the recessive Werdnig Hoffmann gene I carried, that causes the most severe form of muscular dystrophy disease which killed my son Brandon, was a death threat to any future children I *might conceive.*

- **a mother to daughter**, **Sarah**, who was conceived several months after Brandon's death, following the Christmas Season when that small still inner voice from God confirmed a child would be birthed – Sarah was born healthy one day before my birthday.

- **an adult daughter**, who cared for her disabled mother for ten years, together holding each other's hands, as I watched her track and talk to Angels, as she was near death.

- **a business associate of a firm for whom I worked under contract**, and who might have sold its soul to the Devil if there was a penny to be made; didn't keep them from stealing hundreds of my proprietary clients.

- **a mother to daughter**, **Sarah**, who is a business partner, best friend and mother of our grandchild, Howard Edward IV (Howie), given the option to terminate the pregnancy, she chose instead to endure a high-risk and stressful 36-week pregnancy, her baby born prematurely with gastroschisis (i.e., his small intestines outside of the body), who, after his original four weeks in the Neo-natal Intensive Care Unit and months of follow-up procedures, has become our joy, knowing today he is an intelligent and healthy boy; and

- **the spouse of my husband**, **Dr. John**, who has had several near death cerebral strokes along with an aggravated blood clotting disorder, and a recent heart-valve replacement a year after Baby Howie's birth.

Adversity is your springboard to BECOMING YOU! Pick yourself up and start moving!

WALKING THROUGH THE PERFORMANCE DOOR

Let me make this very clear, there are two "states of understanding" you must achieve, sequentially, one after the other, to Become a Consistent Performer after you have "Opened and Walked Through" the **PERFORMANCE DOOR**.

First: you must understand who you have become as a woman or man. I gave you a glimpse of six episodes of adversity I had overcome with a seventh that is an ongoing battle, because more than anything these experiences have tapped into whatever is at my core to shape who I am today. The way I – and you, can tap into this understanding is to use, as I did, something referred to as identifying the "vocabulary of experiences" related to the life episodes you identify. It is your point of reference or your overcoming compass for you to look back and gauge those experiences that gave you strength that will get through the next adversity and trust me it will come. Adversity comes when we least expect it.

Basically, you need to create your own list of episodes of overcoming adversity or of achievement, and then assign different behavioral and emotional experiences to each. But importantly, don't lace your experiences with psychobabble; just sort out the bad from the good – what worked and what didn't, have enough faith and trust in that inner voice – then just go do it!

Second: you must understand how Serendipity, Wisdom Bites and Life-Living Strategies work together to ORGANIZE your approach to Consistent Performance.

Very simply, Serendipity represents an unplanned fortuitous discovery you can readily view as one of the cornerstones of your performance consistency. Why? Foremost, because of its eternal flexibility and adaptability, and more pointedly in how you can, for example, appreciate its value in helping you identify the abrupt appearance of "wisdom bites" (i.e., concepts and ideas you dream-up, stumble upon, or intentionally create to motivate you to behave a certain way to achieve self-defined goals).

I'll write it once, and it'll always be the same: "Wisdom bites" are *entirely subjective*—that is, your "Wisdom bites" create opportunities for the development of *entirely subjective life-living strategies* to achieve general and/or more immediately specific outcomes for your life, be these personal, social, familial, relationship or business goals. Some people think of life-living strategies as "attitude shapers" to help them reinforce the good habits or behaviors they want to espouse, while other people see life-living strategies as opportunities to make very bold statements or affirmations of their personal values or professional priorities. As a Consistent Performer you'll have many opportunities to explore every life-living strategy option.

To reinforce the connection between "wisdom bites" and life-living strategies, I've shared four "wisdom bites" and corresponding life-living strategies (LLS1-4) that were titled and defined by a Visioning Group of 7 (i.e., their collective subjectivity) after the group was given the following *Statement* to study for 30 minutes: *"Most of us today are the product of patchwork families, friends, co-workers and communities that reflect and often embrace the many differences and qualities we've gleaned from a spectrum of life experiences."*

1. Title: <u>Be Color-Blind</u>: accept others' apparent outward differences and expressed beliefs. The Visioning Group's companion Life-living Strategy LLS1: "You're free to disagree with others, even find faults in their beliefs, style of dress, language and peculiarities, etc., BUT YOU MUST remain committed to tolerance and acceptance."

2. Title: <u>Embrace Cultural Differences</u>: there's lots of unused space and circuitry in our brains. LLS2: "Choose the information that you believe will be most useful in multiple personal and professional settings."

3. Title: <u>Spread the Love of Understanding</u>: the true power in this "wisdom bite" is in the "marketing" of goodwill and truth. LLS3 "Marketing goodwill and truth builds incalculable wealth."

4. Title: <u>Be Courageous</u>: yes, not as a Gladiator, but in thought, deed, and in expressing yourself. You may be called on to lead, as others may see you as a natural leader and may want to follow you, but LL S-4: "Your most potent influence in people's lives may well be in your patience, and in how well you handle your reaction to matters that trouble your conscience – because others will be watching you!

The Visioning Group was challenged to freely exchange their own subjective reactions to the *Statement*. If you're like me you're saying, "I didn't see anything about "Love of Understanding" in the *Statement*, and most certainly there was no mention of "Courageous Leadership" anywhere. And you're correct!

Precisely why this was so profound a process, because "collective subjectivity" can only work when the people involved are *consistent performers* who allow free thought and serendipity to enter the scenario. As we watched the Visioning Group function, we saw them scramble the ingredients in the *Statement* and then create a new menu. Their achievement was nothing short of profound; they got it!

Now, use their example of scrambling up some of your challenges and see what kind of "wisdom bites" you can create on your own, and with a sense of confidence, integrity, hopefulness, and strength, identify life-living strategies to overcome each and every obstacle you encounter to out-think it, out-wit-it, or in effect destroy it! As a consistent performer, expect success, while gaining mastery over nagging life challenges.

GETTING PERSONAL

Okay, that's it for the "attitude & perspective" coaching; not that I haven't been at all transparent, but there are a couple of matters that are essential to who I am as a professional and a woman.

Basic to me are two Rules:

1) Be genuine

2) Be transparent

Sometimes it's a bit diplomatic, and it's an either/or, but it's always one or the other, and this applies to all levels of the obvious and not-so-obvious. A good example of the not-so-obvious is our commitment to "Paying it Forward." It is a core principle of our business culture. Very simply, it's much like the biblical tithe: 10% of our net business income is automatically donated to Dreams Foundation, Inc., a separate non-profit 501(c)(3) Corporation that uses 99% of the donations it receives to directly fund the full range of charitable services it provides to children, families, persons with special needs, seniors, veterans, animals and health care facilities providing specialized services.

<u>Stewardship</u> implies ownership driven by some set of principled or ethical standards (and certainly legal standards). Our company's Stewardship practice of "Paying it Forward" funding has yielded several hundreds of thousands of dollars of charitable giving!

We have been both a known and unknown contributor/sponsor of many success stories, yet recognizing successful performance is the public story, while our internal story is remaining consistent performers!

Much of my professional career I've talked about birthing Million Dollar Ideas…yes, really! It's not usually the "light bulb" clicks on and there's the idea, but it's more of a transformational process. I can't in all honesty write a performance piece and not discuss this topic. Think about it. Transformation implies change; transformational suggests the change is dynamic and moving; transformational thinking suggests the birth of your million dollar idea is indeed afforded time because of its dynamic and moving nature – the latter two concepts are open to your unique interpretation and explanation!

Consistent performance commands that the same kind of dynamic nature of your physical, social, and behavioral actions remain committed to your performance goals and aspirations, whatever they are, and all those activities necessary to achieve them. With this performance mindset, it is normal to expect to anticipate advanced training opportunities, courses, travel, mentors, and the like. You get it…budget accordingly. It'll be fun!

The question is not "Can you put these concepts to work for you; but, how soon can you do so?" In closing, let me leave you with this one overriding theme: we all have talents, skills, abilities, and million-dollar ideas tucked away in us. We view these as learned, acquired, inherited or

God-given. Yes, I favor the latter God-given, but would never discount the others. We're all in this together!

Although I find there are times where it seems easiest to accept the premise that the real need to our confusion is to replace doubt with faith, and to live with our eyes open to see where each of us is going in life – where we are called by our innate abilities and faith to be, I know that's not realistic. But, I think I have another way of putting it all in perspective, and let's try saying this another way! How about we all agree to get rid of the junk in our trunks and be who God created us to be; no more wearing masks, no more pretending, no more lies, just genuine and transparent. Just be who God created you to be! There is just one of you in the whole universe. Not another like You…. A genuine piece of God's art.

I'm sure each of us could contribute something to the junk pile…

ABOUT TERRY

Terry Rasner-Yacenda is no ordinary person, as against all odds she's remained a personally responsible, professionally-capable woman who has, and continues to, achieve successful performance competition to keep her on top of her game, while creating a platform for her to help so many other women find achievement in their professional lives!

Every successful businesswoman has points of anchorage: "stuff" upon which she is built, or from which she launched her career. Terry has earned a pair of college degrees, the second she earned being a Bachelor of Arts in Liberal Arts from the University of Nevada. Three reasons it was important to her: 1) a single mother of a young child, the degree would be their safety net; 2) the Liberal Arts course exposure would broaden her exposure to other professionals while learning; and 3) the degree gave her "academic tires" – that is, no one could ever take away her terminal degree!

Terry's "stuff" helped to shape her professional performance year after year, leading to an impressive list of national awards for leadership from the National Association of Women in Real Estate Businesses, and in her home State of Nevada, being named Nevada's *Most Distinguished Woman in Real Estate.*

What Terry learned well, and you may well want to yourself, is that every highly visible and every smart Professional surrounds herself with half-wild, half-tame courageous risk takers who value personal and professional ethics more than a paycheck. She found and developed teams throughout her career in Human Services where she worked on developing enrollment models for Nevada's Children's State Health Insurance Program, to her Real Estate Teams who received an *Excellence in Achievement Award* from the Wall Street Journal as Nevada's #4 and Reno's #1 and # 20, Real Estate Team for Sales and Sides and Volume. Not enough? She was named among the top five percent in her field for American Registry's prestigious, *"America's Most Honored Professionals" Award.*

Not to out-do herself, Terry is the author of the book, *She Is All Business,* and through seminars and one-on-one coaching, she mentors women professionals and women desiring to make their mark in the business world. She is the CEO of Capital City Investments, Inc. and She Is All Business, which has its own website that provides a number of training materials and self-paced self-discovery tools at no cost to readers. As well, she founded the Reno/Tahoe Realty Group, LLC (RTRG), and was one of three co-founders of Dreams Foundation, Inc., and WE BUY ALL MOBILE HOMES.

So, when Terry waxes and wanes on Performance, Business, Personal Growth and Taking Risks, you can know she's for real!

BY MICHAEL CHENG

HOW TO WIN IN LIFE

Bouncing Back From Failure When Hard Work Just Ain't Enough!

After plenty of dark, depressing years, I now live an amazing life. I'm 36 years young, and my real estate development company is preparing to break ground on over $500M worth of projects. I feel closer to God than ever before. I got married days ago and my first newborn is on the way. I have all the time, energy, and money I need for my family, friends, and business, while traveling between Shanghai and New York and expanding globally. I live an amazing life because I learned that the key to having it all begins with "priming" our brains every day -- a morning ritual which has the power to permanently alter our thought patterns, mental energy, and by extension, our realities.

Before I learned how to prime myself, I fell into the deep hole of drifting through a negatively-charged life. During my teens and 20's, a few years of my life were at best filled with ups and downs, while the majority were spackled with depression, lack of faith, absence of hope, and the 3 F's:

- fear I wasn't enough
- fear of what others thought about me
- fear of failure

Yes, I had big plans and ambitions, but I felt I was often being shortchanged and I had an extremely unbalanced life. I was always chasing success but never quite happy with myself, and always frustrated that I never got the results I wanted. I was a ticking emotional timebomb, frequently running out of mental or physical energy, and unable to maintain a happy relationship with my family or keep a significant long-term romantic relationship.

In 2013, I was in my seventh year of building a startup, an online language school, my passion project at the time. I had invested every last penny of my savings and was averaging 80-100-hour work-weeks. The company was not reaching sales targets, I was in poor physical health, and over $150K in credit card debt. I decided to shut the doors in 2013 before my anxiety and depression took away what was left of me. I hated myself, I felt like a loser, nothing was possible, and that I was destined to be a failure. The next two years were an extremely difficult uphill battle to get back my edge, to believe in myself and feel like I could be a success again. I thought I would never dare to have goals or dream again. I struggled because I lacked the tools or skills I needed to bounce back quickly and get back on my feet.

Winston Churchill said, "Success is the ability to move from one failure to another without loss of enthusiasm." Consider yourself lucky if you were one of the few who succeeded in hitting that hole-in-one. When I was in school, I never failed at anything because all I had to do was study the material my teachers gave me, and I had a blueprint for success. When I was building my startup, I thought I had a blueprint for success since

Don't play small in the shadows, in the fear of judgment, because regret is more painful than failure.

I had gone to many motivational seminars and studied sales, marketing and management. But listening to the hype or studying business tactics is not the same as a blueprint for success in life.

So what makes a blueprint for success? A great blueprint for success will always keep you fully confident and engaged whether you're on pace to reaching your goals or when you don't have immediate results. It will keep you energized and focused whether people are cheering you on or telling you it's not going to work. It will allow you to begin every day with joy, gratitude, and excitement, rather than with fear, anxiety, or boredom, give you power for living and purpose for growing whether you're on track or behind schedule. Whether you're hitting all your milestones or experiencing tremendous setbacks and unexpected losses, the right blueprint for success will keep you calm, cool, and collected. It will reprogram you to realize that success is in the journey, not the destination.

Between 2013 and 2015, I worked with several life coaches and delved even deeper into self-help and personal development. I synergized all the best methods for success and they helped me formulate this blueprint for success.

In 2015, following this blueprint, I was able to take a huge leap out of my seemingly bottomless hole, and to compound time so that within three months, I became a completely different person from the inside-out. Here are my seven proven principles for success:

1. Get your endorphins flowing.

It's so easy to overlook how vital bloodflow and sweating are for mental cleansing. Most of us are lazy to some degree, but a good workout makes it easier to stay calm during the storm. I like to workout for 60-90 minutes every day, as it gives me quiet time alone to reflect and mentally unwind. When I'm rushed for time, I start the day with an "adrenaline shot" of a set of 25 burpees. It's hard to be consumed by negative thoughts when your heart is thumping, you're sweating, gasping for breath, and the burn from your workout is all that's on your mind, followed by the endorphins which are the feel-good brain hormones that take over shortly thereafter.

2. Prime yourself for success with a morning ritual.

This will shock you, but having a daily morning ritual that primes you for success is winning 80% of the battle. Our subconscious minds are bombarded with messages from friends, family, mainstream news and advertisements every day. This noise tells you how we're supposed to feel and to live in fear or beware of everything that could go wrong. It's easy to become driven by fear and anxiety, unless we actively tune our brains to be driven by gratitude and love.

Just like your computer needs to be rebooted so it doesn't lag up, humans need to do the same if they want their minds to function at the highest potential. The human subconscious mind can't tell the difference between what is real and what is imagined. If we start worrying about all the things that could go wrong in our day every morning (and many people do without even knowing it), such as "am I good enough?", "will I close the deal today?", or "nothing I try seems to be working", it's inevitable that we will be plagued with anxiety from our fears and our stress hormones will overtake us. On the flipside, if we program our minds with thoughts that give us joy, gratitude and feelings of love, then as Tony Robbins teaches, "it's impossible for us to feel fearful and anxious at the same time we are feeling joy and gratitude."

After your morning workout, while your heart is still beating fast, play your favorite song that brings you feelings of peace, joy, relaxation, or gratitude. It's not always easy to clear your mind at will, so try something else. Instead, close your eyes and visualize a moment from your childhood that had brought you feelings of joy, love, or excitement. Really allow yourself to re-live the experience and hold on to that feeling. Then find another moment and repeat the process. Do it for three memories or as many as it takes until you really start feeling the joy from stacking these positive emotions. Then think of one of your biggest goals or dreams in life; perhaps a project you really want to finish, an amount of money you wish to earn, or a lifestyle you wish to have. Imagine yourself on the day you finally reached that goal.

What are your family and friends saying when you've succeeded in reaching it? What are you feeling inside? Are you smiling? Are you laughing? Hold onto that feeling and repeat this with three or more other goals you wish to accomplish.

If you repeat this exercise every morning consistently for about a month, it trains your brain to feel positive thoughts. Just like training your muscles require daily repetition, so does training your mind. Repeating this daily allows you to imprint the song(s) in your mind with these feelings of joy, love and gratitude. The emotional stacking conditions your mind, and after a month or two, simply hearing the song will actually allow you to feel some of those feelings.

3. Give gratitude to your spiritual source, feed your soul.

Always remember to be grateful to God if you're religious, and to your family and friends, for anything that has ever or will bring you happiness. Even if you don't believe in God, it's easier to go through life believing in some higher power because inevitably there will come a time when your challenges are harder than you wish to face alone; being spiritual intrinsically allows one to place greater value on the greater good than one's self. If your purpose is to serve a greater good, then this higher calling is more likely to give you all the strength you need to excel and conquer your challenges. While you certainly can reach great heights by just believing in yourself, this is a very lonely and onerous path to take.

4. Use Power Statements to build confidence, energy, and excitement.

Also referred to as affirmations, Power Statements are phrases we repeat to ourselves that help us override limiting thoughts and beliefs. Think about the things in your work, relationships, and life that you have been afraid of, or goals you have that you don't believe will come true. Then turn around that thought or statement so it becomes a positive, invigorating statement and write it down. For example, you might have been consumed by the question, "Am I ever going to get rich and make a million dollars?" An intense Power Statement would be "I'm a ---ing deal magnet and money flows to me like an avalanche of wealth!"

If you've primed yourself properly and opened your mind to be joyful and grateful, then you shouldn't be driven by fear or anxiety and it will be easier for you to tell yourself this truth (it's a truth that just hasn't happened yet.) The consistent repetition and invocation of Power Statements on a daily basis will force your subconscious mind to acclimate to the truth of these statements. If repeated for weeks and months, the statements will become the focus of your subconscious mind. You may not believe it, but your mind will invoke these statements and turn them into realities over time, as per the Law of Attraction. Steps 1-4 are like putting the Law of Attraction on steroids! For more info on how this works, read up more about the Law of Attraction.

5. Be a possibility thinker, have BIG goals, and don't listen to naysayers.

If you've done the previous steps correctly and consistently for a few days, then you should become open and bold enough again to start having bigger goals and dreams again.

If your goals and dreams are great enough, then the prospect of achieving them will outweigh the fears and anxieties that fill the road ahead to reach them. It's crucial to have goals that are so big they will get you through the tough times and give you the motivation to overcome the challenges. Dare to have goals that are bigger than your problems, and most of your problems will go away.

6. Be extremely patient and NEVER GIVE UP!

Despite all the priming and planning you can do, life is full of hiccups and nothing usually goes exactly as planned. There's no need to get frustrated if you anticipate things will take a lot of time. It's OK to shift directions if you find your actions are no longer in line with your dreams and passions. Priming yourself on a daily basis creates exponential personal growth, and it's natural for your goals to evolve quite often. Always be ready to adapt and adjust. Recalibrate your plans and execute again.

Instead, close your eyes and visualize a moment from your childhood that had brought you feelings of joy, love, or excitement.

7. Give Back.

Always remember to give back as you begin to reap rewards. There's magic in tithing. This is a secret to success that many wealthy folks use, and it's multiplied my business manifold. Consider donating 10% of your income and you will very quickly discover how real karma works.

Give yourself permission to be authentic. Live with passion. Follow your heart. Don't play small in the shadows, in the fear of judgment, because regret is more painful than failure. After all, failure only happens when you begin telling yourself that you no longer have the time, energy or resources to move forward in the face of a great challenge. If you're truly passionate about what you're working towards, then never tell yourself you've run out of resources. Instead, become more resourceful. Feed your mind the right thoughts, and continue to cultivate the voice within you. These are timeless principles that will allow you to build the life of your dreams.

ABOUT MICHAEL

In 2018, Michael Cheng launched GoalMogul (www.goalmogul.com), the social network for masterminding, which connects users based on what's most important: friends helping each other achieve their deepest goals, dreams, needs, and values. He also co-founded New York-based real estate development companies Epos Development (www.eposglobal.com) and Faith Venture Partners (www.fvpartners.com), which are developing over $550M of residential, commercial, religious and hotel projects.

Cheng's work has been featured on FOX, ABC, NBC, NY1, NY Daily News, USA Today, and the Chinese World Journal. He was a co-author of *Adventures in Manifesting*, a compilation of inspirational stories along with Brian Tracy, Joe Vitale, and others. Mike has also lectured at NYU Steinhardt School of Education and at American Express. Mike received his undergrad degree in Marketing with a specialization in Entertainment, Media, and Technology at the Stern School of Business at NYU.

Michael is very active in his local community in Flushing, NY and frequently travels to Asia. Having lived in Shanghai for over three years, he also frequently fundraises in Singapore and Vietnam. As a community leader, Cheng was a former Hillary delegate, and serves on the Board of Advisors at the Asian Real Estate Association of America (NY-East Chapter), Queens Community Board 7, Flushing Town Hall, Flushing Y, and the Flushing Chamber of Commerce. He attends church at Faith Bible Church, and his favorite charity is Pencils of Promise. He resides in Flushing with his wife Makiyo.

You can contact him at:

mike.cheng@eposglobal.com

www.mikecheng.com

BY MIKE RIEDMILLER

YOUR FINANCIAL SUCCESS PLAN!

Think about what your ideal retirement looks like. Really take some time to ponder this…

- What types of memories would you like to create with your family and friends?

- What are some of the things you would like to do and places you would want to travel to?

- What kind of experiences would you like to enjoy?

- What are some things you have always wanted to do but have not done yet?

Have a **crystal-clear picture** in your mind of exactly **where** you would be, the **people** you would be with and what you would be **doing** together… because life should be about **experiencing joy, doing good and helping others.**

Remember some of your happiest times that you had in your life. It's likely you were with people you cared about doing things that were enjoyable. Consider the **impact and lasting memories** you can create with the people that are important to you. This might be a trip to Disney with the grandkids or an Alaskan cruise with some friends. It could mean doing something you have thought about for many years but have not done yet. Go out and do it. It can also mean having added peace of mind knowing you have more than enough money for financial and medical emergencies, and also being prepared for inflation.

All of this is important because there are **two very different groups** of people. Which group you are in has **nothing** to do with your net worth, social status or political views. It has **everything** to do with whether you have a written financial plan to help you accomplish the things that are important to you. It is quite simple…

You either have a specific written financial plan, or you do not.

It is extremely important to have an actual written financial plan in place that is based on your life goals, and not on numbers or rates of return alone. It does **not** benefit you to have a large amount of money (whatever this means to you) if you do not have a plan in place so you can experience true enjoyment and added peace of mind. There are some people with large portfolios who still experience stress because they do not have the confidence that a written plan can offer. Several studies have shown that people who have written goals are much more likely to achieve them compared to those who do not have them.

For example before a house is built, you start with a written blueprint which lists the dimensions of each room. Can you imagine trying to build a house without a written plan in advance? It is unlikely that you would get the type of home with all of the amenities that you wanted. The structure might not even be stable.

A financial plan is **not** your monthly brokerage account statement which lists your different stocks and mutual fund investments. If the purpose of your investments is not clearly defined in writing then it's likely you do **not** have a financial plan. There can be many potential downsides and risks associated with this.

If you fail to plan, you are planning to fail. ~ Benjamin Franklin

1. Your New Financial Future

When approaching retirement or if you are already retired, many people have experienced the benefits of working with a new financial advisor that is a fiduciary – in which they have your best interests and needs ahead of their own.

The difference between success and failure of your financial future can be the result of working with the proper financial professional.

If you have been working with somebody who calls themselves a financial advisor, how many pages is your written financial plan? If you do not have any type of written financial plan with specifics, then it could be time to work with a new advisor. Consider that they either do not offer a written financial plan for clients such as yourself, or worse yet, they do offer it but they have never taken the time to do this for you. This can be very risky!

Not all financial advisors are equal and neither are the results they produce. Several people found this out the hard way during difficult economic times and stock market downturns like we saw in 2001 and 2008. Some had to go back to work. Others had to cut back on their lifestyle. Unfortunately, some people lost their homes or even filed for bankruptcy. This can be difficult to think about, but it is reality.

Trying to predict where the stock market is headed next can be like guessing or even gambling – which is usually a losing proposition. When you have a financial plan in place, then you can be ready regardless of which direction the markets move next. The time to properly prepare for future events is **before** they occur. **Now** is the best time to get your financial house in order.

Think about why people travel long distances in order to have a different doctor treat them. The reason is because not all doctors and surgeons create the same results. It can be a matter of life and death in some cases. It can be similar for your financial situation. **Different financial advisors will produce different results**. Just because you have an advisor that you have known for a number of years who has helped you up until this point does not mean that they are the right advisor for you in the future.

Unfortunately, there are people in the financial industry who call themselves financial advisors but they are nothing more than salespeople. Their goal is to have you invest your hard-earned money in their stocks, bonds and mutual funds. These are usually **commission brokers** (who used to be called stock brokers). Or it could be somebody that has only talked to you about insurance or annuities. This would be an **insurance agent**. Many times people are not aware of how their financial advisor is licensed and the potential bias and conflicts of interest that can arise.

Thinking that a commission broker can give you a real financial plan would be like going to a fast food restaurant and expecting a healthy meal. It is likely not going to happen.

Insanity is doing the same thing over and over again and expecting different results.
~ Albert Einstein

2. Dangers of Doing It Yourself

Perhaps you do not have a financial advisor and have been handling your investments on your own up until this point. Or maybe you were part of a company 401(k) or 403(b) plan. There can be many potential benefits to working with a fiduciary financial professional. Think about your job or profession. It's likely you had years of training in order to stay qualified in your field. Doctors, dentists, attorneys, architects and engineers attended many years of college to get the needed credentials. In addition, they have continuing education since there are always new advances and updates.

Would you hire any of these types of professionals if they had not acquired the needed training, and instead had "self-taught" themselves by reading some articles on the internet? I doubt you would try to perform surgery on yourself if you had a medical problem by doing some research online. It would not be smart to try to fly an airplane by surfing the internet or watching a few videos on the subject.

3. When it comes to your financial future it is vital to have the most accurate information and work with a professional in the industry.

Research has shown that people who work with a financial advisor can gain greater returns on average of 3% annually (even after factoring in fees). For example, if they had been earning 5% on their money prior to working with an advisor, they might start earning 8% or more on their money after working with an advisor. This can produce a substantial impact of additional hundreds of thousands or even millions of dollars in future gains factored over the course of a couple of decades.

> *To begin with the end in mind means to start with a clear understanding of your*
> *destination. It means to know where you're going so that you better understand*
> *where you are now and so that the steps you take are always in the right direction.*
> ~ Stephen Covey, *The 7 Habits of Highly Effective People*

4. Increase Your Success Probability

When you work with the proper financial professional and also have a real financial plan in writing, then your chances of **success can increase** by many times. This does not have to be a confusing 20-page financial plan that is hard to understand. What I am referring to is a simple, yet potentially powerful 1 to 3-page financial plan that is clear and concise. This would help you accomplish your important financial goals. For the first time, you really understand how all of your investments are working together to help you accomplish your financial objectives.

Steve Jobs founded Apple back in the 1976. He and his team built the company, and then he was ousted by the board of directors in 1985. Jobs was brought back as the CEO in 1997 and helped to bring Apple back from the verge of bankruptcy. Today, Apple is a multi-billion-dollar company which is one of the largest and most admired in the entire world.

Let's think about athletics. We have all seen college and professional sports teams that had losing records for many years. A new coach is hired, and the next year the same team has a winning record. What changed? The team had a new plan along with new leadership.

In both examples, we clearly see how having the right coach can make all of the difference. This coach brings with them a plan for success.

RESULTS IN ADVANCE FINANCIAL PLANNING

There is a proven process called **"Results in Advance Financial Planning"** in which the following is analyzed:

1. Your current investments that are performing well and meeting your goals.

2. Your current investments that are not performing as well.

3. Different investment options that you have been considering but have not yet implemented.

Perform a **stress test** to see your potential results in advance moving forward. This is accomplished by analyzing your historical rates of return, risks, fees and other factors. Many times some **simple change and improvements** can have a big impact.

The end result can give you a **"Mathematically Correct Solution"** for your investments and financial future which includes:

- *Growing your money while reducing your risk of losses.*

- *Make sure you never run out of money regardless of whether the stock market performs the way we want it to or not.*

- *Option for residual lifetime income immediately or in the future.*

- *Preserve your lump sum principal.*

- *Build in your desired liquidity and flexibility.*

- *Reduce your risks and reduce your fees.*

- *Be as tax efficient as possible.*

To accomplish this, it begins with **reverse engineering** your investments based on your goals. Then systematize as much of your portfolio as possible so things happen automatically. Future reviews and corrections can help to ensure things stay on track for the rest of your life.

<u>YOUR NEXT STEPS</u>

1. **Write down the things most important to you from the questions at the beginning of this chapter.** This should include whatever the first things that you think of are. Add items to this list over the course of time. Really put a lot of thought and consideration into this. Do not continue to the next step until you complete this.

2. **Gather all of your account statements.** This can include your brokerage accounts, bank, life insurance, annuities and all other investments so you have everything in one file.

3. **Define the purpose of each account in writing.** If you do not know the purpose of an account then it might not be right for your situation. This would be like a pilot taking off in an airplane without a flight plan and not knowing where the final destination was. This can be dangerous.

4. **Look at your investments that have potential for risk of loss.** What percentage of your portfolio is this? What could happen during the next major stock market downturn? How could this negatively impact your portfolio, goals and lifestyle?

5. **Take the necessary action steps to improve your financial situation based on your written goals**. At this point, all of your accounts should have a defined purposes and be tied to your financial objectives and the things important to you. Produce a 1 to 3-page written plan listing all of your investments, action steps and financial goals along with other financial data.

These are steps you can attempt on your own. The key is to get started and complete the process.

Just like you could try to build your own house or perform surgery on yourself, there are several obvious benefits to working with the proper financial professional. Do your own research. **The internet can be a great way to discover what a financial advisor offers.** Top advisors probably have **videos and educational resources** online that you can review so you know how they have helped other people just like yourself. Contact one or more advisors so you can learn how they could help you with this important process.

Knowledge is power, but only if you act upon the knowledge that you have. Just knowing is not enough. It is a combination of knowing along with action. Your better financial future will not happen by chance or accident.

Congratulations on completing these steps, making improvements and having your **NEW WRITTEN FINANCIAL PLAN** in place. Now go and create those lasting memories with your family and friends. It is time to enjoy the rest of your life and retirement to its fullest!

The best way to predict the future is to create it. ~ Abraham Lincoln

ABOUT MIKE

Mike Riedmiller is the president of Riedmiller Wealth Management, an independent financial firm that is free from the product-focused, sales-driven environment that can be prevalent at other financial firms. He is a fiduciary financial advisor and the best-selling author of the book, *The Road To Success*, (Amazon 2016). In addition, he is the creator of the "Smart Money Planning" educational course and a Forbes BrandVoice Contributor.

Your financial success is Mike's #1 goal. He focuses on retirement planning and wealth management. Mike believes it is important for people to be educated about money and their options so they can secure their financial future. His goal is to build long-term relationships with people in order to help them achieve their important life goals and financial objectives. Mike Riedmiller has a fiduciary responsibility to always act in the best interest of every client.

Riedmiller Wealth Management is proud to be part of a large nationwide network of highly vetted financial professionals who are passionate about helping their clients. This group is supported by one of the fastest-growing private investment companies in the United States. Mike and his team continually advance their education by attending several investment conferences throughout the United States every year.

Mike and his wife, Carisa, have three children – Madison, Sophia and Dillon. They enjoy spending time with family and friends, biking, snorkeling, hiking, reading, and meeting new people. They have traveled throughout the United States and to foreign countries in order to have new experiences and lifetime memories with their family. They actively support a number of charities with the goal of helping others to have better lives and to leave a legacy.

You can discover more about Mike Riedmiller's financial planning strategies and connect with him at: www.RiedmillerWealth.com

BY LIZZIE DEMENT, M.ED.

LEADING WITH "WHY"

Growing up, I was always a high achiever. If I knew someone in an organization, I was trying to join it; if there was a competition on campus, I was trying to win it; if there was an opportunity to be celebrated, I was working towards it. But I never really understood what motivated me to do this. Everyone has a reason why they are working to achieve certain goals, whether it is to make an income to live on, because of a personal passion; but whatever it is – there is a reason. But growing up, I didn't understand my "why" – the drive that pushed me to always do better.

My need to achieve drastically changed when I was 25 years old, and my mom passed away from breast cancer. She had been sick for a while, but her death still drastically impacted me. I chose to quit my job in Arizona and move home to Florida to be with family and deal with her things. After this move home, restarting my life was challenging. I was fortunate to find a job in only a few months, but I felt disconnected from a lot of things in my life. The hardest part of everyday was driving home from work. Back in Arizona, during my drive home from work I would call my mom every day to update her on crazy office stories, my accomplishments of the day, and the plans I had for the next day. Even if I didn't have a major reason behind these calls, they were part of my life and I drastically missed them.

The other major challenge that affected me was selling my mom's house. My family continued to support and push me to sell her house, but I was afraid to confront the issues that surrounded selling her house. Most specifically, I could not commit to going through all of her possessions and choosing what had value to me and what did not. Additionally, there was nothing that motivated me to sell this house. My "why" for accomplishing tasks like this in my life had disappeared. It took longer than I had hoped, but with a lot of help I was finally able to get the house cleaned out and on the market a year and a half after her death. I didn't understand the importance of this accomplishment until we received a bid the first day it was on the market. The day it really hit me that this was happening was the day we finalized all of the paperwork, and I began crying in a FedEx store as I mailed off all of the paperwork. I wasn't upset about selling the house, the tears were filled with joy because I felt proud of myself and for the first time in almost two years, I felt accomplished.

But the "why" shows us the foundation of the task and the ultimate goal that we are constantly working towards.

In the months after selling the house, I continued to reflect on why this was such a challenging experience for me. But after some reflection (and wine), I realized that in losing my mom, I didn't just lose my parent, but I had lost my "why". I had always been a high achiever because I wanted to make my mom proud, I was motivated to join an organization because it would make my mom proud, and I was motivated to be recognized for my achievements because my mom would have loved to hear about these accomplishments each day. Losing my "why" made me lose the motivation that I had become comfortable with, and on a daily basis, we go back to comfort constantly – because it is what we know works. Not having comfort and purpose in our goals adds extra steps that need to be completed, and hesitation in believing that what we are doing is right.

I had grown to drastically miss our daily phone calls because this little call provided me motivation every day to be the best me I could be.

Something as simple as a phone call had kept me motivated and driven. I had grown up with a mother that was always proud of me, but it motivated me more and more every day to achieve things that made her happy. My mom had been my "why".

As leaders, it is our responsibility to always go back to our "why". Because our "why" is our driving force, our "why" creates the priority and purpose behind the project, our "why" determines how much we are willing to wager to accomplish that goal. On a day-to-day basis, it can be challenging to focus on the "why" because time gets in our way. It is much easier to focus in on the task list that needs to be checked off to make it through the day. But the "why" shows us the foundation of the task and the ultimate goal that we are constantly working towards.

Additionally, the "why" helps us gain buy-in from those that we are leading. As a team member, understanding the "why" of your assignments can make you feel important and connected to the overall purpose of the group. After all, if someone does not understand the purpose behind a task or a project, how will they fulfill it to its fullest?

Leading with "why" can impact many key parts of your goals, your team, and your organization. Begin leading your organization with your "why" today through a variety of outlets:

1. **Start with "why" when launching a new goal or initiative** – Rather than starting with a task list of projects and assignments to accomplish the next project/goal, help unite your team by starting with the motivating factor behind the goal. Providing context and purpose can help your team unite in a direction and a commitment. For example, rather than just telling your team that you will be hosting an event in the upcoming weeks, help them understand why your organization saw the need for this initiative, and what you hope to accomplish with this event. This will help your team see value and purpose in the initiative, rather than seeing it as "just another event."

2. **Understand that the "why" can be different for various people and groups involved in the goal** – Goals often have many stakeholders involved in the development and execution of the goal. With many people and perspectives, it is important to note that these various stakeholders have different motives for completing the goal, and that's okay. For example, if your organization is trying to launch a new brand to support your mission and the interest of your consumers, your "why" may be to broaden your organization's outreach, but the marketing consultant you hire may have a "why" centered on bringing in their required income of the month. It is okay that you both have these different motivations, but it is important to understand/recognize these motivating factors so you can understand the perspective you are both coming from, as you work together toward your goal.

3. **Be transparent about the personal "whys" in your life** – Often the easiest way to connect with others is through personal stories. Sharing with your colleagues, employees, and partners your personal story and motivating factors can quicken the development of trust and respect because of an understanding of your choices and actions. When I first started working at a college in Florida, I was pretty determined to share my motives for moving back to Florida with my office. From this, my colleagues understood the priority family had in my life, and better understood what I prioritized both personally and professionally. As people, we often make assumptions about the reasoning behind the choices and actions of others, but having a direct understanding will limit false assumptions and build connections in similar motivations.

4. **Get to know the "whys" of those you lead** – Depending on your leadership role, you could be managing as few as two individuals or as many as a thousand. Leadership roles are constantly different, but this does not detract from the importance of understanding those you manage and how to support them throughout their role. Previously, I had a supervisor who asked all new employees to complete an info sheet about themselves in their first week. Initially, I thought this was going to be the classic/usual questions like my emergency contact. But instead, the sheet was filled with questions like, "How do you hope to grow while working in this position?" "What motivates you to get out of bed every morning?" "What is your favorite snack?" Some of these questions seemed weird at first glance, but it truly allowed our supervisor to understand our "why" and ways to motivate us throughout our work (even if it was through a candy bar). Understanding the "why" of your employees can help them also feel more valued and significant within the organization.

5. **Challenge those you lead to connect to the "whys" of your organization** – As an organization, having a strong and transparent "why" will often recruit employees with similar motivations in their life. As people, we have a natural need to find happiness in our lives and doing work that aligns with our beliefs and purposes increases happiness in our life. That's why individuals are willing to take lower paying jobs in the non-profit and education sectors because they know they will feel more fulfilled from their work. Even if you have employees that do not fully align with the ultimate why of your organization, it is important to help those you lead to connect back to the ultimate purpose of the organization. Encourage your staff to answer: Why is our organization important to you? What about the purpose of our organization motivates you to come to work each day? Why is our organization important to our consumers? Why is our organization crucial to our community? While some of these questions may be easier to answer than others, this can be a beneficial way to gauge the motivation of your employees and their understanding of the overall direction of your organization.

6. **When a "why" is not present, evaluate the need of the initiative** – If you ultimately cannot figure out the "why" behind an initiative, it is important to focus on why that initiative even exists. When I started my job in Florida, we had processes in place that no one could explain. For example, the sharing of spending information with a colleague who did not manage the budget or supervise the area that oversaw that budget. It did not make sense, and no one was able to explain the reasoning behind it. After deeper conversation, it was uncovered that it was an extra step that once had purpose, but now it was simply adding extra work to our already busy days. After evaluating, we removed this step and moved on to support tasks that supported our "why".

Our "why" may change throughout our lives or may be different depending on the project, but that does not diminish the importance of supporting it each and every day. After losing my mom, I had to take some time to reevaluate what pushed me to achieve things throughout my life. Working in higher education, my "why" is constantly my students – going back to their growth and development constantly pushes me to advocate and push initiatives to be at their best. Centering on much of my personal life, my "why" comes back to my family, my dog, my friends, and my overall well-being.

As strong leaders, we need to bring this personal and organizational connection to the forefront of what we lead. We need to be transparent to our employees, colleagues, and consumers about this "why" to get all of us on the same page to move forward. Change can be hard to lead, but it gets easier if all of the stakeholders understand the reasoning and purpose behind the change. Bring your organization back to its ultimate "why" and begin leading with a little more purpose today.

As strong leaders, we need to bring this personal and organizational connection to the forefront of what we lead.

ABOUT LIZZIE

Lizzie Dement is a higher education professional focused on supporting the leadership development of college students. Lizzie earned her B.S. in Political Science & Social Science at Florida State University, and her M.Ed. in Higher Education and Student Affairs at the University of South Carolina. Throughout her education, Lizzie found a passion for leadership development in students because of the opportunity to prepare students to make a positive impact on their peers, their future profession, and their community. Lizzie currently serves as the Assistant Director of Leadership Development at Stetson University, where she has designed a variety of leadership initiatives focused on developing, supporting, and recognizing the leadership of students across campus.

Lizzie is also a certified CliftonStrengths Coach with Gallup, in which she utilizes the Strengths assessment to coach individuals and teams to apply their strengths in leadership, management, team development, and holistic well-being. Lizzie currently oversees Strengths development at Stetson University and serves as a Strengths consultant for individuals and organizations.

You can connect with Lizzie at:

lizziedement@gmail.com

Linkedin.com/in/lizziedement

BY 'B. TAYLOR'

1 LIFE, 1 MIRACLE

For as long as I can remember people have asked me what the title "1 LIFE, 1 MIRACLE" means. Well it begins with me as a little baby, born at the Air Force Academy Hospital in Colorado Springs, Colorado. On the way home from the hospital I stopped breathing and everyone thought I wasn't going to make it. On top of that, I was diagnosed as being pigeon-toed and the doctors had to break my feet to correct that. They told my parents that I would never walk or run straight and there was nothing that could be done. Fortunately, that was not God's plan or my plan either. I went on to become a high school standout student athlete who went on to play football and basketball at the University of Missouri while studying engineering. While at Missouri, there were things that didn't make me happy so I decided to transfer to another school, however the NCAA Clearinghouse had my transfer as ineligible for me to play. Determined not to give up, I thought I could join the Navy ROTC program and continue sports and academics. I joined the Navy while testing into the Nuclear Engineering Program, but ROTC was not granted to me. It left me discouraged but still determined. I then took the second most prestigious job in the Navy as an Aviation Electronics Technician.

The will to succeed led me to graduate at the top of my class and I was selected to meet with Chief of Naval Operations, Admiral Vern Clark (Ret.) and former Secretary of The Navy, The Honorable Richard Danzig. They recognized my will to achieve greatness, wrote personal letters on my behalf and chose me to play on the U.S. All Navy and Military Team USA Basketball teams. On top of that they allowed me to obtain an agent and try out with the NFL after my first tour duty. During my time in the Navy, I was offered the opportunity to play piano for Snoop Dogg at his mother's birthday and wedding. This chance meeting led to me being the first hip hop artist/producer ever discovered by Motown's First Group and Founding Members of *Smokey and The Miracles*, led by Miracle member Pete Moore. As you could imagine I was honored and on cloud nine and so was the U.S. Secretary of The Navy Office. However, despite these new and exciting developments, there was still negativity around. I was told by record executives that being a hip hop artist, bridging Classic Motown Legends and The U.S. Military (Dept of Defense) was corny and would never work in modern entertainment.

Fortunately, that was not God's plan or my plan either.

Then one day, my mentor Pete Moore sat me down and told me his story. He went on to explain how he was the youngest of 14. His mother gave birth to him when she was 50 years old in the 1930's and there was a 10% percent chance of mother and infant surviving such circumstances in those days. Again, God had a plan for him as well. While he was playing in the backyard as a 10-year-old, he touched a live wire that threw him 30 feet in the air. Miraculously, it didn't electrocute him because he was so little and he didn't stay grounded to the Earth. He went on to excel in high school with the intention of going to college to become an engineer, but his boyhood singing group met Berry Gordy, founder of Motown Records. He was told his group, *Smokey and The Miracles*, sounded too different for the times and it was unlikely ghetto kids from Detroit would ever make it mainstream. Despite having the deck stacked against them, that group revolutionized music, the entertainment business and discovered acts who would go on to become cultural icons. That dynasty lives today and is known as Motown.

Pete Moore even served two years in the U.S. Army while with The Miracles, and they saved his money. From that day, I used all the values

I learned from my parents, the "never-quit-get-it-done" training I received in the military, and The Motown Legends guidance and I haven't looked back since. I went on to chart #1 on the Billboard Singles Chart with *Fire In Your Eyes* featuring NCIS actress Pauley Perrette, performed for President Bush's family, President Obama, Mrs. Obama, worked with notable entertainers, became the first to film a music video on The USS Midway Aircraft Carrier, received the HillVets Top 100 Most Influential Veteran Award, was named Global Ambassador & Advocate of Music and Entertainment for the U.S. Military, Veterans, First Responders and their Families, and signed a partnership through Combs Enterprises with owners Sean P. Diddy Combs and Mark Walberg as their Aquahydrate Alkaline Water Military Ambassador, and many other achievements. Pretty much myself and Pete Moore were destined to meet and work together because God gave us this **"1 Life"**, worked a miracle on us both so that we could share our great message to the world as **"1 Life, 1 Miracle"**.

Through my experiences of ups and downs in life, there have been 10 characteristics that I used to obtain winning performances and a life full of meaningful accomplishments.

They are the following:

1. **God** – My belief in God has kept me grounded. Even when times were rough and doors closed, I was able to get on my knees and pray for him to give me the strength that I needed to keep going forward.

2. **Faith and Confidence** – In order to achieve what you want, you must have faith in yourself. If you don't have faith in yourself, how can you expect others to have faith in what you are doing?

3. **Perseverance** – When things don't go your way and the walls are crumbling down, you must stand your ground. You must weather the storm and dig deep within yourself. Tell yourself I can do this and I am not going to stop or give up no matter what it takes to reach your dream.

4. **Organization** – The key to reaching your goals is being organized. The more organized you are the more you can get done and your business will reap the rewards. A disorganized person spends all day juggling tasks, but really doesn't get anything accomplished. Don't be that person!

5. **Respect** – One thing my parents taught me was to respect others. In order to get respect you must give respect as well. The military was really big on respect and you learn that from day one. By serving in the number one organization in the world, I respected those in authority and in return they rewarded me over and beyond my wildest dreams.

6. **Humility** – If you stay humble and grateful, others will always want to help you achieve your vision. The minute you shy away from that and become arrogant or cocky you will lose a lot of great people and business. It might not happen at the beginning but what energy you put out always comes back to you twice fold!

7. **Discipline** – Growing up, my father and mother had strict rules and were disciplinarians. When I joined the military, discipline was the forefront of our training. These rules shaped me into who I am and I was able to accomplish far more because of having this trait.

8. **Consistency** – In anything you do you must be consistent to hitting your mark. Whether you are selling something, promoting something, etc. be consistent with who you are. Don't try to change or appease other people. Be consistent in who you are and what you do at all times and you will see a positive outcome.

9. **Health** – I was always active in sports and never did drugs. I felt that if I try to take care of my health I could obtain more goals. If the body is healthy on the inside then you make better decisions. When you make better decisions, it results in greater success.

10. **Goals** – Write down your goals and dreams. Every month hit a goal and then write down another goal and hit that goal. Repeat this all the time and when you speak your goals and dreams into existence you will notice yourself achieving them.

ABOUT 'B. TAYLOR'

Renowned musician, 'B. Taylor' has been deemed 'the Stevie Wonder of Hip Hop' due to his musicianship and ability to play four instruments – piano, drums, guitar and organ. But that's only the beginning of his story. Discovered by Smokey Robinson and The Miracle's Pete Moore, he has been endorsed by *The Miracles, The Supremes, The Temptations, The Marvelettes, The Vandellas, The Four Tops,* The Gordy Family and the iconic Cash Family of country music for his unique talents as a Hip-Hop artist, producer and songwriter with consummate musicality.

As a No. 1 billboard-charted musician, writer, producer and performer, the Peoria, Illinois native became a decorated sailor in the U.S. Navy, and was awarded special duty and an honorary discharge by the Secretary of the Navy in order to pursue the NFL and his savvy entertainment career professionally. B. Taylor maintains an active presence as a Global Ambassador of Music and Entertainment for the U.S. Military, Veterans, First Responders and Their Families speaking to over 250,000 youth and military personnel while also being supported by many top-ranking officials from all four branches of the U.S. Military (Navy, Army, Air Force and Marines) as well as Department of Defense officials. B.Taylor is also a Co-Chair of The Veterans Task Force Committee formed by U.S. Congressman and Vice Chair of The U.S. Veteran Affairs Committee Gus Bilirakis.

He earned 2 Grammy Nomination Considerations in 2012 for his single "Fire In Your Eyes," featuring NCIS star actress Pauley Perrette, which reached No. 1 on the Billboard's Hot R&B/Hip Hop Singles Sales Chart. Taylor has also performed for President Bush's family, President and First Lady Obama, Christy Walton (Walmart Owner), and opened for Pitbull, Snoop Dogg, Ray J, and many other notable entertainers. He has also garnered a national presence on ESPN, Extra, The Insider/Entertainment Tonight, Fox, CBS, NBC and ABC, as well as features in *Billboard Magazine, BRE Magazine (Black Radio Exclusive Magazine), Yo Raps Magazine, Respect the Grind, The A&R Chronicles, El Diario,* BET, VH1, allhiphop.com, and much more.

This rising young mogul has received over 60 endorsement letters(awards) and testimonials from top government officials, military officials, Fortune 500 executives, educators, legendary entertainers, and continues to redefine the music industry with his impeccable brand. B. Taylor has changed the culture and is the first artist to bridge the gap between hip hop urban/pop culture, Classic Motown, the U.S. Military, and Motorsports. His **"1 Life"** movement is a positive powerful force, as he is helping, changing, and saving lives all through the universal power of music.

BY ELLA RIVKIN

FINANCIAL FREEDOM IS IN YOUR HANDS!

All our lives we are taught to believe that happiness only exists if we have lots and lots of love, money and health. After all, without money, you lack the proper resources. Without health, you don't have the energy to pursue new opportunities or dreams. And ultimately, without a partner to share it with, what use are life's many riches?

However, all too often, we follow the same pattern we are taught to believe is the one path for everyone. It starts with beliefs, mindsets and stories passed down from generation to generation to us by our parents, school and society. Go to school, study hard, get a good education so you can find a good-paying and secure job in a big company to work all your life and then retire with great benefits. It's natural that as we develop as young people, we focus on money and careers and build our lives based on a set of recommendations given to us.

My client had followed a similar set of beliefs all her life. She became a nurse practitioner and found a secure job. Her parents told her that if you do your best, the best will surely come to you. She followed this advice closely by working hard to have her dream life as a nurse practitioner in the hospital for 20 years. She and her family lived in a big house, owned nice cars and went on vacation twice a year.

This is also the same advice that the mama pig gave to her little piglets in the famous story of *The Three Little Pigs and The Big Bad Wolf*.

Remember?

This is the story of how three little pigs left home to start their own lives. Momma Pig told them "Whatever you do, do it the best that you can because that's the way to get along in the world." This story is the perfect analogy for three types of people in this world:

1. The first little piglet who took the easy way out and built a house out of straw. When the big bad wolf came, he blew it down with ease and ate the first little piglet.

2. The second little piglet put in slightly more effort and built a house out of wood. However, when the wolf came, he managed to blow it down with ease again and ate the second little piglet.

3. The third little piglet took his time, though. He laid a strong foundation and built his house out of brick. The big bad wolf tried and tried and tried again to blow it down but was powerless against the sturdy brick house.

I love this story because it represents a key concept we should apply to lives every day:

WHEN IT COMES TO OUR FINANCES, MOST PEOPLE ARE STILL MAKING THE SAME MISTAKE!

Let's look at this story again but from the perspective of real life:

The **first little piglet** represents people who choose not to do anything, or the bare minimum. Often they have very little education, no vision, low ambition and settle for low-paying jobs. Their lives are a constant struggle, as they have no contingency plan against the big bad wolf of debts, spending beyond their limit, and not saving or investing wisely.

Now the **second little piglet** represents two kinds of people:

    a. Those who work hard all their lives to make a living.

    b. The get-rich-quick types who are constantly looking for the next scheme.

The problem is that both of these mentalities have already passed their due dates that lead these people to get stuck in the same spot indefinitely.

They might have gone to school, received a great education, worked hard and made money, but they never learned how money works, so they spend their lives working for money without really knowing how to build wealth. By the time they get the money they think they need, their health, relationships or both have started to deteriorate.

They are very susceptible to market crashes or unexpected turns in their lives for which they are unprepared and left devastated. The prime example of this is the Baby Boomer generation. In fact, most people are stuck in the second 'wooden' house for life.

The **third little piglet** represents individuals who work hard but are also very smart and took the time to lay a strong financial foundation for themselves.

- The reason their house is built out of brick is because they have a vision, the right mindsets, goals and know the value of diversification.
- They have created multiple streams of income, investments, and a crystal-clear plan for the future.
- They have prepared against the "what-ifs" and know how to take advantage of unexpected events in the stock and real estate markets.
- They have great relationships and take care of their health.

Can you see the differences between the three types?

Can you see where you stand right now and where you should be going?

Life is a game, money is how we keep score.

This adage holds true; money is one form of power, but that power is completely useless without financial education. Money comes and goes, but once you understand how money works you are able to make good financial decisions and can begin building financial freedom.

You must gain control over your money or the lack of it will forever control you.

Now, lets get back to my client, the nurse practitioner. She started to experience severe difficulties: she divorced her husband and could no longer afford her children's college tuition and struggled with her health. She was also forced to put her house on the market for less than the purchase price. After the sale, she still didn't have enough funds to cover her debts since she never established a pension plan nor a savings account. She was on the verge of bankruptcy.

Lack of planning and ignorance can destroy opportunities and future success.

I remember working closely with a business owner many years ago. When he first came to me, he was financially comfortable - his business was very profitable. His company's bookkeeper was taking good care of his financial reporting, but the client didn't have a complete understanding of his business's cash flows.

Without understanding and planning for the future, every profitable business can go broke.

I suggested he get more involved in the finances of his business to anticipate issues and make better strategic decisions. He chose to ignore my advice because he "didn't understand numbers."

His business ran smoothly for the next few years, until his bookkeeper left, and he lost his grasp of the company's financials. He squandered years of earnings within six months and lost his company. What could have continued to be a profitable enterprise became a lost opportunity, due to a lack of understanding and planning.

Thinking is one thing no one has ever been able to tax.

I have been practicing for over twenty years and have over a thousand clients, yet very few ask me to teach them about money. They ask me for a discount, obsess about how much I charge, seek to pay less taxes, but very rarely do they ask me about how they can generate more income, save more for the future, and generally build a financial foundation.

For all my years as a professional, I have noticed that most clients will spend the best years of their lives working for money, saving by looking for sales and bargains, buying clothes, eating out, improving their houses, driving nice cars . . . in a word increasing their liabilities. All the while they don't understand the concept of money management - what do you do with the money once you earn it, how you keep it and make it work for you?

Save money and money will save you.

Our school system is woefully bad at teaching financial responsibility. Kids often graduate with a marketable degree but little or no financial education. They work hard but spend carelessly and live easy until the moment when, one day, sleepless and in debt, they find the American Dream slipping away. Some respond by searching for a way to get rich quick, others accept a future of living hand-to-mouth. I call it "Mass production of wooden houses" (à la second little piglet). It doesn't have to be this way.

Those who don't manage their money will always work for those who do.

One recurring problem I see stems from how we relate to the money we have and want. In fact, these are often at opposites with one another. Yet, all too often, people do not analyze their own spending habits or set reasonable goals. If financial freedom is a priority to you, here is an exercise you can do to help you set expectations and make improvements for the future gains.

Activity #1 – Your Numbers

On a piece of paper write down the following (this can be ballpark; it does not need to be the precise figure):

- How much do you have?
- How much do you make?
- How much do you spend?
- How much do you want to make?
- Where do you invest or keep your money?

Activity #2 – Pie Chart

With some of the same data points as above, draw two circles. Above the first circle, label "My Money." Above the second circle, write "Money Goals." You will probably want to do this in pencil to make adjustments as needed.

For "My Money," use pieces of the pie to represent where your total income goes. Give round estimates, such as 40% to your mortgage or 10% to childcare. Maybe 20% is the cost of take-out food, or perhaps another 20% is the cost of gas.

For your "Money Goals" chart, review your numbers. Are there areas where your expenses can increase (e.g., taking the train into work instead of driving, or planning meals differently)? Perhaps there are areas you wish to increase – like a travel budget, or retirement fund. Carve out those increases from the 100% as best as you can.

Wealth is not about having a lot of money.
It's about having a lot of options.

One of my clients of over 10 years is a receptionist, and her husband is a factory worker; they don't make a lot of money. During our first meeting they told me the story of their retired parents, who were having trouble making ends meet. Her mother worked all her life as a bank teller, accumulating a meager pension. Her father was a taxi driver who was having trouble repaying the mortgage on his taxi medallion, because its value had fallen significantly after Uber disrupted the taxi business. Although their house was completely paid off, they had only a small pension and social security check to live on. Due to their small income, they were unable to access the equity stored in their home. Their golden years were stripped of their luster. Understandably, my clients wanted to avoid the same fate.

It's ok to live a life others don't understand.

With that goal set, and their resolve strong, we started working on their financial position, their relationship, and wellness education. We covered many important topics, and in less than in a year, the results of their hard work bore fruit. They make regular contributions to a retirement plan, are invested in several real estate properties, and have a diversified portfolio of business and equity investments.

She is a member of the "Master Mind" club, a group of likeminded individuals dedicated to long-term financial success, and she attends monthly educational seminars to stay sharp and seek out new opportunities.

Fortunately, my client was able to identify that she was stuck in the proverbial wooden house and made a firm commitment to upgrade her potential to be worthy of the brick house. By mastering the key areas of her life, like financial responsibility, physical wellness, and relationship success, she laid the foundation of a home that can withstand all the howling and buffeting that the winds of life sometimes send our way.

Most people fail to realize that financial independence is less about the amount of money you make, and more about your relationship with the money you keep.

I believe you can build a strong foundation for yourself by mastering the following areas of your life:

The mind is just like a muscle – the more you exercise it, the stronger
it gets and the more it expands.

• Change your mindset – The most powerful asset we all have is our mind. If trained well, it can create massive wealth. Constantly develop yourself personally and professionally by reading, attending seminars and workshops.

It's not your salary that makes you rich. It's your spending habits.

• Learn to manage finances – establish a relationship with money.

An investment in knowledge pays the best interest.

• Invest in financial intelligence - have mentors, be part of mastermind clubs and surround yourself with like-minded people.

Health is like money,
We never have a true idea of its value until we lose it.

• Take care of your health - without good health we have nothing. Learn how to create a healthy life style by eating better, exercising and meditating.

Money can feed the body.
Love will feed the soul.

• Take care of your personal relationships - spend time with those you love.

And remember: "It's all in your hands!"

ABOUT ELLA

Ella Rivkin is the founder and CEO of ERPS Group, Inc., a Business Development Center company that reflects her heart and determination. In addition, ERPS is also a wonderful companion to her additional work as a life, business, and health coach, where she has the honor of offering her 20+ years of business expertise coupled with her strategic advisory background to clients. This makes her a unique asset to a number of businesses in a variety of niches and industries. Through her coaching, she offers her proven expertise to entrepreneurs and individuals, helping them to make their dreams come true through consultations and personal aid to assist in business start-ups. In addition to this high-level coaching, she assists with the intricate details involved in business planning, insurance and payroll services, tax preparation, and daily business operations.

Ella's life experiences have provided her with some of the greatest inspiration, motivation, and education one could have in their life. Born in Moscow, Russia, Ella was raised by someone she says is "one of the strongest and most determined women on earth" … her mother. In 1989, when the Soviet Union was going through vast political reforms, Ella's mother emigrated with her two small children to the US in search of a better future. Although small, Ella was inspired by her mother's determination, especially since she only had $300.00 to her name. But she was committed, a quality that Ella greatly admires to this day. All these experiences inspire her work, relationships with others, and her desire to help people recognize opportunity and achieve success.

ERPS Group is a Business Development Center that offers educational seminars. Through the ERPS Group Foundation established by Ella, she has created a way to give back to the community; especially elderly people and children in need. The focal point of this organization is to help teenagers and adults find purpose in their life, attain financial freedom, and overall happiness and comfort in life. This inspires Ella to continuously seek out new and efficient ways to share her knowledge with others. This is busy work…and rewarding work.

Ella has continued to see success as a best-selling author. Her writing can be found in the book, *Cracking the Code for Success*, co-written with renowned author Brian Tracy.

Today, Ella never forgets her blessings in both her personal triumphs and professional pursuits. In addition, she is thankful for her opportunity to be here in America, a country that has offered her so much. Through helping others find their happiness and purpose, she is constantly reminded of what a great gift those two things are. In her free time, Ella cherishes spending time with her two daughters, teaching them about the spirit of service to others, and also enjoys reading anything that promotes personal development. She loves being creative in the kitchen and delights in sporting activities such as biking, swimming, and running.

BY PETER WOLFING

UPGRADE YOUR THINKING FOR GREATER PERFORMANCE

The world's greatest computer consists of the grey matter between our ears. Too often we take it for granted. In our search for greater performance and productivity, we look outside ourselves for solutions. We tend to ignore the ancient wisdom of Ralph Waldo Emerson which tells us, "The law of laws is cause and effect." We are responsible for our actions. We must develop the entrepreneur on the inside first, which is the single best use of our time and resources, because it will yield the best results by amplifying our actions.

To increase your performance manyfold, you must do two things.

FIRSTLY, YOU MAKE ROOM AND UNLEARN:

I owe so much to my military training. As a USMC Sergeant, I was able to learn crucial skills of leadership, delegation, respect, and professionalism. But by far, I feel the greatest value I have gained from my time in the service was the transformational mindset of overcoming any obstacle.

While arriving at boot camp in Parris Island, SC we rolled in at 4 is in the morning on a bus with an expectation. We all had life experiences built up over time. We would react to stress each in a certain way specific to us. We would all be able to take orders differently.

The primary task of the drill instructor is to break us down. We could be then more easily remolded as a United States Marine. We are pounded, day-in and day-out to in effect, reprogram us. This reprogramming is critical. As Yoda said, "You must unlearn that which you have learned." The extra space is made for the input of new information. If you are full already, it becomes very difficult to accomplish this.

Stay with me as I lay a foundation.

You may already be full of prior programming from years of indoctrination by authority figures in your life from the day you were born. How many bad habits do you have? Is it possible some of what you were taught is wrong and not servicing you today?

For those of you that can't relate to this, let me explain it with a metaphorical example with which I think most of us can identify:

Our conscious and subconscious mind is the INTERFACE between the SPIRITUAL and PHYSICAL world. When was the last time you had an UPGRADE? If you can't identify with that, look at the spiritual as a 'connection to' via a frequency or vibration.

What do I mean? Think regarding a laptop which is what I am using now. It has a keyboard and internal hardware, like a processor, etc. Our mind is like the software we use to connect the physical (laptop) to the spiritual (internet) in that I am physically typing my thoughts into this word processor and as I post, it will be transmitted to the internet. Think of the internet as the spiritual or vibrational aspect of my example.

We create our dreams twice, first in our mind, and then we make it physical. We are the interface between the non-physical world and the physical world. How we think about and both act and react to everything is run through this hardware and software configuration.

In the computer and data entry world, we all have heard of "Garbage In, Garbage Out", right? The programmed data from our life experiences flowing into the sensory input of the laptop such as the webcam, audio jack and keyboard will have an impact on what comes out. The quality of experience you get, the decisions you make (or do not make), basically every aspect of your life will drastically be affected. We all know this to be true. So here is the big question, "If we know the above to be true, why do we treat ourselves this way?"

SECONDLY, YOU HAVE TO OPTIMIZE YOUR CURRENT THOUGHT PATTERNS AND USE WHAT YOU CURRENTLY HAVE:

What this means is that, as a creative being with the gift of choice, you are in control of what you think, thus you have the choice to take control of your thinking. Why not upgrade your software. Many people are still running on 30-40-50-year-old programming in their thinking! Many are running themselves on DOS programming.

How do we start? It is not as easy as it seems.

To increase productivity, you must first wipe the hard drive of past programming (unlearn). You need to make room for the new programming so it will not clash with your prior mental mindset. Our physical body is like the physical parts of the laptop. The software we run on it is our conscious and subconscious mind, and they need to be working together.

As Wallace D. Wattles says in his classic book, *The Science of Getting Rich*, "We need to do things in a Certain Way."

Wattles says that to do things the way you want, you have to develop your ability to use your mind and this is the first step, to think what you want to, which is the first step towards getting rich. Rich is, of course, subjective because there are countless forms of being rich and not just the monetary way we usually think.

Have you ever purchased and installed a software program only to use only a small fraction of its capabilities? Experts say, on average, we only use a small fraction of the software we purchase. In much the same way, we do the same to our potential inside of us.

Do you want to have a 1000-fold productivity increase in your business and personal life?

It's imperative that we learn how our programming works, how we become a product of our environment, how the process of "enculturation" works, and most importantly of all, what we can do about it if we don't like the program we have.

Your conditioning wasn't your responsibility at first. It's the same for all of us. Same for me. Same for you. You've ended up a product of your environment. You've ended up being the person that you are. So, it wasn't your responsibility that you've become who you are, *but it is your responsibility to change it if you're not getting the results that you want!* Those that have had a 180-degree productivity turn-around were not afraid to challenge even their longest-held and most-cherished beliefs.

How do we come to believe what we believe? Better yet, how can we re-engineer our beliefs and believe something different? Your beliefs are not the reflection of the reality that we often think that they are, but actually, they're just the result of a subjective learning process. Yes, we can change the process and manipulate the process to learn something, and as a result, become something different.

Bootcamp was a grueling thirteen weeks. Three four-week sections and a one-week break where we did odd duties around the base. The first four weeks was the basic conditioning and break-down. We then did the technical skills such as rifle qualification and field work where we would physically do what we were taught. We had our beliefs re-engineered. I remember it so clearly, after the second four weeks. We came back to the base from being out in the field. I started with little confidence. When the ninth week ended, I was so proud, walked taller, and was a different person.

So how does this help us with our business? Let me set this up for a moment.

The conscious and the subconscious are not in equal halves, but much more like an iceberg, where you've got the sort of vast bulk of the iceberg is underneath the water and just the teeny little bit that you see at the top. That's more indicative of the conscious mind, and the subconscious is this vast invisible bulk underneath.

So that may be a more helpful way to sort of think about the two, because the subconscious is very, very powerful and is running the show. This subconscious is doing almost everything. We have an illusion of control in the conscious mind, but it is just an illusion. The subconscious is vast. It's very fast regarding processing, and the conscious mind is very slow regarding processing.

Those of you who learned to drive a car will have experienced this first hand. In fact, those of you who've learned any complex skill because initially, everything has to be run by the conscious mind, doesn't it? Do we have to think about everything that we're doing because how else can we do it? We want to drive the car. We need to steer. We've got the gears, the handbrake.

So you need to look up in the rear-view mirror. You've got your side mirrors. You've got other traffic, cars emerging, cars overtaking you. So you've got a great deal going on, and you need to think about everything that's happening.

But you can learn it, and at some point, your subconscious will take over, and you no longer have to think of all these things. Think about how many times you drove to work and don't even remember anything of the entire time it took you to get there. That's because that entire time was all subconsciously driven.

Ninety percent and more of the lives of most people are habit driven, which is why I often say most do very little thinking at all. It's just regurgitated thinking of the day before.

The same thing happens as we learn the skills to build our business. It's painful at first. What do I say? How do I do a presentation? You stumble over your words. Your tone of voice is all wrong. Your posture is off physically and mentally. You essentially have to think about every aspect of your tasks. It seems overwhelming, doesn't it?

But over time, you start to program yourself to become a conscious competent and not have to physically think with our conscious mind for every aspect of the business, and it becomes a habit.

So here's the paradox. Is it possible to learn incorrect as well as correct habits? Of course. If you are learning a golf swing, one of the most frustrating things to learn, I can attest to that, if you practice for a year with the bad technique it means you've committed a bad technique to memory.

Your inner game is the most important aspect of your business. Developing the entrepreneur inside you FIRST will multiply your results 1,000-fold. The mental game is at much as 90% of the success or failure of your business. You are the cause of your results, no one else. Most try to treat the symptom and not the cause. The sooner you realize this vital fact, the sooner you will be on the path to stellar results through increased productivity. Every task you do will become more efficient, effective and deliver a more powerful result if you first give yourself a tune-up on the inside.

Work ON your business, not IN your business. Once you understand and become self-aware of what your business can do FOR you, you will fall in love with it.

You surrender your most valuable asset which you can never get back again. . . Your time. It's more valuable than diamonds, gold, silver or even bitcoin, yet we give it away freely. You allow individuals, co-workers, media, authority figures and yes, even our loved ones to monopolize that time and to program your thought patterns without question. Then you wonder why you aren't getting the results we want. You have to be a proper steward of your time as well as what goes into your mind, and guard it like the precious commodity that it is.

TO SUMMARIZE:

In summary, make room for new ideas. Question old belief systems. Do they serve you currently? Are they getting you any closer to your goals and dreams? If not, you owe it to your future to replace them with new and updated programming!

You have the choice to not only get a new hand dealt in the game of life, but you have the choice to be the dealer if you choose to do so. You can even keep dealing until the right combination happens. No longer do you have to play the cards you're dealt. That's corrupt thinking. You can optimize yourself with the most up-to-date programming as you continue to feed yourself quality content.

The only difference between those who make it and those who don't isn't for lack of information. The knowledge for anything we wish to know is everywhere. It's because those who are not reaching their true potential are not willing to pay the price. That price could be monetary and also not being willing to accept new "programming" and staying with their old operating system, i.e., Windows 95. The choice is always yours.

Are you ready for your upgrade?

ABOUT PETER

Peter Wolfing is not your average entrepreneur. He traces his entrepreneurial desire back to a very young age while in grade school. He's learned practical knowledge through real-world experiences. While a Sergeant in the USMC, he learned the crucial skills of leadership, delegation and problem-solving.

Peter will also be featured on Times Square TV Live to be aired on ABC, NBC, CBS, and FOX affiliates. He has close to three decades of experience creating original content in the 100-billion-dollar e-learning space.

Over the past two decades, Peter has developed many online platforms that have attracted a membership base of over 2 million people around the globe. He's mentored countless people, many of which have gone on to develop 6- & 7-figure incomes.

Peter's been called the "Uber" of his industry because he's an out-of-the-box thinker and has revolutionized the online home-based business model. Much like Uber shook the foundation of the automobile travel industry by deconstructing it and completely simplifying the model, Peter has shaken the foundation of the network marketing industry by disassembling the cumbersome infrastructure and completely streamlining the system. He has virtually re-invented the industry. The result? A more efficient, more effective, less complicated, online business model. Limited risk, high upside potential, and incredibly fast growth.

His most recent project is providing the driving force for WizKids.org, a 501(c)(3) not-for-profit charitable organization which coaches and mentors young entrepreneurs.

Peter's an expert trainer, mentor, and author of multiple books. One is co-authored with Brian Tracy – titled *The Will To Win* – and is destined to be a bestseller. He has just completed a new book called, *The Warrior Within Domesticating Fear*, which has been endorsed by Kevin Harrington, a founding member of the hit TV show *Shark Tank*, which can be found at: www.domesticatingfear.com.

Peter is an in-demand speaker and trainer on such topics as leadership, communication, sales, digital products, affiliate and network marketing and he is a certified John Maxwell Team Executive Director.

Are you stuck and can't seem to break through? Peter can help you. You can find him on:

Facebook, Instagram, YouTube /peterwolfing

Or go to his website:

www.peterwolfing.com

BY PAUL FULFORD

SUCCESS SECRETS BY ANALYSIS AND PLANNING

The 5 Prosperity Pillars

S uccess, *noun*:

1. the favorable or prosperous termination of attempts or endeavors; the accomplishment of one's goals.

2. the attainment of wealth, position, honors, or the like.

3. a performance or achievement that is marked by success, as by the attainment of honors.

4. a person or thing that has had success, as measured by attainment of goals, wealth, etc.

5. beneficial outcome.

What is success? Is it as simple as the definition above? Does this define success to you? In my career I have been asked to define many things, success being one of them. It wasn't until recently when I felt I was able to gain clarity on defining success.

I recently lost my father very abruptly due to a multitude of ailments that had gone undiagnosed. I had to quickly pull it together so that I could speak at his funeral and express the impact he had on me, paying him the ultimate respect he deserved. In my eulogy, I covered a wide range of life experiences and characteristics of my father. Specifically, in discussing how he raised me and my brother I said, "If I am able to instill 50% of the disciplines into my daughter that he instilled in me, I would consider that a success." I didn't think much about success at the time. I was simply making a statement and dealing with the loss of my father. When sitting down to write about this topic I realized that what I did at my father's eulogy was much more than give funny stories and discuss what he meant to me. I was sharing his success with everyone. Additionally, many of the people that were there had been there alongside him for it or were affected by it.

Success is much more than a single achievement. Success is much more than having a lot of money or your position at work. Successful people build solid relationships. They leave something behind that impacts and provides better well-being for others. This is what my father had done for the people in the room that day. Everyone was better off for knowing and sharing their life with him.

So, can we only understand, recognize, or designate success once our life is at the end? No. Success happens every day, it's just simply a matter of perspective. In my opinion, success is a journey that leads to other journeys. I am a person that sets goals. When I successfully achieve a task or endeavor, that achievement becomes the new normal. I then have to set a new goal to work towards. In this goal setting process, I have discovered many times that some of my most significant successes came while achieving the goal and not actually the goal itself.

In my current position I have been given the honor of assisting in moving my company in a new direction. I was put in the role because of previous success doing something similar. I went into it trying to do everything on my own. The remainder of this chapter will explain how to achieve success in two different ways:

1. One must set aside pride and ego and realize the end goal ultimately is to win.

2. Take steps that were successfully created working collaboratively to provide a plan for success to our customers.

The new direction for my company was to create a field-based support team to help our customers drive utilization of devices they purchase from us. The goal is to get them to profitability through a variety of strategies designed to attract customers to them and increase conversions once the customers were attracted. Prior to my arrival to the company, we already had a program that was similar in design just done remotely. This program is effective and is run by my colleague, Sarah Brice. Sarah and I are responsible for all matters relating to "Post-Sales Support" for our company.

Sarah and I came into our roles from "opposite sides of the track," so to speak, in our industry. Sarah is a registered nurse. Earlier in her career she was approached by a friend who wanted to open a storefront medical spa with a focus on laser tattoo removal. She was deeply involved in the development and establishment of multiple locations across the country. She basically had to go to the school of trial and error to learn how to effectively market the services for the spas. She then went into the clinical training side for a laser manufacturer. That manufacturer was purchased by another company and she was one of two employees retained from the acquisition. In the transition, she was asked to put together a marketing program that had a clinical angle. This program was to be made available to customers and she would provide them marketing assistance remotely. Since she had successfully launched multiple medical spa locations prior, this was a seamless transition for her and she thrived.

I found myself on the post-sales side of the business coming from the capital equipment sales side. My entire career prior had been in sales. I had achieved success in sales in different industries working my way up through the ranks. What I started realizing was that there was a disconnect between sales and marketing. So, I began to teach myself how to design marketing pieces. I took classes on effective design, taught myself the Adobe suite, and also went to the school of trial and error. I am in the role I am in now because, through marketing, I was able to increase B2B sales while also helping the customer get to profitability 3 to 5 times faster by assisting them with their marketing B2C. Word got out and people obviously saw value in purchasing lasers from a company that would assist them in their ROI and drive profit.

Through this execution of my duties, I was asked to spearhead a program that went along with a new product my company was launching at the time. The goal was to assist every customer who purchased this device with all of their marketing needs, and to provide this service with onsite handholding, patient attraction strategies, and coaching.

Upon arrival at my current company, Sarah was already there running her program successfully. She was asked to assist with the development of the onsite program. With both of us having created successful programs, naturally there can be a sort of reluctance to share ideas and concepts. We had both worked extremely hard to establish our credibility in similar functions. Early into our time together, we sat down and addressed the elephant in the room. We discussed hypothetical insecurities and checked our pride and egos at the door. We are both extremely passionate about what we do. We are both also very loyal to our leadership counterparts as they are a large reason we are both at the company. We realized that the end goal was for the company to win and that by combining our expertise we could create a thorough and complete program that had never been seen before in our industry. So that is what we did. In doing this, we created a systematized step-by-step program for our customers success. The steps can be simplified for use on a broader spectrum. Below are those steps – *The 5 Prosperity Pillars*:

1. **Clarity Gives Command –** Decide what you want and set measurable goals with targets.

2. **Teamwork Makes the Dreamwork –** Set ego aside and work together toward your collaborative goals.

3. **Systems Solve Situations –** Thoroughly analyze where you are, then design a step-by-step plan with targets based on measurable goals, to get where you want to go.

4. **Action & Implement –** Take immediate action, define key stakeholders, follow the plan, and track results.

5. **Follow the Feedback –** Analyze the feedback. adjust, and establish the new set of targets…then repeat.

This is not as simple as it sounds of course, or everyone would be experiencing success. Again, checking pride and ego at the door, one of the first things we realized was that we hoped our customers would grasp that they needed experts to assist. For our customers, the "what-they-want" is to get to profitability as fast as possible through increased usage of our product post sale. We designed an in-depth tool to thoroughly analyze where they are. We have designed a step-by-step measurable plan based on the analysis they can implement. We assist them in identifying people within the business to assign tasks. We help them implement the plan, make adjustments, and refocus to continue moving forward – always providing continuing education onsite and remotely. That is the value in our program. We take the guess work out of it.

For your specific business, you will need to identify what your HPAs (High Payoff Activities) are. It's a lot like how baseball has looked for and found specific analytics to best determine roster performance. What are the activities in your current business that have the greatest impact on your desired result? Let's use "Field Sales" for a simple example. A salesperson needs to make a certain number of contacts or touch points (phone calls/onsite stop-ins/emails) before setting an appointment. Then, they have to have a certain number of appointments with prospects before hopefully accomplishing the end goal of converting those prospects into customers. See the visual below:

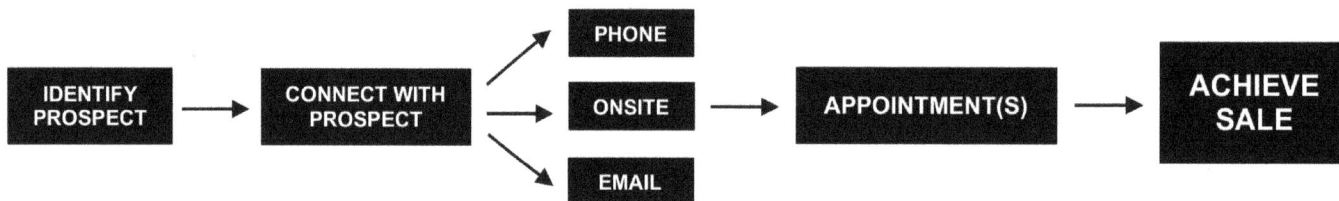

The goal in identifying the steps for the visual is to determine your HPAs. These are the numbers you want to track. You first have to establish a baseline. If you don't know your numbers, how do you know if you're growing? Then, once you have numbers you can identify where they are once the goal is achieved. For example, let us look at the work of two sales persons below:

SALESPERSON A:

In one month - 250 touch points, 10 appointments, 6 sales

• AVG: 25 touch points to set an appointment / 1.7 appointments to make a sale

SALESPERSON B:

In one month - 200 touch points, 30 appointments, 4 sales

• AVG: 6.7 touch points to set an appointment / 7.5 appointments to make a sale

In these examples, there are different areas in which improvement in a particular area should merit an increase in sales. Salesperson A has a 60% conversion ratio of appointments to sales. While Salesperson B has a 13% conversion ratio. When comparing touch points to appointments, Salesperson B has a 15% conversion ratio. While Salesperson A has a 4% conversion ratio. This is a common makeup amongst sales teams.

The coaching points are clear though. Salesperson A needs to improve on converting touch points to appointments. Salesperson B needs to improve on appointments to sales. This is your baseline and these are the areas you have now identified to coach each individual. If you have a positive culture in your organization, pairing these two up along with your coaching can assist in expediting results.

When it comes to success, we know there is no pill someone can swallow to be successful. What I've noticed in people who achieve success is that they work hard toward something they are passionate about, and that moves them to action, and they work with steadfast resilience. You can't be afraid to fail. If you fail to accomplish at first, all you've done is figure out a way not to do something. You can cross that off the list and move on. As passionate as you are about the goal, you can't be attached to the outcome because it blinds you and doesn't allow you to take a step back and regroup.

Anytime I've ever felt overwhelmed working on something, I've written the issue down on a piece of paper. Then, I stand up and look down at what I've written. That is how small it is compared to me. Nothing is bigger than we are! A person can accomplish anything when they realize they are a part of something bigger. A team of people that share the same conviction can truly affect change and find success. Success is available to anyone who wants it, you just have to want it.

ABOUT PAUL

Whether it is as a sales rep for his company, the customer that purchases one of his company's devices, or the people he is responsible for, helping people is what gets Paul Fulford excited to do his job every day. Paul is passionate about helping people. Throughout his career across three different industries, both in Sales and Marketing, helping people get what they want has been a consistent outcome for him.

Paul is currently the Director of Practice Support Marketing for Cutera, Inc., where he and his colleague Sarah Brice lead all things Post Sales for the company. Paul chose to work for Cutera because he is extremely congruent with the company culture and philosophy. Cutera's philosophy is powerfully simple—define the forefront of medical aesthetics with devices exquisitely engineered to deliver the highest level of performance, safety, and efficacy. Cutera devices address a wide range of Face + Body medical aesthetic applications—with results that drive patient satisfaction and practice growth. Practice growth for Cutera's customers is his focus.

Paul regularly speaks on practice growth, marketing strategies, and how to achieve this with Cutera products at weekend symposium events and online webinars. He has had the pleasure of working with over 1,000 aesthetic practices, some of which are considered the best in their respective spaces. With this work, he has helped catalyze these customers ROI with the products they implemented though email marketing, social media, search engine optimization, onsite events, personalized staff coaching, and all other areas that assist them in attracting new customers.

You can connect with Paul at:

pfulford@cutera.com

www.ingramcontent.com/pod-product-compliance
Lightning Source LLC
Chambersburg PA
CBHW051929190326
41458CB00026B/6455